E. M. FORSTER

LITERATURE AND LIFE: BRITISH WRITERS

Complete list of titles in the series available from the publisher on request.

E. M. FORSTER

Claude J. Summers

UNGAR • NEW YORK

For some colleagues who are convinced that our life is a state
of some importance and our earth not a place to beat time on:

DOROTHY LEE, NEIL FLAX, CHRIS DAHL, and TED again

1987
The Ungar Publishing Company
370 Lexington Avenue, New York, N.Y. 10017

Printed in the United States of America

Library of Congress Cataloging in Publication Data

Summers, Claude J.
  E. M. Forster.

  (Literature and life series)
  Bibliography: p. 387
  Includes index.
  1. Forster, E. M. (Edward Morgan), 1879-1970—
Criticism and interpretation.   I. Title.   II. Series.
PR6011.058Z8464   1983   823'.912   82-40624
ISBN 0-8044-6893-1 (pbk.)

Acknowledgment is gratefully made to Random House,
Inc. for permission to quote from the following works of W. H.
Auden: "To E. M. Forster" from *W. H. Auden: Collected Poems*,
edited by Edward Mendelson, copyright © 1976 by Edward
Mendelson, William Meredith and Monroe K. Spears, Execu-
tors of the Estate of W. H. Auden; from "September 1, 1939"
and from "Sir, no man's enemy" from *The English Auden*,
edited by Edward Mendelson, copyright © 1977 by Edward
Mendelson, William Meredith and Monroe K. Spears, Execu-
tors of the Estate of W. H. Auden.

Contents

Chronology

1879   E. M. Forster is born January 1 at 6 Melcombe Place, Dorset Square, London.

1880   His father, Edward Morgan Llewellyn Forster, dies of consumption on October 30.

1883–93   Forster and his mother, Alice Clara "Lily" Whichelo Forster, live at Rooksnest, near Stevenage in Hertfordshire.

1887   Forster's great-aunt Marianne Thornton dies, leaving him £8,000 in trust, the legacy he later describes as his "financial salvation."

1890–93   Attends Kent House preparatory school in Eastbourne.

1893–97   Forster and his mother live in Tonbridge, where he attends Tonbridge School as a dayboy.

1897–1901   Attends King's College, Cambridge, where he falls in love with fellow undergraduate H. O. Meredith.

1901   Elected member of the Cambridge Conversazione Society, the "Apostles."

1901–02   Travels with his mother to Italy, Sicily, and Austria.

1902   Teaches a Latin class at London's Working Men's College, an institution that he will serve as part-time lecturer for over twenty years.

1903   Travels in Italy and Greece. His first published story, "Albergo Empedocle," appears in *Temple Bar*.

1904   He and his mother move to Weybridge, where they will live for twenty years. He works alternately on an edition of the *Aeneid* and on his first three novels. He becomes a regular contributor to *The Independent Review*.

1905   Travels to Pomerania to serve as tutor to the children of the Gräfin von Arnim. His first novel, *Where Angels Fear to Tread,* is published.

1906   Meets Syed Ross Masood, a handsome young Indian with whom he falls in love.

1907   His second novel, *The Longest Journey,* is published.

1908   *A Room with a View,* his third novel, is published.

1910   *Howards End,* his fourth novel, is published. Forster becomes active in Bloomsbury circles and is treated as a literary celebrity.

1911   *The Celestial Omnibus and Other Stories* is published. He writes "Heart of Bosnia," a play that is never produced.

1912   Begins "Arctic Summer," a novel that he abandons after a few chapters. Begins close friendship with Florence Barger.

1912–13 Visits India with G. Lowes Dickinson and R. C. Trevelyan; meets the Maharajah of Dewas Senior.

1913   Visits Edward Carpenter and George Merrill at Millthorpe, where he conceives *Maurice.*

1915   Visits D. H. Lawrence in Sussex; begins a friendship with Lawrence that soon collapses.

1915–19 Works in Alexandria as a Red Cross volunteer officer. In Alexandria, he meets Constantine Cavafy, whose poetry he introduces to England, and falls in love with a young tram conductor, Mohammed el Adl, with whom he shares his first fully satisfying sexual relationship.

1919   He writes a historical introduction to a Fabian pamphlet, *The Government of Egypt.*

1920   He is employed briefly as literary editor of the *Daily Herald.*

1921–22 Serves as private secretary to the Maharajah of Dewas State Senior; enjoys reunions with Syed Ross Masood and Mohammed el Adl.

1922   Mohammed el Adl dies. *Alexandria: A History and a Guide* is published. Begins friendship with J. R. Ackerley.

1923   *Pharos and Pharillon,* a collection of Alexandrian

vignettes, is published. Begins friendship with W. J. H. Sprott.

1924   *A Passage to India* is published to great acclaim, establishing Forster as a major voice in contemporary literature and a discerning critic of imperialism. Begins friendship with T. E. Lawrence. Forster and his mother take up residence in West Hackhurst, a house in Abinger Hammer designed by his father.

1925   Ackerley and Sprott introduce him to London's working-class homosexual milieu; he begins an affair with Harry Dailey.

1927   He delivers Clark Lectures at Trinity College, Cambridge. The lectures are published as *Aspects of the Novel*.

1928   He rallies literary world to protest suppression of Radclyffe Hall's *The Well of Loneliness. The Eternal Moment and Other Stories*, Forster's second collection of short fiction, is published.

1930   Hostile obituaries for D. H. Lawrence spur Forster to proclaim Lawrence "the greatest imaginative novelist of our generation." He begins his long relationship with Bob Buckingham, a young police constable.

1931   Begins career as broadcaster with BBC.

1932   Begins friendship with young novelists Christopher Isherwood and William Plomer. Bob Buckingham marries, sparking a duel between Forster and Buckingham's wife, May.

1933   His godson, Robin Morgan Buckingham, the son of Bob and May Buckingham, is born.

1934   Becomes first president of National Council of Civil Liberties and leads campaign against the Sedition Act. *Goldsworthy Lowes Dickinson*, his biography of a friend and former teacher, is published.

1935   He leads the British delegation to the International Congress of Writers in Paris, addressing the meeting on the subject of "Liberty in England." T. E. Lawrence is killed in a motorcycle accident.

1936   *Abinger Harvest*, a miscellany of essays and reviews, is published.

1937   Syed Ross Masood and the Maharajah of Dewas Senior die.

1938   He contributes "What I Believe" to the "Living Philosophies" series sponsored by the *Nation* (New York).

1939   He defends Auden, Isherwood, Gerald Heard, and Aldous Huxley when they are attacked for "deserting" England at a time of peril.

1940   *Nordic Twilight*, an anti-Nazi pamphlet, is published.

1941   He inaugurates a regular program of book talks broadcast to India.

1942   He presides at a PEN conference to celebrate the tercentenary of Milton's *Areopagitica*.

1945   Lily Forster dies. He makes his third visit to India.

1946   He is forced to leave Abinger. He accepts appointment as Honorary Fellow of King's College, Cambridge, where he lives for the rest of his life.

1947   He visits the United States for the first time, lecturing at Harvard University and elsewhere.

1949   Accompanied by Bob Buckingham, he returns to the United States.

1951   *Two Cheers for Democracy*, his second miscellany of reviews and essays, is published. Benjamin Britten's opera *Billy Budd*, featuring a libretto co-authored by Forster and Eric Crozier, premieres at Covent Garden.

1953   He is awarded the Companion of Honour by Queen Elizabeth II. *The Hill of Devi*, based on letters written home from his visits to India, is published.

1956   *Marianne Thornton*, his biography of his great-aunt, is published.

1958   He completes his final major work of short fiction, "The Other Boat."

1959   King's College, Cambridge, honors him at a lavish eightieth birthday celebration.

1960   He testifies as defense witness in the sensational
        Lady Chatterley's Lover obscenity trial. He re-
        vises *Maurice* for publication after his death.

1962   His godson, Robin Morgan Buckingham, dies of
        Hodgkin's disease.

1964   He suffers his first stroke.

1967   J. R. Ackerley dies.

1969   On his ninetieth birthday, he is awarded the Order
        of Merit by Queen Elizabeth II.

1970   He dies in Coventry, at the home of Bob and May
        Buckingham, on June 7.

1971   *Maurice,* his novel of homosexual love, and *Al-
        bergo Empedocle and Other Writings,* a collection
        of fugitive essays and stories, are published.

1972   *The Life to Come and Other Stories,* a collection
        of stories, mostly on homosexual subjects and
        themes, is published.

1978   His *Commonplace Book* is published.

1980   *Arctic Summer and Other Fiction,* a collection of
        fragmentary novels and unfinished stories, is
        published.

1

The Mirror to Infinity: A Biographical Sketch

When E. M. Forster died in 1970, he had earned an international reputation as an incisive interpreter of the human heart and a champion of the liberal imagination. For the last two decades of his life, he was regularly—even predictably—described as England's greatest living novelist and almost universally respected as the saintly sage of King's College, Cambridge. He had become that public figure he always faintly distrusted, a "Great Man."

Forster adapted to this role with some reluctance, for he believed passionately in the creed of personal relations and in the supreme value of the private life. As he wrote in *Howards End,* "It is private life that holds out the mirror to infinity; personal intercourse, and that alone, that ever hints at a personality beyond our daily vision." But one measure of his greatness is that the public Forster was a faithful image of his private self: sensitive, considerate, plucky. The mirror to infinity held out by his private life reflected above all the holiness of the heart's affections, the Keatsian criterion that made him so unusual a public figure. The story of his life is as much a history of friendships as a chronicle of a career.

He was born in London on New Year's Day 1879, the son of a promising architect, Edward Morgan Llewellyn Forster, and Alice "Lily" Whichelo Forster,

a protégée of Edward Forster's formidable aunt Marianne Thornton and daughter of a drawing master.[1] At
birth, the infant was registered under the name Henry—
in honor of his father's uncle Henry Thornton—but was
christened Edward Morgan by mistake. He thus began
his life at the center of a muddle, that spirit of confusion that entangles so many of his characters.
Throughout his life, he was called Morgan. When his
father died in October 1880, he became the favorite
nephew of the eighty-three-year-old Marianne Thornton, who competed unsuccessfully with the Whichelo
family for his allegiance.

The Whichelos were artistic, easygoing, and poor,
while the Thorntons were unimaginative, serious-
minded, and rich. Prominent bankers, the Thorntons
had been one of England's most public-spirited and
philanthropic families for three generations; their
home—Battersea Rise in Clapham Common—had
been the headquarters of the Clapham Sect, a group of
evangelical Christians devoted to good works. Their
associates included such public figures as William
Wilberforce, James Stephen, Zachary Macaulay, and
Hannah More.[2]

From the Whichelos, Forster inherited a love of
spontaneity and humor, while from the Thorntons, he
received his intellectual seriousness and deep sense of
commitment. More materially, Marianne Thornton
left him a legacy that enabled him to attend Cambridge and travel afterward. He was always ambivalent about his Clapham Sect heritage, but in his last
book—an affectionate but not uncritical biography of
his great-aunt—he declared that "she and no one else
made my career as a writer possible, and her love, in a
most tangible sense, followed me beyond the grave."

Forster was a precocious child. He taught himself
to read at age four and soon thereafter began inventing
stories for his own amusement. Cosseted by a host of
female relatives, especially by his adored mother and

beloved grandmother, he enjoyed a happy and perhaps overprotected childhood. Much has been made of his long "love affair" with his mother, with whom he lived for most of his life. They were indeed emotionally dependent on each other for many years, but Forster's intellectual toughness and independence of thought and feeling were too strong to permit any caricature of him as tied to his mother's apron strings. His relationship with her was one of the richest in his life, and it surely contributed to his art. His skill at depicting elderly ladies and his sensitivity to the nuances of Edwardian etiquette probably reflect his close observation of his mother and her friends.

From 1883 to 1893, he and his mother lived in Rooksnest, a house in Hertfordshire that captured his imagination. Forster later used it as the model for Howards End, and the loss of it haunted the rest of his life. At Rooksnest Forster's love of the English countryside and fear of urban sprawl were developed. There, too, he met a garden boy named Ansell, with whom he played and whose image never left him. To his brief encounter with Ansell, Forster probably owed his romanticized attitude toward the natural man, his respect and empathy for the lower classes, and his hatred of the English class system.

In 1893, Forster and his mother moved to Tonbridge, where he entered Tonbridge School as a dayboy. At school he excelled academically, developing a lifelong love of classical literature. But he was subjected to the cruel taunts of his classmates and suffered acutely from the atmosphere of unkindness. His experience at Tonbridge left him feeling inadequate to cope with the "real world" and despising the entire English public school mentality.

In his scathing portrait of Sawston School in *The Longest Journey*, Forster avenged himself on Tonbridge. But the alienation he experienced there probably contributed to his empathy for the underdog and his love for the individual and suspicion of the group. It also made him aware of the hypocrisy and cant so prevalent in middle-class society, generating the anger that permeates his novels. In 1933, he remarked that "School was the unhappiest time of my life, and the worst trick it ever played me was to pretend that it was the world in miniature. For it hindered me from discovering how lovely and delightful and kind the world can be, and how much of it is intelligible."[3]

He discovered the world's loveliness and intelligibility at that revered place Cambridge, where he matriculated at King's College in 1897. Many years later—in his biography *Goldsworthy Lowes Dickinson*—he described the university as a place where "People and books reinforced each other, intelligence joined hands with affection, speculation became a passion, and discussion was made profound by love." In this atmosphere of kindness and free inquiry, of masculine fellowship and affection, he flourished. He made lasting friendships and explored his own powers. He studied classics and history and came under the influence of such dons as Oscar Browning, G. Lowes Dickinson, and especially Nathaniel Wedd. A militant atheist and iconoclast, Wedd not only taught Forster classics, he also encouraged him to write and introduced him to modern European literature, an interest that helped make Forster one of the least parochial of English novelists. He came especially to admire Tolstoy, Ibsen, Gide, and Proust.

Forster also fell in love with a fellow undergraduate, H. O. Meredith. Brilliant, handsome, and intellectually arrogant, Meredith later served as the model for Clive in *Maurice*. Just as Clive demolishes Maurice's conventional religious opinions and leads him to acknowledge his homosexuality, so Meredith guided Forster to the two great discoveries of his youth: his agnosticism and his passion for men.

Forster's homosexuality is a crucial aspect of his personality and his art. It gave him that feeling of standing "at a slight angle to the universe" that he later detected in the poet Cavafy, and it fueled his anger at social and political injustice, making him contemptuous of the conventions that separate individuals and impede instinct. His acute consciousness of the homophobia that poisoned the dominant culture of his day—as most graphically illustrated by the persecution of Oscar Wilde, which occurred during Forster's late adolescence and early manhood—haunted his imagination throughout his life. When he was almost eighty-five years old, he noted in his diary "how *annoyed* I am with Society for wasting my time by making homosexuality criminal. The subterfuges, the self-consciousness that might have been avoided."[4]

Significantly, however, Forster never felt guilty for his sexuality, and, accepting homosexuality as part of the wholeness of his personality, he never wished to be heterosexual. When Leonard Woolf asked him whether he would like to be "converted" to heterosexuality, he answered without hesitation, "No." Some recent critics of his homosexual fiction, themselves anachronistically regarding homosexuality as pathology, have distorted Forster's life and work by confusing his deeply felt anger at injustice with feelings of guilt or shame.

His relationship with Meredith was an emotional bond similar to that of Clive and Maurice, including kisses and embraces but probably not genital sexuality. Forster was not to experience a fully satisfying sexual relationship of any duration until 1917, and his sexual frustration undoubtedly influenced his novels almost as much as his homosexuality itself, contributing to the emphasis in the early work on the need for wholeness and sexual fulfillment. The affair with Meredith lasted for a number of years and then gradually dissolved.

Meredith sponsored Forster's membership in the "Apostles," the Cambridge Conversazione Society, the university's most prestigious discussion group. Through the Apostles, Forster felt keenly the experience of intellectual and social acceptance, that sense of brotherhood celebrated in the opening pages of *The Longest Journey*. Although he considered himself incapable of abstract thought, he nevertheless imbibed the philosophy of G. E. Moore and J. M. E. McTaggert, Cambridge's leading philosophers of the day and active participants in the Apostles. From Moore, Forster probably received philosophical justification for his belief that personal relations and the contemplation of beauty yield life's most valuable states of mind.

His membership in the Apostles probably also led to Forster's immersion in the works of such radical writers as Nietzsche, Shaw, Hardy, Butler, Carlyle, and Swinburne. It certainly led to close ties with many of his friends later to be associated with Bloomsbury, including Lytton Strachey, John Maynard Keynes, and Roger Fry. Forster's belief in individualism and the sanctity of personal relationships, his scorn for conventionality and religion, his passion for truth and friendship, his unaffected love for art and his intellectual romanticism all either sprang from or were reinforced by his university experience.

At Cambridge, Forster began a novel but abandoned it, unconvinced that he was really a writer. After graduating in 1901, uncertain of what career to pursue, he decided to travel. He and his mother spent a year abroad, traversing the length of Italy and visiting Sicily and Austria as well. This trip provided material that he would later use in his Italian novels and in some of the short stories. More fundamentally, however, Italy warmed his imagination and made him confident of his talent. In Ravello, the first chapter of "The Story of a Panic" rushed into his mind, convincing him of the genuineness of his inspiration. For this vision, Forster always remained grateful to Italy, thinking of it as a place where people knew how to live.

In 1902, Forster began teaching a weekly class in Latin at London's Working Men's College, an institution with which he would be associated in a part-time capacity for more than twenty years. He returned to Italy and traveled to Greece in 1903 and again felt direct inspiration. Back in England, he began outlining *The Longest Journey*, drafting what would become *A Room with a View*, as well as beginning *Where Angels Fear to Tread* and completing several short stories and essays and lectures.

The years 1903 and 1904 were pivotal in Forster's development as a writer. During this period, he worked alternately on a number of different projects and seemed overwhelmed with ideas and inspiration. But not only did he overflow with creativity, his distinctive style suddenly matured. The Forsterian voice—confidential and relaxed and gentle and nearly always tinged with sadness, even when lyrical or ironic—suddenly perfected itself. Soon after completing *Where Angels Fear to Tread*, he traveled to Pomerania, where he spent six months as tutor to the children of the eccentric Gräfin von Arnim, who may have served as the model for Mrs. Failing in *The Longest Journey*.

Where Angels Fear to Tread appeared in October 1905 to excellent reviews. The power of the book surprised many of Forster's acquaintances, who had mistakenly interpreted his demure appearance and soft-spoken gentleness as signs of weakness. The passion of all the novels tended to shock people who remembered Forster from school or knew him only casually.

In 1906, he met Syed Ross Masood, a striking young Indian with a rare talent for friendship. Forster gradually fell in love with Masood, but when he confessed his desire, the Indian was baffled and unresponsive.

Although it was never fulfilled sexually, the relationship with Masood became one of the most important in Forster's life. The emotional and extravagant Masood broadened the Englishman's horizons and finally introduced him to India and helped him understand a new civilization.

With the favorable reception of *The Longest Journey* in 1907 and *A Room with a View* in 1908, Forster became a minor literary celebrity. With the publication of *Howards End* in 1910, he became a major one. *Howards End* was acclaimed almost unanimously, and Forster was marked as a writer of enormous promise. Curiously, the praise filled him with dismay. In his diary entry for December 8, 1910, he wrote: "Let me not be distracted by the world. It is so difficult—I am not vain of my overpraised book, but I wish I was obscure again. Soon it shall be, let me re-enter it with sweetness. If I come an unholy smash let me never forget that one man and possibly two have loved me." As P. N. Furbank observes, Forster here—and at several other points in his life—"showed symptoms . . . of the psychology which Freud describes in his paper 'Those Wrecked by Success.'"[5] Forster's fear of fame is an important aspect of what Lionel Trilling diagnoses as his "refusal to be great."[6]

Concomitant with his recoil from the praise so deservedly accorded *Howards End,* Forster also began to fear sterility as a writer, a fear that haunted him the rest of his life. Although this reaction may seem perverse, coming as it did at the end of one of the most fertile periods ever enjoyed by a writer, it was nonetheless real and painful. In six years, he had published four of the finest novels of the Edwardian era and several stories and essays and reviews, yet he doubted whether he would—or could—write any more.

In 1911, he collected six of his short stories into a volume—*The Celestial Omnibus and Other Stories*—

and began a new project, a novel to be called "Arctic Summer." After several chapters, he abandoned the novel. What is most remarkable about the fragment is its flatness. Although competently written in a recognizably Forsterian manner, "Arctic Summer" is almost completely barren of the poetry that infuses the earlier published novels. One cause for his sterility, he confided to his 1911 diary, was his overweening "Weariness of the only subject that I both can and may treat— the love of men for women & vice versa."[7] Soon afterward, he began writing homoerotic short stories, which he shared with no one. He also attempted, with very limited success, a play, which he entitled "Heart of Bosnia!" He completed this drama, but it was never produced.

In 1912, he cemented his relationship with Florence Barger, the wife of one of his Cambridge classmates. She became Forster's closest woman friend, a confidante and source of strength and solace. She probably fell in love with him, yet she loyally supported his pursuit of homosexual passion. Although he sometimes complained of being smothered by women, Forster had a deep-seated need for female companionship, and he and Florence Barger remained devoted to each other until her death in 1960. In 1912, he also began a long-lasting friendship with the Belfast novelist Forrest Reid. This relationship began with Forster writing Reid a fan letter, a practice that Forster continued throughout his life, encouraging in this way such young writers as J. R. Ackerley, Eudora Welty, and Donald Windham.

With his friends G. Lowes Dickinson and R. C. Trevelyan, he visited India in 1912.[8] The journey was a remarkable success. Not only did he enjoy a happy reunion with Masood—the principal motivation for the trip—he also made a number of new Indian friends and began his long love affair with the mysterious subcontinent. He was appalled by the racist attitudes and unkindness of the British administrators of India, the "Anglo-Indians," and he began to develop a serious interest in the problems of imperialism. He was captivated by the Maharajah of Chhatarpur, whose passions were friendship, philosophy, and beautiful boys, and by the Maharajah of Dewas Senior, whom he was later to serve as private secretary.

When Forster returned from India, he began work on an Indian novel. After a few chapters, he found that he could not complete it, and his feeling of sterility increased. In the midst of this crisis of confidence in 1913, he visited Edward Carpenter. A pioneer in the early gay liberation movement, a Whitmanesque poet and proponent of the simple life, Carpenter lived with his working-class lover at Millthorpe in Derbyshire. Forster had admired Carpenter for several years and probably modeled Mr. Emerson in *A Room with a View* on him, and the 1913 visit was in the spirit of a pilgrimage. The meeting proved more momentous than the novelist could have hoped, for on a subsequent visit to the "shrine" at Millthorpe he conceived in a flash of inspiration *Maurice*, the novel of homosexual love that was to occupy him for so many years thereafter.

He wrote the novel's first draft quickly and with a sense of exaltation. He knew that he could not publish it, given the absurd obscenity laws in England, but he thought that having completed his novel of homosexual passion, his period of sterility would be over and he could turn to other work. "However, now, to his dismay," remarks Furbank, "he discovered that life had played a trick on him. To have written an unpublishable novel, he found, was no help at all towards producing a publishable one."[9]

The outbreak of World War I in 1914 increased Forster's depression. He saw the war as the logical culmination of the gross materialism of the modern world, a materialism that he had exposed in *Howards End*, and he knew that the war would accelerate the destruction of the greenwood, that symbol of natural harmony to which he had clung so poignantly in *Howards End* and *Maurice*. He also knew that the Great War would profoundly alter English society, and he spent much of the rest of his life attempting to adapt the best tenets of Victorian liberalism—especially individualism—to the various heartening or frightening challenges posed by the twentieth-century cultural and political revolutions.

Forster knew as well that he could not produce creative writing under wartime conditions, but he undertook a critical study of Samuel Butler, whose work he greatly admired. He finally abandoned the book in despair.

In 1915, he began an uneasy relationship with D. H. Lawrence. Despite some crucial similarities between the writers, especially their fierce opposition to materialism and sexual repression, the men were fundamentally incompatible, and their friendship soon collapsed. Lawrence thought Forster "bound hand and foot bodily," as he remarked in a letter to Bertrand Russell, asking rather naively, "Why can't he take a woman and fight clear to his own basic, primal being? Because he knows that self-realization is not his ultimate desire. His ultimate desire is for continued action which has been called the social passion—the love for humanity—the desire to work for humanity."[10] Lawrence's contempt for Forster existed side by side with grudging admiration. He later referred to Forster as "the last Englishman," characteristically adding, "And I am the one after that."[11] The younger writer's contempt is especially ironic since Lawrence's early work is deeply indebted to Forster and since he was later to model *Lady Chatterley's Lover* on *Maurice*.[12]

For his part, Forster respected Lawrence, later defying the literary establishment by declaring him "the greatest imaginative novelist of our generation."[13] But he saw clearly that Lawrence flirted dangerously with totalitarianism. He naturally resented the younger writer's hectoring and humorlessness, and he found Lawrence remarkably blind to the homosexual dimension of his own personality. When Lawrence spoke offensively of Edward Carpenter, Forster realized that he could never be a close friend.

During this period near the beginning of the war, Forster increased his contacts with Bloomsbury, which was a kind of London extension of the Apostles, with the addition of the talented Stephen sisters, now Vanessa Bell and Virginia Woolf.[14] He became particularly close to Lytton Strachey and Virginia and Leonard Woolf. He was deeply gratified when Strachey praised *Maurice* very highly. Forster consequently developed a new respect for Strachey, whom he had earlier regarded as cynical and affected. Many years later, when Bertrand Russell attacked Strachey, Forster vigorously defended his friend, praising the historical writer's passion, style, and natural gaiety.[15]

In the years before the war, Virginia Woolf gradually became dependent on Forster's critical opinion of her work. She confided to her diary in 1919 that "Morgan has the artist's mind; he says the simple things that clever people don't say: I find him the best of critics for that reason."[16] He resembled, she thought, an elusive butterfly, timid and difficult to pin down. Forster's friendship with Virginia continued until her death in 1941, but he was always guarded with her, perhaps fearing her emotional instability. She was one of the few close friends whom he did not ask to read *Maurice*. On the other hand, he looked to Leonard Woolf as a practical man who could be counted on for good advice. In 1912, Woolf taught him to improve his horseback riding in preparation for his Indian journey, and Forster later credited him with providing much needed encouragement to finish *A Passage to India*.

In 1915, Forster volunteered to go to Alexandria as a Red Cross hospital "searcher," that is, one who interviews the wounded for information about missing soldiers. His Alexandrian experiences proved extraordinarily valuable, both personally and professionally. He did not find modern Alexandria as interesting as India, but he became fascinated with the city's colorful past, conceiving it as a city of the spirit, a city of love.

In Alexandria, he discovered the great poet Constantine Cavafy, then almost totally unknown to English readers. Cavafy considered himself a "Hellene" rather than a Greek, and he helped broaden Forster's own Hellenism. He stimulated the novelist's interest in Alexandrian history and influenced his technique in the historical vignettes of *Pharos and Pharillon* (1923), which Forster wrote in homage to the city, a companion volume to his history and guide, *Alexandria* (1922). Forster subsequently worked tirelessly—and successfully—to bring Cavafy to the attention of the British literary public.

Most important of all, in Alexandria Forster fell in love with a young tram conductor, Mohammed el Adl. His relationship with the Egyptian was his first fully satisfying sexual affair. As Furbank remarks, "It was the realization of all his secret ambitions. He had, or so he felt, broken through the barriers of class and colour; and this had been the fruit of courage and persistency— of that 'athletic love', or taking trouble over relationships, which he had often preached."[17] The sexual fulfillment that Forster enjoyed in this affair may explain the fact that in *A Passage to India* sexuality is not a major preoccupation. Having experienced sexual joy, he was no longer quite so obsessed with the issues of repression that dominated the early novels.

Even after leaving Alexandria in 1919, Forster remained devoted to Mohammed el Adl. Soon after Forster's departure, the young man was cruelly imprisoned by British occupation forces, an incarceration that wrecked his health. The injustice visited upon his friend undoubtedly influenced Forster's increasingly bitter opposition to the excesses of imperialism. Mohammed el Adl probably also contributed, along with Syed Ross Masood, to the character of Aziz in *A Passage to India*.

When Forster returned to England in 1919, he believed that his career as a novelist was probably over. He devoted himself more and more to literary journalism, frequently reviewing books for such journals as the *Nation* and the *Daily News* and the *Athenaeum*. He also became increasingly active as a critic of imperialism. He contributed, for example, a historical introduction to a Fabian pamphlet on the Egyptian question, *The Government of Egypt*. But he continued to despair over his inability to create. When in 1921 he received an invitation from the Maharajah of Dewas Senior to serve as his private secretary for six months, he accepted immediately, seeing it as an opportunity for reunions with Mohammad el Adl and Syed Ross Masood and hoping that contact with India might stimulate work on the Indian novel he had abandoned soon after his return from his first visit to the subcontinent.

Forster's sojourn in India in 1921 proved crucial to the growth of *A Passage to India*. He was not able to write in Dewas; the opening chapters of his early draft seemed to go dead when confronted with the reality of his experience in the bewildering land. But many of his observations of Dewas were incorporated into the novel, as became apparent in 1953, when he published *The Hill of Devi*, a narrative of his visits to India constructed from his letters home. In *The Hill of Devi* he characterizes his stay in Dewas as the "great opportunity of my life." Not only did it yield his masterpiece, it also led to one of his most valued friendships.

The Maharajah of Dewas Senior, Sir Tokiji Rao III, ruled an absurd little state in central India, intersected by the equally muddled state of Dewas Junior. Dewas was for Forster an anachronistic and rich civilization equally threatened by the faint stirrings of nationalism and by the Western righteousness personified in the British government of India. The maharajah failed to cope successfully with the chaos that surrounded him, but he was a genius and possibly a saint, an apostle of the creed of personal relations and a devout Hindu. When Rao's life ended in catastrophe some years later, Forster eulogized him as a person possessed of "incomparable qualities as an individual: he was witty, gay, charming, hospitable, imaginative, and devoted, and he had above all a living sense of religion which enabled him to transcend the barriers of his creed and to make contact with all the forms of belief and disbelief."[18]

En route to India, Forster enjoyed a rewarding visit with Mohammed in Port Said, and they arranged to spend several weeks together on the writer's return from the subcontinent. But when the Englishman reached Egypt in 1922, he found his friend gravely ill. He embarked for England heavyhearted, convinced that Mohammed was dying. In this crisis, Forster turned to Leonard Woolf, who advised him to give up reviewing and devote himself exclusively to his half-written Indian novel. At this time, Forster also destroyed many of his homoerotic stories, not out of a sense of shame but from a belief that they somehow prevented his work on the novel. He learned on May 17, 1922, that Mohammed was dead.

When *A Passage to India* appeared in 1924, it was hailed as a masterpiece. Much of the early commentary on the novel debated its political dimension, especially the accuracy of the depiction of Anglo-Indians. The acclaim and the controversy jointly established Forster as a major voice in English fiction and a discerning critic of imperialism. Again, he was disturbed by his triumph, a success consolidated by the unexpectedly enthusiastic reception accorded his series of lectures at Cambridge in 1927, *Aspects of the Novel*, and by his second collection of short stories, *The Eternal Moment and Other Stories* (1928), all of which had been written before the Great War. He seems to have known at this point that he would produce no more novels, but he also determined not to despair. He turned to nonfiction forms and to occasional stories on homosexual themes.

In the early 1920s, Forster established important friendships with T. E. Lawrence, W. J. H. Sprott, and J. R. Ackerley. He fervently admired *Seven Pillars of Wisdom* and regarded Lawrence as confirmation of his belief that sensitivity and active heroism could be combined. He served as literary adviser to Lawrence until the latter's death in 1935, their friendship strengthened by Lawrence's rapturous response to his homoerotic story "Dr. Woolacott." Forster was probably in love with Lawrence, though he knew very early in their relationship that Lawrence's abhorrence of the physical precluded the complete union that he now demanded.

W. J. H. "Sebastian" Sprott was a psychology student at Cambridge, a member of the Apostles, and associated with Bloomsbury as the friend and lover of John Maynard Keynes. As Furbank remarks, Sprott's elegant and "exquisite" manner "was, in a way, misleading, for his true wish was not for a 'gilded' Cambridge existence but for a hearty, egalitarian, sexually promiscuous low-life."[19] Forster developed a protective attitude toward him, and though they were never lovers, they became loyal and affectionate friends until the end of Forster's life. Somewhat to Forster's surprise, Sprott became a successful academic psychologist and writer.

The bond with Ackerley began as a result of Forster's writing the young and then totally unknown writer a flattering response to a poem of his published in 1922. Ackerley became one of Forster's closest friends, and when Forster began spending two or three nights a week in London in the late 1920s, the two men saw a great deal of each other. Forster helped arrange Ackerley's appointment as private secretary to the Maharajah of Chhatarpur, the experience that led to Ackerley's *Hindoo Holiday*. Later, when Ackerley became literary editor of *The Listener*, he persuaded Forster to contribute frequent reviews and commentary. Ackerley led a very frenetic life in pursuit of his "ideal friend," to be found, he thought, among young guardsmen and petty criminals. He frequently turned to Forster for advice and support, and the older writer functioned for him as a father figure, a role that Forster often played with younger friends in his later years.

Through Ackerley and Sprott, Forster became involved in London's homosexual working-class milieu. He first established a relationship with Harry Dailey, a charming and outrageous policeman whose closest friends and lovers were criminals and cat burglars and writers. Then Forster fell in love with a good-looking and intelligent police constable named Bob Buckingham.

Forster met Buckingham in 1930, when the constable was twenty-eight years old, and they quickly sealed a bond that lasted until Forster's death forty years later. Their relationship survived even Buckingham's marriage in 1932. After a period of bitter struggle over Bob, Forster and May Buckingham became close friends.[20] The Buckinghams named their son Robin Morgan and designated Forster his godfather. The role of godfather pleased him very much,

for he had always wanted a son and—as the novels testify—had always been interested in continuity from
one generation to another.

If Forster feared his fame, he nevertheless made
excellent use of it, especially as a means to promote
civil liberties, the abiding cause of his middle age. In
1928, when Radclyffe Hall's lesbian novel *The Well of
Loneliness* was prosecuted as obscene, he vigorously
protested, undoubtedly spurred by knowledge of the
fate that would face *Maurice* were he to publish it. He
persuaded Virginia Woolf, Lytton Strachey, and Arnold
Bennett to join his campaign. He was among a group of
distinguished writers prepared to defend Hall's novel
when it came to trial, but the magistrate peremptorily
refused to hear expert evidence. Thirty years later,
however, Forster successfully testified in the equally
sensational trial of *Lady Chatterley's Lover*, strongly
supporting the publication of a novel heavily indebted
to his own suppressed book, which Lawrence had read
in manuscript.

Forster's former teacher and close friend G. Lowes
Dickinson died in 1932. At the request of Dickinson's
sisters, he undertook his friend's biography, producing
in *Goldsworthy Lowes Dickinson* (1934) a moving
tribute to the value of personal relations. In 1936, he
issued *Abinger Harvest*, a miscellany of some eighty
essays and reviews that spanned the period from 1905
to 1935. Named for Abinger Hammer, the Surrey village where he and his mother had lived since 1924, the
volume dramatically illustrated the wide range of
Forster's interests and affirmed the new direction of
his career as a penetrating observer of his age and a
sensitive critic of his contemporaries.

During the 1930s, he embarked on a career as a
broadcaster—offering regular book talks on the
BBC—and as a political activist. He served for several
years as president of the National Council for Civil

Liberties, and he frequently appeared at writers conferences to speak out on the dangers of censorship. Forster's political involvement was never parochial or narrow, but it was a natural redirection of the political concerns that had infused the novels. During this period, he became England's foremost exponent of humane values in a world increasingly threatened by the clash of totalitarian ideologies. He summed up his liberal humanism in a series of memorable essays, most notably in "What I Believe" (1938), in which he announced his abiding faith in personal relations and asserted that "if I had to choose between betraying my country and betraying my friend, I hope I should have the guts to betray my country."

In the 1930s Forster became a moral presence, a liberal conscience that countered the excesses of left and right alike. Especially for such angry young writers as C. Day Lewis, W. H. Auden, Christopher Isherwood, and William Plomer, he functioned as a symbol of committed humanism and responsible intelligence. For them, he was a figure of sanity in a world gone mad. In Auden's beautiful sonnet "To E. M. Forster," which served as the dedication to the Auden-Isherwood *Journey to a War*, he is saluted as an exemplar of enduring values who is endangered but not silenced by the international evil:

> Here, though the bombs are real and dangerous,
> And Italy and King's are far away,
> And we're afraid that you will speak to us,
> You promise still the inner life shall pay.
>
> As we run down the slope of Hate with gladness
> You trip us up like an unnoticed stone,
> And just as we are closeted with Madness
> You interrupt us like the telephone.[21]

For Isherwood, who was greatly influenced by Forster both as a man and as a writer, he was the epit-

ome of the antiheroic hero. He was both "the only living writer whom he would have described as his master" and a father figure on whom he relied for encouragement and support. In a memorable passage from
Down There on a Visit—based on diary entries during
the Munich crisis of 1938, when Neville Chamberlain
returned from his conference with Hitler unconvinc-
ingly proclaiming peace in our time—Isherwood movingly conveys the extraordinary admiration he felt for
Forster at a time of doubt and despair:

> When the newspapers compare Chamberlain to Abe
> Lincoln and Jesus Christ, they aren't being in the least
> sacrilegious, because *their* Lincoln and *their* Christ are
> utter phonies, anyhow. The newspapers are moved to
> tears by the spectacle of a gentleman standing his
> ground against a non-gentleman. So they call him
> "England."
>
> Well, *my* "England" is E. M.: the antiheroic hero, with
> his straggly straw mustache, his light, gay, blue baby
> eyes and his elderly stoop. Instead of a folded umbrella
> or a brown uniform, his emblems are his tweed cap
> (which is too small for him) and the odd-shaped brown
> paper parcels in which he carries his belongings from
> country to town and back again. While the others tell
> their followers to be ready to die, he advises us to live as
> if we were immortal. And he really does this himself, al-
> though he is as anxious and afraid as any of us, and
> never for an instant pretends not to be. He and his
> books and what they stand for are all that is truly worth
> saving from Hitler; and the vast majority of people on
> this island aren't even aware that he exists.[22]

During the war itself, Forster vigorously responded to the fascist threat, attacking anti-Semitism,
race consciousness, and intolerance. At the same time,
however, he was aware of the danger of the war mentality to English culture and liberty, and he frequently
pointed out the risk of destroying freedom while ostensibly defending it. In looking beyond the war to the

new society that would emerge from it, he confronted the classic liberal dilemma of the mid-twentieth century: the conflict between individualism and collectivism. In resolution, he endorsed libertarianism in the realm of personal relations and socialism—tempered by due regard for rural tradition—in the realm of economics. He also broadcast many political and literary talks, regularly preparing a book program broadcast to India.

In 1945, Lily Forster died. She was ninety years old and had been declining for some time. In 1937, Forster had written to Ackerley that women "are important to one's comfort and stability" and offered his relationship with his mother as proof of the observation: "Although my mother has been intermittently tiresome for the last thirty years, cramped and warped my genius, hindered my career, blocked and buggered up my house, and boycotted my beloved, I have to admit that she has provided a sort of rich subsoil where I have been able to rest and grow. That, rather than sex or wifiness, seems to be women's special gift to men."[23] The death of his mother was a great blow to Forster, and he mourned her for years.

In 1943, the influential American critic Lionel Trilling published an important monograph on Forster's work, which in turn stimulated enormous interest in the novels, leading to a "Forster revival" that quickly established the novelist as a major figure in contemporary literature. All through the rest of his life, his literary renown expanded, prompting the waggish observation that his reputation grew with every novel that he did not write.

The question of why one of our most acclaimed novelists wrote no novels in the final forty-six years of his life is a fascinating one that admits of no simple answers. One reason is the explanation Forster himself frequently gave: as a homosexual, he grew bored with writing marriage fiction, and he could not publish his work on homosexual subjects. This is no doubt true to a certain extent, but it oversimplifies a complex problem, especially since *A Passage to India* is hardly marriage fiction. In addition to the frustration he felt in not being able to explore homosexual issues openly in his fiction, he was probably also affected by the fact that the world he knew best had ended in 1914, with the beginning of the Great War. Even his final major effort at short fiction—"The Other Boat," completed in 1958—is set in the years just before World War I. His conviction of belonging to an anachronistic tradition probably tended to inhibit his creative imagination. But perhaps the major reason Forster abandoned the writing of novels is the simplest one of all. He probably felt that he had fully expressed (and exhausted) his vision in his six novels and that in any future novel he would only repeat himself. Complicated as well by his fear of success, Forster's long silence as a novelist remains among the most intriguing puzzles in modern literary history.

However, Forster reacted to his new eminence in the 1940s with considerably more equanimity than he had earlier responded to his moments of fame. For instance, he enjoyed the opportunities now afforded him to return to India in 1945 and to travel to the United States in 1947 and again in 1949. Tellingly, however, his greatest pleasure on these journeys came in reunions with old friends and in the forging of new friendships rather than in the public functions he performed as eminent author.

In 1946, Forster was forced to leave his home in Abinger, his lease having expired. He bitterly resented having to abandon the house built by his father for his aunt, in which he and his mother had lived for over twenty years. But his unhappiness was considerably eased by an invitation from King's College, Cambridge, to reside in the college as Honorary Fellow. For the rest of his life, he made his home in Cambridge, though he continued to spend much time in London with Ackerley and in Coventry with the Buckinghams.

Forster's later years were spent as "The Old Man of King's." He found the role of sage both trying and frustrating. He was frequently besieged by admirers, especially visiting Indians and academics and other individuals who had been particularly affected by his novels. He felt that he had indeed become wise, but he also believed that wisdom was incommunicable; it "goes with our learning into the grave," he wrote in his *Commonplace Book*.[24] But his chief objection to the fame that he was now burdened by was that it induced idleness and pretentiousness.

In fact, however, Forster never became pretentious, and he was very active during the decade of the 1950s. He co-authored the libretto for Benjamin Britten's opera *Billy Budd* (1951); he collected his second miscellany of essays and reviews, *Two Cheers for Democracy* (1951); he published his account of his Indian visits, *The Hill of Devi* (1953); and he wrote his great-aunt's biography, *Marianne Thornton* (1956). He also found time to continue tinkering with *Maurice* and to write stories, completing one of his most powerful—"The Other Boat"—in 1958, when he was almost eighty.

His final years were marred by a series of losses, including those of his godson, who died of Hodgkin's disease in 1962, and of Joe Ackerley, who died in 1967. But he continued to review books, to write prefaces for the works of promising or neglected writers, and to speak out on questions of censorship and culture. He had earlier declined a knighthood and an honorary degree from Oxford, but in 1952 he did accept appointment as Companion of Honour, and in 1959 King's College recognized him at a lavish birthday luncheon, where a telegram from Auden aptly characterized him as "famous loved yet not a sacred cow."[25] On his nine-tieth birthday in 1969, he was awarded the Order of Merit.

On June 7, 1970, after a stroke suffered in his rooms at Cambridge, Forster died in Coventry at the home of Bob and May Buckingham. He had left instructions forbidding religious observances, but at Bob Buckingham's direction, Forster's body was cremated to the accompaniment of Beethoven's Fifth Symphony, which he had described in *Howards End* as the "most sublime noise that has ever penetrated into the ear of man."

For all his reluctance to assume the mantle of greatness, Forster merited the title, most obviously by virtue of having produced a body of work that ranks among the finest of the century, but also because his public career mirrored those private qualities he loved. He was himself a member of that spiritual aristocracy he sketched so memorably in "What I Believe"—"an aristocracy of the sensitive, the considerate and the plucky"—and thus a reassuring exemplar of the "true human condition, the one permanent victory of our queer race over cruelty and chaos." In J. R. Ackerley's summation, "Morgan lived to a great age, but he never grew old excepting in his body in the last few years of his life, he never became a blimp or a bore, the scientific age was not to his taste but he never ceased to care about the state of the world, and he never lost faith in human values and human relationships."[26]

2

〰〰〰〰〰〰〰〰〰〰〰〰〰〰〰〰〰〰〰〰〰〰〰

Homage to the Complexity of Life: *Where Angels Fear to Tread*

Where Angels Fear to Tread is a minor masterpiece. Issued in 1905, when Forster was twenty-six years old, this first published of his books is astonishingly assured. Indeed, it may be the most perfectly controlled and flawless of his novels. As C. F. G. Masterson wrote in an unusually prescient 1905 review, "*Where Angels Fear to Tread* is a remarkable book. . . . It is told with a deftness, a lightness, a grace of touch, and a radiant atmosphere of humour, which mark a strength and capacity giving large promise for the future."[1]

In its controlled irony, its rich texture of allusions and leitmotifs, its perfect balance of comedy and pathos, its deep insight into character and social nuance, and its steady preoccupation with the inner life and with the difficulty of achieving wholeness, *Where Angels Fear to Tread* anticipates Forster's more ambitious works. Yet this strangely sad comic novel is ambitious in its own right, for it explores the complexities of character and of moral choice in a world that conspires to simplify both. Moreover, as an account of the complexity of life, *Where Angels Fear to Tread* remains curiously contemporary even now that the Edwardian society it faithfully mirrors has long since vanished.

The title of the book provides a clue to the narrative point of view that controls the wide tonal range as the plot incorporates elements of social comedy, melodrama, and even tragedy. Forster originally named his novel "Rescue" and then "Monteriano." The original publishers, the Edinburgh firm of William Blackwood, requested another title and finally chose "Where Angels Fear to Tread" from two suggested by Forster's friend E. J. Dent. Forster was not entirely happy with the choice, but "Where Angels Fear to Tread," he declared in a letter to his mother, "has the merit of describing the contents."[2]

An allusion to Pope's famous line in "An Essay on Criticism," "For *Fools* rush in where *Angels* fear to tread,"[3] the title perfectly captures the narrator's attitude toward the characters and the action. The narrator recounts the novel's events and explores the inner lives of the central characters from a vantage point of superior knowledge and lofty vision. The effect of this distance is not merely to create condescension toward fools and their machinations. It also facilitates the novel's irony, and it establishes intimacy between the narrator and the reader, who is assumed to share the narrator's sophistication. The condescension toward the central characters gradually dissipates as they grow toward self-knowledge and as their inner lives are explored with increasing seriousness. Concurrently, the comic surface of the novel is gradually exposed as a veneer beneath which lies an intractable sadness.

Where Angels Fear to Tread is also firmly controlled by the masterful manipulation of leitmotifs—what Forster in *Aspects of the Novel* calls "rhythm" or "repetition plus variation"[4]—the recurrent use of particular diction and tableaus to develop theme and establish symbols. The words "saved," "interfere," "transfigure," "duty," "influence," "forbid," and "mystery," for example, are repeated throughout the book, often with subtly different meanings and contexts. These repetitions help unify the novel and focus its irony.

The use of the word "saved" is particularly important. Initially used ironically, it finally helps define the book as a serious study of salvation, not from a conventional religious perspective but from the point of view of individual transfiguration and self-awareness. The religiously charged words function both to satirize conventional religiosity and to heighten Forster's moments of visionary experience, which are spiritual but not religious. Forster's reliance on Wordsworthian moments of transcendence reveals his romantic sensibility, while his endorsement of a Hegelian secular spirituality places him in a Victorian tradition of non-Christian quests for freedom from the limitations of material existence.

Throughout the novel, particular images, such as violets in a dark wood and the towers of Monteriano and crimson cheeks, are evoked again and again; and various tableaus are reenacted with significant variations. This rhythmic technique unifies the novel by "internal stitching" and elevates tone by "its lovely waxing and waning to fill us with surprise and freshness and hope."[5] As Frederick Crews observes, this technique can be successful only "in a work whose themes and authorial point of view are under perfect control from the beginning."[6]

Forster's mastery of characterization is also evident in *Where Angels Fear to Tread*. Using a combination of "flat characters" constructed around "a single idea or quality" and more complex "round characters" who are capable of development and growth, of "surprising in a convincing way,"[7] Forster translates a plot rife with melodrama into a vehicle for the study of character. Indeed, *Where Angels Fear to Tread* is Jamesian in its analysis of the interior lives of its central characters, and in fact the novel is probably indebted to James's *The Ambassadors*. At the same time, however, Forster impressively marshals the flat characters to further the plot and stimulate the growth of round characters. Flat characters such as Mrs. Herriton and her daughter Harriet are among his most successful satiric creations.

In *Where Angels Fear to Tread*, an important test of the growth of the central characters is their rejection of Victorian sexual values. As Lionel Trilling observes, the book "is a story of questioning, disillusionment and conversion. It is a criticism of the great middle class. It is a novel of sexuality."[8] Not surprisingly, Forster's celebration of sexual passion influenced D. H. Lawrence. But *Where Angels Fear to Tread* presents sexuality so discreetly that contemporary readers accustomed to explicit depictions of sexual activity in recent novels may not at first reading even recognize it. Paradoxically, however, the necessity to veil sex and to discuss sexual questions euphemistically actually invests sexuality in *Where Angels Fear to Tread* with mystery and charges it with force and significance. Forster exploits the power of reticence to suggest a wealth of emotional experience lurking behind respectable facades. His understanding of the centrality of the sexual instinct marks him as distinctly modern. *Where Angels Fear to Tread* both reflects and transcends Edwardian attitudes and contexts.

Perhaps Forster's greatest achievement in *Where Angels Fear to Tread* is his early and complete mastery of a particular tone of voice. This voice is intimate and relaxed, gentle and confidential, understated and dryly ironic, often whimsical and romantic, sometimes devastatingly satirical or brightly humorous, occasionally lyrical and even rapturous, and nearly always lightly brushed with sorrow and uncertainty. It is inimitable, and it is inseparable from the humane values it articulates.

The novel opens with the Herriton family of Sawston gathered at London's Charing Cross railway station to bid farewell to Lilia Theobald Herriton, the thirty-three-year-old widow of the family's eldest son Charles, and to Caroline Abbott, a sensible young lady from Sawston who is to accompany Lilia on an extended tour of Italy. Lilia, who has the "knack of being absurd in public," is an acute social embarrassment to her formidable mother-in-law, Mrs. Herriton. The Italian trip has been suggested by Lilia's young brother-in-law Philip Herriton as a means of safely removing her from the temptations of an unsuitable marriage to a "chinless curate" or otherwise reflecting badly on her in-laws.

While visiting the small town of Monteriano in central Italy, however, Lilia becomes infatuated with Gino Carella, the handsome twenty-one-year-old son of a dentist. Mrs. Herriton immediately dispatches Philip on a rescue party to break off the engagement. But when he arrives, he learns that Lilia and Gino are already married. The marriage proves a disaster as Lilia discovers that the restrictions on women in Italy are even worse than the social conventions of Sawston and that Gino is unfaithful. She dies giving birth to a son.

The Herritons pretend ignorance of the child until Gino begins to send postcards to young Irma, Lilia's daughter by her first marriage. Prodded by Caroline Abbott, who feels guilty for having encouraged the misalliance between Gino and Lilia, Mrs. Herriton—reluctantly but with fierce determination—decides to adopt the baby. She sends Philip and her inflexible daughter Harriet, who "had bolted all the cardinal virtues and couldn't digest them," on another rescue party. When they arrive in Monteriano, they discover Caroline already there.

Gino refuses to allow the Herritons to adopt his son. Having surrendered to the charms of Italy, Philip and Caroline accept his decision. Harriet, however, kidnaps the baby, and in an accident as they are leaving Monteriano, he is suffocated in her lap. Philip returns to confront Gino with the bad news and is nearly murdered by the enraged father. Caroline separates the men and reconciles them. As Caroline and Philip return to England, he realizes that he is in love with her. But just as he is on the verge of proposing marriage, she confesses her love for Gino, explaining, "I dare tell you this because I like you—and because you're without passion; you look on life as a spectacle; you don't enter it; you only find it funny or beautiful." The two resign themselves to the fact that "all the wonderful things had happened."

Where Angels Fear to Tread thus opens with a train departing for Italy and closes with one returning to England. It begins with broad domestic comedy, turns toward scathing satire, flares into melodrama, flirts with tragedy, and modulates into a sober, tenderly ironic coda. The two rescue attempts structure the novel as an exploration of the effects of Italy on the "undeveloped hearts"[9] of the four English characters who venture from the safety of their home.

Central to the novel is the contrast of Monteriano and Sawston. A "suburb of all the deadly virtues," as Wilfred Stone describes it,[10] Sawston epitomizes the limitations of the English upper middle class. Rich, clean, efficient, charitable, it is also narrow-minded, conventional, dull, and pretentious. In Sawston, decorum and duty are more valued than spontaneity and joy, appearances are more important than reality, and vulgarity is a sin more despised than any other. Caroline Abbott accurately summarizes Sawston as a place of idleness, stupidity, respectability, and "petty unselfishness," a place where people "spent their lives in making little sacrifices for objects they didn't care for, to please people they didn't love . . . they never learned to be sincere—and, what's as bad, never learned how to enjoy themselves." Governed by simplistic morality, Sawston lacks depth. It represses instinct and inhibits desire.

The presence of Mrs. Herriton dominates Sawston, and her character helps define it as prosaic and unimaginative. A vital and shrewd woman, Mrs. Herriton is one of Forster's most incisive portraits. Though an accomplished diplomat, she is incapable of recognizing the complexity of human relationships, as illustrated by her belief that Lilia must either be engaged to her admiring curate or not, "since no intermediate state existed," and by her remark when Gino rejects her offer to adopt his son: "For some perverse reason he will not part with the child." Her lack of imagination is evident in the fact that she does not "believe in romance, nor in transfigurations, nor in parallels from history, nor in anything else that may disturb domestic life."

Mrs. Herriton carefully cultivates an appearance of refinement, yet she has a will of iron—"when she wanted a thing she always got it"—and she is capable of cruelty. Her reaction to the news of Lilia's engagement reveals both her pettiness and her tenacity: "Suddenly she broke down over what might seem a small point. 'How dare she not tell me direct! How dare she write first to Yorkshire! . . . Bear witness, dear'—she choked with passion—'bear witness that for this I'll never forgive her!'" When Caroline Abbott refuses to accept her initial, insincere efforts to secure Gino's child, Mrs. Herriton's reaction frightens her son: "This outburst of violence from his elegant ladylike mother pained him dreadfully." Her aim in life is the "repression of vigour," and her motivation is pride. She launches the expedition to rescue the child only because she "could not bear to seem less charitable than others." Philip finally comes to recognize her as "a well-ordered, active, useless machine."

In contrast to Sawston, Monteriano represents instinct and passion, beauty and naturalness, mystery and complexity. When Philip is dispatched on his first rescue party, he leaves the "cold March night" of Sawston and arrives in Monteriano's "advancing tide of spring," evident in the riot of violets that cover the ground of the little wood through which the road to the town passes. Monteriano is dirty and inefficient, but like Gino's bedroom, its "shocking mess" is "the mess that comes of life, not of desolation." It is a place "where people have lived so hard and so splendidly," where they "know how to live."

The town is distinguished by its seventeen towers: "all that was left of the fifty-two that had filled the city in her prime. Some were only stumps, some were inclining stiffly to their fall, some were still erect, piercing like masts into the blue." These towers are phallic, and they suggest the masculine sexuality that dominates Monteriano. As the frequent scene of violence throughout the centuries, they also are witness to the brutal passions latent in the apparently peaceful community, passions not unconnected with male sexuality. But the towers also imply a comprehensiveness that is as alien to Sawston as sex and physical violence. Of one of the largest towers, Philip remarks, "It reaches up to heaven . . . and down to the other place." This comment indicates Monteriano's ability to embrace the entire range of human experience, including the demonic as well as the angelic, the brutal as well as the spiritual.

The wholeness of Monteriano is also suggested by the piazza "with its three great attractions—the Palazzo Pubblico, the Collegiate Church, and the Caffè Garibaldi: the intellect, the soul, and the body." This completeness defines it as a city in contrast to Sawston's status as a suburb. The distich out of Baedeker that is repeated over and over in the novel—"Poggibonizzi, fatta in là, / Che Monteriano si fa città!"—emphasizes this point; it may be translated, "Men of Poggibonsi, move on, / Monteriano is becoming a city!" When Philip stands in the center of the piazza, he thinks "how wonderful it must feel to belong to a city, however mean."

The charm and naturalness of Monteriano rebuke the ugliness and pretentiousness of Sawston. But Forster's contrast of the two locales is not simple, and Monteriano is not offered as an ideal. If life in Sawston is characterized by injunctions to duty and profit, so these notions also infect personal relationships in Monteriano. Gino's attraction to Lilia is mercenary, and his prime requisite in a second wife is that she know her duty toward his son. Moreover, Italian society is as convention-ridden as English society. "Italy is a delightful place to live in," the narrator remarks, and then adds the crucial qualification, "if you happen to be a man." In the democracy of the café, Italy achieves the "brotherhood of man," but "it is accomplished at the expense of the sisterhood of woman." Though the son of a dentist, a "troublesome creature, whom careful people find difficult to class," Gino manages to escape the worst restrictions of his society by virtue of being "that glorious invariable creature a man." Nevertheless, he conventionally decrees that "his wife should visit nowhere rather than visit wrongly."

The experience of Lilia poignantly illustrates the limitations of Monteriano and the difficulty of transcending cultural barriers. Fleeing the domination of the Herritons and the repression of Sawston, she is understandably attracted to Gino, whose beauty and charm promise fulfillment and freedom. At the beginning of their relationship, she is the dominant partner. But as Gino matures, he asserts the privileges of Italian manhood and accepts what he sees as the burden of his sex, the responsibility of managing his wife.

In marrying Gino, Lilia merely exchanges one form of bondage for another: "in the most gentle way, which Mrs. Herriton might have envied, Gino made her do what he wanted. . . . He had a good strong will when he chose to use it, and would not have had the least scruple in using bolts and locks to put it into effect." She becomes literally a prisoner, and from the vantage point of her "captivity," Sawston looks quite different from its previous appearance: "It seemed impossible that such a free, happy life could exist."

Lilia's disillusionment and suffering, which give her surprising dignity and genuine pathos, must be seen against the backdrop of female passivity in Monteriano. Whereas Lilia's suffering arouses her to escape attempts and passionate pleas for help, the city's patron saint, Santa Deodata, establishes Monteriano's ideal of feminine conduct by suffering passively: "So holy was she that all her life she lay upon her back in the house of her mother, refusing to eat, refusing to play, refusing to work. The devil, envious of such sanctity, tempted her in various ways. . . . When all proved vain he tripped up the mother and flung her downstairs before her very eyes. But so holy was the saint that she never picked her mother up, but lay upon her back through all, and thus assured her throne in Paradise."

The legend of Santa Deodata functions in the novel to illuminate the impassivity of Philip, but it is also important as a symbol of Monteriano's attitude toward women, an attitude sharply different from that of Sawston, where the decorous activity of Mrs. Herriton and Caroline Abbott is fully sanctioned. From this perspective, the unhappiness of Lilia's marriage results not merely or even primarily from her incompatability with Gino but from cultural differences that transcend individual ones. "No one realized," the narrator explains, "that more than personalities were en-

gaged; that the struggle was national; that generations
of ancestors, good, bad or indifferent, forbade the
Latin man to be chivalrous to the northern woman, the
northern woman to forgive the Latin man."

Against this background of social and cultural
contrasts and restraints, Forster explores the emotional
lives of Philip Herriton and Caroline Abbott. *Where
Angels Fear to Tread*, in fact, chronicles their sexual
and intellectual awakenings. The allusions to Dante's
celebration of his love for Beatrice, *La Vita Nuova*, in
the repeated phrase "the New Life," and to the *Divine
Comedy*, in the opening lines of the *Inferno* that Gino
recites in the second chapter, help define the book as a
life pilgrimage, a *Bildungsroman*. The lines from the
Inferno—"Midway this way of life we're bound upon,
/ I woke to find myself in a dark wood, / Where the
right road was wholly lost and gone"[11]—describe the
awkward plights of Philip and Caroline. Forster com-
passionately but unsentimentally examines their attempts to discover the right road out of the dark wood
in which they experience their late awakenings.

The novel's two central characters attain growth
and degrees of self-knowledge, but they do not
achieve the wholeness they seek. Their failure results
both from their individual limitations and from the social pressures that realistically impinge on their lives.
The integration of the outer and the inner lives—the
harmonizing of what Caroline Abbott's father describes as "real life" and what Philip refers to as the
"real you"—never takes place, yet this integration
functions as an ideal against which the characters'
growth and final accommodations are measured. The
awareness of the difficulty of achieving wholeness
contributes to the peculiar poignancy of the novel's
conclusion, in which the ironic perspective is less satirical than tender.

Philip Herriton is the quintessential Forsterian

hero: intellectual, overcivilized, self-conscious, and repressed. He may, in fact, be an ironic self-portrait or, in Stone's words, a "kind of experimental self for Forster, a portrait of the artist as a young man exploring his own possibilities for experience."[12] Although he is tall, he is physically unprepossessing, a "weakly-built young man, whose clothes had to be judiciously padded on the shoulder in order to make him pass muster." In compensation, he has developed two gifts, "a sense of beauty and a sense of humour." His sense of beauty leads him to an affected aestheticism: "It caused him at the age of twenty to wear parti-coloured ties and a squashy hat, to be late for dinner on account of the sunset, and to catch art from Burne-Jones to Praxiteles. . . . All the energies and enthusiasms of a rather friendless life had passed into the championship of beauty."

His aesthetic view of life leads him to romanticize Italy and to despise Sawston. From his first trip to Italy at the age of twenty-two, he "came back with the air of a prophet who would either remodel Sawston or reject it. . . . In a short time it was over. Nothing had happened either in Sawston or within himself." He thus comes to rely more and more on his second gift: "If he could not reform the world, he could at all events laugh at it, thus attaining at least an intellectual superiority." *Where Angels Fear to Tread* traces Philip's growth from aestheticism and romanticism toward active participation in reality.

Philip has a large capacity for self-deception and for pretending to emotions that he does not actually feel. His aestheticism is itself a form of insincerity and his romanticism a "spurious sentiment." It is the "idea of Italy" that intoxicates him; it is only "in theory" that he is unconventional. He thinks that he believes the advice he gives Lilia in the novel's opening scene: "don't, let me beg you, go with that awful tourist idea that Italy's only a museum of antiquities and art. Love and understand the Italians, for the people are more marvelous than the land." Ironically, he is more guilty of tourism than Lilia is, and he is the one most shocked when she adopts quite literally his injunction to love the Italians.

Real life constantly and painfully intrudes on Philip's romantic preconceptions. When he learns that Lilia is infatuated with the son of a dentist, he gives "a cry of personal disgust and pain. . . . A dentist in fairyland!" His reaction to Gino on their first meeting exposes both the hypocrisy of his pretended unconventionality and the voyeurism of his tendency to distance reality by interpreting it aesthetically: "Philip had seen that face before in Italy a hundred times—seen it and loved it, for it was not merely beautiful, but had the charm which is the rightful heritage of all who are born on that soil. But he did not want to see it opposite him at dinner. It was not the face of a gentleman."

Philip's salvation is accomplished in a number of stages. His disillusioning encounter with the real Italy of cads and dentists deprives him of the worst aspects of his sentimental romanticism, and he comes to find his unpleasant habit of laughing at others less and less satisfying. His gradual recognition of the meaninglessness of his mother's life also prepares him for liberation from Sawstonian values. "To what purpose was her diplomacy, her insincerity, her continued repression of vigour?" he asks of his mother's machinations. "Did they make anyone better or happier? Did they even bring happiness to herself?" But it is in Italy that he achieves insight into himself by learning concretely that "human love and love of truth sometimes conquer where love of beauty fails."

Caroline Abbott's journey parallels Philip's. Beneath her genteel appearance lies an adventuresomeness that is kept in check only by a highly developed

sense of propriety. Like Philip, she rebels against Sawston and then becomes disenchanted with Italy. She
admires Lilia for having "somehow kept the power of
enjoying herself with sincerity," and she encourages—
unconsciously for her own vicarious pleasure—Lilia's
infatuation with Gino, to whom she herself is attracted.
Thus she blames herself when the marriage turns out
badly and Lilia dies in childbirth. She comes to think
of Monteriano as a "magic city of vice, beneath whose
towers no person could grow up happy or pure," and
she regards the rescue of Lilia's baby as her "sacred
duty."

The heart of *Where Angels Fear to Tread* is the
second encounter of Philip and Caroline with Italy and
their consequent "homage to the complexity of life."
Accompanied by Harriet, who is "acrid, indissoluble,
large; the same in Italy as in England—changing her
disposition never, and her atmosphere under protest,"
Philip goes to Monteriano "as a puppet" of his mother,
approaching his task as a disinterested spectator, "in
the spirit of the cultivated tourist." Having arrived before them, Caroline has already encountered Gino
briefly and has been forced to acknowledge "in spite
of herself" the tangle of beauty, charm, vulgarity, and
mystery that is Monteriano. This tangle is nowhere
more evident than in the performance of *Lucia di
Lammermoor* that Harriet, Philip, and Caroline
attend.

The scene at the opera is among the most vivid in
the novel. As Alan Wilde remarks, "This is Forster's
Italy at its best: music and laughter, high spirits bounding back and forth from stage to audience, art as a living force, as something shared, and majestic bad taste
which 'attains to beauty's confidence.'"[13] Not surprisingly, Harriet is appalled by the raucousness of the audience, finally bolting with the cry, "Call this classical?
. . . It's not even respectable!" Significantly, the im-

mediate cause of Harriet's unhappiness is a bouquet of
welcome containing a billet-doux intended for the
prima donna. Philip and Caroline take the welcome to
heart and fully participate in the performance. Caroline "chatted and laughed and applauded and encored,
and rejoiced in the existence of beauty." Philip forgets
both his mission and his status as a tourist: "He was not
even an enthusiastic visitor. For he had been in this
place always. It was his home."

The evening ends with Harriet leaving in outrage,
dragging Caroline behind her. Philip, however, is
greeted by Gino as a long-lost brother, lifted into the
young Italian's box, and introduced to his friends.
Philip is not yet altogether free of self-consciousness,
but he responds to Gino's warmth and courtesy. He
"would have a spasm of horror at the muddle he had
made. But the spasm would pass, and again he would
be enchanted by the kind, cheerful voices, the laughter
that was never vapid, and the light caress of the arm
across his back." As John Sayre Martin observes, it is
one of the novel's "finer ironies" that Philip, the per-
petual spectator, should "while attending an opera be
pushed and jostled into life."[14]

For Philip and Caroline, the scene at the opera is
crucial. They both reawaken to the charm of Italy and
to the natural sexuality of Gino. Like Philip's, Caroline's head "was full of music, and that night when she
opened the window her room was filled with warm
sweet air. She was bathed in beauty within and without, she could not go to bed for happiness." Ashamed
of her sexual response, she "began to beat down her
happiness, knowing it to be sinful." But that night she
dreams of a "joyless, straggling place, full of people
who pretended." When she awakens, she recognizes
the ugly dreamscape as Sawston.

In a desperate reaction against her emerging consciousness, Caroline decides to attempt to secure the

child herself. Her mission is doomed to failure, however, for she encounters a moral complexity that
causes her once again to question the superficial Sawstonian code. When she sees the baby, she realizes that
it is not an abstract principle but a "real thing": "It was
so much flesh and blood, so many inches and ounces
of life—a glorious, unquestionable fact, which a man
and another woman had given to the world." Observing Gino with his son, she confronts the "horrible truth,
that wicked people are capable of love. . . . She was
in the presence of something greater than right or
wrong."

As she helps Gino bathe the child, she is "strangely
exalted by the service," and she determines to abandon the quest for the baby, "to exert no more influence
than there may be in a kiss or in the vaguest of the
heartfelt prayers." When Philip enters Gino's room, he
sees Caroline seated with the baby in her arms, Gino
kneeling by her side, and behind them twenty miles of
view: "to all intents and purposes, the Virgin and
Child, with Donor."

The bathing scene and Philip's aesthetic interpretation of it are revealing of the strengths and limitations of Gino, Caroline, and Philip. Just as the three
great attractions of Monteriano's piazza symbolize the
intellect, the soul, and the body, so do Philip, Caroline,
and Gino also represent these parts of an entire person.
The bathing scene crystallizes the quality that dominates each character. Taken together, Philip, Caroline,
and Gino may seem peculiarly complementary, with
their individual strengths combining harmoniously.
But the dominance in each of a particular aspect of
human life also suggests their individual incompleteness and their fundamental incompatibility, especially
since the positive quality in each has been developed
at the expense of deficiency in other areas. The under-
lying sadness of *Where Angels Fear to Tread* stems

from its apprehension of the atomized self, of the near impossibility of connecting the intellect, the soul, and the body, either in a balanced individual or in complementary relationships.

In Gino is represented the dominance of the body. From the very beginning of the novel, he is described in terms of the physical. He is, as Caroline admits to Philip, "Very good-looking. All his features are good, and he is well-built." He has served in the crack regiment, the Bersaglieri,[15] and he is an athlete, a proficient player of *pallone*, "that entrancing combination of lawn-tennis and fives" that Philip loves to watch. Throughout the book, Gino is associated with unconscious sexuality and physicality, functioning as a kind of Pan figure. But his greatest desire—as the bathing scene underlines—is not sexual but paternal: "He stood with one foot resting on the little body, suddenly musing, filled with the desire that his son should be like him, and should have sons like him, to people the earth. It is the strongest desire that can come to a man—if it comes to him at all—stronger than love or the desire for personal immortality." Gino's passion for his child is elemental, and the death of his son will unleash savage cruelty. Such passion and such concern for continuity mock Philip's indifference to life.

Caroline, on the other hand, functions as the soul figure. When she flees the bathing scene, she goes to pray in Santa Deodata's, where Philip tracks her as a "wounded soul." Throughout the book, she is associated with works of charity and moments of exaltation. Caroline's spiritual aura is her greatest attraction. Gino recognizes it as that elusive quality *simpatico*, and Philip—in a reversal of the Neoplatonic progression—finally comes to love her by the "spiritual path: her thoughts and her goodness and her nobility had moved him first, and now her whole body and all its gestures had become transfigured by them." Both men come to regard her as a goddess. Ironically, the spiritual quality they sense in her is actually the reflection of an internal struggle between Sawstonian morality and her awakening sexual response. Consequently, and even more ironically, her greatest attraction is also her greatest barrier to fulfillment. Her spirituality blinds Gino to her physicality and inspires only the intellectual passion of Philip, itself a displacement of his sexual attraction to Gino. Philip's identification of Caroline as the Virgin in the tableau of the bathing scene is cruelly appropriate.

In Philip, the intellect dominates. Described as "the clever one of the family," he is conscious throughout the book of his intellectual superiority to others, even when he allows them to manipulate him. This consciousness is at one with his aestheticism, his distance from reality, and his persistent interpretation of life in terms of art. Appropriately, in the bathing scene he is a voyeur of the tableau rather than a participant in it. He diagnoses his problem, complaining that "I seem fated to pass through the world without colliding with it or moving it," and he recognizes the justice of Caroline's criticism that "It's not enough to see clearly . . . your brain and your insight are splendid. But when you see what's right you're too idle to do it." Fittingly, as Caroline chastises him, Philip gazes on a fresco depicting the death of Santa Deodata, who "in her death, as in her life . . . did not accomplish much."[16] Ironically, the intellectual faculty proves singularly ineffectual in this novel, for Philip consistently fails to understand Caroline's spiritual struggle and Gino's paternal passion. By the end of the book, Philip attains a level of engagement and resolution, but his approach to life continues to be more intellectual than spiritual or passionate.

Caroline tells Philip that "I wish something would happen to you, my dear friend," and in the novel's bril-

liant close, the focal characters find themselves
tangled in a web of violent action almost unique in
Forster's canon. The catalyst of this violence that leads
to confrontation between the major characters and
within each is Harriet. Motivated by a simplistic evangelical morality that denies the complexity of life and
fortified by her Bible, she steals the baby. The scene of
kidnaping and death is as somber and foreboding as
the scene at the opera is light and joyful. In the dark
wood "where violets were so plentiful in spring," as
the English visitors descend the hillside in the rain "as
if they were traveling with the whole world's sorrow,"
the carriage accident kills the child and propels Philip
with a broken arm into his painful but redemptive encounter with real life.

Philip accepts responsibility for the baby's death,
and in his detachment and failure of involvement he is
almost as guilty as Harriet. At last forced to act, he
takes the news to Gino. In the violence that ensues,
Philip participates in a range of experience heretofore
foreign to him, a range that includes the physical and
the spiritual, the demonic and the angelic. In his rage,
Gino reacts savagely, demonically, and Philip refers to
him as a "brute" and a "devil." But Philip is not merely
Gino's passive victim. In the bloody fight, the Englishman strikes out at his adversary, knocks him unconscious, and then tenderly, lovingly, almost sexually
revives him, only once again to be stalked and then attacked by the grieving father, who obscenely tortures
and almost kills him. Philip's capacity for the brutal
and demonic is further illustrated when he deliriously
murmurs to Caroline, "Kill him! Kill him for me." The
point that needs emphasis is that in this painful confrontation Philip is forced to express the physical and
emotional passion that he has hitherto scrupulously
avoided. This participation prepares him for further
growth.

Philip's immersion in the physical is complemented by a vision of the spiritual. Caroline ends the
fighting, announces "I will have no more intentional
evil," and seals the reconciliation of the two men by
administering a sacrament of milk. To Philip she seems
like a goddess. As she comforts the suffering father,
Philip observes, "Her eyes were open, full of infinite
pity and full of majesty, as if they discerned the boundaries of sorrow, and saw unimaginable tracts beyond.
Such eyes he had seen in great pictures but never in a
mortal." If Philip here continues to engage in voyeurism and to interpret life in terms of art, there are nevertheless some important differences. Now he recognizes the genuineness of life as well as art, and in fact,
he here validates art by reference to his experience of
life rather than vice versa, as has been his custom. He
looks away from the scene, "assured that there was
greatness in the world." The narrator adds: "Quietly,
without hysterical prayers or banging of drums, he
underwent conversion. He was saved."

Philip's salvation is not, to be sure, a conventional
religious conversion. Rather, it is an epiphany of the
spirit, an apprehension of wholeness, and it transfigures him. It promises success in his quest for secular
spirituality, for freedom and self-determination. Observing Caroline cradling Gino's head to her breast and
brushing his brow with her lips, Philip glimpses an existential union of the physical and the spiritual, of the
body and the soul. This union is not the "aesthetic
whole" into which he had earlier absorbed Italy but an
emblem of connection in real life and an image of exalted sexuality. It signifies the triumph of human love
and love of truth where love of beauty fails.

The central irony of this ironic novel is that Philip
himself misinterprets the vision. He thinks that it is
Caroline's spirituality—her agency as a goddess—that
saves him. But as the conclusion makes clear, her re-

sponse to Gino is not that of a superior being but of a
sexually aroused woman. It is appropriate that Philip's
transfiguration be triggered by a vision of sexuality
that he misinterprets, for his own sexuality has been so
repressed that he misunderstands it as well.

Philip's real sexual attraction is not the weak intellectual response he develops for Caroline "by the spiritual path" but the physical passion he feels for Gino.
Philip himself is not conscious of the implications of
this attraction, though he does acknowledge ties to the
young Italian "of almost alarming intimacy." This failure to know himself well constitutes Philip's most severe limitation; it is a measure of the distance he has
yet to traverse on the road out of the dark wood. The
homosexual subtext of the novel is suggested obliquely
but unmistakably, and it is important to a full understanding of Forster's masterful conclusion, which is at
once tender-spirited and tough-minded.

The final chapter is both a grim comedy of frustration and yet another homage to the complexity of
life. It records the apparent triumph of the outer life
over the inner life, of social conventions over individual fulfillment; and in its account of the failure of
Philip and Caroline to connect, it anticipates the ending of *A Passage to India*. Yet beneath the irony and
among the sadly comic misinterpretations on which
the novel closes are grounds for optimism.

The concluding chapter opens with the news that
Gino is committed to marrying the widow he had
chosen as a second wife to take care of his son; it
would be too expensive to break off the engagement
now. Philip—"convalescent, both in body and spirit"—
has decided to live in London and devote himself to
his law practice. Yet he is aware that though life was
greater than he had supposed, "it was even less complete. He had seen the need for strenuous work and for
righteousness. And now he saw what a very little way

those things would go." In an attempt to attain wholeness, he is on the verge of declaring his love for Caroline, a love whose weak physical component has not
flowered naturally but has been coached into being by
Gino.

The elliptical quality of the conversation between
Caroline and Philip as they leave Italy indicates the increased difficulty of communication as they approach
Sawston. Each completely misinterprets the intentions
of the other. Just when Philip thinks that Caroline will
demurely signal her love for him, she bursts forth with
a confession of passion for his Italian friend: "I'm in
love with Gino . . . I mean it crudely—you know what
I mean. . . . If he had asked me, I might have given
myself body and soul." She has been "saved" from
sexual happiness and social ostracism—and, more ominously, from the fate of Lilia—by the fact that Gino
regarded her as "a superior being—a goddess" and
hence did not respond to her awakening sexuality. The
use of the word "saved" is not altogether ironic, at least
not in any simple or merely satiric sense, for the experience of Lilia testifies to the power of social conventions and cultural barriers in turn-of-the-century Europe. From this perspective, the triumph of the
Sawstonian code is not entirely a defeat for Caroline.

Philip recognizes that "the thing was even greater
than she imagined." He now sees her as a goddess of a
different sort than he had perceived earlier. He com-
pares her with classical figures of inappropriate and
unrequited passion: Pasiphaë, whom Poseidon cruelly
caused to become enamored of a bull, and Selene the
moon, who loved Endymion, the most beautiful
of men, but could embrace him only in sleep. Caroline's attitude, however, is not romantic. Declaring that
"I and my life must be where I live" and convinced
that all the wonderful things had happened, she determines to return to Sawston. The intimate conversation with Philip "had made her life endurable."

The conclusion is realistic in its depiction of social restraints that inhibit happiness and profoundly sad in its recognition of the difficulty of achieving wholeness. Yet *Where Angels Fear to Tread* is not entirely pessimistic. Completeness is difficult but not impossible; the failures of Caroline and Philip are individual, not universal. Moreover, both characters grow in the novel, and the disappointment of their failure to connect sexually with each other is mitigated by recognition of Philip's homosexual nature.

Caroline's description of Philip as his old self—a passionless spectator—is a serious misinterpretation on her part. Even if he has not yet come to understand his own sexuality, at least he has come to a more complex view of sexuality itself than he had held previously. When Caroline declares her passion, Philip discards the old categories of "refinement" and "unrefinement," and the narrator intrudes to explain Philip's growth: "Out of this wreck there was revealed to him something indestructible—something which she, who had given it, could never take away." This is an oblique hint that Philip may eventually be saved by his homosexuality, as are so many characters in Forster's explicitly gay fiction.

Philip's decision to leave Sawston and move to London is yet another sign of maturity. It indicates his break with his mother, and it offers opportunities for sexual fulfillment, since a city—as opposed to a suburb—is a symbol of wholeness in this novel, written before Forster came to envision cities as sterile and satanic. Most important, Philip has grown to appreciate the greatness of life, to understand that human love and love of truth can conquer where love of beauty fails. He continues to approach life intellectually and primarily as an observer, but now his intellect is larger and his sight sharper. More than ever before, he pays homage to the complexity of life.

Where Angels Fear to Tread is an impressive

achievement. This apparently slight book about "the improvement of Philip," as Forster described it in a 1905 letter to R. C. Trevelyan,[17] trenchantly confronts issues of continuing importance and pressing interest: individuality and social restraints, involvement and commitment, repression and fulfillment. In its dissection of simplistic morality, it is vital and forceful. And in its insistent concern with fashioning the self, with achieving wholeness of being, the novel is remarkably contemporary, addressing what is still a dilemma in the late twentieth century with insight and compassion.

Forster's first book embodies fully matured his characteristic gifts of commanding intelligence, ironic observation, whimsical comedy, and deep pathos. A novel both powerful and subtle, *Where Angels Fear to Tread* marks an auspicious beginning to a career that would produce books more ambitious, more complex, and more penetrating but none more perfectly controlled.

3

Bubbles on an Extremely Rough Sea:
The Longest Journey

The Longest Journey (1907), Forster's second published novel, is his most problematic. A work of great passion and vitality, it is lyrical, resonant, intense, and painful. It is undeniably moving, yet it strikes many readers as sentimental and confused.[1] Certainly it is marred by unconvincing characterization and by a lack of proportion and perhaps as well by an imperfect reconciliation of the allegorical and the realistic. Still, it was Forster's own favorite among his novels,[2] and it is his most clearly autobiographical work. Moreover, it marks an important breakthrough in his development as a novelist.

As a *Bildungsroman, The Longest Journey* has affinities with *Where Angels Fear to Tread.* Both novels pivot on a series of symbolic moments, the acceptance or rejection of which signifies the acceptance or rejection of life, and the protagonist of each is similarly voyeuristic. *The Longest Journey* also anticipates *Maurice*, especially in the exploration of homosexual love. But homosexuality in *The Longest Journey* is explored covertly, and whereas *Maurice* chronicles its hero's salvation through sexual fulfillment, *The Longest Journey* relentlessly depicts the consequences of its protagonist's failure to acknowledge his true nature, his real self.

Most of all, however, *The Longest Journey* looks

forward to *Howards End* and *A Passage to India*. It shares with them frank ambition, complex and expansive symbolism, and genuine breadth of vision. Its mythological dimension and its reverence for the English countryside link it to *Howards End*, while its persistent posing of metaphysical questions anticipates *A Passage to India*. It is also similar to *A Passage to India* in that its external plot is finally dwarfed by a layer of meaning communicated primarily through subtly orchestrated symbolism.

The Longest Journey is divided into three unequal sections, "Cambridge," "Sawston," and "Wiltshire." These sections mark the stages of Rickie Elliot's life journey, and the places reflect different responses to life: the bookish humanism and truth seeking of the university, the sterile conventionality of the suburb, and the natural, instinctual pastoralism of the countryside. Corresponding to the movements of a doleful sonata, this tripartite structure also mirrors the Hegelian pattern of thesis-antithesis-synthesis. The synthesis that the novel ultimately proposes is the union of the best values of Cambridge and Wiltshire, as epitomized by the alliance of Rickie's friend and his half brother, Stewart Ansell and Stephen Wonham.

As the "Cambridge" section opens, Rickie is an undergraduate who has discovered in the camaraderie of the university some respite from the loneliness and unhappiness of a friendless childhood. An orphan and a congenital cripple who loathes the memory of his hateful father and idolizes that of his beloved mother, he is an idealistic and naive young man who writes romantic stories heavily laden with fantasy. On a visit to family friends, he chances upon Agnes Pembroke and Gerald Dawes making love and voyeuristically discovers heterosexual desire. When Gerald is suddenly killed, he urges Agnes to "mind," to "remember that the greatest thing is over."

Two years later, Agnes visits Cambridge and, in a secluded womblike dell, seduces Rickie. Despite the passionate objections of his friend Stewart Ansell, Rickie and Agnes become engaged. At Cadover, "the perilous house," the Wiltshire home of his unpleasant aunt Mrs. Failing, Rickie learns that his aunt's uncouth ward Stephen Wonham is actually his half brother. Rickie recognizes that the revelation offers him a "symbolical moment," and he believes that such a "real thing" as brotherhood ought to be acknowledged. But Agnes persuades him to reject both the moment and the brother.

In the "Sawston" section, Rickie and Agnes marry. He accepts a teaching position at Sawston School, and under the influence of Agnes's older brother Herbert Pembroke, he becomes more and more conventional. A "shadow of unreality" increasingly darkens his world. Agnes gives birth to a badly deformed daughter, who soon dies. The relationship between Rickie and Agnes deteriorates, especially when he discovers that she is partially responsible for Stephen's expulsion from Cadover. When Stephen and Ansell simultaneously appear in Sawston, they scuffle and then become fast friends. Ansell recognizes the unpolished shepherd as "one of the greatest people I have ever met." Agnes attempts to bribe Stephen not to reveal his kinship with Rickie to the world at large, but Stephen is insulted by the offer and angrily leaves Sawston. Ansell, however, remains to denounce Rickie's cowardice and to reveal that Stephen is the illegitimate son not of Rickie's despised father but of his adored mother.

The "Wiltshire" section begins with a flashback detailing the relationship of Rickie's mother and Stephen's father, a farmer named Robert; their flight to Sweden; and Robert's death by drowning seventeen days later. Rickie's knowledge that Stephen is his mother's son causes him to regard his half brother very differently; when Stephen returns to Sawston, Rickie embraces him as a brother. Stephen warns Rickie against viewing him as a reincarnation of their mother rather than as an individual in his own right, and the two leave Sawston together, seeking refuge with Ansell.

When Rickie visits Cadover, Mrs. Failing tells him to "beware of the earth," for "conventions . . . will claim us in the end." Rickie rejects the advice, but his fragile faith in the earth, in Stephen, and in people generally is shattered when his half brother breaks a promise and gets drunk in a local pub. Discovering Stephen unconscious, his body draped across railroad tracks, Rickie saves him from an oncoming train but loses his own life. In an epitaph for Rickie, Mrs. Failing describes him as "one who has failed in all he undertook." The novel ends with Agnes having remarried, Herbert having become a clergyman, Mrs. Failing having died, and Rickie's stories having achieved posthumous success. Accompanied by Ansell, Stephen moves to Wiltshire, marries, and fathers a child, whom he names for his and Rickie's mother. He believes that "he guided the future of our race, and that, century after century, his thoughts and his passions would triumph in England."

The plot of *The Longest Journey* is unwieldy and, especially in the brief "Wiltshire" section, too hurried. But the frequent flashbacks, meditations on the past, and projections into the future are central to the novel. As J. K. Johnstone observes, the book "looks back to the prehistoric dawn of Stonehenge, and forward, down the stream of time, through the arches of the years."[3] This perspective is neatly crystallized by the intersection of an ancient Roman road and a modern railroad line at which several children—and eventually Rickie himself—surrender their futures in death.

Forster's awareness of the complex ways in which the past impinges on the present and the present on the future gives Rickie Elliot's bleak journey scope and significance and helps define the novel itself as nothing less than a search for meaning in life. This search assumes both the continuity of "a little earth, for ever isolated from the rest of the solar system" and the fragility of any individual existence: "we are all of us bubbles on an extremely rough sea." *The Longest Journey* in effect dramatizes Byron's conception of the mystery of life, as expressed in the famous final stanza of Canto 15 of *Don Juan:*

> Between two worlds life hovers like a star,
> 'Twixt Night and Morn, upon the horizon's verge.
> How little do we know that which we are!
> How less what we may be! The eternal surge
> Of Time and Tide rolls on and bears afar
> Our bubbles; as the old burst, new emerge,
> Lashed from the foam of ages; while the graves
> Of Empires heave but like some passing waves.[4]

The pervasive water imagery in *The Longest Journey*, including the conception of time as a stream rushing into the future, emphasizes the flux of life. The recurrent chalk imagery, on the other hand, testifies to the strength and durability of the earth, itself doomed eventually to disintegrate. Significantly, chalk is neither strong nor durable in any absolute sense: it is so only in comparison to the sea. Forster's distrust of absolutes is at the heart of the novel and of his humanism, and it helps account for the muted pessimism that accompanies even his epiphanies.

The transitoriness of life is underscored by the numerous deaths casually recounted in the novel. As Rickie and Agnes arrive in Wiltshire on their first visit to Cadover, a child is killed by their train, thus anticipating Rickie's own death. Rickie's mother, though apparently in good health, survives his father by only eleven days. The fifth chapter opens with the notorious sentence "Gerald died that afternoon." Robert's death by drowning and Rickie's daughter's death of pneumonia are equally sudden. The arbitrariness of death gives urgency to the book's search for meaning and the characters' need to find stability in the flux of life. It signifies the cruelty of nature, "to whom our refinement and piety are but as bubbles, hurrying downwards on the turbid waters. They break, and the stream continues."

In *The Longest Journey*, a test of each character is an attempt to discover a metaphysical reality, a "Spirit of Life" that makes sense of a universe apparently devoid of meaning. The novel defines decent people as those who are "convinced that our life is a state of some importance, and our earth not a place to beat time on." In this book, Forster does not offer any conclusive answers to the metaphysical questions that he raises. He does, however, suggest that there is, in fact, meaning to life, meaning that—though it cannot be articulated clearly—can be apprehended both intellectually and instinctively. And he emphatically condemns social conventions such as marriage, organized religion, and the class system—and all the suburban ideals represented by Sawston School—as artificial, unnatural, and life-denying impositions of order on a universe that is fundamentally indifferent to individual human happiness. Suburbanization, the class society, and the conventions all distance men and women from the earth, in whose durability and cyclical rhythms resides the spirit of life. As James McConkey explains, "the earth represents the continuity which exists within the eternal change of nature; it provides the means whereby man can perceive his connection with his ancestors and with all the past as well as with his fellows."[5]

The very title of Forster's novel repudiates the social convention of marriage, at least insofar as marriage represents Rickie's attempt to achieve stability through "eternal ownership" of another person. Taken from Shelley's "Epipsychidion," the title indicts Rickie's disastrous marriage as an ill-advised effort to invest the "dreariest and longest journey" with significance by conforming to the "code / Of modern morals" that requires one to select "Out of the crowd a mistress or a friend, / And all the rest, though fair and wise, commend / To cold oblivion." It condemns his decision to travel to his "home among the dead" with "one chained friend, perhaps a jealous foe."[6] Rickie's marriage fails because it is an act of conformity and a denial of his own nature.

To his ultimate grief, Rickie regards his brief glimpse of Gerald and Agnes making love as a symbolic moment. Coming upon them in each other's arms, Rickie discovers Eros for the first time and is profoundly affected:

He only looked for a moment, but the sight burnt into his brain. . . . He thought, "Do such things actually happen?" and he seemed to be looking down coloured valleys. . . . He stood at the springs of creation and heard the primeval monotony. Then an obscure instrument gave out a little phrase. . . . The phrase was repeated and a listener might know that it was a fragment of the Tune of tunes. Nobler instruments accepted it, the clarionet protected, the brass encouraged, and it rose to the surface to the whisper of violins. In full unison was Love born, flame of the flame, flushing the dark river beneath him and the virgin snows above. His wings were infinite, his youth eternal; the sun was a jewel on his finger as he passed it in benediction over the world. Creation, no longer monotonous, acclaimed him, in widening melody, in brighter radiances. Was Love a column of fire? Was he a torrent of song? Was he greater than either—the touch of a man on a woman?

Following this deliberately overwritten outburst of sentimental lyricism, the narrator adds laconically, "It was the merest accident that Rickie had not been disgusted."

The weak passion that Rickie eventually develops

for Agnes is similar to the spiritual love that Philip Herriton finally develops for Caroline Abbott in *Where Angels Fear to Tread*. Just as Philip's love for Caroline is a displacement of his physical passion for Gino Carella, so Rickie's love for Agnes is aroused by his unconscious desire for Gerald, a brainless soldier who had mistreated him at school, "a young man who had the figure of a Greek athlete and the face of an English one. . . . Just where he began to be beautiful the clothes started." At the height of his erotic awakening, Rickie imagines Gerald as the young Athenian in Aristophanes's *The Clouds*, "perfect in body, placid in mind, who neglects his work at the Bar and trains all day among the woods and meadows, with a garland on his head and a friend to set the pace." The longing for love implicit in this fantasy is especially poignant in light of the lame Rickie's question as a child: "Shall I ever have a friend? . . . I don't see how. They walk too fast."

Rickie's romantic conception of the brutal Gerald is inaccurate, the narrator says, for "Mr. Dawes would not have bothered over the garland or noticed the spring, and would have complained that the friend ran too slowly or too fast." Similarly, Rickie's love for Agnes, developed "through the imagination" rather than "through the desires," is also inappropriate and unreal. His conception of her as a "kindly Medea, a Cleopatra with a sense of duty" is, in Ansell's diagnosis, "the subjective product of a diseased imagination." It also illustrates Rickie's characteristic tendency to filter reality through a romantic sensibility that distorts rather than illuminates.

In contrast to the misconceived Gerald and Agnes, Ansell—who genuinely loves Rickie—is real, and he literally wears a garland in a crucial scene, a symbolic moment that Rickie fails to recognize. This scene, set in the secluded dell in which Agnes will later seduce

Rickie, juxtaposes heterosexuality and homosexuality and helps explain Rickie's desire to marry. As he and Ansell converse, Rickie thinks of the "irony of friendship—so strong it is, and so fragile. We fly together like straws in an eddy, to part in the open stream." He thinks that friendship (or homosexuality) offers no stability against the flux of time, for "Nature has no use for us: she has cut her stuff differently. Dutiful sons, loving husbands, responsible fathers—these are what she wants, and if we are friends it must be in our spare time."

Convinced that physical procreation offers the only source of continuity, he muses: "Abram and Sarai were sorrowful, yet their seed became as sands of the sea, and distracts the politics of Europe at this moment. But a few verses of poetry is all that survives of David and Jonathan." He wishes that "we were labelled," that "there was a society, a kind of friendship office, where the marriage of true minds could be registered." The allusions to David and Jonathan and to Shakespeare's Sonnet 116 clearly establish homosexuality rather than more conventional male friendship as the subject of this conversation. Rickie's preoccupation with labels and despair over the physical sterility of homosexuality are crucial aspects of his character.

Ansell later rejects the idea of marriage as "ordained by nature" with the fierce response, "The point is, not what's ordained by nature or any other fool, but what's right." Here, however, he does not grasp Rickie's questioning of their friendship, and after the two romp like lovers in the dell, he allows Rickie to jerk away and hurry off to his fatal appointment with Agnes. She seduces him in a peculiarly maternal manner in the dell that John Sayre Martin describes as a "retreat from the uncertainties of life, a natural womb that partly compensates [Rickie] for the loss of his mother."[7] As they embrace, he tells Agnes, "What

[Gerald] gave you then is greater than anything you will get from me." Understandably, the young woman shivers "with the sense of something abnormal."

Rickie's failure to accept—or even to recognize—his homosexual nature is in large part responsible for his tragedy. Like Oedipus, to whom he is linked by his limp and his obliviousness to the true circumstances of his family origins, he lacks self-knowledge. Indeed, as the narrator later points out, "he knew nothing about himself at all." When he heard of a "sordid village scandal" involving homosexuality, he "blushed at it like a maiden lady, in spite of its having a parallel in a beautiful idyll of Theocritus." As Wilfred Stone writes, Rickie's "latent homosexuality is one of the realities of his nature. He must either courageously face this knowledge and its consequences or else try to force his life into an alien, conventional mold."[8]

Rickie's choice of conformity, of socially approved labels as a source of stability on his journey, is a rejection of the "wine of life" in favor of the "teacup of experience." To accept passively this teacup time after time is to become "quite sane, efficient, quite experienced, and quite useless to God or man." The challenge the novel offers its characters (and its readers) is to say, "I will experience no longer. I will create. I will be an experience." To make this declaration is not easy: "to do this we must be both acute and heroic." Significantly, all the characters in *The Longest Journey* who might be described as acute and heroic, who drink the "wine of life," either defy social conventions or are by birth or background placed beyond the bounds of respectability. Ansell is a homosexual Jew, Stephen is a bastard, Rickie's mother and Robert violate both her marriage vows and the class barrier, and Mr. Failing, who is present in the novel through his posthumously published collection of essays, is an agrarian socialist, an apostle of universal brotherhood.

In *The Longest Journey,* a novel dedicated "Fratribus," social conventions typically destroy fraternity.[9] Thus, Rickie's marriage is not only unnatural for him as a repression of his deepest instinct, it is destructive of brotherhood as well. Agnes not only alters the relationship of Rickie and Ansell, she also intervenes to prevent Rickie from seizing the symbolic moment when he learns that Stephen is his half brother. As Stephen calls up to Rickie's room at Cadover, Agnes halts her fiancé's advance "quite frankly, with widespread arms."

Because Stephen is a bastard, first Agnes and then Rickie regard him as "illicit, abnormal, worse than a man diseased." Reflecting the same prejudice, a nonconformist Christian who gives Stephen a ride when he is expelled from Cadover labels him "a blot on God's earth." Stephen's bastardy—his status as a "natural" child—enhances his role as opponent of respectability and artificiality. This role is intimated by the occasion when as a naked child he climbed to the roof of Cadover, thereby inspiring Mr. Failing to a vision: "I see the respectable mansion. I see the smug fortress of culture. The doors are shut. The windows are shut. But on the roof the children go dancing forever." Not coincidentally, Stephen later smashes with lumps of chalk the closed windows of the respectable mansion in protest against the exploitation Mrs. Failing sanctions.

The novel exposes the hypocrisy and destructiveness of suburban respectability and of the class system. The Silts, Rickie's cousins, are proud that his small fortune is "unspoiled by trade," and Agnes insults Stewart's sister Maud by cattily reminding her of the Ansells' lack of status as drapers. Such attitudes reveal the pettiness and absurdity of English social customs. The elaborate map of class, with the "line between the county and the local, the line between the laborer and the artisan," with everything "graduated" ostensibly so that "things could be kept together," actually promotes division rather than unity. It destroys the possibility of personal intercourse by accenting the differences that separate people rather than the similarities that link them. It mocks Mr. Failing's ideal of the brotherhood of man.

Rickie is not acute and heroic, but what distinguishes him from the characters wholly addicted to convention, such as Agnes and Herbert, is his respect for the imagination and the intellect, for those who attempt "to dispel a little of the darkness by which we . . . are surrounded." This sets him apart from Herbert, who "for all his fine talk about a spiritual life . . . had but one test for things—success: success for the body in this life or for the soul in the life to come," and from Agnes, who responds "balder-dash" when Rickie observes that the ancient Greeks knew that "poetry, not prose, lies at the core." Herbert is contemptuous of philosophy, and Agnes lacks the capacity to "detect the union of adamant and shadow that men call poetry." Rickie's earnest desire to apprehend meaning in life renders his increasing bewilderment the more poignant. He becomes painfully aware that "beyond the yearning there remained a yearning, behind the drawn veil a veil that he could not draw."

Rickie's respect for the intellect is a legacy of Cambridge. The university, which never pretends to be the "great world," is sharply contrasted with Sawston School, which proclaims itself "the world in miniature." The watchwords of Sawston—"'Organize.' 'Systematize.' 'Fill up every moment.' 'Induce *esprit de corps.*'"—are destructive, for "they ignored personal contest, personal truces, personal love." Sawston School is a "beneficent machine" that promotes cruelty and conformity. In contrast, the tutors and resident fellows at Cambridge "taught the perky boy that he was not everything, and the limp boy that he might be something. They even welcomed those boys who were neither limp nor perky, but odd. . . . And they did everything with ease—one might almost say with nonchalance,—so that the boys noticed nothing, and received education, often for the first time in their lives." When Rickie crept to Cambridge, "cold and friendless and ignorant . . . preparing for a silent and solitary journey," the university "had taken and soothed him, and had laughed at him a little."

Ansell functions in *The Longest Journey* as the "undergraduate high priest of that local shrine" Cambridge,[10] the representative of the intellect. Interestingly, his intellect is not coldly rational. In the discussion of whether a cow is "real" if no one is there to see it, he abandons the laws of logic and evidence to assert, "She's there for me. . . . Whether I'm in Cambridge or Iceland or dead, the cow will be there." Ansell brings to bear on the questions of existence his own willed faith and intuition, and his judgments are infallible. "If you ask me what the Spirit of Life is," he declares, "I can't tell you. I only tell you, watch for it. Myself I've found it in books. Some people find it out of doors or in each other. Never mind. It's the same spirit, and I trust myself to know it anywhere, and to use it rightly." Ansell recognizes Agnes's lack of seriousness and truthfulness, her unreality, from the very beginning, just as he will later immediately conclude that Stephen naturally intuits the spirit of life. Throughout the novel, Ansell articulates Forsterian values.

Ansell's habit of drawing a circle within a square within a circle within a square indicates his quest to discover an ineffable reality. This symbol is repeated throughout the book, sometimes obliquely as in the descriptions of the Cadbury Rings and of the British Museum Reading Room. It serves as a constant reminder of the need to discover "what is good and true" and "what lies behind everything." This need can never be fully satisfied, for ultimate meaning will remain hidden; it is represented by the innermost circle, "the one in the middle of everything, that there's never room enough to draw." But despite the impossibility of penetrating ineffable reality, the effort to discover meaning is what defines Forster's characters as most fully human. Ansell knows that his life is not ignoble: "It was worth while to grow old and dusty seeking for truth though truth is unattainable, restating questions that have been stated at the beginning of the world. Failure would await him, but not disillusionment."

Ansell is an intellectual, yet he is also capable of action. "When the moment comes," he declares, "I shall hit out like any ploughboy. . . . Nothing's easier than action. . . . But I want to act rightly." His test for the rightness of any fact or action is the Keatsian criterion, "the holiness of the heart's imagination," a test that emphasizes the personal rather than the conventional or the abstract. If he is in many ways pedantic—as, for instance, when he ineffectually warns Rickie against Agnes by appealing to books, specifically to "Epipsychidion" and to the first Canto of *Don Juan*, in which Julia declares that "Man's love is of man's life a thing apart, / 'Tis woman's whole existence"—at least "his pedantry lay close to the vineyards of life—far closer than that fetich Experience of the innumerable teacups." The association of Ansell with agricultural imagery—"ploughboy," "vineyards of life"—and the fact that his uncles are farmers help elevate him in this novel in which a classical scholar declares that editing Sophocles is "second best" to planting potatoes.

Ansell, who has continued to love Rickie even as the lame young man has steadily deteriorated, is the appropriate person to shock him into a recognition of reality and brotherhood, both of which Rickie has denied in rejecting Stephen. In his dramatic confrontation with his friend, Ansell seems "transfigured into a Hebrew prophet passionate for satire and truth." In the Sawston School dining hall, he exposes Rickie's guilty secret; attacks Rickie, Agnes, and Herbert as "fools"; and reveals the shattering reality that Stephen is the son of Rickie's mother.

The news is shattering to Rickie because his conception of his mother is as much the "subjective product of a diseased imagination" as was his early conception of Agnes. He has so idealized Mrs. Elliot that she has become less a mortal person than a symbol, a "standard of the dead." When he assumed Stephen to be his hated father's son, he bitterly lamented that his half brother "would have children: he, not Rickie, would contribute to the stream; he, through his remote posterity, might be mingled with the unknown sea." Now, with the knowledge that Stephen is his mother's son, Rickie welcomes the prospect, for he sees in Stephen the possibility of his mother's resurrection. He regards him as a "symbol of redemption." The only thing that matters is that "the Beloved should rise from the dead."

Rickie's falsely romantic conception of his mother leads to his falsification of Stephen. Rickie's tendency to invest individuals with unreality is evidence of his spiritual bankruptcy, his soul's attempt to mint counterfeit currency, to create moral absolutes. "We do but shift responsibility by making a standard of the dead," the narrator explains. Stephen firmly rejects Rickie's new view of him as their mother's resurrection: "'Last Sunday week,' interrupted Stephen, his voice suddenly rising, 'I came to call on you. Not as this or that's son. . . . I simply came as I was, and I haven't altered since. . . . I haven't risen from the dead.'" He tears up Rickie's treasured photograph of their mother, exclaiming, "You talk to me, but all the time you look at the pho-

tograph. . . . I've my own ideas of good manners, and
to look friends between the eyes is one of them."

Stephen finally invites Rickie to leave Sawston
with him, but "as a man. . . . Not as a brother; who
cares what people did years back? We're alive together, and the rest is cant." Ironically, however,
Rickie accepts the offer but not the terms in which it is
proffered. As Stephen speaks, his brother hears the
voice of their mother: "In the voice he had found a
surer guarantee. Habits and sex may change with the
new generation, features may alter with the play of a
private passion, but a voice is apart from these. It lies
nearer to the racial essence and perhaps to the divine;
it can, at all events, overleap one grave." Rickie's persistent regard of Stephen as primarily a reincarnation
of Mrs. Elliot assures his disillusionment and tragedy.

Rickie's passionate concern with continuity crystallizes a dominant theme in *The Longest Journey*, the
question of whether individuals can transcend their
narrow life-spans to connect with past and future generations. This theme is suggested in a number of ways,
from Rickie's concern with the physical sterility of
David and Jonathan to Stephen's function as guardian
of England's future. Even the congenital lameness that
Rickie inherits from his father and transmits to his
doomed daughter seems to illustrate the connection of
past and future generations, as does the promise of the
Roman Catholic Church in Cambridge that "watches
over the apostate city, taller by many a yard than anything within, and asserting, however wildly, that here
is eternity, stability, and bubbles unbreakable upon a
windless sea." But the transmission of hereditary disease is actually yet another instance of the cruelty of
nature, its indifference to individual happiness, rather
than a viable example of connection. And Christianity
in *The Longest Journey* is disparaged as a system of
belief. Professing Christians such as Gerald, Agnes,

Herbert, and Mrs. Failing are fundamentally unserious and singularly lacking in spirituality, while the characters who most embody the novel's code of values—Ansell and Stephen—are not Christian. Moreover, the Church's wild assertion contradicts reality: the sea of life is not "windless" but "extremely rough."

Rickie's hope for individualized immortality for his mother through Stephen's participation in the stream of life is similarly unfounded. When Stephen takes his role at the end of the novel as guardian of the race, he governs the paths between the "dead who had evoked him" and the "unborn whom he would evoke." But this is not equivalent to the personal resurrection Rickie envisions, any more than Agnes's child by her second marriage—whom she names Herbert—ought to be regarded as a token of the Pembrokes' immortality. Yet Stephen's impersonal need to marry ("I expect that sometime or other I shall marry. . . . For it's something rather outside that makes one marry . . . not exactly oneself") and his procreation of a child do signify the continuity of the race and the apotheosis of his mother's spirit, an apotheosis that Rickie himself makes possible by sacrificing his own life to save Stephen's.

It is as the natural embodiment of the Greek spirit of life—as localized in Wiltshire—that Stephen inherits England. Stephen's intuitive absorption of the Greek spirit contrasts with Rickie's studied literary Hellenism. Rickie's artificial idealization of the ancient Greeks falsifies and distances, whereas Stephen's unconscious Hellenism translates ancient ideals into living values. Stephen "lived too near to the things he loved to seem poetical," and he dismisses Rickie's fantasies of "getting into touch with Nature, just as the Greeks were in touch" as "cant," for, living close to nature himself, he recognizes the artificiality of Rickie's pastoralism. Although the young shepherd "worried infinity as if it was a bone," he represents the body rather than the brain, intuition rather than intellect. He resembles "an animal with just enough soul to contemplate its own bliss. United with refinement, such a type was common in Greece." Forster's persistent condemnation of bookishness and aestheticism is yet another manifestation of his fundamental romanticism, even in this novel that attacks falsely romantic attitudes.

When Ansell first sees Stephen, the philosopher is convinced that the young shepherd "has been back somewhere—back to some table of the gods, spread in a field where there is no noise, and that he belonged forever to those guests with whom he had eaten." Stephen is described in echoes of Keats's "Ode on a Grecian Urn": Mrs. Failing remarks cynically of him, "You are a joy forever," and Ansell observes seriously that his face is "beautiful, if truth is beauty." Referring to Stephen, Ansell muses that "Certain figures of the Greeks, to whom we continually return, suggested him a little." Indeed, Stephen is repeatedly associated with such mythological characters as Pan, Dionysus, and Orion. In *The Longest Journey*, the living vitality of Greek mythology itself signifies continuity and the direct apprehension of reality. As the classics scholar Mr. Jackson notes, "the Greeks looked very straight at things, and Demeter or Aphrodite are thinner veils than 'The survival of the fittest' or 'A marriage has been arranged' and other draperies of modern journalism."

As a shepherd, Stephen is linked with Pan, the anarchic goat god who represents liberation from restraint and convention. Stephen's contact with the great god Pan leads to a troubled adolescence reminiscent of Eustace's in "The Story of a Panic" but less extreme. For Stephen, the onset of puberty is marked by "a violent spasm of dishonesty." His "sacred passion for alcohol," on which the novel's conclusion pivots, connects him with Dionysus, a figure of sexuality, ecstasy, and rebirth, while his frequent associations with the constellation Orion make him emblematic of cyclical renewal and of mystery. The link with Orion also makes Stephen symbolic of adventure and aspiration, nobility and freedom. The photograph of Demeter of Cnidus that he keeps in his attic room at Cadover and in the Wiltshire farmhouse at the end of the novel reveals his natural kinship with his mother, who is frequently identified with Demeter, the goddess of agriculture and the representative of life and sorrow, the giver of corn and tears.

Stephen is not the resurrection of Mrs. Elliot, but he embodies the same ancient harmony of man and earth that his parents did, and he represents the novel's best hope for the attainment of that harmony in England. As John Magnus has demonstrated, Forster's elaborate system of mythology, ritual, and mysticism culminates in a symbolic reincarnation that "signifies the salvation of the race through a return to the forsaken earth and to an agricultural society which takes Demeter . . . to represent its basic values."[11] Significantly, this reincarnation is made possible by Rickie's unconscious function as a kind of Hermes figure who restores the spring in the person of Stephen's daughter.

The social theorist of the agricultural society that the novel envisions is Stephen's foster father, Anthony Failing. Himself a voice speaking from beyond the grave in his posthumously published essays, he functions as the guardian of the earth and the opponent of life-denying convention. An agrarian socialist who "would often stretch out the hand of brotherhood too soon or withhold it when it would have been accepted," he is a visionary whose watchword is "Attain the practical through the impractical." Although his experiment with socialism at Cadover does not suc-

ceed, "In after years his reign became a golden age."
Opposed both to the severe aestheticism of his wife
and the conventionality of the Pembrokes, he sacrifices the pleasure of art "to have more decent people in
the world," and he redefines vulgarity as the "primal
curse, the shoddy reticence that prevents man opening
his heart to man, the power that makes against equality." His creed is most fully stated in the passage Rickie
reads to Mrs. Failing on his final visit to Cadover: "Let
us love one another. Let our children, physical and
spiritual, love one another. It is all that we can do. Perhaps the earth will neglect our love. Perhaps she will
confirm it, and suffer some rallying-point, spire,
mound, for the new generations to cherish."

Perhaps intended to echo the despairing final
stanza of Arnold's "Dover Beach," in which personal
love is the only comfort in a joyless world, Mr. Failing's creed is the novel's creed as well. The book offers
no certainty that the earth will confirm human love,
but in Mr. Failing's non-Arnoldian allusions to the spire
and the mound there is hope. They are symbols that
assert, in Frederick Crews's words, the "persistence of
human love amidst the forgetfulness of nature rather
than apart from it."[12] The mound refers to the Cadbury Rings, which the agnostic Stephen cherishes; the
spire, to Salisbury Cathedral, which is valued not for
its Christian dogma but because generations "have
found in her the reasonable crisis of their lives." These
monuments—as well as Stonehenge and Old Sarum—
identify Wiltshire as a place where man's life is naturally in tune with the earth. The chalky Salisbury plain
"is the heart of our island: the Chilterns, the North
Downs, the South Downs, radiate hence. The fibres of
England unite in Wiltshire, and did we condescend to
worship her, here we should erect our national shrine."

At the center of the plain is the Cadbury Rings,
the prehistoric burial grounds that repeat the geomet-

ric pattern Ansell draws to illustrate the ultimate mystery of the universe. It is in the natural pastoralism of Wiltshire that Stephen effortlessly imbibes the spirit of life. This pastoral harmony distinguishes Wiltshire both from a suburb, like Sawston and the one where Rickie spent his childhood, and from a city like London, whose inhabitants Mr. Failing describes as sterile. Cambridge, however, is subtly connected with Wiltshire both by Ansell's mandala and by the chalk that forms Rickie's magic dell, giving the enclosure a sense of timelessness.

The novel's injunction—"Let us love one another. . . . It is all that we can do"—does not promise that the earth will confirm individual love. Indeed, the pairing of Mrs. Elliot and Robert, the only example of fulfilled love in the book, illustrates the earth's indifference to individual relationships as well as the truth of Mr. Failing's belief that love is all we can do in the face of such indifference. Robert's regard for the earth strikes a responsive chord within Mrs. Elliot, the novel's Demeter figure: "As he talked the earth became a living being— or rather a being with a living skin,—and manure no longer dirty stuff, but a symbol of regeneration and of the birth of life from life." But the couple share only "one little interval between the power of the rulers of the world and the power of death." He drowns, and she returns to her cruel husband, prepared for a life "of beating time till I die."

Significantly, however, Mrs. Elliot learns that for her "there is no such thing as beating time," and her experience of passionate love actually increases her capacity to love others. She draws strength from the "heroic past" and loves her new child, which in turn causes her to love her first one. Yet just as she anticipates a "glorious autumn, beautiful with the voices of boys who should call her mother, the end came for her as well." Forster's point is that in the face of a universe

profoundly indifferent to individual human happiness,
love is its own reward: "It is all that we can do."

Mr. Failing warns that Swinburne's "Love, the Beloved Republic" will not be achieved by love alone,
but by "Self-sacrifice and—worse still—self-mutila-
tion." Rickie's rescue of Stephen, in which he is both
mutilated and sacrificed, illustrates this sad truth. The
self-sacrifice comes on the heels of a bitter disappointment in his brother, a disappointment that reveals
Rickie's basic conventionality even after he has ostensibly rejected the hostess of the "innumerable teacups," as personified in Mrs. Failing. He dies believing
that his mother "would die out, in drunkenness, in de-
bauchery, and her strength would be dissipated by a
man, her beauty defiled in a man. She would not continue." As he expires, he whispers to Mrs. Failing, "You
have been right," thus endorsing her belief that "people are not important," that conventions "are majestic
in their way, and will claim us in the end. We do not
live for great passions or for great memories, or for
anything great." Mrs. Failing pronounces Rickie "one
of the thousands whose dust returns to dust, accom-
plishing nothing in the interval."

But Mrs. Failing's epitaph is more appropriate for
herself than for Rickie. Although she imagines herself a
cold-eyed Ibsenesque heroine, "Really she was an
English old lady, who did not mind giving other people a chill provided it was not infectious." Intelligent,
cultured, supercilious, and cruel, she sees life as an unpleasant comedy. She takes "life with a laugh—as if
life is a pill." When she was young, the "world had not
been so humorous . . . but it was more important."
She lives in Wiltshire, but she cares for neither the land
nor the people. Her refusal to bridge the railroad crossing indicates her indifference to human life. Like her
brother, she falsifies life and fears the earth. She becomes one of those people who will die "and nothing

will have happened, either for themselves or for others." Significantly, the same is not true of Rickie.

Like Mr. Failing, Rickie dies a most unhappy man, "Not knowing that the earth had confirmed him." But his mutilating self-sacrifice for his brother actually makes possible that very continuity he has come to doubt. In his disillusionment, Rickie believes that the "mystic rose and the face it illumined meant nothing," referring to the incident in which he and Stephen launched flame boats in a stream. As Stephen lights the paper boat, Rickie examines him and notices a "new spirit" in his face, the image of his mother; the paper boat bursts into a "rose of flame" that soon vanishes for Rickie but flares for Stephen "as if it would burn forever." Rather than meaning nothing, the mystic rose and the face it illumines prophesy Stephen's triumph and the apotheosis of his mother's spirit at the end of the novel. The triumph and the apotheosis are made possible only by the sacrifice of Rickie, and thereby he too contributes to the stream of life. Although his spirit flees in agony and loneliness, his sacrifice makes possible Stephen's salvation and contributes to the future realization of "Love, the Beloved Republic."

In the final chapter, many of the book's themes and symbols coalesce. The stream of time, the chalk of the earth, the silence of rural fields, the sweet peas associated with Robert and Mrs. Elliot, the sky of Orion, the pink tint of the evening that recalls the mystic rose, the railroad train of death and modern technology, the Cadbury Rings that recapitulate Ansell's mandala: all are present. With Ansell and Stephen's wife in another part of the house, Stephen and Herbert haggle over the profits of Rickie's literary remains. Much as Ansell did earlier, the young farmer rebukes Herbert's idea of "the world in miniature." He jerks the newly ordained clergyman around to observe a quiet valley and in it "a rivulet that would in time bring its waters to the sea," just as in time Stephen's own thoughts and passions will triumph in England. "Look even at that—and up behind where the Plain begins and you get on the solid chalk," he tells Herbert, "that's the world. . . . There's one world . . . and you can't tidy people out of it."

The novel ends with Stephen wondering how he can repay Rickie, whose sacrifice has made possible his salvation. After Herbert leaves, Stephen gathers up his daughter and abandons the house to sleep beneath the stars. As he worries metaphysical questions, the whistle of Herbert's train sounds, "and a lurid spot passed over the land—passed and the silence re- turned." In tribute to his brother, whose body is now dust and thus unable to share any ecstasy of his, Ste- phen bends down and reverently salutes the child, to whom he has given the name of their mother. The novel thus concludes in a tableau that suggests renewal and continuity, for which Stephen and Rickie are jointly responsible. In crediting them equally for this renewal, Forster implies the symbolic achievement of the physically impossible: fraternity has begotten progeny. This suggestion is intensified by the fact that Rickie's marriage, the impetus for which was to avoid the physical sterility of homosexuality, produced no heirs and by the virtual anonymity of Stephen's wife, who functions in the novel as a means to fulfill the life force embodied in Stephen rather than as a character in her own right.

The apotheosis of Mrs. Elliot does not imply the possibility of transcendent personal immortality. In- deed, the novel warns against conventional religious faith, asking "Will it really profit us so much if we save our souls and lose the whole world," thus reversing the biblical question of Matthew 16:26. Nevertheless, *The Longest Journey* insists on the individual's duty to re- state "questions that have been stated at the beginning of the world," to regard life as a matter of importance, to embrace a Hegelian secular spirituality. Hence, the book ends with Stephen "musing on his happy tangible life," wondering "why he was here," marvelling "why he, the accident, was here." "By whose authority?" he persistently asks, a question the novel does not answer but by the posing of which it judges all the characters.

Immortality in *The Longest Journey* is not exclusively a matter of procreation, of racial continuity, or even of earth worship. The spirit of life may be discovered through books and individuals as well as through the outdoors, and the children whom Mr. Failing implores to love one another are spiritual as well as physical. Ansell's presence in Stephen's house at the end of the novel and the continuing presence of Mr. Failing in his essays are important indications of the validity of intellectual and spiritual attempts to apprehend life's meaning, attempts that complement the instinctive understanding of Stephen. Rickie himself attains a kind of immortality through his material and spiritual legacy to his brother, the long posthumously successful story about "A man and a woman who meet and are happy." Presumably, this is the story of Robert and Mrs. Elliot, who discover meaning in life through love for each other as well as through their reverence for the earth. Perhaps the only form of personal immortality is the persistence of "images of the dead," images that literature can freeze in an eternal present. But the very notion of earthly immortality is qualified by the knowledge that the earth itself will not continue forever. As Robert explains, "In time the fire at the centre will cool, and nothing can go on then."

The Longest Journey is an important book, especially as an early expression of the peculiarly Forsterian blend of skepticism and mysticism that culminates in *Howards End* and *A Passage to India,* a vision at once pessimistic and hopeful. Imaginatively manipulating mythic and romance motifs, the novel is richly suggestive. Its first two sections—the chronicle of the steady deterioration of a sensitive and serious young man who lacks the self-knowledge that might have saved him from the vulgarity of Sawston—are extraordinarily moving. Moreover, its depictions of such characters as Rickie, Ansell, Agnes, Herbert, and Mrs. Failing are convincing and insightful, revealing Forster's large and humane understanding of character. In addition, the novel is brilliantly stitched together by rhythmic echoes and an elaborate yet subtle network of symbolism, and it is written in prose of unusual resonance and allusiveness.

Nevertheless, for all its continuing fascination and unquestionable successes, the work is deeply flawed. Its most obvious flaws are the sentimental and unconvincing characterization of Stephen as a mythic figure and the imperfect harmonizing of the mythic and realistic dimensions. Stephen's implausibility nearly renders ludicrous Forster's sophisticated ideology of reverence for the earth. Stephen simply cannot support the symbolic weight he is asked to bear.

Indeed, despite the deftness Forster displays in manipulating symbols, such as the subtle evocations of Orion and the recurrent yet unobtrusive imagery of water and chalk, the symbolism threatens to overpower the action. The characters are frequently coerced into fulfilling allegorical roles that are unconvincing from a realistic perspective. For instance, Ansell's immediate recognition of Stephen as "one of the greatest people I have ever met" is not a natural response; it is all too obviously contrived to validate the scholar's earlier boast about the spirit of life: "I trust myself to know it anywhere."

More seriously, Rickie's despair over Stephen's drunkenness is too extreme and follows too suddenly his literal breaking of the "teacup of experience" to be

convincing. His sacrifice and mutilation are thus insufficiently motivated on the realistic plane of action.
Consequently, he seems victimized rather than confirmed by the earth, forced into playing a mythic role
as a Hermes figure, the unconscious servant of his
mother Demeter in assuring the return of spring in the
person of Stephen's daughter.[13] This victimization
suggests the intervention of supernatural forces in
human lives, an impingement that contradicts the novel's insistence on the universe's indifference to individuals. The mythology that informs the work thus becomes deterministic rather than merely expressive of
man's participation in the great rhythmic movements
of psyche and nature. Moreover, the final brief section
of the novel compresses too much action spanning too
much time to create a satisfying sense of proportion.

The unmistakable autobiographical elements in
the characterization of Rickie, who writes stories
about "getting in touch with Nature" that are almost
identical in plot to Forster's own early short fiction,
may also constitute a flaw in the novel even as they inevitably spark interest in the relationship between
character and creator. In response to the question, "Do
any of your characters represent yourself at all?" Forster once replied, "Rickie more than any."[14] Actually,
Rickie is less a self-portrait than a projection by Forster of what his life might have become had he yielded
to any lingering temptation toward conformity. The
characterization of Rickie may have functioned for
Forster as a kind of exorcism.

Nevertheless, the fierce hounding of the Forster-
like Rickie to his death—coupled with the simultaneous celebration of the boorish Stephen—is deeply disturbing. Ansell's function in the novel as a balance to
Stephen is schematically clear, but the civilized philosopher is so overshadowed by the heroic farmer at the
book's conclusion that one is tempted to see in the epi-

phany of the natural man a repudiation of Forster's own poetic imagination, broad culture, wide learning, and love of literature. Stephen is, of course, attributed qualities of intelligence and considerateness, but his bumptiousness and lack of education are made to seem virtues rather than limitations. Forster's closeness to the novel may account for the lyricism and passion that distinguish it, but these distinctions are bought at the expense of the ironic distance that is his most characteristic gift.

Finally, however, *The Longest Journey* is more successful than not, and its flashes of brilliance earn it a special place in the Forster canon. The loving characterizations of Cambridge and Wiltshire, the scathing account of Sawston School, and the tender but unfulfilled relationship of Ansell and Rickie are particular glories of the novel. The exposure of the conventional and the celebration of the personal are deeply felt and genuinely moving.

But most important of all, *The Longest Journey* espouses Forster's mature humanism. This philosophy is epitomized in the combination of Mrs. Elliot's belief "that facts are beautiful, that the living world is beautiful beyond the laws of beauty, that manure is neither gross nor ludicrous, that a fire, not eternal, glows at the heart of the earth" and Mr. Failing's injunction, "Let us love one another. . . . It is all that we can do." This humanism is the hallmark of the Forsterian world view. The ambitiousness of Forster's second published novel marks it as pivotal in his development, and the passionate intensity with which it is written makes it almost unique in his canon, rivaled in this regard only by *Maurice*.

4

◊◊◊

The Holiness of
Direct Desire:
A Room with a View

Forster's third novel, *A Room with a View* (1908), was begun in 1903, before *Where Angels Fear to Tread*, and completed after the publication of *The Longest Journey* in 1907.[1] At first reading, *A Room with a View* seems deceptively lightweight. But its appearance of slightness conceals a steady preoccupation with large and complex issues, and its happy ending is shadowed by a typically Forsterian tentativeness. The book is a fascinating composite of social comedy in the manner of Jane Austen and prophetic utterance of a kind later associated with D. H. Lawrence. Indeed, *A Room with a View* perfectly illustrates Forster's comment that he learned from Jane Austen "the possibilities of domestic humor" but that he "tried to hitch it on to other things." The "other things" to which Forster hitches domestic comedy are celebrations of sexuality and democracy that anticipate the work of Lawrence, whose first novel, *The White Peacock* (1911), is heavily indebted to *A Room with a View*.[2] The social comedy and the Lawrentian prophecy are complementary: together they define the novel as an epiphany of the natural and the instinctive within a context that acknowledges the power of convention and repression.

    A Room with a View lacks the painful intensity of *The Longest Journey* and the fierce satire of *Where Angels Fear to Tread*, but like the earlier works, it chronicles a search for meaning and a sexual awakening. Like Forster's first novel, *A Room with a View* pivots on the contrast of Italian passion and English decorum, but it also shares the love for rural England that is expressed in *The Longest Journey* and *Howards End*. In its repudiation of aestheticism and in its reliance on symbolic moments, *A Room with a View* is reminiscent of the two earlier novels, while its political dimension—especially its feminism—and overt romanticism anticipate *Howards End* and *Maurice*. Forster's most genial novel, *A Room with a View* is especially interesting for the subtlety of its manipulation of imagery and rhythm. The novel's symbolism finally suggests the presence of a mythic counterplot that deepens the surface plot in a manner similar to the technique of *The Longest Journey* and *A Passage to India*.

The first part of the book is set in Florence, where young Lucy Honeychurch of Summer Street, Surrey, and her older cousin Charlotte Bartlett of Tunbridge Wells have begun their Italian tour. At the Pension Bertolini, which is owned by a Cockney and caters exclusively to English clients, Lucy and Charlotte are disappointed to discover that their rooms have no view. Overhearing their distress, an old Englishman, Mr. Emerson, and his son George offer the ladies their rooms. Offended by the Emersons' presumption and lack of delicacy, Charlotte refuses the offer. She relents only upon the intervention of Mr. Beebe, a clergyman who is scheduled to be assigned to Lucy's home parish. The cousins are quickly taken up by their fellow tourists at the pension—the elderly spinsters Miss Teresa and Miss Catherine Alan, and the lady novelist Eleanora Lavish—and by the Reverend Cuthbert Eager, a member of the English colony in Florence who presides over the Anglican church there and whose custom is "to select those of his migratory sheep who seemed worthy, and give them a few hours in the pastures of the permanent."

The action of the first part of the novel centers on Lucy's encounters with the Emersons. Having been abandoned without her Baedeker by Miss Lavish, Lucy joins the Emersons for a tour of Santa Croce. Mr. Emerson implores her to help George overcome his despair that "things won't fit" and remarks that "By understanding George you may learn to understand yourself." When Lucy wanders alone to the Piazza Signoria, she witnesses a murder and faints. She is revived by George, who holds her in his arms and then escorts her back to the pension. The experience convinces Lucy that she "had crossed some spiritual boundary" and George that he wants to live after all. On an outing to Fiesole arranged by Mr. Eager and Mr. Beebe, Lucy stumbles onto a little terrace awash in violets and overlooking the Val d'Arno. Standing at its brink is George, who rushes forward to kiss her. The embrace is broken by the appearance of Charlotte, who rebukes George, comforts Lucy, and arranges a hurried departure to Rome.

The second half of the novel is set at Lucy's Summer Street home, Windy Corner, presided over by her mother Mrs. Honeychurch and her brother Freddy. Lucy accepts a proposal of marriage from Cecil Vyse, an aesthete who has read Walter Pater and who regards his fiancée as Leonardoesque. When a neighboring villa becomes vacant, Lucy suggests that it be rented to the elderly Alan sisters, but Cecil, as a joke on the landlord Sir Harry Otway, whom he considers vulgar, arranges its rental to the Emersons, whom he once met in London's National Gallery. Lucy first encounters George in Summer Street as he emerges naked from a local pond—Sacred Lake—in which he, Freddy, and Mr. Beebe had been swimming. At a tennis party, Cecil calls attention to a new

novel that he finds amusing, a pseudonymous book actually written by Miss Lavish that contains a scene
based on the encounter between George and Lucy in
the little terrace overrun with violets. His courage
sparked by the memory of the original embrace,
George again kisses Lucy.

Recruiting Charlotte as chaperone, Lucy boldly
confronts George, who warns her against marrying
Cecil: "He should know no one intimately, least of all a
woman." Lucy rebukes the young man for impertinence and sends him away, but when later that same
afternoon Cecil refuses to make up a fourth at tennis,
she abruptly breaks off her engagement and unconsciously echoes George in the process. Because Lucy
refuses to acknowledge her true feelings for George,
she temporarily joins the "vast armies of the benighted, who follow neither the heart nor the brain,
and march to their destiny by catch-words." Only
through an encounter with Mr. Emerson is Lucy saved,
a meeting perhaps made possible by Charlotte's
subconscious desire to aid the couple. The old man
convinces Lucy of the "holiness of direct desire." In
the final chapter, she and George are spending their
honeymoon in Florence at the Pension Bertolini. In
their physical and emotional fulfillment, they are conscious of a love yet "more mysterious" than their personal gratification.

The special charm of *A Room with a View* resides
in its curious combination of the mundane and the
mysterious, the comic and the serious. The actual
events of the novel may seem inconsequential and the
importance attributed to two kisses on the cheek disproportionate. But the apparently trivial events gain
significance by being played out against a backdrop of
romance, violence, heightened sexuality, politics, and
metaphysics. Even the plot's reliance on coincidence,
which at first glance may seem a flaw, is used themati-

cally to enhance the mysteriousness of the union of Lucy and George, a union that comes to seem at once tenuous and fated. With considerable artistic daring, Forster translates the material of romantic comedy into a novel of ideas.

An idea at the heart of *A Room with a View* is the "holiness of direct desire," a lesson that finally liberates Lucy's soul. All three substantives in the phrase are important. Sexuality in the novel is a physical manifestation of spirituality. As Mr. Emerson explains, "love is of the body; not the body, but of the body." The fulfillment of direct desire resolves life's existential "muddle" and diminishes the "world sorrow" that George experiences intellectually and Lucy feels intuitively. The directness of desire is a measure of its purity, its naturalness. Hence the novel attacks social conventions, class shibboleths, stereotypical sex roles, aestheticism, and organized religion. All are forces that impede instinct and deflect desire by substituting "catch-words" for independent thought and natural emotion. As Frederick Crews points out, these forces are especially dangerous because they provide "an illusion of completeness to lives, such as Lucy Honeychurch's, that are actually very constricted."[3]

As the novel opens, Lucy and George are both troubled by the sense that "things won't fit." Lucy's unease is vague and unarticulated, indicated mainly by the restiveness of her piano playing, her inchoate rebellion against the ideal of the "medieval lady," and her susceptibility to attacks of nerves. Her awakening is explored at great length and with intimacy, but George's more intellectual conflict gives philosophical depth to the book. Having been raised free of the social and religious cant that threatens Lucy, the young man experiences an existential crisis more profound yet simpler to resolve than Lucy's. It is symbolized by the "sheet of paper on which was scrawled an enormous note of interrogation" that Charlotte discovers in his room.

George's "world sorrow" stems from his inability to find a satisfying answer to the "why" of existence. His father quotes the opening stanza of A. E. Housman's "From far, from eve and morning" and asserts that "We know that we come from the winds, and that we shall return to them; that all life is perhaps a knot, a tangle, a blemish in the eternal smoothness." But Mr. Emerson does not understand why this should make his son unhappy. Alluding to Carlyle's *Sartor Resartus*—a book whose radical romanticism, "supernatural naturalism," and belief in the body as the garment of the spirit inform *A Room with a View* at every turn[4]— he implores Lucy to make George "realize that by the side of the everlasting Why there is a Yes—a transitory Yes if you like, but a Yes." The key to George's despair may be found both in the Housman poem and in the contrasting reactions of the two Emersons to Giotto's fresco "The Ascension of St. John the Evangelist" in Santa Croce.

Giotto's fresco depicts St. John ascending into heaven, where he is greeted by Christ and the Apostles.[5] Flanking this central event are two groups of people; one group gazes adoringly at the ascension while the other group stares amazedly into an open grave. The elder Emerson objects to the work of art as untruthful: "Look at that fat man in blue! He must weigh as much as I do, and he is shooting into the sky like an air-balloon!" In contrast, George declares: "It happened like this, if it happened at all. I would rather go up to heaven by myself than be pushed by cherubs; and if I got there I should like my friends to lean out of it, just as they do here." He adds: "Some of the people can only see the empty grave, not the saint whoever he is, going up. It did happen like that, if it happened at all." This contrast is important, for it reveals George's spiritual hunger, his need to discover a transcendental reality. He is skeptical of the Christian dogma reflected in the fresco, but he dissociates himself from those who can see only the empty grave, thus indicating his desire to believe in a continuity of life beyond death. His desire to connect with friends is significant as well in this novel where personal intercourse is elevated into a spiritual test.

The Housman poem is also important as a gloss on George's unhappiness. As Mr. Emerson indicates, the poem accounts for human existence by reference to the twelve winds that blow together the "stuff of life" and then disperse it. But the poem also emphasizes the brevity of life and the consequent yearning to establish intimacy in the face of death. In stanzas not quoted in the novel, the speaker of the poem pleads, "Take my hand quick and tell me, / What have you in your heart. . . . Ere to the wind's twelve quarters / I take my endless way."[6] George's unhappiness can be assuaged only by a similar communion, one that offers tangible meaning to life's brief sojourn. He finds glimpses of such meaning in his encounters with Lucy, whose home is appropriately named "Windy Corner," first in the Piazza Signoria and later on the terrace overlooking the Val d'Arno.

These scenes establish the novel's pervasive imagery of light and shadow, ascent and descent, music and water; and they resonate with passion and sexuality.[7] When Lucy goes into the Florentine twilight on the evening of the murder in the Piazza Signoria, she is conscious of "strange desires," of discontent with "the august title of the Eternal Woman" that insulates her from contact with real life. Earlier that afternoon she had played Beethoven and had become "intoxicated by the feel of the notes: they were fingers caressing her own; and by touch, not by sound alone, did she come to her desire," an account of her playing that links her

frequent immersion in music with her repressed sexuality and that implies her ripeness for experience.

Lucy finds the great square in shadow, a state that
appropriately symbolizes ambiguity, for the piazza is
to be the site both of murder and of love: "Neptune
was already unsubstantial in the twilight, half god, half
ghost, and his fountain plashed dreamily to the men
and satyrs who idled together on its marge. The Loggia showed as the triple entrance of a cave wherein
dwelt many a deity, shadowy but immortal, looking
forth upon the arrivals and departures of mankind."
The description of the Loggia, which suggests feminine
sexuality, is matched by the phallic symbolism of the
tower, "like a pillar of roughened gold . . . throbbing
in the tranquil sky." Loggia and tower together intimate the mystery of sexuality and its function in assuring the continuity of life, a continuity symbolized as
well by the water of the Neptune fountain and the tur-
bulent river.

One of only two chapters designated by number
rather than title, the Fourth Chapter is crucial. The violent passion that erupts in the piazza brings George
and Lucy together and furthers their maturity. The
connection between the murder and the developing
sexual attraction of the English couple is not coinci-
dental, for both are spontaneous and vital, and both
signify the crossing of spiritual boundaries. In this regard, it is telling that the murderer attempts to kiss his
victim before surrendering to the police, thus anticipating the later kisses of George and Lucy and her subsequent surrender to authority. When Lucy faints at
the sight of the blood flowing from the dying man's
mouth, George rushes to hold her in his arms. Suddenly, he is not looking at her "across" anything; they
are in direct contact. The embrace impresses Lucy
greatly: "The whole world seemed pale and void of its
original meaning." George is aware that "something

tremendous has happened." In fact, he determines that
life may have meaning after all. "I shall probably want
to live," he explains.

As George and Lucy walk along the banks of the
Arno, George throws something into the river. Lucy
suddenly remembers her photographs of famous art
works, including Botticelli's "Birth of Venus," that she
had asked him to retrieve. The young man confesses
that he tossed them into the swirling water, for "They
were covered with blood . . . it seemed better they
should go out to the sea." This incident neatly juxtaposes the stasis of art and the flux of life, the unrealistic
idealization of art and the messiness of real life. Lucy's
reaction to George's confession reveals her immatur-
ity, the distance she has to travel before she can embrace life and truly appreciate the holiness of direct
desire: "He had thrown her photographs into [the
river], and then he had told her the reason. It struck
her that it was hopeless to look for chivalry in such a
man." Her continuing reliance on such "catch-words"
as chivalry precludes her acceptance of the symbolic
moment that she is offered here. Yet there is hope for
Lucy as she contemplates the River Arno, "whose roar
was suggesting some unexpected melody to her ears."

The expedition to Fiesole organized by Mr. Eager
and Mr. Beebe offers George and Lucy another symbolic moment. This chapter, distinguished by the
book's most elaborate title, is also pivotal. Although intended by the incongruously named Mr. Eager as his
own *"partie carrée,"* the outing is actually, as Alan
Wilde remarks, "presided over by the god Pan
. . . conducted by the forces of love, of spring, and of
the earth."[8] The carriage is driven by Phaethon—"a
youth all irresponsibility and fire"—who is accompanied by his girl friend Persephone. When Phaethon and
Persephone kiss, Mr. Eager violently objects and Mr.
Emerson stoutly defends them. "To be driven by

lovers—A king might envy us," he declares, and quotes Lorenzo de Medici, "Don't go fighting against the spring," a line as applicable to Lucy as to anyone else. When she sees the young couple "sporting with each other disgracefully," she has "a spasm of envy."

Phaethon himself leads Lucy to George as a result of a perceptive misunderstanding. When she asks, "Dove buoni uomini," intending to request directions to the clergymen, he takes her instead to the "good man" George, shouting, "Courage and love," as she falls onto an open terrace and is enveloped in light and beauty. This terrace—on which "violets ran down in rivulets and streams and cataracts, irrigating the hillside with blue, eddying around the tree stems, collecting into pools in the hollows, covering the grass with spots of azure foam"—is the "primal source whence beauty gushed out to water the earth," a description rife with sexual overtones. In this setting of light, metaphorical water, and primal beauty, George steps forward to kiss Lucy. But before she can react to his embrace, the magical moment is destroyed by Charlotte, standing "brown against the view." Even Phaethon's benediction, "Courage and love," is mocked by Mr. Eager's "catch-word" in the midst of the storm that follows: "Courage and faith."

The first part of the novel thus ends with the rout of the forces of nature and instinct and the triumph of those of respectability and repression. More particularly, the triumph belongs to Charlotte, who "had worked like a great artist; for a time—indeed, for years—she had been meaningless, but at the end there was presented to [Lucy] the complete picture of a cheerless, loveless world of precautions and barriers which may avert evil, but which do not seem to bring good, if we may judge from those who have used them most." Yet as Lucy prepared for her flight to Rome, she "felt that the candle would burn better, the pack-

ing go easier, the world be happier, if she could give
and receive some human love." This need promises
that Lucy may indeed "learn better" than to accept the
world of precautions and barriers that Charlotte represents. Like George, the young woman hungers for
truth and maturity. She cries out in her sleep, "I wish
not to be muddled. I want to grow old quickly."

Lucy's escape from muddledom is not easy, for
the second half of the novel records a series of deceptions by which she attempts to avoid "that king of ter-
rors—Light." In her muddle, light especially terrifies
her because—as her name indicates—it is equivalent to
self-knowledge. To embrace light is to accept the philosophy of George, who recognizes the inevitability of
shadow but who advises her to face the sunshine.
Lucy's struggles validate Samuel Butler's description
of life as "a public performance on the violin, in which
you must learn the instrument as you go along," a description that Mr. Emerson quotes in the penultimate
chapter.[9]

The first of Lucy's self-deceptions is her conviction that she loves Cecil Vyse, who falls in love with
her in Rome and is finally accepted on his third proposal of marriage. Although Cecil would prefer that
Lucy connect him with the open air, she actually thinks
of him as in a room without a view. This conception
recognizes his narrowness and artificiality, his overre-
finement and lack of vision. As long as Lucy is committed to Cecil, she will never face the sunshine or
glimpse possibilities beyond the confining limits of
aestheticism and domesticity.

Cecil epitomizes those qualities which Forster denounces as medieval: "Tall and refined, with shoulders
that seemed braced square by an effort of the will, and
a head that was tilted a little higher than the usual level
of vision, he resembled those fastidious saints who
guard the portals of a French cathedral. Well edu-

cated, well endowed, and not deficient physically, he remained in the grip of a certain devil whom the modern world knows as self-consciousness, and whom the mediaeval, with dimmer vision, worshipped as asceticism." Anticipating George's later charge that Cecil is incapable of intimacy, Mr. Beebe describes him as an "ideal bachelor." His asceticism is a pronounced aspect of his character, for he has "depths of prudishness in him." He is also supercilious, citified, and snobbish. He finds Summer Street society too "narrow," but he fails to realize that Lucy "had reached the stage where personal intercourse alone would satisfy her." As his Christian name suggests, he is "dim-sighted."[10]

The central irony of Cecil's passionless love for Lucy—actually "a profound uneasiness"—is that what he interprets as her Leonardoesque qualities of "shadow" and "reticence" are actually signs of her confusion and repression.[11] He finds her enchanting as a work of art when she obliquely reflects mystery, but whenever she directly expresses deep human emotion, he is disappointed. For instance, when Lucy angrily punctures his pretense to democratic ideals as an explanation for his arranging the Emersons' move to Summer Street, the young aesthete "stared at her, and felt again that she had failed. . . . Her face was inartistic." Similarly, when Lucy vigorously condemns the egregious Mr. Eager for having insinuated that Mr. Emerson had murdered his wife, Cecil is confused: "It was as if one should see the Leonardo on the ceiling of the Sistine. He longed to hint to her that not here lay her vocation; that a woman's power and charm reside in mystery, not in muscular rant." The startling image of a Leonardo portrait on Michelangelo's Sistine Chapel ceiling is not only typical of Cecil's habit of interpreting life in terms of art, it also connects Lucy with George, who is described as "Michelangelesque" and whom Lucy imagined she saw in Rome "on the ceiling of the Sistine Chapel, carrying a burden of acorns."

Cecil's self-consciousness and awkwardness as a lover are depicted vividly when he kisses Lucy for the first time ever, several days after their engagement. His courage faltering, he timidly requests permission to embrace her. The kiss itself is a comic fiasco: "At that supreme moment he was conscious of nothing but absurdities. . . . As he approached her he found time to wish that he could recoil. As he touched her, his gold pince-nez became dislodged and was flattened between them." This kiss is the antithesis of direct desire. It lacks spontaneity. "Passion should believe itself irresistible," Cecil acknowledges to himself. "It should forget civility and consideration and all the other curses of a refined nature. Above all, it should never ask for leave where there is a right of way." He fantasizes quite a different scene, with Lucy "standing flower-like by the water," yielding to his manly demands. But Cecil's belief that "women revere men for their manliness" is not only incongruous with his priggishness, it is also symptomatic of his medievalism. It is an extension of Charlotte's medieval notion that the mission of ladies is "to inspire others to achievement rather than to achieve themselves."

Cecil's ineptitude as a lover locates his own sexual inadequacy as the source of his conventional views as to sex roles. He "always felt that he must lead women, though he knew not whither, and protect them, though he knew not against what." He is an exemplar of attitudes toward women that have "kept Europe back for a thousand years." He cannot conceive of a relationship that is not "feudal: that of protector and protected." His regard of Lucy as a work of art and a creature to be shaped to his aesthetic taste stifles her individuality and limits her growth. The novel opposes to this chivalric code a Whitmanesque ideal of comradeship, embodied in Mr. Emerson's belief that the sexes will be equal "when we no longer despise our bodies" and in George's declaration to Lucy that "I want you to have your own thoughts even when I hold you in my arms."

This ideal of comradeship is exemplified in the second of the novel's two chapters designated only by number, Chapter 12. This episode at Sacred Lake echoes the eleventh section of Whitman's "Song of Myself," with its "Twenty-eight young men and all so friendly" dancing and laughing and bathing by the shore. As in Whitman's poem and in numerous other homoerotic bathing scenes in late nineteenth-century literature and visual art, Forster's scene is a celebration of the body and of the democracy of the flesh.[12] It reflects as well the Carlylean notion expressed in *Sartor Resartus* that man is a naked animal whose clothes are masks that conceal his soul.

Mr. Beebe, Freddy, and George sport in the sun and water, abandoning class and age differences and exulting in comradeship. When the unexpected arrival of Mrs. Honeychurch, Lucy, and Cecil interrupts the party, however, Mr. Beebe remembers "that after all he was in his own parish" and hides his nakedness in the water on which floats his underwear. Freddy and George, on the other hand, confront the intruders, unashamed of their bodies. "Barefoot, bare-chested, radiant and personable against the shadowy woods," George calls out to Lucy, who returns his greeting with a bow. Henceforth, George—unlike Cecil—is invariably linked in Lucy's mind with the open air.

The bathing scene in Sacred Lake is characterized as a "call to the blood and to the relaxed will, a passing benediction whose influence did not pass, a holiness, a spell, a momentary chalice for youth." This description unmistakably links the scene to the holiness of direct desire. The experience cements the friendship of

George and Freddy, who has always been distrustful of Cecil. It also cures George of the depression into which he had lapsed as a result of Lucy's precipitous flight from Florence. As Mr. Beebe remarks of George soon after the bathing episode, "He is waking up," thus indicating his arousal from the somnambulism that—according to *Sartor Resartus*—makes difficult the posing of the crucial question, "Who am I; what is this ME" (p. 54). In addition, the scene illustrates the sway that convention finally exerts over Mr. Beebe even after he momentarily relaxes in the comradeship of Sacred Lake. Most important of all, however, the bathing scene reflects the Carlylean doctrine of the human body as a "Revelation in the Flesh" (*Sartor Resartus*, p. 239) and establishes the Whitmanesque celebrations of democracy, the body, and sexual equality as goals against which to measure Lucy's progress to self-awareness.

The feminist and democratic consciousness of *A Room with a View* is inextricably linked to its search for a new chivalry, a new aristocracy of the spirit. In this regard, it is significant that Lucy and George both hold anomalous positions within the rigid English class system. Lucy's father was a "prosperous local solicitor," and although the Honeychurches are mistaken "for the remnants of an indigenous aristocracy," in fact Lucy's social status is "more splendid than her antecedents entitled her to." As a clerk, George's position is even more ambiguous. He is the grandson of a laborer and the son of a socialist journalist who "made an advantageous marriage." George's descent from a journalist father may be especially important in light of Carlyle's belief that journalists "are now the true Kings and Clergy" (*Sartor Resartus*, p. 45). Thus set apart from the class system, Lucy and George are appropriate embodiments of the spiritual aristocracy that Forster later defines in "What I Believe": "Its members are to be found in all nations and classes, and all through the ages, and there is a secret understanding between them when they meet."[13]

Lucy's soul comes to yearn for the comradeship that Cecil is unable to provide, a comradeship both sexual and political in nature. Her experience in Italy expands her senses and teaches her to distrust class divisions: "she felt that there was no one whom she might not get to like, that social barriers were irremovable, doubtless, but not particularly high." George's embarrassment in Summer Street at Charlotte's appearance teaches Lucy that "men were not gods after all, but as human and as clumsy as girls; even men might suffer from unexplained desires, and need help." She naturally longs for "equality beside the man she loved." That equality is offered by George; although she rejects his offer, she nevertheless echoes his ideas when she breaks her engagement to Cecil, a necessary preliminary to her salvation.

Lucy's disengagement speech attacks Cecil's medieval attitudes toward women and his aestheticism. She tells her startled fiancé that "I won't be protected. I will choose for myself what is ladylike and right. To shield me is an insult." She accuses Cecil of conformity and of distancing himself from life: "you may understand beautiful things, but you don't know how to use them; and you wrap yourself up in art and books and music, and would try to wrap up me. I won't be stifled, not by the most glorious music, for people are more glorious, and you hide me from them." As she talks, Cecil finds her "each moment more desirable," seeing her for the first time as a living woman. He startles her by agreeing with her charges against him, and his exit from her life is dignified: "nothing in his love became him like the leaving of it."

Lucy's passionate declaration that people are more glorious than the most glorious music promises the fulfillment of Mr. Beebe's earlier prediction that some day she will be wonderfully proficient in life and music both. "The water-tight compartments in her will break down," he remarks, "and music and life will mingle. Then we shall have her heroically good, heroically bad—too heroic, perhaps, to be good or bad." But at this point the compartments hold, music continues to be a substitute for Lucy's participation in life, and she fails to attain the Nietzschean heroism Mr. Beebe predicts. She determines never to marry. In making this decision, she disregards her head and heart and relies on yet another "catch-word." She is terrified that she will be accused of what is, after all, the truth—of being in love with someone else while having been engaged to Cecil. Her fear of the "world's taunts" causes her to sin against passion and truth, "against Eros and Pallas Athene." She yields to "the enemy within" and joins the "vast army of the benighted," just as Charlotte had done thirty years earlier.

The decline into which Lucy falls is indicated by increasing images of darkness in the novel and by her compulsive playing of a song from Scott's *The Bride of Lammermoor*, a historical romance whose heroine is also named Lucy:

> Look not thou on beauty's charming.
> Sit thou still when kings are arming,
> Taste not when the wine-cup glistens,
> Speak not when the people listens,
> Stop thine ear against the singer,
> From the red gold keep thy finger;
> Vacant heart and hand and eye
> Easy live and quiet die.

This song, given to Lucy by Cecil, is approved of by Mr. Beebe but condemned by Freddy: "The tune's right enough . . . but the words are rotten." The lyrics, of course, advise asceticism, the renunciation of life;

and Lucy's compulsive playing of this song represents a desperate attempt to convince herself of the rightness of her rejection of George and her decision never to marry. But just as the "soaring accompaniment" criticizes the words that it adorns, so the song itself is criticized by the Housman poem that Mr. Emerson quoted earlier in the novel. Even as Lucy tries to deceive herself into asceticism, her very action illustrates the need for comradeship that she shares with the speaker of the Housman poem: "Take my hand quick and tell me, / What have you in your heart."

By the end of the novel, Lucy achieves the comradeship she needs. The allied deities Eros and Pallas Athene are reconciled. Lucy acknowledges passion and truth, and she is rescued from the armies of the benighted. Mr. Emerson makes her look within herself: "as he spoke the darkness was withdrawn, veil after veil, and she saw to the bottom of her soul." This insight causes her to confess her deceptions and to believe with her elderly, secular saint of a mentor that "we fight for more than Love or Pleasure; there is Truth. Truth counts, Truth does count." Functioning as a kind of Teufelsdröckh, Mr. Emerson echoes the hero of Carlyle's *Sartor Resartus*, who clings to the love of truth even as he confronts the Everlasting No (p. 161). In robbing "the body of its taint" and "the world's taunts of their sting," Mr. Emerson enables Lucy to achieve a sense of completion: "It was as if he had made her see the whole of everything at once."

Crucial to Lucy's salvation is the agency of Charlotte Bartlett, who makes possible the troubled young woman's interview with Mr. Emerson in the rectory. Charlotte's temporary defection from the armies of the benighted is foreshadowed by Mr. Beebe's early observation that she "might reveal unknown depths of strangeness" and by her own roguish announcement when Lucy rejects the young Emerson: "Well, it isn't every one who could boast such a conquest." On their honeymoon, George convincingly explains to Lucy Charlotte's surprising action as the result of a subconscious sympathy with the lovers: "from the very first moment we met, she hoped, far down in her mind, that we should be like this. . . . The sight of us haunted her. . . . She is not frozen, Lucy, she is not withered up all through. She tore us apart twice, but in the Rectory that evening she was given one more chance to make us happy."

One of Forster's most successful satiric portraits, Charlotte throughout the novel functions as a warning of what Lucy may become if she is not redeemed by the holiness of direct desire. Although Lucy is younger and thus more open to experience, the cousins are nevertheless similar in their basic conventionality. At one point early in the novel, Mr. Emerson gently criticizes Lucy by telling her, "I think that you are repeating what you have heard older people say." The criticism is equally applicable to Charlotte, whose last name—surely intended to suggest Bartlett's *Familiar Quotations* (first published in 1855)—identifies her as the novel's leading exponent of "catch-words."

The difference between the cousins is indicated early in the book when, after exchanging rooms with the Emersons in the Pension Bertolini, Lucy flings open her window to breathe fresh air and relish the view. In her room, however, Charlotte blocks out the view. She fastens the window shutters and locks the door. Significantly, Lucy, after rejecting George's love, becomes more and more like Charlotte. Mrs. Honeychurch even remarks exasperatedly of her daughter, "How you do remind me of Charlotte Bartlett!" Charlotte is too old for the salvation that Lucy finally experiences, but the older woman's sympathetic action on the lovers' behalf is a sign of optimism. For all the power of the forces of convention in *A*

Room with a View, the victims of repression are never-theless capable of small acts of charity, even if (as in the case of Miss Alan) such charity is against their bet-ter judgment.

Perhaps as surprising as Charlotte's unexpected aid to the lovers is Mr. Beebe's chilly opposition. In many ways the novel's most elusive character, the clergyman functions consistently to focus attention on Lucy's potential for heroism. He is intelligent and in-sightful, tolerant and humane. Early in her stay at the Pension Bertolini, Lucy exclaims of him: "He is nice. . . . He seems to see good in every one. No one would take him for a clergyman." In his liberality and good humor, he is the antithesis of the narrow-minded and pompous Mr. Eager. But like his fellow cleric, Mr. Beebe also fights against the spring and erects barriers between himself and the fullness of experience. He fi-nally joins the forces of medievalism, as illustrated when he is spurred into "knight-errantry" by the pros-pect of delivering Lucy from "some vague influence . . . which might well be clothed in the fleshly form."

Mr. Beebe's alliance against the lovers is rooted in his repression of his own homosexual nature. His homo-sexuality is suggested early in the novel. "Mr. Beebe was, from rather profound reasons," the narrator re-cords, "somewhat chilly in his attitude toward the other sex, and preferred to be interested rather than enthralled." A confirmed bachelor, he regards himself as "better detached." His belief in celibacy, "so reti-cent, so carefully concealed beneath his tolerance and culture," finally exposes him, as Judith Scherer Herz points out, as a servant of "religion and all the institu-tions that stifle instinct."[14] Mr. Beebe's justification of his celibacy—and of his negative attitude toward mar-riage—is revealing: "'They that marry do well, but they that refrain do better.' So ran his belief, and he never heard that an engagement was broken off but with a slight feeling of pleasure." His opposition to marriage is tellingly based on St. Paul's condemnation of sexuality in I Corinthians 7:9, in a passage that also provides the locus of Christian opposition to homosexuality. Mr. Beebe's celibacy is thus a conscious repression of his own nature.

This insight is validated by Mr. Beebe's curious participation in the bathing episode in Sacred Lake. He accompanies Freddy and George to the pond in a spirit of voyeurism rather than of active involvement. As the young men disrobe and plunge uninhibitedly into the water, the fully clothed clergyman holds back. He "watched them, and watched the seeds of the willow-herb dance chorically above their heads." He joins the revelers only after looking around to make certain that there are in the vicinity "no parishioners except the pine-trees, rising steeply on all sides, and gesturing to each other against the blue." The phallic imagery, the implied Hellenism, and the tableau traditionally associated with homoeroticism all promise release from repression. For a moment, he exults in the freedom and comradeship of Sacred Lake. But with the appearance of human parishioners, Mr. Beebe rejects the "call to the blood." His opposition to the lovers is thus a consequence of his self-denial, a function of his own repression. Mr. Beebe can best be understood as a victim of social and religious attitudes that he has embraced to his own detriment, and of Forster's criticism of what Glen Cavaliero describes as "the cautious, self-punishing homosexual consciousness that acquiesces in the verdict of religion and society."[15]

The depiction of Mr. Beebe as a victim is consistent with Forster's compassionate view of his characters in this novel. Although many of the subsidiary characters are portrayed satirically—Miss Lavish and Miss Alan, for instance—the satire is far gentler than that of the previous novels, and some characters—such as Freddy and Mrs. Honeychurch—are depicted with genuine affection even as their limitations are exposed. With the exception of Mr. Eager, who does not appear in the second half of the book, there are no villains. Charlotte, Cecil, and Mr. Beebe, the most interesting characters in the novel, are not willful perpetrators of evil. Their predicaments illustrate the difficulty of moral choice in a society that stifles instinct and individuality. As victims, they function as exemplars of the tremendous power of repression, a power that ultimately defeats the natural instincts of even an intelligent individual like Mr. Beebe. His and Charlotte's failures testify yet again to the difficulty of achieving wholeness.

This difficulty is also indicated by Forster's daring reliance on coincidence in uniting Lucy and George. The string of improbabilities that finally results in their union makes their success seem almost miraculous, the result of chance as much as of any intrinsic virtue in the lovers. At the same time, however, the coincidences come to seem emblematic of the workings of a life force, of what George and Lucy define as fate. For instance, Lucy regards the expedition to Fiesole, which she tried to avoid, "as the work of Fate." And when Mr. Beebe attempts to explain away the coincidences that bring the tourists of the Pension Bertolini to Summer Street, George protests: "It is Fate. Everything is Fate. We are flung together by Fate, drawn apart by Fate—flung together, drawn apart. The twelve winds blow us." Fate is thus credited with George's discovery of at least a "transitory Yes" at Windy Corner.

The suggestion that George and Lucy are manipulated by a life force greater than themselves is consistent with Forster's attempts throughout the novel to portray them as simultaneously both realistic characters in a domestic comedy and allegorical figures in a

mythic romance. The romance elements are most obvious in the outing to Fiesole, where George and Lucy
are driven by Phaethon and Persephone. But mythological allusions pervade the novel, and George and
Lucy frequently are associated with archetypal characters. They function finally as latter-day, pagan in-
carnations of Adam and Eve, symbols of fertility and
continuity, natural innocence and unashamed sexuality.

These allegorical roles are suggested in a number
of ways, including Lucy's identification of George
with one of the acorn-bearing *ignudi* in the framing
panels of Michelangelo's Sistine Chapel ceiling,[16] an
imaginative association that gains fleshly reality when
she sees him nude at Sacred Lake, and in Cecil's projection of Lucy herself onto the Sistine ceiling. Moreover, Lucy is identified with Eve by the parallel between Forster's description of his young heroine's
"thousand little civilities that create a tenderness in
time" and Adam's commendation of Eve's "graceful
acts, / Those thousand decencies that daily flow /
From all her words and actions mixt with Love" in Milton's *Paradise Lost* (VIII.600–602).[17] In addition, the
literal meaning of George's name—"a husbandman"—
recalls Adam's function as first tiller of the land and
cements the metaphorical identification.

Most insistently, however, the allegorical roles are
suggested by the frequent references to gardens, from
the garden at Windy Corner to the gardens in Gluck's
Armide and in Wagner's *Parsifal* to the primal garden
of violets on the little terrace overlooking the Arno and
to the Garden of Eden itself. The Edenic paradise, Mr.
Emerson declares, is not in the past but in the future:
"We shall enter it when we no longer despise our
bodies."

Thus, when Lucy learns to acknowledge her sexuality, she assumes her role as neo-pagan Eve beside
George's Adam, and together they enter a new Edenic

garden. Their marriage then truly becomes—in Mr. Emerson's prophecy—"one of the moments for which the world was made." The "love more mysterious" than merely their personal happiness that George and Lucy are conscious of on their honeymoon is this fated pairing of archetypes, a pairing that may yield a new society rising phoenixlike from the ashes of a dying one, as predicted in *Sartor Resartus* (pp. 231–38). That this pairing promises the continuity of life is suggested by the melody of the River Arno, "bearing down the snows of winter into the Mediterranean." George and Lucy hear this elemental music even after Phaethon's honeymoon serenade of "passion requited, love attained" fades away.

The allegorical dimension of the novel is implicit and subordinate rather than explicit or dominant. The mythic aspect deepens the surface comedy and imparts heightened significance to the surface plot's account of the union of a rather ordinary English couple, a couple who are actually less intrinsically interesting than several of the subsidiary characters. The restrained use of symbolism and the natural harmonizing of the allegorical and the realistic are evidence of Forster's consummate control in *A Room with a View*, especially as contrasted with *The Longest Journey*. This firm control, coupled with the happy ending, may explain the greater popularity of Forster's third novel.

The popularity of *A Room with a View* may also be attributable to the fact that it is Forster's fullest celebration of heterosexual love. Ironically, however, the novel is actually the product of Forster's self-conscious attempt to discover a homosexual literary tradition, and it is suffused with homoeroticism and with the ideology of the late nineteenth-century homosexual emancipation movement. In an entry in his diary for New Year's Eve 1907, during a period when he was writing *A Room with a View*, Forster constructed a list

of famous homosexual authors and artists, including
A. E. Housman, William Shakespeare, John Addington
Symonds, Walter Pater, Walt Whitman, Edward Car-
penter, Samuel Butler, H. S. Tuke, Luca Signorelli, and
Michelangelo, all of whom are quoted in the novel or
are otherwise influential on it.[18]

Housman and Butler are quoted directly; Michelangelo and Luca Signorelli are explicitly evoked, the
latter being the artist that the Emersons discuss in the
National Gallery when Cecil first encounters them.
The remark that "nothing in [Cecil's] love became him
like the leaving of it" alludes to *Macbeth*, while Lucy's
discovery that "men were not gods after all" but susceptible to "unexplained desires" echoes a speech by
Desdemona in *Othello*. Pater's influence is apparent in
Cecil's aestheticism, and Whitman and Tuke influenced the bathing scene in Sacred Lake, which establishes comradeship as the ideal human relationship.

In the late nineteenth and early twentieth centuries, the word "comrade" itself possessed strong homoerotic connotations, especially in the work of Edward Carpenter, on whom Forster probably based the
character of Mr. Emerson, as John Colmer suggests.[19]
Whitman's English disciple and a pioneer in the early
English gay liberation movement, Carpenter begins
his *Homogenic Love* (1894) by declaring that "Of all
the many forms that Love delights to take, perhaps
none is more interesting . . . than that special attachment which is sometimes denoted by the word Comradeship," and throughout he uses "comrade-love" as a
synonym for homosexuality. *Homogenic Love* may
also have influenced Forster's contrast of chivalry and
comradeship, for Carpenter comments of the medieval period: "its ideal was undoubtedly rather the chivalric love than the love of comrades."[20]

Although Forster did not become friends with
Carpenter until after the publication of *Howards End*,

Carpenter's work and personality are important influences on *A Room with a View*. On the centenary of
Carpenter's birth in 1944, Forster wrote a generous
tribute, describing the social pioneer as a "remarkable
fellow, lovable, charming, energetic, courageous, possibly great."[21] And in the "Terminal Note" to *Maurice*,
Forster describes Carpenter in terms evocative of Mr.
Emerson: "He was a rebel appropriate to his age. He
was sentimental and a little sacramental. . . . He was a
socialist who ignored industrialism and a simple-lifer
with an independent income and a Whitmannic poet
whose nobility exceeded his strength and, finally, he
was a believer in the Love of Comrades, whom he
sometimes called Uranians. It was this last aspect of
him that attracted me in my loneliness."

But perhaps the greatest influence of this group of
artists whom Forster believed to be homosexual is
John Addington Symonds, whose anonymously issued
poem in honor of Whitman, "The Song of Love and
Death" (written in August 1871), may be the source
both for the crucial scene on the violet-strewn terrace
overlooking the Arno and for the novel's general
search for a new chivalry and a new Eden. The following passage from Symonds's poem reads like a pro-
grammatic guide to *A Room with a View*:

> There shall be comrades thick as flowers that crown
> Valdarno's gardens in the morn of May;
> On every upland and in every town
> Their dauntless imperturbable array,
> Serried like links of living adamant
> By the sole law of love their wills obey,
> Shall make the world one fellowship, and plant
> New Paradise for nations yet to be.
> O nobler peerage than that ancient vaunt
> Of Arthur or of Roland! Chivalry
> Long sought, last found.[22]

The point that needs emphasis is not that *A Room
with a View* is a disguised homosexual love story with

Lucy actually "a boy *en travesti*," as K. W. Gransden refers to her,[23] but that the holiness of direct desire has homosexual as well as heterosexual application. Indeed, Forster's vision of a new Garden of Eden to be attained "when we no longer despise our bodies" is a vision that emerges directly from the ideology of homosexual comradeship as developed by Whitman, Carpenter, and Symonds. The novel's search for a new chivalry based on sexual and social equality is firmly rooted in the homosexual emancipation movement. Thus, Forster's attempt to discover a homosexual literary tradition yielded both his celebration of homosexual passion in *Maurice* and his depiction of fulfilled heterosexual love in *A Room with a View*.

Although *A Room with a View* is the sunniest of Forster's novels, it is not without shadows. At the end of the book, Lucy is estranged from her family, who are "disgusted at her past hypocrisy." Both she and George are alienated from Mr. Beebe, and in reaction to their elopement, Cecil has developed a cynical attitude toward women. While Lucy expresses confidence that "if we act the truth, the people who really love us are sure to come back to us in the long-run," George is less confident. There is no question as to the happiness of the young lovers in the Pension Bertolini, who exult in the holiness of direct desire. Their union presages a new order in the relationship of men and women, as implied when George asks his bride to put aside the darning of his sock and partake of the view. But the novel does not disguise the cost at which their happiness and this promising new order have been purchased, and it does not underestimate the strength of the forces of repression. Forster's happy ending is qualified and tentative.

A Room with a View is a rich and vital book. It is especially interesting as a bold hybrid of social comedy and sexual celebration, of domestic humor and mythic romance. A novel of great charm and warmth, it is energized by its commitment to feminism and by its opposition to "catch-words" of all kinds. Moreover, as an articulation of the ideology of homo-erotic comradeship—however assimilated into the heterosexual plot—*A Room with a View* is particularly important as an expression of Forster's self-acceptance of his own role in a homosexual literary tradition.

The novel suffers from the slightness of its two central characters in their surface manifestations, but this failure is partially compensated for by their function on the mythic level and by their being surrounded by a number of fascinating subsidiary figures. The compassion with which Forster treats almost all of his characters marks a new maturity, and his masterful control of image and symbol harmonizes the novel's surface plot and its mythic vision. Perhaps Forster's best-loved book, *A Room with a View* is at once romantic and serious, charming and visionary.

5

~~~~~~

Hope This Side of the Grave: *Howards End*

Howards End (1910), Forster's fourth novel, is a major achievement. It ranks among the most important works produced in the period between the death of Queen Victoria and World War I, and it concretely embodies the tensions and conflicts of that superficially placid age. At once a social comedy, an unusual love story, and an ambitious attempt to confront responsibly those dualities of body and soul, individual and society, personal fulfillment and social repression that haunt Forster's earlier novels, *Howards End* articulates more completely than they a comprehensive social vision. Yet the liberal humanism of *Howards End* has metaphysical as well as political dimensions, and the novel can best be understood as a plea for connection and reconciliation, including the reconciliation of the seen and the unseen.[1]

Howards End is especially distinguished by its mature exploration of the role of the individual in society. Like the earlier novels and like *Maurice*, it traces the growth of a focal character, but it presents this development within a broader context than the earlier works, and it displays a larger spirit of tolerance. As a metaphysical novel, *Howards End* is a reminiscent of *The Longest Journey*, and it anticipates *A Passage to India*. Like *The Longest Journey*, Forster's fourth novel asks the question, "Who shall inherit England?"

and it is similarly imbued with love for the English
countryside. In its concern with achieving wholeness
of being, it is reminiscent of *Where Angels Fear to
Tread* and *A Room with a View*. Like the latter novel,
Howards End displays a compassionate view of character and has a happy ending. Curiously, however, the
qualifications of its conclusion link the novel with the
willed happiness at the end of *Maurice* while simultaneously evoking the tentativeness of *A Passage to
India*.

The tentativeness of *Howards End* results from
the clarity of its vision, from its apprehension of the
vulnerability of liberal values in a changing world.
Forster exposes his liberal humanism—which may be
characterized as a belief in the sanctity of the individual, a respect for diversity, a faith in personal relations,
an unaffected appreciation of art, a reverence for the
inner life, a love for rural tradition, and a distrust of
conformity and a fear of urban homogeneity—to the
challenges of the machine age and the forces of rampant capitalism, imperialism, impersonality, and exploitation.[2] In the ensuing conflict, the liberal position
is unquestionably vindicated, but not without honestly
acknowledging its inner weaknesses and contradictions.[3] The triumph of liberalism in *Howards End* is
neither complete nor secure, and Forster's sense of the
vulnerability of his most cherished values contributes
to the book's urgency and integrity.

One measure of the book's integrity may be found
in its epigraph, the quintessential Forsterian motto,
"Only connect. . . ." The idea of connection fuels the
novel's attempts to fuse into wholeness individuals divided within themselves and a society equally frag-
mented and to reconcile the various dualities of existence: the inner life and the outer life, the past and the
present, the body and the soul, the masculine and the
feminine, the city and the country, the visible and the

invisible, the prose and the passion, life and death. The novel does not find each half of every duality equally valuable, but the need for reconciliation implies at least some value for each half, and in this acknowledgment lies the novel's honesty. The vision of *Howards End* resides in its conviction both of the need for connection and of its possibility, however much that possibility rests in faith rather than reason.

The book begins by immediately pitting the Schlegels against the Wilcoxes. The Schlegel family— consisting of Margaret and her younger siblings, Helen and Tibby—are of Anglo-German origin, the children of a moneyed English mother and an intellectual German idealist. They believe passionately in personal relations, art, and the life of the mind. The Wilcoxes— Henry and Ruth and their children, Charles, Paul, and Evie—are wealthy imperialists, enamored of motor cars and *laissez faire* capitalism. Helen, visiting the Wilcox family at Mrs. Wilcox's ancestral home in Hertfordshire, Howards End, writes Margaret that she has fallen in love with Paul. Unable to leave Tibby, who is ill, Margaret dispatches Aunt Juley Munt on a mission to assure her sister that "it is not a criminal offense to love at first sight." But by the time Aunt Juley arrives at Howards End—and after a comic contretemps with Charles Wilcox, whom she mistakes for Paul—the sudden alliance between Helen and Paul has been broken off, leaving Helen embarrassed and contemptuous of the "panic and emptiness" beneath the Wilcox facade of confidence and practicality. The Wilcoxes again encounter the Schlegels when they temporarily occupy a flat opposite the Schlegels' London home. Margaret and Mrs. Wilcox quickly become unlikely but close friends. In her final illness, Ruth Wilcox scrawls a message leaving Howards End to Margaret, a bequest her family ignores. As a memento of her friend, they send Margaret a silver vinaigrette.

Two years later, the Schlegel household is disrupted by the appearance of Jacky Bast, a slatternly wife in search of her missing husband Leonard, a bookish but poor young man whom the Schlegels had met at a concert in Queen's Hall. When Leonard himself arrives to apologize for his wife's vague accusations, Margaret and Helen recognize in him the possibility of something real, something beyond the "husks of culture" that fill his brain; and they determine to "show him how he may get upwards with life." When Mr. Wilcox remarks that Leonard's employer, the Porphyrion Fire Insurance Company, will soon smash, the women advise the young man to find another job. Meanwhile, Henry and Margaret are increasingly attracted to each other. He finally proposes marriage, and despite Helen's strenuous objections, Margaret accepts the proposal.

Margaret and Henry plan to be married soon after his daughter Evie's lavish wedding at Oniton Grange, the Wilcox home in Shropshire. On the evening of Evie's wedding, Helen—with the Basts in tow—makes an unexpected appearance. Henry's information about the Porphyrion Fire Insurance Company turns out to have been inaccurate, with disastrous consequences for the Basts. Acting on Henry's advice, Leonard had quit his job to accept a lower-paying one with a safer company, only to be fired in a general retrenchment. Helen holds Henry directly responsible for Leonard's ruin and demands that he make amends. Margaret agrees to intercede with Henry on Leonard's behalf, but her efforts are abruptly halted when Henry encounters a drunken Jacky, who addresses him familiarly. Henry confesses that some ten years ago he had had an affair with Jacky, and he offers to release Margaret from their engagement. Margaret declines the offer and dismisses the Basts. After unsuccessfully attempting to give Leonard almost half her fortune, Helen departs for Germany.

Margaret and Henry are married in a quiet ceremony. They live together in Henry's London home and store the Schlegels' furniture in Howards End. Margaret's happiness is shadowed by Helen's continuing estrangement. When Aunt Juley becomes ill, Helen returns to England but refuses to see Margaret and Tibby. Concluding that her sister must be mentally imbalanced, Margaret agrees to Henry's plan to lure Helen to Howards End and capture her there. The sisters are thus reunited, and Margaret discovers that Helen is pregnant with the child of Leonard Bast. Helen asks Margaret to spend the night with her in Howards End, where their old furniture has been unpacked by Miss Avery, a neighboring farm woman who had earlier told Margaret, "You think that you won't come back to live here . . . but you will." When Henry refuses permission for the sisters to sleep at the house, Margaret turns on him, accusing him of being "criminally muddled" for embracing a double standard by which he excuses his own fallibility and yet condemns Helen.

Defying her husband, Margaret joins Helen at Howards End. The next morning, however, Leonard and Charles both appear. The men scuffle, and Leonard dies of a heart attack. Margaret determines to leave Henry and live with Helen in Germany, but when Charles is charged with manslaughter, Henry breaks down. He pleads with his wife "to do what she could with him." She establishes a home at Howards End with her husband and pregnant sister. The novel ends fourteen months later. Helen has given birth to Leonard's son, Charles is in prison, and Henry has made a will leaving Howards End to Margaret, who in turn plans to leave the house to her young nephew. When Margaret learns that Henry's will is the fulfillment of Ruth Wilcox's original bequest, the news "shook her life in its inmost recesses, and she shivered."

As the bare outline of the highly contrived plot in-

dicates, *Howards End* is an extraordinarily complicated novel, focusing on issues of economics, class,
family relationships, sexual morality, and the supernatural. Forster's great triumph in the novel is to invest
these abstract issues with the concrete reality of life.
The book is structured schematically as a contrast between families and individuals and classes and ways of
life; it presents a series of antitheses that are variously
resolved in the conclusion. But what gives power to
this rich book is its sure sense of character and its masterful yet subtle manipulation of image and symbol to
alter tone and create meaning.

Howards End is beautifully written in arresting
and evocative prose. It is brilliantly unified by pervasive water imagery that constantly expands to convey
both the disorderly flux of modern life and the mysterious flow of time by which individuals merge with infinity. As James McConkey points out, "There is a
wonderfully realized sense of motion, of rising and falling, throughout"; the novel becomes a modern epic,
tracing the sea voyage of its homeless characters to
their ultimate destination, Howards End, which is
"sighted frequently but never spiritually reached until
the . . . conclusion."[4] The farmhouse and its associated symbols—the wych-elm, the meadow, the un-
prolific vine, the hay, and the Danish tumuli nearby—
promise stability against the tumultuous tides of
change.[5] They symbolize the "help from the earth" by
which the meaningless motion of progress can be
gentled into the flow of life's "deeper stream" that
connects the past, present, and future.

In Margaret Schlegel, Forster creates one of the
most memorable women in modern literature, someone who is "not beautiful, not supremely brilliant, but
filled with something that took the place of both qualities—something best described as a profound vivacity,
a continual and sincere response to all that she encoun-

tered in her path through life." Margaret and Helen
and Henry and Aunt Juley all function as representa-
tives of social classes and ideological positions, but
they also breathe the air of life, and as a consequence,
the novel is a distinguished social comedy.[6] In scenes
such as Aunt Juley's duel of "capping families" with
Charles, the concert at Queen's Hall, the luncheon
party Margaret arranges for Ruth Wilcox, the Wilcox
family conference after Ruth's funeral, and Margaret's
attempt to convince an uninspired Tibby of the virtues
of work, Forster perfectly captures the texture of English middle-class life at a particular moment in history.
Not all the characters are equally convincing—the
Basts, for instance, are unbelievable and wooden; and
Ruth Wilcox, though beautifully realized, is a figure
from myth rather than from reality, more a symbol
than a person—yet the success of the book depends in
large measure on Forster's masterful depiction of individuals who are also social types.

The recognition of individuality leads to important
distinctions within the novel's competing groups. The
Wilcoxes and the Schlegels are contrasted, for instance,
but so are the individual members of each family.
Margaret and Helen are sharply differentiated—one is
stable and moderate, the other impulsive and extreme—and Tibby, an aesthete who " had never been
interested in human beings," is in many ways unlike
either. Similarly, Ruth Wilcox is very different from
the other members of her family. Despite her marriage,
she remains a Howard rather then a Wilcox; as her
Christian name suggests, she spends her family life
among alien corn. Henry also has qualities that distinguish him from his superficially similar children. More
obviously, Leonard and Jacky Bast are unlike each
other. The differences between the individual characters in the various groups help make the novel seem
less schematic while also contributing to an important

theme, the celebration of diversity. In the final pages of the book, Margaret speaks of individual idiosyncrasies as "part of the battle against sameness." She asserts that differences—"eternal differences"—are "planted by God in a single family, so that there may always be colour; sorrow perhaps, but colour in the daily grey."

Margaret's apprehension of the need for color in the daily grey helps establish her as the novel's heroine and the spokesperson for Forsterian values. The increasing drabness of English society is a depressing reality particularly associated with London, with capitalism, and with the dominance of the outer life of "telegrams and anger" at the expense of the life of the spirit. The search for "something beyond life's daily grey" becomes a measure of character. As Margaret explains in an important conversation with Leonard, "Haven't we all to struggle against life's daily greyness, against pettiness, against mechanical cheerfulness, against suspicion? I struggle by remembering my friends; others I have known by remembering some place—some beloved place or tree. . . ." The novel offers as a solution to the ennui of prosaic existence the possibility of constructing a "rainbow bridge that should connect the prose in us with the passion." This salvation, "latent . . . in the soul of every man," promises the exaltation of human love by uniting the inner and outer lives in a harmonious whole.

Margaret functions as the book's agent of connection because she alone recognizes the worth of both the inner and the outer lives. She tells Helen, "The truth is that there is a great outer life that you and I have never touched—a life in which telegrams and anger count. . . . This outer life, though obviously horrid, often seems the real one—there's grit in it." In contrast, Helen—after her brief flirtation with the Wilcoxes, during which she even enjoys Henry's bluff ridicule of women's suffrage, tolerance, social equality, and other

Schlegel tenets—violently rejects the notion that the outer life might be valuable. She correctly perceives that the Wilcoxes' competence is insufficient, that they lack inner resources, that behind their veneer of masculine assurance lurks the "panic and emptiness" of life that cannot be dispelled by denial. But she fails to recognize that the outer life fosters—in Margaret's words—"such virtues as neatness, decision, and obedience, virtues of the second rank, no doubt, but they have formed our civilization."

Margaret's acknowledgment of the value of the outer life is a result of her Arnoldian attempt to "see life steadily and to see it whole."[7] She attributes to the Wilcoxes those practical virtues which are a necessary prelude to culture. "If Wilcoxes hadn't worked and died in England for thousands of years," she tells Helen, "you and I couldn't sit here without having our throats cut. There would be no trains, no ships to carry us literary people about in, no fields even. Just savagery. . . . Without their spirit, life might never have moved out of protoplasm." Similarly, she is skeptical of imperialism but nevertheless capable of appreciating the "heroism that builds it up." Late in the novel, when Miss Avery explains how Henry had saved Howards End, declaring that "Wilcoxes are better than nothing. . . . They keep a place going," Margaret adds: "They keep England going."

Margaret's generous recognition of qualities very different from her own may also result from her guilty awareness that her life of culture and personal relations is made possible by men like Henry Wilcox. "More and more," she exclaims, "do I refuse to draw my income and sneer at those who guarantee it." She forthrightly recognizes the importance of money and its impact on every aspect of her life. As she tells Aunt Juley, "You and I and the Wilcoxes stand upon money as upon islands. It is so firm beneath our feet, that we forget its very existence. . . . I stand each year upon six hundred pounds, and Helen upon the same, and Tibby will stand upon eight, and as fast as our pounds crumble away into the sea they are renewed—from the sea."

Her respect for money is also shown by her proposal in the discussion club that the best way to aid Leonard Bast is to give him a large sum of money. When someone asks "what it would profit Mr. Bast if he gained the whole world and lost his own soul," her reply echoes the passage about the soul's currency in *The Longest Journey* and illustrates again her function as an agent of connection: "Nothing, but he would not gain his soul until he had gained a little of the world."

Among the novel's genuine distinctions is its honest recognition of money as the basis of modern society.[8] Margaret's openness about her fortune challenges the hypocrisy of the conventional attitude that considers it vulgar to discuss money, an attitude illustrated both in Leonard's suspicion when the Schlegel sisters attempt to warn him about the state of the Porphyrion Fire Insurance Company and in Henry's inability to confide his net worth even to his fiancée. Although some members of the discussion group are shocked by Margaret's assertion that money "is the warp of civilization, whatever the woof may be" and consequently think the outspoken sisters "a little unspiritual," Margaret's shout "Hurrah for riches!" is not an expression of complacency. Her awareness that money protects her from the abyss that threatens to claim Leonard fuels her deep concern with the effects of poverty. She admits "that an overworked clerk may save his soul in the superterrestrial sense, where the effort will be taken for the deed, but she denied that he will ever explore the spiritual resources of this world, will ever know the rarer joys of the body, or attain to clear and passionate intercourse with his fellows."

But the novel also acknowledges the ineffectuality of liberalism's efforts to alleviate poverty, thus again implying the need for a Shavian connection between the forces of inner vision and those of practicality. The famous passage that begins Chapter VI—"We are not concerned with the very poor. They are unthinkable, and only to be approached by the statistician or the poet"—is a statement that not only limits the scope of the book but also acknowledges the limitations of the liberal ethos that governs it. Similarly, Margaret's intensely personal altruism is severely limited in its application to the problems of an industrial society. She rejects Henry's smug evasion of personal responsibility, as when he asserts that "our civilization is molded by great impersonal forces . . . and there always will be rich and poor." But her own efforts do not promise widespread relief: "she only fixed her eyes on a few human beings, to see how under present conditions, they could be made happier. Doing good to humanity was useless: the many-coloured efforts thereto spreading over the vast area like films and resulting in a universal grey. To do good to one, or . . . to a few, was the utmost she dare hope for."

Tellingly, in the discussion club debate, her position is defeated. The reactionary religious idealists and the radical political economists form an uneasy coalition against her and succeed in maintaining control of the hypothetical millionaire's money. Moreover, when Helen actually tries to put into effect Margaret's plan to rescue Leonard by giving him a large sum of money, he refuses to accept the gift.

The limitations of liberalism in this regard stem not so much from its personal approach to the question of poverty as from the nature of the "present conditions." The gross materialism of modern society is a fairly recent development, as indicated by the assurance that had Leonard lived some centuries ago, "in

the brightly coloured civilizations of the past," his
plight might not have been so bleak: "he would have
had a definite status, his rank and his income would
have corresponded." In the machine age, however, the
social relationship between the higher and lower classes
is neither personal nor human. There is no longer that
sense of reciprocal obligations that linked the classes in
the past.

The materialism of modern society results from
distorted values. What the Schlegels' idealistic father
said of Germany is equally applicable to England:
"you only care about the things that you can use, and
therefore arrange them in the following order: Money,
supremely useful; intellect, rather useful; imagination,
of no use at all." Significantly, while Margaret's own
ranking is quite different—"money is the second most
important thing in the world"—the Wilcoxes adhere to
the German priorities, as indicated by their reaction to
Ruth Wilcox's bequest of Howards End to Margaret:
"To them Howards End was a house: they could not
know that to her it had been a spirit, for which she
sought a spiritual heir." For materialists, houses are
real property to be bought and sold; they cannot conceive that "possessions of the spirit" might be be-
queathed or that the soul may have offspring.

The materialism of modern society is expressed
most frighteningly in the urbanization of England.
London, a "tract of quivering grey, intelligent without
purpose, and excitable without love," epitomizes the
rootlessness and alienation of a society in relentless
pursuit of material values. It represents "eternal form-
lessness; all the qualities, good, bad, and indifferent,
streaming away—streaming, streaming for ever." In
continual flux, London is a place where buildings are
constantly in the process of construction or demolition,
their "bricks and mortar rising and falling with the rest-
lessness of the water in a fountain, as the city receives
more and more men upon her soil."

London separates man from nature and destroys individuality at an ever increasing rate: "month by month the roads smelt more strongly of petrol, and were more difficult to cross, and human beings heard each other speak with greater difficulty, breathed less of the air, and saw less of the sky." Its loneliness fosters crude, anthropomorphic religion, for "the continuous flow would be tolerable if a man of our own sort . . . were caring for us up in the sky." Even its numbers are deleterious to personal relations. As Margaret tells Helen, "The more people one knows, the easier it becomes to replace them. It is one of the curses of London. I quite expect to end my life caring most for a place."

The imminent loss of the Schlegels' home at 2 Wickham Place makes Margaret particularly sensitive to the city's "architecture of hurry." The millionaire who plans to demolish her home and erect "Babylonian flats" on the site is very similar to Henry Wilcox: "He was not a fool—she had heard him expose Socialism—but true insight began just where his intelligence ended, and one gathered that this was the case with most millionaires." An exemplar of the outer life, the landlord is indifferent to the sense of continuity represented by a home and insensitive to its spiritual value. His eventual destruction of the Wickham Place house renders the Schlegels poorer, for it "had helped to balance their life, and almost to counsel them," without making him spiritually richer: "He has built flats on its site, his motor-cars grow swifter, his exposure of Socialism more trenchant. But he has spilt the precious distillation of the years, and no chemistry of his can give it back to society again."

Significantly, even in her preoccupation with her own death, Ruth Wilcox intuitively grasps the social and spiritual diminishment such destruction entails. She is horrified to learn of the plan to demolish the home. "It is monstrous, Miss Schlegel; it isn't right," she declares. "To be parted from your house, your father's house—it oughtn't to be allowed. It is worse than dying. . . . Can what they call civilization be right, if people mayn't die in the room where they were born?"

Ironically, Ruth Wilcox herself is not permitted to die in the room where she was born. Her husband, who believes that the "sick had no rights," places her in a nursing home. This action is symptomatic of the spread of urban values even into the countryside, and it imparts urgency to the novel's poignant recognition of England's loss of rural stability. Indeed, the real danger of London is that it is but a foretaste of a nomadic society that threatens to alter human nature itself. By reverting to the "civilization of luggage," by accumulating "possessions without taking root in the earth," the English middle classes are in danger of becoming an imaginatively impoverished "nomadic horde." "Under cosmopolitanism," Margaret muses, "we shall receive no help from the earth. Trees and meadows will only be a spectacle, and the binding force that they once exercised on character must be entrusted to Love alone." The question of whether love alone is equal to the task haunts the book.

The Wilcoxes are in the vanguard of the "civilization of luggage," owning as they do homes in Hertfordshire, Shropshire, and London, among other places. They shuttle back and forth between them and make commercial expeditions to the Continent and to various colonial outposts. For the Wilcoxes, houses are measured in terms of profitability and convenience. Thus, even Howards End is regarded as "picturesque enough, but not a place to live in." They are indifferent to tradition, as is apparent from their staging of Evie's wedding in Shropshire, where they have never actually lived. Although the banns are read in the local church, "the Wilcoxes have no part in the place, nor in any place. It is not their names that recur in the parish register; it is

not their ghosts that sigh among the alders at evening.
They have swept into the valley and swept out of it,
leaving a little dust and a little money behind." Their
elaborately orchestrated caravan of wedding guests
from London quite literally constitutes a nomadic
horde.

The Wilcoxes see life steadily, but "with the stead-
iness of the half-closed eye." They avoid the personal
and are oblivious to the unseen. They are representative
of the "inner darkness in high places that comes with a
commercial age." They regard the earth as a resource
to be raided, and their imperialism partakes of that
vice of the vulgar mind described by Ernst Schlegel:
"to be thrilled by bigness, to think that a thousand
square miles are a thousand times more wonderful
than one square mile, and that a million square miles
are almost the same as heaven." As imperialists, they
hope to inherit the earth, but—the narrator warns—
"though [their] ambitions may be fulfilled, the earth
[they] inherit will be grey."

The symbol of the new cosmopolitanism is the
motor car that facilitates the encroachment of London
into the countryside. Particularly associated with Charles Wilcox, the motor car leaves clouds of dust and the
reek of gasoline wherever it passes. It desecrates the
Great North Road—which "should have been bordered
all its length with glebe" except that "Henry's kind had
filched most of it"—by reducing it "to such life as is
conferred by the stench of motor cars, and to such culture as is implied by the advertisements of antibilious
pills." The automobile makes "porridge" of natural
scenery, blurring the delicate structure of the Hertfordshire countryside, robbing its passengers of any
sense of space and proportion.

The destructiveness of the motor car is crystallized
on the "unreal" journey from London to Shropshire for
Evie's wedding, during which an automobile strikes a

cat. When Charles refuses to stop, Margaret leaps from
his car, injuring her hand. She reflects, "They had no
part with the earth and its emotions. They were dust,
and a stink, and cosmopolitan chatter, and the girl
whose cat had been killed had lived more deeply than
they." The motor car intrudes even upon Howards
End, whose paddock becomes the site of a garage,
built near Ruth Wilcox's beloved wych-elm, the protective "comrade" that shelters the house with a tenderness born of strength.

The threat posed by cosmopolitanism is international as well as local, illustrated in the fate of Germany
as well as England. The emergence of Germany as an
imperial force, a commercial and naval power, "with
colonies here and a Forward Policy there, and legiti-
mate aspirations in the other place," prompts Ernst
Schlegel's flight to England. A countryman of Hegel
and Kant, he hoped "that the clouds of materialism
obscuring the Fatherland would part in time, and the
mild intellectual light re-emerge." But at the time of
the novel, shortly before the Great War, materialism is
rampant in both countries, and the rivalry between
them is ever increasing. This rivalry is dramatized
comically in the competing chauvinisms of Aunt Juley
and the Schlegels' German cousins and in the Wilcoxes'
dislike of foreigners, especially Germans. More ominously, the threat of war is rendered more likely, the
narrator remarks, by the incessant repetition of the
slogan "England and Germany are bound to fight" by
the "gutter press" of both nations. The internationalism
of the book is also indicated by the imperialistic ven-
tures of the Wilcoxes and by the dependency of the
Schlegels on foreign investments.

A principal victim of the new cosmopolitanism is
Leonard Bast, "one of the thousands who have lost the
life of the body and failed to reach the life of the spirit."
The grandson of agricultural laborers, he has been

"sucked into the town" and submerged into an economic system that is impersonal and life-denying. He
is an exemplar of the dehumanizing effect of the machine age on the worker, who has become merely a resource to be exploited and discarded at will.

In his search for "something beyond the grey," for
"the unknown," Leonard pathetically aspires to the
Schlegels' life of "books, literature, clever conversation,
culture," a world for which he is not prepared and
which his poverty precludes. Only in his honest response to nature during his adventuresome walk in the
Surrey night does he glimpse something greater than
the books he reads so assiduously and so futilely: the
spirit that led the authors to write them. His need for
adventure is a sign of inner vitality, of the "poetry" that
even the dreariness of his London existence cannot ex-
tinguish completely, and it finally redeems his life. As
the unconscious embodiment of a natural spirit of adventure, Leonard—though finally swallowed by the
abyss of urban poverty—nevertheless qualifies as the
genetic donor of the heir to Howards End, in whom
resides the novel's faint hope for England's future.

It is under these "present conditions" of materialism, urbanization, and cosmopolitanism that *Howards
End* poses the question, "Who shall inherit England?"
This question is given a lyrical resonance shortly after
Margaret tells Helen of her intention to marry Henry.
The two women, visiting Aunt Juley at Swanage, gaze
across Poole Harbor and watch the tide return. "England was alive, throbbing through all her estuaries, cry-
ing for joy through the mouths of all her gulls, and the
north wind, with contrary motion, blew stronger against
her rising sea," the narrator records, and then asks:
"What did it mean? For what end are her fair complexities, her change of soil, her sinuous coast? Does she
belong to those who have moulded her and made her
feared by other lands, or to those who had added noth-

ing to her power, but have somehow seen her, seen the whole island at once, lying as a jewel in a silver sea, sailing as a ship of souls, with all the brave world's fleet accompanying her towards eternity?" These questions are at the heart of the book. More crudely stated, they ask whether England belongs to the imperialist or to the yeoman, to those who see life steadily or to those who see it whole, to the prosaic or to the poet. Put another way, they ask whether the inheritors of England are to be people of action or vision.

Howards End disguises neither the growing power of materialism nor the ineffectuality of liberalism to counter it in the public arena. Even liberalism's power in the private forum is questioned by the example of Tibby, who despite the influence of his sisters grows into a selfish if amiable aesthete. Unlike them, he has no interest in social justice. He "neither wished to strengthen the position of the rich nor to improve that of the poor." He possesses "leisure without sympathy" and thus despises "the struggling and the submerged." Sent to Oxford, "he took into life with him, not the memory of a radiance, but the memory of a colour scheme." Tibby's effeminacy represents a tendency of liberal culture that parallels the far more dangerous tendency of the Wilcoxes toward brutality, as illustrated in the example of Charles.[9] But perhaps the failure of liberalism in both the public and private realms is illustrated most completely—and most ironically— in Helen's treatment of Leonard Bast. She violates his personal integrity by objectifying him as a cause and contributes as well to his submersion in the abyss of poverty.[10] Her proposed gift of money to her former lover is uncomfortably reminiscent of the Wilcoxes' practice of giving their servants money for Christmas.

But Ernst Schlegel's dreamy "Imperialism of the air" and his daughters' desire "that public life should mirror whatever is good in the life within" are not neg-

ligible forces in this novel that insists on the superiority
of insight to intelligence. A soldier who "beat the Aus-
trians, and the Danes, and the French, and who beat
the Germans that were inside himself," Mr. Schlegel
bequeathes to his daughters "that interest in the universal which the average Teuton possesses and the average Englishman does not." Thus Margaret and Helen
inherit resources beyond their "islands" of money, resources that the book asserts are of practical value. Indeed, *Howards End* illustrates that "There are moments when the inner life actually 'pays,' when years
of self-scrutiny, conducted for no ulterior motive, are
suddenly of practical use," thus provocatively translating the soul's currency into capitalist coin. The novel's
faith in the possibility of reconciling the seen and the
unseen offers "hope this side of the grave." This faith is
justified by Margaret's success, finally, in seeing life
both steadily and whole.

Whereas the Wilcoxes see life steadily, only Margaret, Ruth, and Helen see it whole. Only they are able
to glimpse the transcendent as well as the mundane.
They are examples of the Carlylean speculative person,
who in "meditative, sweet, yet awful hours . . . in
wonder and fear . . . ask[s] . . . that unanswerable
question: Who am I; the thing that can say 'I' . . . ?
The world, with its loud trafficking, retires into the
distance; and, through the paper-hangings, and stone
walls, and thick-piled tissues of Commerce and Polity,
and all the living and lifeless integuments . . . where-
with your Existence sits surrounded,—the sight reaches
forth into the void Deep, and you are alone with the
Universe, and silently commune with it as one mysterious Presence with another."[11]

Helen's capacity for seeing life whole is revealed
in her perception of "heroes and shipwrecks" in the
musical flood of Beethoven's Fifth Symphony, that
"most sublime noise that has ever penetrated into the

ear of man." Helen revels in the music's victorious assertion of "superhuman joy," its depiction of "the gusts
of splendour, the heroism, the youth, the magnificence
of life and death." But she is equally aware of the "goblins" that walk quietly over the universe from end to
end and that Beethoven does not dismiss as merely the
"phantoms of cowardice and unbelief." The goblins
that stalk the universe testify that "all is not for the best
in the best of all possible worlds," that panic and emptiness lie at the core of worldly achievement. The goblins thus deepen human experience by purging it of
superficiality and complacency.

Helen's understanding of how "the Invisible
lodges against the Visible" is evident as well in her passionate insistence that "Death destroys a man: the idea
of Death saves him."[12] Death places in perspective the
materialism of the Nietzschean "superman" who "can't
say 'I'": "Injustice and greed would be the real thing if
we lived for ever. As it is, we must hold to other things,
because Death is coming." The value of death is that it
exposes the emptiness of materialism and strengthens
the force of love: "Behind the coffins and the skeletons
that stay the vulgar mind lies something so immense
that all that is great in us responds to it. Men of the
world may recoil from the charnel-house that they will
one day enter, but Love knows better. Death is his foe,
but his peer, and in their age-long struggle the thews of
Love have been strengthened, and his vision cleared,
until there is no one who can stand against him."

The connection between love and death is concretely illustrated when the woodcutter who observes
Ruth's burial plucks a chrysanthemum from the wreath
sent by Margaret to take to his love. In *Howards End*
as in Wallace Stevens's "Sunday Morning," "Death is the
mother of beauty."[13] The resolution of the paradox
that "Death destroys a man: the idea of Death saves
him" is rooted in death's power to enhance life by forc-

ing human beings into an awareness of the spiritual as well as the material. The idea of death thus promises hope this side of the grave, a promise explicitly drawn from the death of Leonard Bast.

Ruth Wilcox, the most elusive character in the novel, is the fullest embodiment of wholeness. In many ways, she is very different from the Schlegel sisters. She is not interested in the social and cultural issues that agitate them, and the luncheon party Margaret stages in her honor is a conspicuous failure. Her quality is ineffable and wisplike, but for all her spirituality, she knows that a house cannot stand without bricks and mortar. She lives her life as she dies: "neither as victim nor as fanatic, but as the seafarer who can greet with an equal eye the deep that he is entering, and the shore that he must leave."

Ruth's respect for the inner life links her to Margaret, and her instinctive understanding of it is fuller than Margaret's more intellectual approach. A descendant of Quakers, Ruth seeks "a more inward light" than that offered by conventional religion, especially for the sake of her materialistic children. Her innocence stems from her strong identification with the earth: she "knew no more of worldly wickedness and wisdom than did the flowers in her garden, or the grass in her field." Her wisdom—actually the reality of the divine wisdom that Margaret seeks through the study of theosophy—is an "instinctive wisdom" bestowed on her by the past, which she in turn bestows on Margaret in her bequest of Howards End, the symbol of the continuity of the past into the future. Just as she cares for her ancestors, and lets them help her, so she guides Margaret, her spiritual heir.

Ruth functions as the novel's spiritual guardian. This role is intimated when, at Ruth's death, Margaret thinks of her as a "great wave" that "had strewn at her feet fragments torn from the unknown," and it is made apparent later when Margaret tells Helen, "I feel that you and I and Henry are only fragments of that woman's mind. . . . She is everything. She is the house and the tree that stands over it." Certainly, Ruth's spirit haunts the book and influences the course of events well after her death. On the occasion of Henry's proposal, Margaret thinks that "Mrs. Wilcox strayed in and out, ever a welcome guest; surveying the scene . . . without one hint of bitterness." Ruth's influence—augmented by the sibylline utterances of Miss Avery—gives the novel a supernatural aura and helps account for the series of coincidences that culminate in Margaret's literal succession as mistress of Howards End. From this perspective, Ruth fulfills the role claimed by Stephen Wonham at the end of *The Longest Journey:* she governs the paths between the dead who had evoked her and the living whom she evokes.

Howards End thus suggests the continuing influence of the dead upon the living, but it also makes Margaret's succession to Ruth realistically convincing as well. Despite the superficial differences that separate the two women, they share a predisposition toward connection. Although they lack common interests, they are instinctively drawn to each other. In this regard, it is worth noting that Helen's visit to Howards End as the novel opens is the result of an invitation originally extended by Ruth to Margaret, whom she had met in Germany.

Their relationship is cemented when Margaret announces her formula for coping with the complexities of life: the achievement of "proportion." "To be humble and kind, to go straight ahead, to love people rather than pity them, to remember the submerged," Margaret begins her litany of Schlegelisms, and then admits: "well, one can't do all these things at once . . . because they're so contradictory. It's then that proportion comes in—to live by proportion. Don't *begin* with proportion. Only prigs do that. Let proportion come in as a last resource." In response, Ruth—"withdrawing her hand into the deeper shadows"—exclaims, "It is just what I would have liked to say about [the difficulties of life] myself." Significantly, this exchange follows Margaret's admission of inexperience—"I have everything to learn—absolutely everything"—and it adumbrates her verdict on Ruth's life when her friend dies: "She had kept proportion." The novel in effect chronicles Margaret's parallel quests for experience and for proportion, pilgrimages that lead her toward the attainment of Ruth's wholeness of vision and of being.

Margaret achieves proportion by making "continuous excursions" into the inner and the outer realms, not seeking some mathematically precise midpoint between the extremes but attempting to combine the best elements of each. She avoids the errors of both the "businessman who assumes that this life is everything, and the mystic who asserts that it is nothing." More pointedly, she eschews the extremes represented by both her obtuse husband and her absolutist sister, each of whom presses competing claims on her loyalty. The novel generates tension as a result of this competition and raises the possibility that in her attempt to connect the inner and the outer lives Margaret may sacrifice herself on the altar of an unsatisfying marriage, that she may herself become a Wilcox not only in name but also in spirit.

Some critics complain that Margaret's decision to marry Henry is inconsistent with her character,[14] but Forster's depiction of their courtship is entirely believable. Indeed, the subtlety with which he develops their attraction for each other is a major achievement of the novel. Margaret's attraction for Henry is a response to his masculinity and decisiveness, his optimism and self-confidence. Not insignificantly, she is also attracted to him sexually. Early in the book, she comments on his handsome physical appearance—"He has a remarkably good complexion for a man of his age"—and later, as she anticipates his proposal, she observes that "His complexion was robust, his hair had receded but not thinned, the thick moustache and the eyes that Helen had compared to brandy-balls had an agreeable menace in them, whether they were turned towards the slums or towards the stars."

Much as Helen did on her original visit to Howards End, Margaret even responds to the patronizing tone and protective attitude that Henry exercises in his dealing with women, finding these characteristics fatherly and charming. Most of all, she is flattered by the attentions of a "real man," particularly one who—unlike most men—prefers her to her prettier sister: "She was not young or very rich, and it amazed her that a man of any standing should take her seriously." As she tells Helen, "It is wonderful knowing that a real man cares for you."

Margaret's response to Henry is also a function of her acute consciousness of the "pressure of virginity" and of her isolation, her sense of incompleteness in a world of couples. When she meets Evie and her fiancé Mr. Cahill for lunch at Simpson's in the Strand, "she saw not only houses and furniture but the vessel of life itself slipping past her." In the party that follows, when Henry joins the trio, ordering lunch for Margaret and commanding her attention, the older pair soon lapse into the "No, I didn't; yes, you did" kind of conversation characteristic of the engaged couple. When Henry actually proposes to her, in one of the finest scenes in the novel, an "immense joy came over her. It was indescribable. It had nothing to do with humanity, and most resembled the all-pervading happiness of fine weather. Fine weather is due to the sun, but Margaret could think of no central radiance here. She stood in his drawing room happy, and longing to give happiness. On leaving him she realized that the central radiance had been love."

But when Helen asks Margaret whether she really loves Henry, Margaret "meditated honestly, and said: 'No.'" What she is confident of when she accepts Henry's proposal is that she will learn to love him, and indeed she does. She characterizes her feeling for Henry as prose, "a very good kind of prose, but well considered, well thought out." She thinks that she knows her future husband's limitations and that she can make of him a better man than he is at present.

Even after their first kiss, which disappoints her in its abruptness and lack of tenderness, she thinks that "Mature as he was, she might yet be able to help him to the building of the rainbow bridge that should connect the prose in us with the passion." She hopes that she can help him reconcile the incompatible fragments of his personality—the beast and the monk in him. This fragmentation precludes a satisfying sexual life, torn as Henry is by an "incomplete asceticism" that permits him furtively to enjoy loveless sex in his affair with Jacky Bast while causing him to "be a little ashamed of loving a wife." But Margaret's sermon, "Only connect, and the beast and the monk, robbed of the isolation that is life to either, will die," falls on deaf ears: "For there was one quality in Henry for which she was never prepared, however much she reminded herself of it: his obtuseness."

Margaret's love for Henry survives its first crisis, the revelation of Henry's affair with Jacky. But Margaret, who distinguishes between unchastity and infidelity and decides that Henry's infidelity had been an offense against Ruth rather than herself, forgives Henry as an act of pity. Certainly, she is correct in her plea for "charity in sexual matters: so little is known about them; it is hard enough for those who are personally touched to judge; then how futile must be the verdict of society." But she is too complacent about the prospects of achieving a fulfilling marriage with someone whom she does not respect and with whom she cannot be fully herself.

"To have no illusions and yet to love," Margaret muses, "what stronger surety can a woman find? She had seen her husband's past as well as his heart." But while Margaret's lack of illusions and her willingness to compromise help assure superficial happiness for her marriage, this happiness is bought at a very high price. The danger that her marriage represents is to her individuality; domesticity threatens to engulf her personality. She is conscious of the superiority of her values to Henry's, yet in her yearning for love and in her desire to forge connections, she comes close to destroying the very basis on which her superiority rests.

Margaret's tendency to submerge her personality in the interests of harmony is apparent during the courtship, as when she pretends to agree with Henry's opinions, suppresses her own ideas, and feigns surprise at his proposal. Even after their engagement and marriage, she continues to play an unnatural role of submissive ingenue. She deliberately pretends to ignorance on the trip from London to Shropshire for Evie's wedding when the overly chivalrous men incorrectly identify the Oxford colleges for the ladies' edification. She artfully allows her brave action in leaping from the automobile to be misinterpreted as hysteria. Henry and Charles readily accept this explanation, for "it fitted in too well with their view of feminine nature." She restrains her deepest impulses in her letter to Henry after the revelation of his affair with Jacky, for "Henry would resent so strong a grasp of the situation. She must not comment; comment is unfeminine."

Margaret is conscious of the tension between the need to "remain herself" and the need to conform to the expectations of her husband, yet she increasingly denies her instincts—especially her feminism—and she stoops to "the methods of the harem." "In dealing with a Wilcox," Margaret acknowledges, "how tempting it was to lapse from comradeship, and to give him the kind of woman that he desired." Henry appreciates having a wife who reads poetry and concerns herself with social issues—"it distinguished her from the wives of other men"—but he especially enjoys the fact that "He had only to call, and she clapped the book up and was ready to do what he wished." *Howards End* is strongly feminist in outlook, and Margaret's attempt to mold herself into a conventionally submissive wife is depicted as unnatural and destructive.[15]

The outward happiness that Margaret and Henry experience at the beginning of their married life is thus based on deception and self-denial. The threat that Wilcoxism may subsume Margaret is nowhere more evident than in her acquiescence to Henry's plan to capture Helen at Howards End, a plan that "clever and well-meaning as it was, drew its ethics from the wolf-pack." But when Henry attempts to leave her behind with his daughter-in-law, Margaret realizes that "he was only treating her as she had treated Helen, and her rage at his dishonesty only helped to indicate what Helen would feel against them. She thought: 'I deserve it: I am punished for lowering my colours.'"

This insight saves Margaret, and when she overhears Henry and the physician calmly speculating as to whether her sister is "normal," she revolts and allies herself with Helen: "How dare these men label her sister! . . . The pack was turning on Helen, to deny her human rights, and it seemed to Margaret that all Schlegels were threatened with her. Were they normal? What a question to ask! And it is always those who know nothing about human nature, who are bored by psychology and shocked by physiology, who ask it. However piteous her sister's state, she knew that she must be on her side. They would be mad together if the world chose to consider them so." Margaret's indignation at the men's measuring of her sister according to some arbitrary scale of normality undoubtedly reflects Forster's own resentment at the persistent labeling of homosexuals as abnormal.

Margaret's reconciliation with Helen is a repudiation of the attempt at connection through self-denial. As she bars the entrance of Henry, the physician, and the chauffeur into the house, "A new feeling came over her; she was fighting for women against men." She apologizes to Helen for behaving unworthily, pointedly asking, "What would our father have thought of me?" The women explore the house, now filled with the Schlegel furniture, and Helen remarks that the house seems alive, "it looks to be ours now." The house, symbol of continuity and of hope this side of the grave, seems to have wonderful powers. "It kills what is dreadful and makes what is beautiful live," Margaret declares.

Surrounded by Schlegel mementos in a house that seems to breathe with the spirit of the past, Margaret and her pregnant sister reap the harvest of their devotion to the inner life: "And all the time their salvation was lying round them—the past sanctifying the present; the present, with wild heart-throb, declaring that there would after all be a future, with laughter and the voices of children." Speaking of the Wilcoxes, Helen tells Margaret, "my life is great and theirs are little. . . . I know of things they can't know of, and so do you. We *know* that there's poetry. We *know* that there's death. They can only take them on hearsay. We know this is our house, because it feels ours." The novel's conclusion, a compound of melodramatic action, rich symbolism, and visionary hopefulness, validates the claim.

Margaret's attempt to secure permission for Helen to spend the night at Howards End marks the end of her flirtation with Wilcoxism. It leads to her permanent return to the liberalism espoused by her father and the spirituality embodied in Ruth. Although Henry tells her that "We are husband and wife, not children," he in fact addresses her as a child, even echoing the cliché that parents use when disciplining their offspring, "Remember that this is far worse for me than for you." But this condescension stirs Margaret to rebellion. She rejects his assumption of male superiority.

As they talk, she gazes at the Six Hills, the ancient burial ground of soldiers, suggestive of her soldier father, of the earth, of the past, of the unseen, and of androgyny, since they are described as "breasts of the spring." Fortified by these associations, Margaret strikes out at her husband when he evokes conventional morality as an excuse to bar Helen from Howards End. She points out the hypocrisy of his attitude, drawing a connection between his conduct with Jacky Bast and his treatment of Helen and violently summing up the muddle of his life: "Do you see the connection? Stupid, hypocritical, cruel—oh contemptible!—a man who insults his wife when she's alive and cants with her memory when she's dead. A man who ruins a woman for his pleasure, and casts her off to ruin other men. And gives bad financial advice, and then says he is not responsible. These, man, are you. You can't recognize them, because you cannot connect." When she later considers this speech, Margaret reflects: "It had to be uttered once in a life, to adjust the lopsidedness of the world. It was spoken not only to her husband, but to thousands of men like him."

The climax of the novel is the death—the "supreme adventure"—of Leonard Bast, whom Helen had loved "absolutely, perhaps for half an hour." In the middle of the night that Helen and she spend at Howards End, Margaret wakes up thinking of Leonard. "Was he also part of Mrs. Wilcox's mind?" she ponders.

The coincidence of his arrival at Howards End while
Margaret and Helen are in residence and when Charles
has arrived to evict them and the highly symbolical
tableau of his death—he dies of a heart attack when
struck by a Wilcox wielding a Schlegel sword and is
swamped by a shower of books, those symbols of the
culture to which he so poignantly aspired—suggest a
supernatural influence.

In considering the "jangle of causes and effects"
that culminate in Leonard's death, Margaret finds significance beyond the "ordered insanity" of logic:

Here Leonard lay dead in the garden, from natural causes;
yet life was a deep, deep river, death a blue sky, life was a
house, death a wisp of hay, a flower, a tower, life and death
were anything and everything, except this ordered insanity,
where the king takes the queen, and the ace the king. Ah no;
there was beauty and adventure behind, such as the man at
her feet had yearned for; there was hope this side of the
grave; there were truer relationships beyond the limits that
fetter us now. As a prisoner looks up and sees stars beckoning, so she, from the turmoil and horror of those days, caught
glimpses of the diviner wheels.

This passage, among the most beautiful in the
book, brings together the various strands of the novel's
persistent concern with how the invisible lodges
against the visible. Progressing from the concrete reality of nature to the ineffability of "diviner wheels," and
encompassing such artifacts of man's life and ambitions
as the house and the tower, Margaret's meditation on
Leonard's death serves up in a microcosm the constit-
uent elements of the connnections necessary to perceive clearly the entirety of human experience on earth,
a whole that includes life and death, past and future,
the mundane and the mysterious. The passage makes
clear the paradox that death enhances life; it insists that
life and death are part of the same continuum of existence; and it asserts the superiority of the transcendent
to the mundane.

Leonard's death cannot be explained satisfactorily as merely the culmination of a logical chain of events. The mystery of life and death defies comprehension by the world of telegrams and anger. Margaret does not know "to what harmony we tend," but she finds in Leonard's death—however squalid it may appear when viewed from the steady but narrow perspective of the outer life—an emblem of wholeness. It promises hope on this side of the grave: "there seems great chance that a child would be born into the world, to take the great chances of beauty and adventure that the world offers." The repetition of the word "chance" shadows this annunciation without denying the possibility of beauty, adventure, and continuity. Because Leonard's death provides a glimpse of the unseen, it is transformed from Squalor into Tragedy, "whose eyes are on the stars, and whose hands hold the sunset and the dawn."

The effects on the Wilcoxes of the crisis prompted by Leonard's death confirm Helen's early view that behind their facade of self-confidence lies panic and emptiness. Indeed, these effects illustrate the novel's conviction that the practitioners of the outer life sorely need the virtues of liberal humanism that they despise. In the scene between Charles and his father, after Leonard's death but before the inquest that indicts Charles for manslaughter, the inability of the two men to express their innermost thoughts is poignantly portrayed. As he watches his father walking up the road toward the police station, Charles thinks that Henry has become "more like a woman," and he is himself filled with "a vague regret—a wish . . . that he had been taught to say 'I' in his youth." The "feminization" of Henry, the collapse of his assumption of masculine authority, leads finally to his salvation. His masculine "fortress" against emotion collapses: "He could bear no one but his wife, he shambled up to Margaret . . . and asked her to do what she could with him. She did what seemed easiest—she took him down to recruit at Howards End."

It is appropriate that the lives of the Wilcoxes and the Schlegels are reordered at Howards End, one of those English farms where "if anywhere, one might see life steadily and see it whole, group in one vision its transitoriness and its eternal youth, connect—connect without bitterness until all men are brothers." There, where men's hours are governed "by the movements of the crops and the sun," lies England's best hope, the breeding of a "nobler stock" of yeoman.

Thus, as John Edward Hardy has demonstrated, the novel's final chapter enacts a fertility ritual: "The mower is 'encompassing with narrowing circles the sacred centre of the field' as the chapter opens; at the end, Helen, with baby on arm, rushes into the house to hurrah the harvest. . . . Nothing could be plainer. 'Circles,' a 'sacred centre,' baby, bumper crop."[16] This fertility is embodied in the fruit of Leonard and Helen's brief liaison. Significantly without a name, the genetic offspring of a Bast and a Schlegel, the heir to a Wilcox and destined to be the lifelong friend of the "wonderful nursemaid" neighbor boy Tom, the baby reconciles the competing families in the novel. Belonging to all of them, he represents the connections by which brotherhood might be realized in England.

But though the nameless child belongs to all the competing groups in the novel, he belongs especially to Helen and Margaret, who are jointly responsible for his future. If in *The Longest Journey* Forster symbolically achieves the impossible feat of having fraternity beget progeny, in *Howards End* he achieves the equally impossible feat of having sorority beget progeny. This suggestion is underlined by the perfunctory nature of Helen's relationship with Leonard and by the fact that the alliance between the sisters is by far the strongest emotional bond in the book.

The novel's harmonious conclusion is engineered by the heroism of Margaret, with the "uncanny" aid of the land and of Ruth. For the first time in the book, Margaret is associated with hay, the symbol of influence from beyond the grave that has previously and persistently been linked with Ruth. Margaret and Henry achieve the "truer relationship" of comrades, a bond that transcends sex roles and is paralleled by the comradeship attributed to the wych-elm and the Howards End house, a relationship that is an emblem "not of eternity, but of hope on this side of the grave." Helen even learns to like Henry, and they both retreat from their most extreme positions.

Henry qualifies his materialism by treating his children generously rather than justly and by acquiescing in Margaret's decision to diminish her income by half and give away a great deal of money. Helen's absolutist belief in personal relations is tempered when she confesses her inability to care for Leonard's memory and her lack of interest in romantic love.

"Don't drag in the personal when it will not come," Margaret tells her as the older sister confides her own indifference to children. She cautions Helen against attempting to conform to some external standard of normality, thus enunciating a doctrine of tolerance that extends to their brother, who had never learned to care for people, and to Ruth, who had derived meaning from devotion to a place: "people are far more different than is pretended. All over the world men and women are worrying because they cannot develop as they are supposed to develop . . . others go farther still, and move outside humanity altogether. A place, as well as a person, may catch the glow." This diversity, Margaret asserts, "leads to comfort in the end." Forster's celebration of pluralism here is undoubtedly influenced by his acceptance of his own homosexuality.

The book thus ends on a note of harmonious

wholeness, but it does not deny the vulnerability of Howards End and the life of connection that it represents. The novel's very title questions whether the values embodied in Ruth Howard Wilcox can be transmitted beyond her lifetime. "London's creeping," Helen remarks, pointing to the horizon of red dust beyond the meadows: "You see that in Surrey and even Hampshire now. . . . I can see it from the Purbeck Downs. And London is only part of something else, I'm afraid. Life's going to be melted down, all over the world."

Margaret admits that the "civilization of luggage" creeps ever closer, but she clings to a faith that defies logic: "Because a thing is going strong now, it need not go strong for ever. . . . This craze for motion has only set in during the last hundred years. It may be followed by a civilization that won't be a movement, because it will rest on the earth. All the signs are against it now, but I can't help hoping, and very early in the morning in the garden I feel that our house is the future as well as the past." The novel's optimism is thus tentative and willed, illogical and mystical. But countering the "ordered insanity" of logic is a faith justified by Margaret's glimpse of the "diviner wheels" on the occasion of Leonard's death and by the presence in the field of the nameless baby who is the living hope of the English countryside's ability "to throw back to a nobler stock, and breed yeomen."

Howards End is a novel of extraordinary ambition and wide scope. Written in prose with the texture of restrained poetry, it is consummately controlled and sure of purpose. It is Forster's most complexly orchestrated work to its date, and it smoothly manipulates imagery and symbolism, plot and character, into an organic whole. In so doing, it gracefully integrates social comedy, metaphysical explorations, and political concerns. *Howards End* tests Forster's liberal humanism, finds it wanting, and proposes a marriage of liberal values to conservative tradition. Without denying the practical contributions of progressivism, it forcefully attacks the mindless materialism that yields rootlessness and spiritual poverty.

Forster's fourth novel successfully captures the texture of life and manners at a pivotal moment in English history. As domestic comedy, it is marred by the unconvincing characterization of Leonard and Jacky and by the strained credibility of the relationships between Henry and Jacky and Helen and Leonard.[17] But the novel brilliantly penetrates beyond the placid surface of its era to the social tensions and the "panic and emptiness" that would lead to the Great War of 1914 and the convulsions afterward. In retrospect, those convulsions seem to have mocked Margaret's optimism and to have destroyed forever the greenwood that her nephew was to have inherited. But our knowledge that some aspects of Margaret's faith were to be mocked by history only increases the urgency of her vision and the poignancy of her optimism.

Most profoundly, however, *Howards End* is a metaphysical novel, one that searches for meaning to the human experience. It finds—tentatively and in defiance of logic—hope this side of the grave. Its optimism is qualified by skepticism and tinged with despair. It is not Forster's masterpiece—that designation belongs to *A Passage to India*, in which divisions are even more intractable and the possibilities of connection yet more remote. But *Howards End*, in its willed faith, in its desperately grasped hope for help from the earth, is a fascinating response to the same sense of isolation that propels the greater and more pessimistic novel. A work of strange tenderness, *Howards End*, like Beethoven's Fifth Symphony, acknowledges the goblins of the universe but nevertheless builds up the ramparts of the world.

6

♈♈♈

The Flesh Educating
the Spirit:
Maurice

Although the existence of a novel by Forster dealing
with homosexual themes was an open secret in the literary world for years, *Maurice* was not published until
1971, the year after Forster's death. It was begun in
September 1913, completed in July 1914, and periodically revised until 1960, when it reached its final state.[1]
The belatedness of the publication of *Maurice* has had
unfortunate consequences. It and the other posthumously published works have been seen as distinctly inferior to the justly celebrated novels and stories published in Forster's lifetime. They have in effect
been relegated to that tiny corner in the back of the
bookstore reserved for gay literature, and their publication has sparked a number of blatantly homophobic
attacks on Forster and an even larger number of reviews and analyses marred by condescension and
thinly veiled contempt.

The attacks inspired by bigotry generally betray
their own absurdity, as, for example, when Cynthia
Ozick asserts that Forster's homosexuality devalues his
humanism.[2] But the division of Forster's canon into
homosexual and heterosexual works is more insidious.
What needs emphasis is what Judith Scherer Herz and
Jane Lagoudis Pinchin point out: that such a division is
artificial, suggested by the publication history of the
works and their external dramatic situations but not by

the fiction itself, all of which embodies a consistent system of belief.[3] As James Malek writes of *Maurice*, "It is wrong to regard the novel as being exclusively or primarily 'about' homosexuality. Its principal concerns are spiritual life, liberation, psychological wholeness, the value of the individual, moral responsibility, the ennobling power of love, responsiveness to life's variety and mystery—in short, most of the human values that characterize all of Forster's work; the novel is 'about' these things, and homosexuality is one means that *may* help *some* people attain these blessings or discover these values."[4]

More to the point, *Maurice* is a significant achievement, deserving of an honored place in the canon of a major artist. Forster's most concentrated novel, it is resonant, subtle, sophisticated, and poignant. Although Forster worried that *Maurice* might be considered only a period piece, its firm rooting in a particular place and time—England in the years before the Great War—actually testifies to the timelessness of its insight into the pain and joy of personal growth. Indeed, the novel dramatizes in deeply felt human terms the most important recent conclusions of sexologists and psychologists—that homosexuality is a set of feelings involving the connection and commitment one individual makes with another and that such feelings predate sexual expression, sometimes by years—while at the same time placing this understanding in the concrete context of Edwardian England.[5] The social setting is important, for *Maurice* also explores the impact of self-awareness on social attitudes, and it is fundamentally a political novel. For Forster, individual growth is always measured in terms of sharpened insight into the nature of convention and repression.

In a fascinating "Terminal Note" drafted in 1960 and appended to the novel, Forster describes the genesis of *Maurice* as the direct result of a 1913 visit to the social pioneer and gay liberation activist Edward Carpenter: "It must have been on my second or third visit to the shrine that the spark was kindled and he and his comrade George Merrill combined to make a profound impression on me and to touch a creative spring." Inspired by Carpenter and his working-class lover Merrill, Forster wrote the novel quickly, guided by the conviction that a "happy ending was imperative."

The happy ending made *Maurice* difficult to publish during most of Forster's lifetime. Since homosexuality was illegal in England until 1967, the novel might have been construed as recommending crime and hence have been subject to prosecution. Nevertheless, the happy ending is an integral component of Forster's vision in *Maurice*. The determination that "in fiction anyway two men should fall in love and remain in it for the ever and ever that fiction allows" is not an expression of wish-fulfilling fantasy but rather a shaping element of Forster's realistic depiction in the novel of his hero's gradual awakening to—and ultimate salvation by—the holiness of direct desire.

In its commitment to the holiness of direct desire and in its faith in the possibility of human happiness even in the midst of repression, *Maurice* most closely resembles *A Room with a View*. Both novels translate the ideology of the early homosexual emancipation movement into ideals against which are gauged individual growth and social health. Like *A Room with a View* and *Where Angels Fear to Tread*, the posthumously published novel is a *Bildungsroman* that traces the growth of its hero toward maturity. The painful intensity of *Maurice* recalls *The Longest Journey*, while its political implications are suggestive of *Howards End* as well.

Howards End and *Maurice* are both thesis novels, though in neither is the thesis narrow or constricting; and both insist, in Margaret Schlegel's words, "that people are far more different than is pretended." The social analysis of *Maurice* is more sweeping in scope but less exhaustive in detail than that of *Howards End*, and in 1913–14 Forster is less willing to compromise and to hope against logic than he had been in 1910. In its vivid dissection of the loneliness of the human condition, *Maurice* anticipates *A Passage to India*, though the former is less profoundly pessimistic than the latter. Less ambitious than *A Passage to India* or *Howards End* and more narrowly focused than the earlier novels, *Maurice* shares with all of them the brilliant manipulation of leitmotifs and rhythm. As controlled as *Where Angels Fear to Tread* and as moving as *The Longest Journey*, *Maurice* deserves far more appreciation than it has received.

The plot chronicles the growth of the eponymous hero from the onset of puberty at the age of fourteen to his sexual and social liberation at the age of twenty-four. The novel opens with Maurice Hall a "plump, pretty lad, not in any way remarkable." The son of a widowed mother and the brother to two younger sisters, he is expected to follow the life journey of his father, who had been "a good citizen, but lethargic." Maurice moves from Mr. Abraham's preparatory school to Sunnington, a mediocre public school, to a Cambridge college patronized by other old Sunningtonians. At Cambridge, he gradually ascends from the "Valley of the Shadow of Life" and cements a friendship with Clive Durham, the scion of a county family and the heir to Penge, a declining country house located near the Wiltshire and Somerset border.

A fastidious intellectual and self-conscious Hellenist, Clive introduces Maurice to Plato's *Symposium* and finally declares his love for the less intellectually gifted young man. At first Maurice is "shocked to the bottom of his suburban soul," but he finally comes to acknowledge that the "only sex that attracted him was

his own." One night he climbs through Clive's bedroom window to tell him that he loves him just as
Clive calls out Maurice's name in sleep. At Clive's insistence, the young men's relationship remains pla-
tonic, romantic but nonphysical. They share an outing
in the Cambridge countryside, and then Maurice is expelled for having missed lectures. Despite several obstacles to their love, including pressure on Clive to
marry and beget an heir, the young men enjoy two
years of happiness. During a prolonged attack of in-
fluenza, however, Clive gradually develops an attraction for women and a "horror of masculinity." On a
trip to Greece, he writes to Maurice that "Against my
will I have become normal. I cannot help it."

Maurice is devastated by Clive's desertion and by
the collapse of his orderly life. He is disturbed as well
by his increasingly insistent sexual urges. After flirting
with suicide, he decides to attempt to become normal.
He confesses to his neighbor Dr. Barry that he is "an
unspeakable of the Oscar Wilde sort," a confession the
old physician dismisses as "Rubbish, rubbish!" Maurice accepts an invitation from Clive and his new
bride, Anne Woods, to spend a brief holiday in the
country. At Penge, he discovers that Clive is almost totally absorbed in an election campaign. Disappointed
at Clive's neglect and even more determined to become normal, Maurice writes for an appointment with
a hypnotist, Mr. Lasker Jones, and he allows Anne and
Clive to believe that he plans to be married. After a
session with the hypnotist, he returns to Penge; in his
sleep that night, he walks to the window of his room
and calls, "Come!" The plea is answered when Alec
Scudder, the estate's handsome undergamekeeper
with "bright brown eyes," climbs up a ladder and into
Maurice's arms.

The next morning, during a cricket match, Maurice
envisions himself and Alec as two comrades fighting

against a hostile world, a reverie broken by the appearance of Clive. Suddenly taken ill, Maurice abruptly
leaves Penge. At home, he receives a letter from Alec
requesting a meeting before the young gamekeeper
emigrates to Argentina. Fearing blackmail, Maurice
ignores the letter. But in his next encounter with the
hypnotist, he fails to enter a trance. Jones tells him that
by "sharing" with Alec, Maurice has "cut himself off
from the congregation of normal men."

Maurice's failure to be converted to heterosexuality actually gives him an inner peace, and he is not disturbed when he receives a threatening letter from
Alec. He asks the young man to meet him at the British
Museum. The encounter there culminates in Maurice's
declaration of love for Alec and in a night of passion in
a cheap hotel. Maurice proposes that his friend not emi-
grate and that they retreat into the greenwood together,
but Alec refuses. When the gamekeeper fails to appear
for the departure of his Argentine-bound ship, however, Maurice hurries to Penge and discovers Alec
waiting for him in the boathouse. Before the lovers
depart for the greenwood, Maurice confronts a disbe-
lieving Clive with the astonishing news. The novel
ends with the squire meditating on "some method of
concealing the truth from Anne."

Just as the heterosexual plot of *A Room with a
View* articulates the ideology of the early English homosexual rights movement, so does *Maurice* also reflect
this ideology. Indeed, the later novel mirrors a significant debate within the Uranian movement. The term
"Uranian" derives from Plato's *Symposium*, in which
Pausanias distinguishes between Heavenly Aphrodite
(Aphrodite Urania) and Common Aphrodite (Aphrodite Pandeumia). According to Pausanias, those who
are inspired by Heavenly Love "are attracted towards
the male sex, and value it as being naturally the stronger
and more intelligent . . . their intention is to form a

lasting attachment and partnership for life."[6] The term was popularized by the Austrian legal official Karl Heinrich Ulrichs in the late 1860s and 1870s and was soon adopted in England. By 1890, there existed a group of writers, artists, and philosophers dedicated to the goal of securing sympathetic recognition of the homosexual (or Uranian) impulse in a repressive society. The two most important ideologues of the movement were John Addington Symonds and Edward Carpenter. Both disciples of Whitman, they preached the love of comrades in numerous poems, pamphlets, and books.[7]

Symonds and Carpenter equally deserve credit as pioneers in sexual reform, but their styles and ideas were quite different, and *Maurice* pivots on the contrast between them. Whereas Symonds tended to be evasive and apologetic, Carpenter was open and visionary. Symonds implied the superiority of homosexuality to heterosexuality, finding the former more spiritual and less bound by material considerations, but Carpenter insisted on the equality of the two emotions, considering neither one more or less spiritual than the other. While Symonds isolated homosexual love as a private experience and minimized physical passion, Carpenter forthrightly acknowledged the physical and linked homosexual emancipation with feminism, labor reform, and social democracy. For Carpenter, the homosexual experience provided an opportunity to question received ideas and to develop a radical critique of society itself.

As Robert K. Martin has demonstrated, *Maurice* enacts a dialectic between these two main branches of Uranian thought.[8] The novel opposes not heterosexuality and homosexuality but two versions of homosexuality, one associated with Symonds, the other with Carpenter. This dialectic is reflected in the very structure of the book, which divides into two parallel sections, the action of each half mirroring the other with significant differences. The first half (comprising Parts One and Two) is devoted to the Maurice-Clive relationship. It traces a false vision of "superior" homosexuality that is platonized and sublimated in the manner of Symonds. The second half of the novel (encompassing Parts Three and Four) is devoted to the Maurice-Alec alliance, and it tracks Maurice's salvation through a Carpenterian homosexuality that includes physical love and leads Maurice to reject class barriers and social conventions. Maurice finally comes to embrace the political consequences of homosexuality and adopt the radical perspective on society conferred by the outlaw status of the homosexual in 1913.

Appropriately, the most significant literary influence on Forster's novel is the work of Victorian England's most famous homosexual outlaw, Oscar Wilde. Sentenced in 1895 to two years' hard labor for homosexual activities and subjected to the cruelest of humiliations, Wilde became the era's most conspicuous martyr to sexual ignorance and intolerance. His long letter from Reading Gaol, *De Profundis*, informs *Maurice* at every turn.[9] The frequent echoes of *De Profundis* serve to incorporate Wilde's work into the very texture of Forster's novel and help establish Wilde's martyrdom as the historical reality that all considerations of the social and political consequences of homosexuality must confront.

Wilde's insistence in *De Profundis* on the transcendent value of self-realization and on the redemptive potentiality of suffering—its ability to transform perspective and deepen character—shapes the development of Forster's hero. Moreover, Wilde's rejection of society and his expectation of solace in nature help explicate the retreat into the greenwood at the end of *Maurice*, a conclusion that has troubled many critics.

What is most impressive about *Maurice* is its superb artistry. Although most critics dismiss it as "thin" and "simple," the novel is actually resonant and complex. Full appreciation of its subtlety depends on several readings. Indeed, *Maurice* demands the reader's engagement in a process of interpretation and reinterpretation. The novel's "double structure," in which the second half (Parts Three and Four) recapitulates the first (Parts One and Two) with crucial differences, is complemented by an elusive narrative technique that combines the point of view of the focal character with frequent though cryptic authorial intrusions. The effect of this sophisticated technique is to force the reader to experience firsthand Maurice's bewilderment and pain and exhilaration and muddle, thus contributing to the book's peculiar poignancy. Only later, on rereading the first section in light of the second, is the reader able to place the early events of the novel in context, thereby correcting his or her original responses; only through this process of reinterpretation can the reader detect irony in the narrator's apparent endorsement of a particular perspective. Much of the novel's pleasure resides in the subtle exposure of unexpected dimensions and unsuspected ironies.

In the "Terminal Note," Forster writes that in his hero, "I tried to create a character who was completely unlike myself or what I supposed myself to be: someone handsome, healthy, bodily attractive, mentally torpid, not a bad business man and rather a snob. Into this mixture I dropped an ingredient that puzzles him, wakes him up, torments him and finally saves him." Like Lucy Honeychurch, Maurice Hall is a very ordinary person who moves painfully from muddle to clarity, from conventionality to heroism. The journey of Forster's hero is from ignorance to truth, from dream to reality, from internal obscurity to the "light within," and from comfort to joy. The "vast curve" of Maurice's life includes a progress to a relationship in which the flesh educates the spirit and develops "the sluggish heart and the slack mind against their will."

The dominant imagery in the novel is that of light and darkness, ascent and descent, sleep and wakefulness. This imagery is crystallized in the recurrent metaphor of the "Valley of the Shadow of Life," surrounded by the lesser mountains of childhood and the greater ones of maturity. The metaphor itself—an ironic reversal of the biblical "valley of the shadow of death" (Psalm 23:4)—may have been suggested by Wilde's comment in *De Profundis* that "I have hills far steeper to climb, valleys much darker to pass through" (p. 30) and by his quotation there of Wordsworth's *Excursion*: "It is so difficult to keep 'heights that the soul is competent to gain'" (p. 60). Wordsworth's poem itself, "containing views on Man, Nature, and Society," and employing imagery of light and darkness, ascent and descent, may also have influenced *Maurice* directly.[10]

In the "Valley of the Shadow of Life," Maurice falls asleep, awakens, and finally scales the constricting mountains to emerge—after periodically slipping back into the abyss of the obscured "I"—into the full light of self-awareness. The emphasis throughout the novel on Maurice's torpor probably reflects Carlyle's description of life on earth as somnambulism, a state that underlines the difficulty of asking the crucial but unanswerable question, "Who am I; what is this ME."[11]

At the very center of *Maurice* is this paradoxical insight about the loneliness of the human condition: the achievement of self-knowledge depends on communion with another. "To ascend," Forster writes of his hero, "to stretch a hand up the mountainside until a hand catches it, was the end for which he had been born." Thus, Maurice's search for his own identity is necessarily bound up with his need for a friend.

Maurice's need for a friend is expressed in the two

dreams he has at school, which Forster says, "interpret him." The first dream is of George, the garden boy, "just a common servant," whose name he whispers as a charm against his fear of the shadowy reflections in the looking glass. In the dream, George runs toward him, naked, bounding over obstacles. Just as the two meet, Maurice awakens, filled with disappointment. Maurice's attachment to his playmate is apparent when he bursts into tears, overwhelmed by "a great mass of sorrow," upon learning that George has left his mother's employment. Only later, after his encounter with Alec, whom he at first also regards as just a common servant, does Maurice realize "very well what he wanted with the garden boy." Only then is he able to accept without fear "the land through the looking-glass."

The second dream is one in which "Nothing happened. He scarcely saw a face, scarcely heard a voice say, 'That is your friend,' and then it was over, having filled him with beauty and taught him tenderness." This dream haunts the novel and establishes the ideal against which Maurice's struggles toward fulfillment are measured: "He could die for a friend, he would allow such a friend to die for him; they would make any sacrifice for each other, and count the world nothing, neither death nor distance nor crossness could part them, because 'this is my friend.'" This exaltation of friendship imparts enormous dignity and simple beauty to Maurice's concurrent quests for self-knowledge and relief from loneliness.

Maurice at first attempts to convince himself that the friend of his dream is Christ; then he thinks that perhaps the friend is a Greek god. He finally accepts the fact that "most probably he was just a man." He gradually comes to regard Clive as the friend "who was more to him than all the world." But the dream achieves fleshly reality only in the person of Alec, whose name appropriately means "Help."[12] The morning after their first night together, Maurice asks the young man, "Did you ever dream you'd a friend, Alec? Nothing else but just 'my friend,' he trying to help you and you him. . . . Someone to last your whole life and you his." He adds, "I suppose such a thing can't really happen outside sleep." But the morning after the night in the hotel, he recognizes Alec as "the longed-for dream."

Forster's vision in *Maurice* is a humanistic one in which "man has been created to feel pain and loneliness without help from heaven." As in Arnold's "Dover Beach," the world of the novel is a land of dreams in which human love offers the only help for pain. This view of human isolation gives urgency to Maurice's plight and depth to his search for a communion of body and soul. The relationship with Clive, the development of which is one of the major achievements of the novel, is a necessary but preliminary step in Maurice's growth. Significantly, Maurice meets Clive as a result of his interest in Risley, a self-proclaimed "child of light" or Uranian.

In *De Profundis*, Wilde describes the "child of light" as perpetually at war against the Philistines and "their heavy inaccessibility to ideas, their dull respectability, their tedious orthodoxy, their worship of vulgar success, their entire preoccupation with the gross materialistic side of life, and their ridiculous estimate of themselves and their importance" (p. 109). Risley wages this battle in the luncheon party arranged by Mr. Cornwallis, and Maurice himself will later assume the same struggle. Wilde and Forster both playfully invert the biblical concept of "child of light" (cf. Luke 16:8, John 12:36, Eph. 5:8, and I Thess. 5:5), and Maurice's eventual achievement of the "light within" will lead him to embrace the darkness without.

Maurice's interest in Risley is a symptom of his loneliness. He is not attracted to the young Uranian, but he feels that "this queer fish" might help him, "might stretch him a helping hand." On his mission for help, Maurice discovers Clive in Risley's rooms, and the two develop a friendship. Maurice responds to Clive's sincere intellect and superior knowledge. Clive, on the other hand, "liked being thrown about by a powerful and handsome boy. It was delightful too when Hall stroked his hair: the faces of the . . . people in the room would fade: he leant back till his cheek brushed the flannel of the trousers and felt the warmth strike through." Soon Maurice's heart is lit with a fire "never to be quenched again, and one thing in him at last was real."

Clive dominates Maurice intellectually, and the latter soon surrenders all his conventional religious opinions. Maurice's orthodoxy is merely conformist and sentimental: "He believed that he believed, and felt genuine pain when anything he was accustomed to met criticism—the pain that masquerades among the middle classes as Faith. It was not Faith, being inactive." In contrast, Clive's rejection of Christianity is a direct result of his early awareness of himself as a homosexual: "He was obliged . . . to throw over Christianity. Those who base their conduct upon what they are rather than upon what they ought to be, always must throw it over in the end."

The young men's debates about religion constitute a courting ritual. Maurice's pose as a theologian is simply a ploy to engage his friend's interest. He has no answer when Clive attacks his "tenth-hand" opinions, questioning whether it isn't improbable that genuine belief could be imparted by parents and guardians. "If there is [a belief for which you would die] won't it be part of your own flesh and spirit?" Clive asks, echoing Wilde's remark that belief "must be nothing external to me. Its symbols must be of my own creating. . . . If I may not find its secret within myself, I shall never find

it: if I have not got it already, it will never come to me"
(pp. 32–33). These debates also provide the first concrete evidence of how Maurice's homosexuality can
shape the curve of his life, saving him from a hollow
existence fed on catchwords like that of his father,
who "was becoming a pillar of Church and Society
when he died." Forster adds: "other things being alike
Maurice would have stiffened too."

Although Maurice loses the debates, "he thought
that his Faith was a pawn well lost; for in capturing it
Durham had exposed his heart." When the two embrace after their return to Cambridge from the long
vacation, Clive declares his love, assuming that Maurice has understood the implications of the *Symposium*, which he had asked his friend to read. Maurice's
shocked response—"a rotten notion really"—causes
Clive to sever his links with the young man, suggesting
in an icy note "that it would be a public convenience if
they behaved as if nothing had happened." This break
forces Maurice into a frenzy of self-examination: "It
worked inwards, till it touched the root whence body
and soul both spring, the 'I' that he had been trained to
obscure, and, realized at last, doubled its power and
grew superhuman. . . . New worlds broke loose in
him at this, and he saw from the vastness of the ruin
what ecstasy he had lost, what a communion."

The pain of Clive's rejection and the introspection
it provokes lead Maurice to an important step toward
maturity. He determines not to "deceive himself so
much." He accepts the fact that "He loved men and
always had loved them. He longed to embrace them
and mingle his being with theirs." He rejects the judgments of the world and determines no longer to be fed
on lies. He haunts the bridge leading to Clive's quarters; and one night, "savage, reckless, drenched with
the rain, he saw in the first glimmer of dawn the window of Durham's room, and his heart leapt alive and

shook him to pieces." Just as he springs into the room, he hears Clive call his name. Part One of the novel thus ends with Maurice's achievement of manhood and communion.

Part Two begins with the new dawn of the communion between Clive and Maurice and ends with the darkness of Clive's repudiation of their relationship. For two years the young Uranians enjoy "as much happiness as men under that star can expect." Their relationship is modeled on Clive's interpretation of the *Symposium*: "The love that Socrates bore Phaedo now lay within his reach, love passionate but temperate, such as only finer natures can understand." The elitism of Clive's assumptions here—and when he tells Maurice, "I feel to you as Pippa to her fiancé, only far more nobly, far more deeply . . . a particular harmony of soul that I don't think women have ever guessed"—reflects his snobbishness and misogyny and the apologia of Symonds.

The relationship is one in which Clive "educated Maurice, or rather his spirit educated Maurice's spirit." It is doomed to failure, as Forster hints early in the book when he describes the bridge leading to Clive's room as "not a real bridge: it only spanned a slight depression in the ground." Maurice's ascent from the Valley of the Shadow of Life requires a helping hand extended from greater heights than Clive has achieved. The Maurice-Clive relationship is limited, for it is based on distrust of the body and on a bookish—hence false—Hellenism.

Clive's distrust of the body and contempt for his sexuality are deeply rooted in his subconscious. They result from his having internalized the Christian prohibitions that he outwardly rejects, and they are reflected as well in his extreme reaction to Maurice's understandable shock at his declaration of love. Clive requests his friend not to mention his "criminal morbidity" to anyone and tells him, "It is a lasting grief to have insulted you."

Clive's commitment even to the spiritualized homosexuality of the *Symposium* is so tenuous that his friend's conventional reaction breaks down his "whole philosophy of life . . . and the sense of sin was reborn in its ruins." When Maurice protests his pain at Clive's rejection and declares that "I have always been like the Greeks and didn't know," Clive characterizes Maurice's pain as "only the Hell of disgust" and the avowal of homosexuality as "grotesque," thus revealing his own self-condemnation. Later, on the eve of his desperate journey to Greece, when he views his attachment to Maurice as unclean and longs for the forgetfulness of Lethe, Clive worries that "beyond the grave there may be Hell." For all his vaunted Hellenism, Clive's emotional life has been shaped by his early Christian conviction that homosexuality is an abomination.

Even on the apparently idyllic expedition into the Cambridgeshire countryside, Clive's distrust of the body is manifest. His refusal to undress in order to swim in the dyke is analogous to Mr. Beebe's failure to participate fully in the homoerotic bathing scene in *A Room with a View* and similarly signifies self-repression. In contrast, Maurice disrobes, shouting, "I must bathe properly." As Robert Martin has noted, this scene in its entirety is wryly ironic, concealing a note of warning beneath its surface of ecstatic prose. The lovers' reliance on a machine—"They became a cloud of dust, a stench, and a roar to the world," like the Wilcoxes in *Howards End*—signals an "opposition between nature and the products of an industrial society,"[13] and establishes an important point of contrast between Maurice's false communion with Clive and his real one with Alec, who is consistently linked with nature and the natural.

Clive's self-imposed repression is equally apparent when he flushes crimson at Maurice's adulation on his first visit to Penge. "I think you're beautiful," Maurice tells him in the Blue Room, the color of which symbolizes the spiritual and cerebral nature of Clive's love.[14] "I love your voice and everything to do with you, down to your clothes or the room you are sitting in. I adore you." Clive responds tepidly, "Those things must be said once, or we should never know they were in each other's hearts," but he insists that their love, "though including the body, should not gratify it." This arrangement initially satisfies Maurice, largely as a result of Clive's "hypnotic" power over him. But Maurice later comes to regret that he had never fully possessed Clive even in their hour of passion and rejects his friend's doctrine that the "less you had the more it was supposed to be."

The conflicting attitudes of the young men toward their sexuality are cast into bold relief by their reactions to the moment they spend in bed together on the eve of Clive's departure for Greece. Clive has already begun to develop heterosexual attractions and to regard his homosexual attachment as something dirty and shameful; as an antidote to these feelings, he asks Maurice if he may join him in bed. The encounter proves unsatisfactory to each, but for tellingly opposed reasons: "They lay side by side without touching. Presently Clive said, 'It's no better here. I shall go.' Maurice was not sorry, for he could not get to sleep either, though for a different reason, and he was afraid Clive might hear the drumming of his heart, and guess what it was." Maurice is sexually excited by the closeness of his lover and fears that Clive may disapprove; in contrast, Clive is confirmed in his disgust at the notion of physical contact with his friend. Maurice and Clive's isolation from each other here is strikingly underlined by the later scenes of bodily communion between Maurice and Alec.

The limitations of the Maurice-Clive relationship
are also evident in its failure to provoke a searching
analysis of their society and their roles in it. The young
men are aware of the hypocrisy around them, from Mr.
Ducie's embarrassment over his sex-lecture diagrams
in the sand and Mr. Cornwallis's refusal to translate a
"reference to the unspeakable vice of the Greeks" to
the Cambridge dons' deeming "it right to spoil a love
affair when they could" and the double standard of
Dr. Barry. Yet the two young men fail to question the
fundamental assumptions of their society. Both are
misogynistic and utterly conformist save for their
Wednesdays and weekends spent together. Although
Clive professes to believe that fertility is not the goal
of love—"For love to end where it begins is far more
beautiful, and Nature knows it"—he does not challenge his family's expectations that he will dutifully
beget an heir for Penge. Although he thinks of himself
as "a bit of an outlaw," he acquiesces in the assumption
that he will succeed his late father as a Member of
Parliament.

The young men placidly step into the niches that
England has prepared for them, Clive as country squire
and Maurice as "suburban tyrant" and successful stock-
broker. "Society received them, as she receives thousands like them," Forster writes, adding: "Behind Society slumbered the Law. They had their last year at
Cambridge together, they travelled in Italy. Then the
prison house closed. . . . Clive was working for the
bar, Maurice harnessed to an office."

This concept of society as a prison house probably
reflects Wilde's comment in the letter to Robert Ross
quoted in the preface to *De Profundis*, "I know that on
the day of my release I shall be merely passing from
one prison into another" (pp. vi–vii), as well as Wordsworth's idea in the "Intimations" ode that "Shades of the
prison-house begin to close / Upon the growing boy"

(11. 67–68). Forster's adaptation of these views in the novel both exposes the shallowness of the Clive-Maurice relationship and anticipates the result of the social analysis occasioned by the Alec-Maurice liaison. That analysis will lead Maurice to reject the life of respectability for a life of freedom, to sacrifice a spurious safety for the struggle that "twists sentimentality and lust together into love."

Even Clive's Hellenism is conventional, distorting ancient ideals as thoroughly as does Maurice's Greek oration at Sunnington. Just as the oration wrenches Greek ideals toward exercise and bodily health in order to glorify the contemporary obsession with war, so Clive distorts the Greek ideal of moderation into abstinence in order to justify his conventional distaste for sexuality, a distaste rooted in Christian rather than classical thought. Although Clive condemns the dean's suppression of references to Greek homosexuality on the grounds of "pure scholarship"—"The Greeks, or most of them, were that way inclined, and to omit it is to omit the mainstay of Athenian society"—his own classicism is equally partial. It ignores the Dionysian and overemphasizes the Apollonian. The "harmony of soul" that Clive proposes is purchased at the expense of the physical and the ecstatic. It represents comfort rather than joy; it is an example not of moderation but of disproportion.

Clive's devotion to an intellectualized classicism reflects the stupidity of his heart and constitutes a retreat from real life. His bookish Hellenism is similar to Rickie Elliot's literary pastoralism in *The Longest Journey*. In the earlier novel, Rickie's artificial idealization of the ancient Greeks blinds him to Stephen Wonham's natural absorption of the Greek spirit. Similarly, Clive's falsely romantic Hellenism causes him to ignore the Dionysian spirit latent in Maurice. This potential is suggested by the consuming "frenzy" Maurice experiences when he first falls in love with Clive. As Forster comments then, "A slow nature such as Maurice's appears insensitive, for it needs time even to feel. . . . Given time, it can know and impart ecstasy." The potential for Dionysian ecstasy is implicit as well in Maurice's "good head" for liquor and in his fur-clad appearance "like an immense animal," both of which link him with Stephen Wonham. But Maurice's Dionysian spirit is fully realized only after his communion with Alec in which the flesh educates the spirit.

Precisely because Clive's Hellenism is artificial and disproportionate, it finds no sustenance in the Greek ruins that the young man visits in a "childish and violent" attempt to preserve his attraction toward Maurice. One of the novel's most revealing ironies is that Clive's tenuous classicism is so utterly routed by the faint stirrings of his incipient and unwilled heterosexuality. The elaborate intellectual edifice he constructs to justify his homosexual tendencies crumbles at the onset of his growing physical attraction toward the opposite sex. Clive defines himself exclusively in terms of his soul and denies his body, yet his change is a result of the body's "inscrutable" will, a "blind alteration of the life spirit" that resists rational explanation. Clive's conversion to heterosexuality vividly illustrates the power of the physical, even in someone who has struggled so long to repress it, "not realizing that the body is deeper than the soul."

Forster does not condemn Clive for his involuntary conversion to heterosexuality. After all, a central premise of the novel is that sexual preference is not a matter of choice. But Clive is exposed as shallow and hypocritical by the eagerness with which he embraces the "beautiful conventions" that earn social approval and by the cruelty with which he denies the reality of Maurice's love for him in the pivotal confrontation scene that ends Part Two. This scene marks the termination of the long

day of spiritual communion between Clive and Maurice
and announces the dawn of "the full human day" that
Clive believes the love of women promises him.

This promise, however, is belied by the evidence
of the confrontation scene itself, which in a series of
subtle contrasts reveals the insipidity of Clive's heterosexuality while simultaneously implying the potential
of Maurice's sexuality for stimulus and growth. Struc-
turally, this scene is parallel to the encounter between
Clive and Maurice that concludes the novel. Both confrontation scenes are set at night and in darkness. At
the end of Part Two, however, Clive's way is lit by
streetlamps, while at the end of Part Four, Maurice's
walk is guided by evening primroses; and the scene in
Part Two takes place indoors, whereas the novel's final
scene is out of doors. These differences signify the limitations of Clive's triumph here—its connection with
the artificial and the societal. They also help explicate
Maurice's fuller triumph at the end of the book, when
he departs into "the darkness where he can be free."

Throughout the bleak final scene of Part Two,
Forster exposes the shallowness of Clive's passion and
foreshadows the depth of Maurice's future commitment to Alec. For instance, as Clive awaits his friend's
arrival, he appreciates the Hall women for the first
time. But significantly, he finds them reminiscent "of
the evening primroses that starred a deserted alley at
Penge," the very place where Maurice will eventually
encounter Alec and bid farewell to Clive. Clive is particularly attracted to Ada, whose voice is similar to
Maurice's. He regards her as a "compromise between
memory and desire," thus establishing a telling contrast
with Maurice's earlier hope for a life without compromise and his later choice of such a life. The knowledge
that he might arouse Ada's love lights Clive's heart
"with temperate fire," thus recalling the fierce fire
"never to be quenched again" that love had ignited in

Maurice's breast and that finally will be sustained by
Alec's matching ardor.

Most pointed of all is the contrast between the
appearances of the two young men when Maurice arrives, looking "like an immense animal in his fur coat,"
to find Clive bandaged like an accident victim, having
happily "submitted his body to be bound" by the sisters. This contrast of animal vitality and voluntary repression crystallizes the differences between the
former lovers and foreshadows their fates. Moreover,
the scuffle between Maurice and Clive over the key to
the Halls' drawing room anticipates Alec's later message to Maurice, "I have the key," a reference to the
boathouse at Penge, where the lovers will meet at the
end of the novel to begin their lives in the greenwood.

The immediate impact of the confrontation with
Clive devastates Maurice. Clive not only affirms the
reality of his heterosexuality, for which he cannot be
blamed, but more culpably, he also coldly rejects the
legitimacy of his former attachment. "I was never like
you," he tells Maurice. To deny one's experience is, in
the words of Wilde's *De Profundis*, "to put a lie into
the lips of one's life. It is no less than a denial of the
soul" (p. 37). Clive's rejection of his past here exposes
him as a hypocrite and casts into doubt the sincerity of
the quality by which he defines himself, his soul. By
characterizing romantic love between men as unreal,
Clive also attacks the very basis of his friend's identity,
for only through his love did Maurice become a "real"
person.

The love affair terminates with an ugly scuffle and
with Maurice sobbing, "What an ending . . . what an
ending." The repeated phrase alludes to Wilde's account of his despondency during his first year of imprisonment, when he "did nothing else, and can remember
doing nothing else, but wring my hands in impotent
despair, and say 'What an ending, what an appalling

ending!'" (pp. 121–22). Significantly, however, the force of this allusion in *Maurice* is positive. It promises a new perspective, for Wilde—having grown as a result of his suffering—continues, "now I try to say to myself, and sometimes when I am not torturing myself do really and sincerely say, 'What a beginning, what a wonderful beginning!'" (p. 122). This allusion suggests the possibility that, like Wilde, Maurice will profit from his pain.

On the surface, however, this appalling ending is bleak, leaving the former lovers enveloped in darkness, both literally and metaphorically. Maurice extinguishes the electric light and sits gloomily alone, while Clive goes out into the night, exchanging "the darkness within for that without." But Clive's promised dawn will culminate in a sexual relationship "veiled in night" and in a marriage marked by deception and ignorance; his deep-rooted distaste for the "reproductive and digestive functions" will continue to limit his communion with others. Maurice, on the other hand, will achieve wholeness of being; he will discover "the light within" and embrace the evening's external darkness as a refuge against ignorance and hypocrisy. The false climax at the end of Part Two thus ironically mirrors the triumphant climax of the novel itself. It is actually a new beginning.

Maurice's new beginning is painful indeed: he "returned in a few hours to the abyss where he had wandered as a boy." As a result of Clive's defection, his life is barren and empty. After abandoning the temptation to suicide, he continues a dreary existence for some time, "proving on how little the soul can exist." Forster poignantly conveys the pain of Maurice's grief, but central to the novel is the meaningfulness of suffering. *Maurice* dramatizes Wilde's contention that suffering is not a mystery but a revelation: "One discerns things one never discerned before. One approaches the whole of history from a different standpoint" (p. 52). Thus, in his loneliness Maurice comes to a firmer understanding of his position in society: "He was an outlaw in disguise." He clings tenaciously to his grandfather's exhortation to discover "the power within the soul: let it out, but not yet, not till the evening." Even in the depths of his despair, he fleetingly entertains the possibility that "among those who took to the greenwood in old time there had been two men like himself."

Maurice's regeneration begins with the stirrings of lust. On the very morning that he learns of Clive's engagement, he is awakened to desire. He glimpses the nude body of Dickie Barry, his young houseguest whom he rouses from a late sleep. He discovers Dickie "with his limbs uncovered. He lay unashamed, embraced and penetrated by the sun. The lips were parted, the down on the upper was touched with gold, the hair broken into countless glories, the body was a delicate amber."[15] This vision of Eros leads Maurice momentarily to abandon himself to joy and then to reproach himself bitterly. Significantly, Maurice faces his predicament with a new frankness: "His feeling for Dickie required a very primitive name. He would have sentimentalized once and called it adoration, but the habit of honesty had grown strong."

Maurice finds his newly awakened passion deeply troubling. His resistance to his body's natural responses leads to a vicious assault on a railway passenger whose "disgusting and dishonorable old age" Maurice fears may prophesy his own. This resistance culminates in a desperate hope for punishment and cure. At the same time, however, Maurice's awakening to physical desire represents "the flesh educating the spirit." It promises the ultimate attainment of the "fresh mode of self-realization" that Wilde speaks of in *De Profundis*: "the mode of existence in which soul and body are one and indivisible: in which the outward is expressive of the inward" (pp. 27, 53). Even as Maurice resists the promptings of desire, his flesh continues to educate his spirit.

Maurice's progress toward wholeness is gradual but inexorable, complicated by his inner contradictions but never halted. For instance, in Part Three he would like to be "at one with society and the law," but he slowly begins to realize the corruption of both. His disastrous visit to Dr. Barry, in which he confesses himself "an unspeakable of the Oscar Wilde sort," is followed by his thrill of recognition when he reads a biography of Tchaikovsky. Although he grasps at the hope that hypnotism might cure him, he is nevertheless aware that "doctors are fools." Moreover, even as he pursues the cure, he knows the cost at which such normality will be bought. "If this new doctor could alter his being," he muses, "was it not his duty to go, though body and soul be violated?" When he does make an appointment with Mr. Lasker Jones, he bids, "Farewell, beauty and warmth."

Maurice's internal contradictions are brilliantly juxtaposed on his visit to Penge, where "he seemed a bundle of voices . . . he could almost hear them quarreling inside him." At Penge he both pursues his appointment with the hypnotist and confirms "his spirit in its perversion," as Lasker Jones will later diagnose the results of his "sharing" with Alec. The visit to Penge also defines the distance Maurice has yet to travel in his quest for wholeness. His flesh can educate his spirit fully only when he escapes the influence of Clive, and he can free himself of Clive's influence only when "something greater" intervenes. Thus it is fitting that Maurice's visit to Penge leads both to his disillusionment with Clive and to his discovery of Alec.

Penge itself functions as a double symbol in the novel, representing the duality within Maurice's own nature in Part Three. As a dilapidated country house, it symbolizes the philistinism of the English upper middle classes, who are declining but still in firm control. Maurice will later reject the bourgeois values of Penge and observe "how derelict it was, how unfit to set standards or control the future." But, located on the Wiltshire border, Penge is also part of the English countryside, embodying the solace of nature and the natural, the greenwood to which Alec and Maurice will ultimately escape.

Penge thus epitomizes the novel's contrast of the indoors and the outdoors, the values of society and those of nature, the life of respectability and the life of the earth.[16] It is the setting both of the Durhams' snobbery, in which Maurice initially joins, and of Alec's natural responsiveness to life, in which Maurice eventually participates. Its dichotomies may best be represented by Anne, whose maiden name—Woods— signifies a naturalness that her upper-middle-class upbringing has stifled through the deliberate inculcation of sexual ignorance. Interestingly, Anne functions as an unconscious agent of connection for Alec and Maurice, being responsible for Alec's employment at Penge and for drawing Maurice's attention to him at a pivotal moment. Presided over by Clive, "whose grievances against society had passed since his marriage," Penge is at once a citadel of oppression and a stimulus to Maurice's growth.

That stimulus is provided most forcefully by Alec, whom Maurice notices as he drives through the park to begin his visit at Penge. Throughout his stay, he is vaguely aware of the undergamekeeper, though in his snobbishness Maurice denies full humanity to the lower classes. Maurice's class consciousness precludes an early union, but that is what each subconsciously desires. On his first two nights at Penge, Maurice gazes from his bedroom into the rainy night, longing for a companion, only later to learn that Alec, filled with a similar yearning, had been waiting on the lawn for his call.

Maurice first acknowledges Alec's individuality when he temporarily leaves Penge for his appointment in London. He offers Alec a tip and is outraged when the young man refuses it. Although Maurice's fierce reaction may seem petty, based as it is on a misinterpretation of Alec's independence as impertinence, it is actually more liberal than Archie London's condescending attitude that "When servants are rude one should merely ignore it." As his carriage leaves Penge, Maurice looks out the window at the dog roses that border the lane and suddenly recognizes Alec:

Blossom after blossom crept past them, draggled by the ungenial year: some had cankered, others would never unfold: here and there beauty triumphed, but desperately, flickering in a world of gloom. Maurice looked into one after another, and though he did not care for flowers the failure irritated him. Scarcely anything was perfect. On one spray every flower was lopsided, the next swarmed with caterpillars, or bulged with galls. The indifference of nature! And her incompetence! He leant out of the window to see whether she couldn't bring it off once, and stared straight into the bright brown eyes of a young man.

This recognition shocks Maurice into an awareness of Alec's beauty and anticipates the perfection of their eventual union. As James Malek remarks of the passage, "This initial association of Alec with nature and perfection leaves a lasting impression and colors our response to him throughout the remainder of the novel."[17] Placed immediately before Maurice's consultation with the hypnotist, the vision of Alec's perfection also renders ironic Lasker Jones's attempt to implant in Maurice's subconscious his own palely conventional aesthetic and erotic responses.

After his interview with the hypnotist, Maurice returns to Penge, thinking that the quiet of the countryside will be therapeutic. Ironically, however, Penge proves stimulating rather than numbing. Anne, believing that Maurice has been to London to court a prospective wife, underscores the importance of Maurice's vision of Alec's perfection by asking, "is she very charming? I am convinced she has bright brown eyes." When Maurice thinks that "he wasn't the same; a rearrangement of his being had begun," he is correct, though he is wrong to credit Lasker Jones with the alteration. The credit belongs to Alec, whom he encounters several times that momentous night in the darkness of the deserted alley starred with evening primroses.

The change in Maurice is evident when he returns from a stroll outdoors with his head all yellow with pollen. Mrs. Durham exclaims, "Oh, don't brush it off. I like it on your black hair . . . is he not quite bacchanalian?" The evening primrose pollen expresses Maurice's Dionysian potential, a potential implicit in his preoccupations as he strolls through the alley and encounters Alec: "Food and wine had heated him, and he thought with some inconsequence that even old Chapman had sown some wild oats. . . . He wasn't Methusaleh—he'd a right to a fling. Oh those jolly scents, those bushes where you could hide, that sky as black as the bushes!" As he goes indoors, expecting to resume his life as a "respectable pillar of society who has never had the chance to misbehave," he bumps into Alec, fittingly a Pan figure, similar in this respect to Gino Carella and Stephen Wonham.[18]

This encounter sharpens Maurice's mind, making him consciously aware of Alec as an individual, a "fine fellow," who "cleaned a gun, carried a suitcase, baled out a boat, emigrated—did something anyway, while gentlefolk squatted on chairs finding fault with his soul." Maurice attacks the clergyman Mr. Borenius's legalistic religion, telling him, "that may be your idea of religion but it isn't mine and it wasn't Christ's," thus echoing Wilde's assertion that Christ "exposed with utter and relentless scorn" the "tedious formalisms so dear to the middle-class mind" (pp. 110–11). As Maurice goes to bed that night, his brain—wreathed with a "tangle of flowers and fruits"—works more actively than ever. He sees commonplace objects with a new clarity, and he redefines darkness as something to be desired: "not the darkness of a house which coops up a man among furniture, but the darkness where he can be free."

Conscious of the irony of having paid a hypnotist to imprison him in a "brown cube of such a room," Maurice drifts off to sleep, dimly aware of alternatives. "There was something better in life than this rubbish," he thinks, half asleep, "if only he could get to it—love—nobility—big spaces where passion clasped peace, spaces no science could reach, but they existed for ever, full of woods some of them, and arched with majestic sky and a friend. . . ." This dream of perfection, of harmony with nature and communion with another, achieves the promise of reality.

Maurice's sleepwalking cry, "Come!" is answered by Alec, who scales a ladder into the Russet Room: "someone he scarcely knew moved towards him and knelt beside him and whispered, 'Sir, was you calling out for me? . . . Sir, I know . . . I know,' and touched him." This consummation, beautiful in its tenderness and simplicity, parallels the communion of Maurice and Clive at the end of Part One. But the sharing of Maurice and Alec in the Russet Room promises the fuller relationship for which both long in the deepest recesses of their beings, a union of body and soul, of the flesh educating the spirit.

Part Four of the novel chronicles the achievement of this promise and the completion of Maurice's journey toward self-realization. Beginning with the bright dawn of a new relationship and ending in the darkness of a confrontation scene, Part Four recapitulates Part Two. But whereas the dawn of Part Two is what Wilde describes as one of the "false dawns before the dawn itself" (p. 116), the new daybreak proves genuine. Similarly, the darkness in which Part Four concludes is the protective cover of the greenwood in which Alec and Maurice discover freedom, not the interior darkness of the earlier climax. And in the confrontation scene that ends the novel, Maurice triumphs unambiguously, having truly earned a new beginning.

Maurice's self-realization is accomplished as the result of a struggle between his real self and the obscured "I" of his social self. When he descends from the scene of communion with Alec "to take his place in society," his suburban gentleman's class consciousness battles with his longing for fulfillment. His life disturbed "to its foundations," Maurice alternates between his conventional distaste for "social inferiors" and his desire for comradeship. As he and Alec play cricket together that morning, Maurice meditates on the possibilities of their union: "They played for the sake of each other and their fragile relationship—if one fell, the other would follow. They intended no harm to the world, but so long as it attacked they must punish, they must stand wary, then hit with full strength, they must show that when two are gathered together majorities shall not triumph." But this reverie of liberation is interrupted by the arrival of Clive, the representative of convention, the future Member of Parliament, the apostle of class loyalty to whom "intimacy with any social inferior was unthinkable." Suddenly sick with fear and shame, Maurice returns to his home, seeking security rather than joy.

But even as Maurice struggles against his deepest instincts, his flesh continues to educate his spirit. That night his body yearns for Alec's: "He called it lustful, a word easily uttered, and opposed to it his work, his family, his friends, his position in society." But, Forster adds, "his body would not be convinced." In a childish and violent expedient analogous to Clive's trip to

Greece, Maurice telephones Lasker Jones for another consultation. This time, however, he is unable to enter a trance. He leaves the hypnotist's office curiously relieved and with new insight.

Walking home, he observes the King and Queen passing through a park. He unthinkingly bares his head in a gesture of respect. Then he suddenly despises these symbols of society, seeing them as victims of the very values that oppress him. This insight gives him a new perspective: "It was as if the barrier that kept him from his fellows had taken another aspect. He was not afraid or ashamed anymore. After all, the forests and the night were on his side, not theirs." This new insight radically alters his previous image of himself wandering "beyond the barrier . . . the wrong words on his lips and the wrong desires in his heart, and his arms full of air." He realizes that "they, not he, were inside a ring fence," imprisoned by conventions.[19]

Maurice's acceptance of himself and his outlaw status here presages his final liberation. He gains new insight into the inequities and limitations of his society. He suggests to his aunt "that servants might be flesh and blood like ourselves." He questions the ethics of his profession, despising his clients' choice of comfort rather than joy, of "shelter everywhere and always, until the existence of earth and sky is forgotten, shelter from poverty and disease and violence and impoliteness; and consequently from joy." He determines himself to seek the "life of the earth" and accept the struggle that may make possible the attainment of love.

Maurice evaluates his own past actions, concluding that he erred grievously in trying "to get the best of both worlds." In a society that criminalizes him and falsifies his experience, he must embrace his outlaw status and be true to himself. Thus, when he receives a threatening letter from Alec containing many words, "some foul, many stupid, some gracious," he agrees to

a meeting. "Both were outcasts," he thinks, "and if it
came to a scrap must have it without benefit of society."
Maurice's point here reflects Wilde's painfully earned
confession from Reading Gaol: "The one disgraceful,
unpardonable, and to all time contemptible action of
my life was to allow myself to appeal to society for help
and protection" (p. 135).

The meeting of Alec and Maurice in the British
Museum is one of the novel's most delightful scenes.
Maurice approaches the encounter "without any plan
at all, yet something kept rippling in his mind like
muscles beneath a healthy skin." He quickly realizes
that Alec's attempt at blackmail "was a blind—a practical joke almost—and concealed something real, that
either desired." The gamekeeper's childish attempt at
extortion is a reaction against Maurice's mistrust and
condescension, a reflection of pain at having been neglected and a sign of interest.

As the two men spar, they are interrupted by Mr.
Ducie, who as always gets "the facts just wrong" as he
tries to remember Maurice's name. When Maurice tells
the schoolmaster that his name is Scudder, the identification of the young men is complete. As Maurice will
shortly realize, "In a way they were one person." Maurice succeeds here in winning Alec's love by approaching him as an equal: "Not as a hero, but as a comrade."
He "stood up to the bluster, and found childishness
behind it, and behind that something else." By suffering, Maurice has learned to interpret the suffering of
others. He has absorbed Wilde's lesson that "behind
sorrow there is always a soul" (p. 133).

Forster's account of the lovers' communion in the
hotel—the mixture of "tenderness and toughness" in
their sharing—beautifully affirms Maurice's success in
grasping the lessons that the flesh teaches the spirit.
Tellingly, the night of passion in a "casual refuge" that
protects them momentarily "from their enemies" is

made possible by Alec's insistence that Maurice cancel the formal dinner party "of the sort that brought work to his firm." The cost of the joyful night thus anticipates the price of "the safety in darkness" that the escape to the greenwood will exact. That retreat requires mutual sacrifice, as Alec acknowledges when he protests that Maurice's vaguely formulated plan "Wouldn't work. . . . Ruin of us both, can't you see, you same as myself." But balanced against the loss of the young men's careers, family ties, and respectability is the prospect of gaining their own souls.

When Alec fails to appear for the departure of the *Normannia*, he surrenders his security and distinguishes himself from the "timorous millions who own stuffy little boxes but never their own souls." Alec and Maurice are thus numbered among those few who, according to Wilde, "ever 'possess their souls' before they die" (p. 82). Their mutual sacrifices give the lie to Mr. Borenius's assumption that "love between two men must be ignoble," and their compensation is one familiar in Forster's novels. Like Stephen Wonham and the child of Helen Schlegel and Leonard Bast, they inherit England: "They must live outside class, without relations or money; they must work and stick to each other till death. But England belonged to them. That, besides companionship, was their reward." This inheritance is the fulfillment of Maurice's early dreams of communion and ecstasy.

After Maurice's confrontation with Clive in the deserted alley at Penge, "where evening primroses gleamed, and embossed with faint yellow the walls of night," Maurice and Alec depart for the greenwood. The final chapter recounts Maurice's repudiation of Clive's influence, "the closing of a book that would never be read again." This ending is a necessary preliminary to the self-confessed outlaw's new beginning with Alec. When Maurice disappears into the night, having

elected a life "without twilight or compromise," he
leaves behind only a "little pile of the petals of the evening primrose, which mourned from the ground like an
expiring fire."

The dying petals, symbolic of the fire that Clive's
love originally inspired within Maurice's breast, signify
the death of Maurice's love for Clive and the enormity
of Clive's loss in failing to appreciate his friend's potential for Dionysian ecstasy. Ironically, however, though
Maurice wrestles free of Clive's influence, the country
squire who smugly denied the reality of homosexual
love will never escape the memory of his incomplete
passion. Maurice will continue to haunt all his days and
nights to come, mocking his timidity and rebuking his
hypocrisy: "To the end of his life Clive was not sure of
the exact moment of departure, and with the approach
of old age he grew uncertain whether the moment had
yet occurred. The Blue Room would glimmer, ferns un-
dulate. Out of some external Cambridge his friend began beckoning to him, clothed in the sun, and shaking
out the scents and sounds of the May term." Clive's fate
is aptly summed in Wilde's description of men who desire to be something separate from themselves, such as
a Member of Parliament. Such a person, Wilde writes,
"invariably succeeds in being what he wants to be. That
is his punishment. Those who want a mask have to
wear it" (p. 119).

Maurice and Alec's retreat into the greenwood has
frequently been scorned by critics as sentimental and
unconvincing. Actually, however, the ending is neither.
Alec and Maurice have earned their happiness through
suffering and sacrifice, and despite their differences in
background and education, they are well matched.
There is nothing sentimental in the notion of hard-won
happiness earned through mutual trust and support.
This happiness is bought at a high price, but their willingness to pay such a toll is what finally enables Maurice

and Alec to transcend the artificial barriers that separate them. Forster's awareness of the cost these individuals must pay to possess their own souls makes their romantic escape into the greenwood less fantastic than realistically necessary.

Still, the ending is flawed. "The problem," as James Malek explains, "is that Forster succeeds more completely on the general level than on the particular. There is no doubt about the value or rightness of the lovers' decision. Nor, on the level of the particular, do we doubt their ability to follow through, but we have not been prepared for the specific form it might take, nor is it easy to imagine since Maurice has talked of it in very general terms."[20] The vagueness of the lovers' future life together probably reflects a compromise between Forster's original vision of two men roaming the greenwood and his postwar realization that "Our greenwood ended catastrophically and inevitably," as he remarks in the "Terminal Note." Although the escape into the "big spaces . . . arched with majestic sky and a friend" is too vaguely formulated and too broadly generalized, it is nevertheless essential to the novel's vision.

The escape into the greenwood expresses Forster's radical critique of his society while also conveying his humanistic faith in personal relationships. The ending of *Maurice* is influenced by the conclusion of *De Profundis*. There Wilde remarks that "we all look at Nature too much, and live with her too little. . . . We have forgotten that water can cleanse, and fire purify, and that the Earth is mother to us all" (pp. 146–47). *De Profundis* ends with a moving coda in which Wilde looks to nature for healing and wholeness: "Society, as we have constituted it, will have no place for me, has none to offer; but Nature, whose sweet rains fall on unjust and just alike, will have clefts in the rocks where I may hide, and secret valleys in whose silence I may weep undisturbed. She will hang the night with stars so that I may walk abroad in the darkness without stumbling, and send the wind over my footprints so that none may track me to my hurt: she will cleanse me in great waters, and with bitter herbs make me whole" (pp. 150–51).

Like Wilde, Forster has no faith in reforming society. Even in the "Terminal Note" of 1960, Forster remains pessimistic about social reform, remarking that "Since *Maurice* was written there has been a change in the public attitude here: the change from ignorance and terror to familiarity and contempt." In his novel "Dedicated to a Happier Year," he shows how the "four guardians of society—the schoolmaster, the doctor, the scientist and the priest"—all condemn the homosexual.[21] Thus, Maurice and Alec must utterly reject society, whose injustices they perceive as a result of their homosexuality. But unlike Wilde's, Forster's pessimism is tempered by belief in personal relations. Hence, Maurice and Alec together accept England's air and sky as their birthright, facing the world unafraid, showing that "when two are gathered together majorities shall not triumph." The escape into the greenwood thus simultaneously renders a summary judgment against society and endorses the possibility of the flesh educating the spirit, even in the midst of repression.

Critics have frequently denigrated *Maurice* as an exercise in special pleading, accusing Forster of claiming that homosexuals have a privileged status, a "heightened sensibility and a more profound aesthetic understanding" than heterosexuals.[22] In fact, however, Forster makes no such claim. As Robert Martin observes, "The novel clearly rejects the idea of the superiority of homosexuality, an idea which is specifically Clive's and derived from Plato, while keeping the idea that homosexuality may provide the occasion for a growth in spiritual awareness."[23]

Forster certainly accepts Wilde's premise that to "become a deeper man is the privilege of those who

have suffered" (pp. 124-25). This "privilege," however, is the result not of a quality innate in homosexuality but of the oppression homosexuals endure in a world
that rejects the legitimacy of their experience. What
Joseph Cady writes of Wilde in *De Profundis* is equally
true of Maurice Hall in Forster's novel: "Branded and
cast out by society for his homosexuality, Wilde develops insight into that society and an opposition to the
way it can arbitrarily impose forms on its members."[24]
Maurice's progress from a homosexuality linked with
Symonds and other apologists to a homosexuality associated with Carpenter is a progress from claims of
superiority to assertions of equality. Forster properly
emphasizes the spiritual and political insight that the
pain of exclusion may confer, but he does not endorse
the claim that homosexuality is in itself either superior
or inferior to heterosexuality.

In general, *Maurice* has been shabbily treated by
critics. The condescension visited upon the novel has
resulted from a misunderstanding of Forster's narrative technique and a consequent refusal to engage in
the process of interpretation and reinterpretation that
the book's "double structure" requires. Thus, the sophisticated artistry, the irony, and the rhythms of the
novel have been largely ignored. In addition, the publication history of *Maurice* has led critics to view it in isolation from the rest of Forster's canon and to read it too
narrowly as a sentimental apology for homosexuality.
But the book is not an apology at all; rather, it is a convincing account of its hero's growth toward wholeness
in a society that makes such growth very difficult. The
human and social values that *Maurice* propounds are
precisely those which energize all Forster's novels.

Admittedly, Forster's "Terminal Note," in which he
writes of his determination that "in fiction anyway two
men should fall in love and remain in it for the ever
and ever that fiction allows," has encouraged critics to

dismiss the happy ending as a sentimental fantasy. But as the "Terminal Note" also indicates, the inspiration for the novel was the example of Edward Carpenter and George Merrill, one of whom was born into the upper middle class and educated at Cambridge, the other of whom was uneducated and of lower-class origins. This gay couple's retreat into the greenwood led to a long and happy relationship that endured from their meeting in 1898 until Merrill's death in 1928. The happy ending of *Maurice* does not strain credibility, provided that one is able to accept the premise that individuals of different classes can forge lives together in opposition to the mores of their society. Not to accept that premise is to deny both the assumptions of liberal humanism and the evidence of empirical reality itself.

Anticipating the reluctance of critics to credit the ending, Forster revised it more often than any other part of the book, finally eliminating an epilogue in which Kitty encounters Maurice and Alec some years later. The final version suffers from vagueness, but it is no more sentimental than the conclusions of *The Longest Journey, A Room with a View*, and *Howards End*, all of which similarly incorporate mythic elements and romance modes and none of which has been subject to the scathing attacks directed toward the happy ending of *Maurice*. One can only suspect that many of these attacks on the novel's alleged sentimentality stem, at least in part, from a homophobic refusal to grant homosexuals the same possibility for happiness routinely granted to heterosexuals in the "ever and ever" afterward of fiction.

This is not to say that all critics who express dissatisfaction with *Maurice* are homophobic. Many of the complaints registered by critics are sincerely motivated even when not entirely persuasive. At any rate, the book is by no means perfect, and it is flawed not only by the overly generalized ending. The extraordinary compression of the plot contributes to the novel's power, but such intensity is bought at the expense of character development and an impression of thinness. For instance, Chapters 18 and 19, which are very brief, summarize two years of the Maurice-Clive relationship. The perfunctory nature of this summarizing technique effectively conveys the relationship's static quality—its failure to stimulate growth—but critics have understandably complained of such gaps in the narrative.

Moreover, some readers do not find the characterizations altogether convincing, and they feel that Forster uses Maurice as a mouthpiece, that his motivations and actions are imposed on him from without rather than developing from within. Certainly, it is true that the steady focus on Maurice renders all the subsidiary characters—except for Clive—shadowy and undeveloped. But Maurice himself is thoroughly convincing, and his journey toward completeness is properly the book's insistent concern.

Although not a perfect novel, *Maurice* is an important achievement. In Forster's canon it ranks not with *Howards End* and *A Passage to India* but with *Where Angels Fear to Tread*, *The Longest Journey*, and *A Room with a View*. Precise distinctions as to the relative value of these works are not particularly helpful, since each of them is so individual an accomplishment. All of Forster's work is of a single thread, yet each novel is also quite distinctive and repays careful study on its own terms. But inasmuch as *Maurice* has been relegated to a position apart from the novels published during Forster's lifetime, it is worth observing that the posthumously published book is more mature than *Where Angels Fear to Tread*, more technically successful than *The Longest Journey*, and more passionate than *A Room with a View*. At the very least, it deserves full integration into Forster's canon.

In total, despite all its real or imagined flaws,

Maurice is a book of haunting beauty, tracing the painful journey of its hero from bewilderment to self-realization. It is preeminently a political novel, for Maurice's education through suffering culminates in a sweeping indictment of his society, an indictment that results directly from his awareness of the political implications of the homosexual experience in a hostile world. At the same time, however, the book transcends the political by affirming the possibility of alleviating the loneliness endemic to the human condition. The communion of flesh and spirit achieved by Alec and Maurice may isolate them from the "congregation of normal men," but it promises help in a universe in which "man has been created to feel pain and loneliness without help from heaven." Subtle and resonant, lyrical and moving, *Maurice* is Forster's most undervalued work. Although it has been attacked as sentimental and chauvinistic, it is actually a "masterly and touching novel,"[25] a worthy addition to the canon of a superb artist.

7

The Friend Who Never Comes: *A Passage to India*

A Passage to India (1924) is Forster's masterpiece and one of the great novels in the language. The most rhythmic of all Forster's works, it is virtually an echoing chamber that resolutely resists definite statement yet continually reverberates with expansive meaning.[1] Rooted in the complex realities of India at a particular moment, the novel also transcends the specifics of time and space to question the nature of meaning itself. Most profoundly, *A Passage to India* explores the limitations of human consciousness and the loneliness of the human condition.

Forster's final novel shares affinities with his earlier work, but it also marks a new departure. Like *Where Angels Fear to Tread* and *A Room with a View*, *A Passage to India* places English characters in a foreign environment and measures their responsiveness to a culture that questions their received ideas about life. But the foreignness of India threatens these characters in ways more basic and more disturbing than the moral complexity of Italy. Like all the earlier works, the final novel wrestles with familiar issues of personal fulfillment and growth, but these issues are dwarfed by a backdrop that threatens to shrink them into insignificance. *A Passage to India* asks many of the same questions posed by the earlier works, but its answers are less certain and more tentative.

181

Forster's final novel resembles *The Longest Jour-ney* and *Howards End* most closely. Like them, it per-sistently poses metaphysical questions and employs complex symbolism to suggest a layer of meaning in-dependent of plot. But *A Passage to India* is more un-settling than these earlier novels, presenting a world in which man no longer receives "help from the earth" and in which the limitations of liberal humanism are more obvious. The final novel shares with the earlier works a romantic disaffection with life's incomplete-ness, but it lacks confidence in their romantic solu-tions. Like *Maurice*, *A Passage to India* conceives of the universe as a place where "man has been created to feel pain and loneliness without help from heaven," but it has less hope in the efficacy of personal relation-ships to relieve the radical loneliness implicit in "our need for the Friend who never comes."

Unlike the earlier novels, *A Passage to India* re-fuses to focus on a single character, presenting instead four focal characters and a very large supporting cast. This diffuseness expands the book's scope and widens its vision, enabling it to explore the subjectivity of per-ception and to view events from a cosmic perspective. This lofty point of view necessarily reduces the stature of individual characters, questions the significance of action, and even casts doubt on the relative impor-tance of humanity. This process of deflation is clear in the description of characters in a tender farewell scene as "dwarfs shaking hands," in the measured assessment at the climax of the trial at the center of the plot—"The Marabar caves had been a terrible strain on the local administration; they altered a good many lives and wrecked several careers, but they did not break up a continent or even dislocate a district"—and in the ob-servation that "It matters so little to the majority of liv-ing beings what the minority, that calls itself human, desires or decides."

The integrity of the novel resides in this remarka-

ble breadth of vision, a scope that permits it to accommodate numerous versions of reality without endorsing any of them. But for all its breadth of vision,
the novel is not detached. However small its characters
may seem from the perspective of the universe, *A Passage to India* is nevertheless passionately committed to
the urgency of questions for which it does not presume
to have answers. And in Cyril Fielding, Dr. Aziz, Mrs.
Moore, Adela Quested, Professor Godbole, and several minor participants in the book, it presents characters who haunt the imagination. Narrated in a voice of
extraordinary subtlety, brushed by comedy, enlivened
by satire, toughened by irony, and tinged with despair,
A Passage to India is a masterful achievement.

The novel is divided into three unequal sections:
"Mosque," "Caves," and "Temple." These divisions
parallel the three seasons of the Indian year in which
they are set—cool weather, hot weather, and monsoon—and they have been interpreted to symbolize
various structural triads, such as prelude-separation-
reconciliation or emotion-reason-love or maturity-
death-rebirth.[2] The tripartite structure is reminiscent
of the form of *The Longest Journey*, and the movements of the two novels are similar in tone. Moreover,
the mandala in *The Longest Journey*—a circle within a
square within a circle—is suggested in the later book in
the image of a square (or perhaps a cross) formed by
intersecting right-angled roads within concentric circles. But the incompleteness of the mandala in *A Passage to India* and its image of expansion rather than
contraction suggest the greater elusiveness of the later
novel; if the earlier book mirrors the Hegelian pattern
of thesis-antithesis-synthesis, *A Passage to India* resists
neat formulations and questions the force of logic
itself. The novel arrives not at a synthesis but at a recognition of limitations. The reconciliations of the conclusion are tender but qualified and self-questioning.

The plot of the novel centers on the injustices of

British colonialism and on the question debated by a group of Indians "as to whether or no it is possible to be friends with an Englishman." In *A Passage to India*, Forster subverts the Kiplingesque tradition of colonial fiction and exposes the cruelty and fear on which the British Raj rested so sanctimoniously in 1924.[3] The classic exploration of colonialism in English literature, it is more obviously a political novel than *Howards End* and *Maurice* and its social satire is equally pointed; but even more insistently than they, *A Passage to India* transcends the political to explore the spiritual. Taking its title from Whitman's poem of the same name, the novel presents India as the home of "primal thought" and spiritual mystery.[4] But it refuses to affirm Whitman's optimistic vision of a "passage to more than India" and finds India "not a promise, only an appeal."

The first section of the book is set in Chandrapore, a small Indian city administered by British officials that "presents nothing extraordinary" except for the Marabar Caves twenty miles away. The section traces the involvement of a sensitive young Moslem physician, Dr. Aziz, with a group of English visitors and residents. Aziz meets an elderly matron, Mrs. Moore, in a mosque, where he is delighted by her unaffected respect for his religion. They immediately establish an unusual rapport. Mrs. Moore and her traveling companion Adela Quested—a young woman who is considering marriage to Mrs. Moore's son, Ronny Heaslop, the city magistrate—are appalled by the racist attitudes of the British officials and their families, the Anglo-Indians. The women yearn to see "the real India" and to meet Indians socially. Reluctantly, Mr. Turton, the district's chief administrator, sponsors a "bridge party" ostensibly designed to bring together Indians and Anglo-Indians. Predictably, the party is a dreary failure, spoiled by the aloofness and condescension of the Anglo-Indians.

Sensing the disappointment of the visitors, Cyril Fielding, the principal of the government college, arranges a smaller, more informal gathering for the English ladies, Dr. Aziz, and Professor Godbole, a devout Hindu who teaches at the school. The party is lively but vaguely disappointing, animated largely by Aziz's nervousness. In his desire to please the ladies, the physician impetuously—and only half seriously—invites the group to accompany him on an expedition to the Marabar Caves, which he himself has never visited. The party is broken up by the unexpected arrival and rude behavior of Ronny, but as the guests prepare to depart, Professor Godbole sings a curiously disturbing song to Shri Krishna, Lord of the Universe. "I say to Him, Come, come, come, come, come. He neglects to come," Godbole explains.

Disappointed by Ronny's wholesale adoption of Anglo-Indian values, Adela decides not to marry him. But on an automobile ride arranged by an influential Moslem landowner, the Nawab Bahadur, Ronny and Adela are jostled together. Their hands touch, "and one of the thrills so frequent in the animal kingdom passed between them, and announced that all their difficulties were only a lovers' quarrel." After an accident in the automobile perhaps caused by a hyena, Ronny and Adela agree to be married. When they tell Mrs. Moore of the collision on the Marabar Road, she shivers and exclaims, "A ghost!" Later, the Nawab Bahadur, who laments superstition among uneducated Hindus, offers the same explanation. Meanwhile, Fielding's friendship with Aziz is sealed when the principal visits the physician's sickbed and is shown a photograph of Aziz's dead wife.

The second section recounts the expedition to the mysterious Marabar Caves. Aziz goes to much trouble and great expense to assure the outing's success, but Professor Godbole miscalculates the length of a prayer, and he and Fielding miss the train. Aziz revels

in the opportunity to entertain his guests, but both Mrs.
Moore and Adela are tired and preoccupied with their
own responsibilities. On her inspection of the first
cave, the elderly woman has an unpleasant experience.
Unnerved by the cave's mysterious echo that reduces
everything to the same dull sound, "boum," Mrs.
Moore refuses to continue the sight-seeing. She comes
to question all her beliefs and the value of life itself
and gradually lapses into apathy and despair.

On her tour of the caves, Adela—accompanied by
Aziz—becomes disoriented and believes herself the
victim of an attempted sexual assault. Frantically trying to escape her attacker, she stumbles down the face
of a precipice into a stand of cacti. Badly injured and
emotionally distraught, Adela is rescued by Miss
Derek, a young woman who volunteered to drive
Fielding to join the expedition. Miss Derek immediately returns to the city with Adela. When the train
bearing the rest of the party arrives in Chandrapore,
Aziz is arrested and charged with the assault.

The accusation against Aziz throws Chandrapore
into a state of turmoil. The Anglo-Indians react viscer-
ally, viewing the assault as an attack on British wom-
anhood and a validation of their bigotry, especially
their conviction that disaster inevitably results "when
English people and Indians attempt to be intimate socially." The prosecution of Aziz unites the hitherto hostile Hindu and Moslem communities and fans antico-
lonial sentiment. Fielding enrages his compatriots by
clinging to his belief in Aziz, a stance that infuriates the
Anglo-Indians even more than the assault itself.
Meanwhile, Adela continues to suffer from her har-
rowing experience, especially from the torment of a
persistent echo. Mrs. Moore grows querulous and
lapses more deeply into listlessness. When she announces that "Of course [Aziz] is innocent," Ronny
hurriedly arranges for his mother to leave India.

The trial is a boisterous affair, punctuated by hysterical outbursts from both sides. When it is revealed that Mrs. Moore has been sent from the country, the chant "Esmiss Esmoor" disrupts the proceedings. Ronny thinks it "revolting to hear his mother travestied into . . . a Hindu goddess," but the chant relieves Adela's echo, and during her testimony, she shocks the courtroom by recanting her accusation against Aziz. As the Indians celebrate their victory, the British renounce Adela. She takes refuge with Fielding at the college, where they learn of Mrs. Moore's death at sea. Ronny asks to be released from his engagement to Adela, and she returns to England.

By appealing to the memory of Mrs. Moore, Fielding finally convinces Aziz not to sue Adela for damages. But Fielding's efforts on Adela's behalf lend credence to Aziz's suspicion that his friend has had an affair with the Englishwoman and intends to marry her. As a result of Aziz's suspicion and Fielding's misunderstanding of its seriousness, the friendship of the two men weakens. When Aziz hears that Fielding, on furlough in England, has married, he assumes that the bride is Adela and becomes even more embittered against the English. Despite his dislike of the Hindus, Aziz determines to secure a position in a Hindu state, where the British presence is less oppressive.

The book's brief third section takes place two years later in Mau, a Hindu state where Aziz is court physician and Godbole the minister of education. Fielding and his wife Stella and brother-in-law Ralph, the children of Mrs. Moore, arrive in Mau during the Gokul Ashtami festival, a celebration of the birth of Krishna. While participating in the celebration, Professor Godbole suddenly recalls Mrs. Moore, whom he had scarcely known. When Fielding and Ralph are attacked by bees, Aziz and Fielding are finally reunited. The physician is delighted to learn that Fielding did not marry Adela but is embarrassed by his blunder in thinking otherwise. Ralph's voice reminds Aziz of Mrs. Moore, and the memory of his old friend stirs him to write Adela a gracious letter of reconciliation. Now a militant nationalist, Aziz looks forward to the expulsion of the British from India, for only then can he and Fielding be friends. "Why can't we be friends now?" Fielding asks, and all the voices of India respond, "No, not yet . . . No, not there."

From the most basic plot level to the most complex layer of symbolism, *A Passage to India* explores the difficulties of connection—of bridging the chasms that divide man from nature, race from race, and individual from individual—and of achieving a transcendent unity. Such difficulties are universal, but they are especially apparent in the vast subcontinent where hostility seems to exude from the very soil and where the manifold gulfs of language and religion and class and culture are particularly prominent. As James McConkey observes, "India is more than a foreign land which the English may leave at their wish; it is the contemporary condition, the separation between all mankind and all earth."[5]

The divisions of India are overwhelming, but so are its amorphousness, lack of outline, and absence of form. Boundaries in India constantly shift; no animal respects the sense of an interior; and everything resists identification, merging into something else. India is at once split by an infinite number of fissures yet threatened by an inclusiveness that blurs all distinctions and defies human comprehension. To Europeans, the reductive, homogenizing tendencies of India are even more terrifying than its inability to unite its many factions and sects into a unified whole.

As much a muddle as a mystery, India resists attempts at connection yet continually suggests the possibility of wholeness. The infinite fissures of the

hundred Indias express a longing for unity even as they
evidence its absence. The novel's power resides in this
combination of tremendous desire and inevitable frustration. All the glimpses of transcendence are suspect,
and always meaning remains just beyond human
grasp: "Outside the arch there seemed always an arch,
beyond the remotest echo a silence." India "knows of
the whole world's trouble, to its innermost depth. She
calls 'Come' through her hundred mouths, through objects ridiculous and august. But come to what? She has
never defined." But the very chaos of India exercises
the mind's need to discover some hidden principle of
order, and the very elusiveness of meaning fans the desire for some ultimate truth.

The book is haunted by the possibility that the
universe is devoid of meaning, that the primal caves
contain not only nothing but nothingness. Countering
this apprehension of a nihilistic absence of value are
the momentary glimpses of transcendence achieved
through the "secret understanding of the heart" or
through poetry, sexual desire, or mystical religious experience. These visions express the loneliness of the
human condition, the elemental need to escape our isolation, "our need for the Friend who never comes yet is
not entirely disproved." The relationship between the
need for communion and the fear of nothingness is
most apparent in the contrapuntal echoes of the words
"come" and "nothing," repeated persistently in various
contexts and colorations. This rhythmic technique establishes almost subliminally the novel's recognition of
the desperate need to believe in a meaningful cosmos
even—perhaps especially—in the face of nothingness.

In its examination of the subjectivity of perception, *A Passage to India* is as much a psychological as a
religious novel. Empirical observation is suspect and
the phenomenal world ambiguous, hence nothing is
ever simply what it appears to be and everything as-

sumes a different appearance by being filtered through a different consciousness. For instance, en route to the caves, Adela mistakenly identifies the stump of a withered palm as a snake; when she attempts to explain her error, "The villagers contradicted her. She had put the word into their minds, and they refused to abandon it." From a suitable distance and in a particular light, even the terrifying Marabar Hills appear romantic. Verbal truth and truth of mood often are incompatible in the novel, and a series of true statements frequently yields a false conclusion.

Sometimes a single character perceives an event in two opposed ways simultaneously, as when Aziz—a poet as well as a physician—observes the "strange looking" Ralph Moore: "The doctor in Aziz thought, 'Born of too old a mother,' the poet found him rather beautiful." And perception is subject to the distorting lens of the caste mentality, as when the Anglo-Indian club decrees that "few Mohammedans and no Hindus would eat at an Englishman's table, and that all Indian ladies were in impenetrable purdah. Individually it knew better; as a club it declined to change." Similarly, a group of Moslems rapidly lose sympathy with Professor Godbole, whom they admire, when they think of him as a Hindu: "He moved them less than when he had appeared as a suffering individual." Moreover, a single event can be seen in contradictory terms, as for example the 1857 mutiny, which for the Indians is a source of pride, while for the Anglo-Indians it is an emblem of native perfidy.

In this context of extreme subjectivity, the various attempts to impose order on a chaotic universe are expressions of a profound psychological need. They are reflections of and reactions to ontological uncertainty. Characters constantly imitate Aziz's propensity for decking the mosque "with meanings the builder never intended." Indeed, the novel conceives meaning itself as a function of perception, a projection of human consciousness rather than an external reality. Hence, almost every event—from the accident on the Marabar Road to the alleged assault on Adela to the "telepathic" communication of Mrs. Moore—receives multiple interpretations that are rarely mediated by the omniscient narrator, and the frequent glimpses of transcendence result either from the interpenetrations of other minds or from the abandonment of personality altogether.

Every system of belief is undercut in the novel, presented as a limited version of reality rather than as truth. This refusal to endorse a particular interpretation of the universe creates a powerful ambiguity. The reader is constantly placed in a position analogous to Ronny's attempts "to decide which of two untrue accounts was the less untrue." Although some readers impose on the novel an affirmation of a particular religious approach, they do so at the cost of ignoring the skepticism that informs the book and qualifies every explanation of infinity. Hinduism is depicted as more comprehensive and more appropriate to India, more capable of accommodating the subcontinent's mysteries—hence "less untrue"—than either Christianity or Islam, but Forster does not endorse the Hindu view of the universe as an accurate reflection of reality. The ambiguity of *A Passage to India* voices a recognition of the limitations of human consciousness; the book questions the possibility of the very quest for truth that it attempts.

The subjectivity of perception is vividly illustrated at the very beginning of the novel. Chandrapore is at first described from the prospect of the Ganges, which "happens not to be holy here." The town is "nothing extraordinary," a collection of mean streets, ineffective temples, and a "few fine houses . . . hidden away in gardens or down alleys whose filth deters all

but the invited guest." Viewed from this perspective,
Chandrapore is a place where the "very wood seems
made of mud, the inhabitants of mud moving. So
abased, so monotonous is everything that meets the
eye, that when the Ganges comes down it might be
expected to wash the excrescence back into the soil.
Houses do fall, people are drowned and left rotting,
but the general outline of the town persists, swelling
here, shrinking there, like some low but indestructible
form of life." This powerful description of Chandrapore as an amoebalike organism that blurs all distinctions as it expands and contracts expresses the paradoxical image of India's simultaneous divisiveness and
inclusiveness.

But when Chandrapore is viewed from a different
perspective it becomes "a city of gardens . . . a forest
sparsely scattered with huts . . . a tropical pleasaunce
washed by a noble river." This account of the Anglo-
Indian compound demonstrates the anomalous nature
of the English experience in India, an unnaturalness
exacerbated by their self-segregation and isolation. So
artificial is the view from their compound that new-
comers find it difficult to believe that Chandrapore is
"as meagre as it is described, and have to be driven
down to acquire disillusionment." The discrepancy in
the descriptions of the city establishes the important
principle that interpretations of reality are necessarily
dependent on perspective. The novel insists further
that all human perspectives are limited views at best.

The most limited views in the novel are those of
the Anglo-Indians. The Anglo-Indians' failure to understand the country they rule is illustrated by the unnaturalness of the intersecting right-angled roads they
construct in the city, forming in effect a square (or a
cross) amid concentric circles. Their attempt to impose a rational and alien order reveals their inability to
perceive—or appreciate—the more subtle and com-

plex forms of order natural to India, as represented by the arches and circles associated with Mohammedanism and Hinduism, respectively. The roads are "symbolic of the net Great Britain had thrown over India." But for all their domination of public life, the Anglo-Indians remain exiles, confined to small pockets of Sawstonian civilization, alienated from a landscape they despise. They eat "the food of exiles, cooked by servants who did not understand it." Attempting to learn native languages only in order to command inferiors, they master "none of the politer forms and of the verbs only the imperative mood."

Ironically, the destiny of the English is that of the earlier conquerors of India, "who also entered the country with intent to refashion it, but were in the end worked into its pattern and covered with its dust." Indeed, the Anglo-Indians are themselves caught in the net they have thrown over the country. Despite their attempts to avoid contact with India, they nevertheless participate in the tendency toward reductiveness and inclusiveness so characteristic of the subcontinent. As Aziz declares in the discussion of whether it is possible to be friends with an Englishman, "They all become exactly the same, not worse nor better. . . . All are exactly alike."

Forster's refusal to distinguish clearly among the individual members of the large group of Anglo-Indian characters corroborates this point, itself an ironic echo of racist comments made by Anglo-Indians. Major Callendar may be particularly brutal, Mrs. Turton especially pretentious, and McBryde somewhat more professional than the others, but in general the Anglo-Indians blur into an undifferentiated mass, constituting yet another caste among India's hundreds of divisions, one more ripple of sand in a desert of humanity that extends "grading and drifting beyond the educated vision."

Forster's critique of colonialism includes its effect on the conquerors as well as on the conquered, and among the effects of the herd mentality assumed by the Anglo-Indians are their loss of individuality and the destruction of their capacity for empathy with others. Fielding says of his countrymen, "they are much nicer in England. There's something that doesn't suit them out here." Uninterested in Indian civilizations and indifferent to their own culture, the Anglo-Indians discourage intellectual curiosity and insist on rigid conformity to their narrow view of the world. As Fielding learns when he fails to rally to the banner of race, "Nothing enrages Anglo-India more than the lantern of reason if it is exhibited for one moment after its extinction is decreed." Adela notices that "India had developed sides of [Ronny's] character that she had never admired. His self-complacency, his censoriousness, his lack of subtlety, all grew vivid beneath a tropic sky; he seemed more indifferent than of old to what was passing in the minds of his fellows, more certain that he was right about them or that if he was wrong it didn't matter."

The Anglo-Indians' failure of sympathy is manifest in their fear of intimacy, their habitual rudeness, their assumption of superiority, and their contempt for the land and people they rule. They distort science to bolster racism, as in McBryde's theory of Oriental pathology.[6] They pervert medicine into an instrument of cruelty, as illustrated by Major Callendar's mistreatment of Nureddin, by a nurse's belief that "One's only hope was to hold sternly aloof" from native patients, and by Mrs. Callendar's declaration that the "kindest thing one can do to a native is to let him die." Most tellingly, they distort Christianity into a grotesque religion barren of love. For prayer, they substitute the national anthem's "curt series of demands on Jehovah," trusting that "God who saves the King will surely support the police." Oblivious to the unseen, they enjoy behaving like little gods, while excluding non-Europeans from heaven. "I am all for Chaplains, but all against Missionaries," one Anglo-Indian lady exclaims.

The novel predicts with remarkable prescience the dissolution of British rule in India, tracing in the experience of Aziz a growing resentment against colonial insensitivity that transforms him from an apolitical surgeon who asks of the English only permission to "get on with my profession and not be too rude to me officially" into a fervent nationalist. Ronny dismisses his mother's insistence that "God put us on the earth in order to be pleasant to each other" as irrelevant to practical politics. The British are in India "to work . . . to hold this wretched country by force. . . . We're not pleasant in India. We've something more important to do," he asserts. But in a country that yearns for "Kindness, more kindness, and even after that more kindness," the Anglo-Indians' lack of love dooms them politically as well as spiritually. As Fielding remarks, "Indians know whether they are liked or not—they cannot be fooled here. Justice never satisfies them, and that is why the British Empire rests on sand."

The distortions of imperialism doom to frustration the yearning for communion between Englishmen and Indians. Interracial friendship is not impossible in the abstract, but under the peculiar conditions of imperialism, in which one race is subject to the other, communication is necessarily limited. Hamidullah recounts with great affection his love for an English family, the Bannisters, but that friendship developed and flourished in Cambridge. He despairs of seeing his friends' son in India, for the "other Anglo-Indians will have got hold of him long ago." Even Mahmoud Ali, the most militantly anti-British of Aziz's circle, speaks affectionately of Queen Victoria, but as Aziz points out, she and Mrs. Bannister are dead. As they play polo together, Aziz and the stray soldier on the Maidan temporarily establish a good fellowship because their "forces were equal." They part with a friendly salute before "nationality exerts its poison," as it does later when the soldier declares, "What you've got to stamp on is these educated classes," ironically unaware that the object of Anglo-Indian hatred is "the one I had a knock with on your Maidan last month." Friendship between the English and the Indians may be possible in other places and in other times, but not here, not now.

A Passage to India is a novel of frustrations and limitations, but perhaps the most poignant of all its frustrations is the disintegration of the friendship between Aziz and Fielding, the relationship that forms the emotional center of the book. For both men, friendship is a consummation devoutly to be wished, for each feels acutely the loneliness endemic to the human condition. They both long for the "secret understanding of the heart" that might soothe their discontents. Grieving for his wife, who died soon after he had fallen in love with her, Aziz knows that "no woman could ever take her place; a friend would come nearer to her than another woman." Fielding, who "had learnt to manage his life and make the best of it on advanced European lines," is plagued by a vague sadness and yearns for communion with another. "The world," he believes, "is a globe of men who are trying to reach one another and can best do so by the help of good will plus culture and intelligence."

Their friendship develops from Fielding's invitation to the physician to attend the small party at the college. Throughout the novel invitations are extended and accepted, but often they are meant insincerely or accepted grudgingly, and frequently the friend never comes. "All invitations must proceed from heaven perhaps," Forster suggests evasively, "perhaps it is futile for men to initiate their own unity." The metaphor of invitation embraces both the secular and religious dimensions of the book, and the repeated refusals of the numerous appeals signify the difficulty of connection and transcendence.[7] But Aziz recognizes in Fielding's invitation "true courtesy—the civil deed that shows the good heart," and though he has not yet met the principal, he anticipates "that the one serious gap in his life was going to be filled."

Aziz arrives early for the party, and he and Fielding are quickly drawn to one another. Aziz is pleased by Fielding's house, which contains some luxury "but no order—nothing to intimidate poor Indians." He is relieved to discover that in the principal's rooms everything is not "ranged coldly on shelves," as he assumes is the case in most Anglo-Indian households. The delicate arches of the house's central hall, a beautiful eighteenth-century room, particularly please Aziz, for they are associated with Mohammedanism and stir him to a fantasy of benevolence worthy of his beloved Mogul emperors. In this reverie, "He was even tender to the English; he knew at the bottom of his heart that they could not help being so cold and odd and circulating like an ice stream through his land." Made nervous by the arrival of the visiting English ladies and the enigmatic Deccani Brahman, Professor Godbole, he talks too much and not always accurately, but Fielding "did not even want to pull him up; he had dulled his craving for verbal truth and cared chiefly for truth of mood."

The friendship is sealed when Fielding visits Aziz some days later. The scene is carefully prepared: Aziz is ill, and Fielding's visit is preceded by the calls of other friends concerned about Aziz's health. Before Fielding arrives, Aziz recites a poem by Ghalib, a nineteenth-century Urdu lyricist:

The squalid bedroom grew quiet; the silly intrigues, the gossip, the shallow discontent were stilled, while words accepted as immortal filled the indifferent air. Not as a call to

battle, but as a calm assurance came the feeling that India
was one; Moslem; always had been; an assurance that lasted
until they looked out the door. . . . And the sister kingdoms
of the north—Arabia, Persia, Ferghana, Turkestan—
stretched out their hands as he sang, sadly, because all
beauty is sad, and greeted ridiculous Chandrapore, where
every street and house was divided against itself, and told
her that she was a continent and a unity. . . . The poem had
done no "good" to anyone, but it was a passing reminder, a
breath from the divine lips of beauty, a nightingale between
two worlds of dust. Less explicit than the call to Krishna, it
voiced our loneliness nevertheless, our isolation, our need for
the Friend who never comes yet is not entirely disproved.

This important passage colors the entire novel. It
reveals Aziz's need to believe in a unified subcontinent
even in the face of overwhelming evidence that India
is anything but unified; it documents the potential for
delusion in the human consciousness, the susceptibility
to belief in such temporary and spurious unities as
those evoked by Ghalib and mocked by the realities of
"ridiculous Chandrapore"; and it reflects a deeper
sadness than the shallow discontents of mundane life
under imperialism. The longing for the Friend—"a
Persian expression for God"—represents the need to
believe in an ordered and benevolent universe, but it
also signifies the elemental and equally spiritual need
to commune with another.

That the need for the Friend who never comes
motivates the Aziz-Fielding friendship is made clear
when Fielding, after leaving Aziz's room, is "stopped
by a call from the house" and returns. "I never expected you to come back just now when I called you,"
Aziz says. He shows Fielding a picture of his dead
wife, gazing bewilderingly at "the echoing contradictory world!" Fielding is astonished at this "outburst of
confidence," feeling like "a traveller who suddenly
sees, between the stones of the desert, flowers. The

flowers have been there all the time, but suddenly he sees them." The sharpened perception that results from the developing friendship promises a heightened awareness of the unseen. Communion with another enables individuals to escape the blinders of self-absorption. It is a secular expression of the spiritual longing that impels Godbole's repeated pleas to Krishna and Aziz's recitation of the poem by Ghalib.

Fielding is saddened that he is unable to reciprocate the sharing of intimacies. His secrets "were so uninteresting, it wasn't worth while lifting a purdah on their account." Aziz explains that were his wife alive, "I should have told her you were my brother, and she would have seen you. . . . All men are my brothers, and as soon as one behaves as such he may see my wife." The scene ends with the men joined as "friends, brothers . . . their compact had been subscribed by the photograph, they trusted one another, affection had triumphed for once in a way." The limitations of the triumph are apparent in the qualification "for once in a way," but this limited triumph promises at least partial fulfillment of the longing that haunts the human consciousness.

The friendship of Aziz and Fielding functions in the novel as an emblem of universal brotherhood, a test of the possibility of bridging cultural and social chasms through Fielding's good will and intelligence and Aziz's spontaneous emotion and intuition. The relationship illustrates the difficulties as well as the possibilities of brotherhood, and its eventual disintegration painfully documents the limits of even so sacred a Forsterian tenet as personal relations. In some ways, the two men are an unlikely pair. Aziz is mercurial, affectionate, and deeply "rooted in society and Islam," whereas Fielding is reticent, undemonstrative, and free of family and social responsibilities. Both consider themselves outcasts, but in vastly different ways. The personal and cultural differences that separate them are sources both of the attraction they feel for each other and of the difficulties that eventually will part them, differences that are exacerbated by the poisoned air of imperialism and the divisiveness of India.

Fielding is a rationalist, "a hard-bitten, good-tempered, intelligent fellow on the verge of middle age, with a belief in education." He is "content to help people, and like them as long as they didn't object, and if they objected pass on serenely." He finds intimacy difficult and he is skeptical of religion, clinging instead to a belief in liberal humanism, as epitomized by individualism. "I believe in teaching people to be individuals, and to understand other individuals. It's the only thing I do believe in," he declares. He defines mystery as "only a high-sounding term for a muddle." His experiences have "helped him towards clarity, but clarity prevented him from experiencing something else."

Aziz, on the other hand, is more emotional than rational and "sensitive rather than responsive. In every remark he found a meaning, but not always a true meaning, and his life though vivid was largely a dream." He is an orthodox Moslem, but "he wavered like the average Christian; his belief in the life to come would pale to a hope, vanish, reappear, all in a single sentence or a dozen heart beats, so that the corpuscles of his blood rather than he seemed to decide which opinion he should hold, and for how long. It was so with all his opinions. Nothing stayed, nothing passed that did not return." Although he is a skilled surgeon, "it was his hand, not his mind that was scientific." Devoted to the faded glories of Moslem conquest, the two themes he prefers in poetry are "the decay of Islam and the brevity of Love." Indeed, he is more a poet than a physician. "There are many ways of being a man," he states, "mine is to express what is deepest in my heart."

The difficulties that finally disrupt the Fielding-
Aziz relationship are presaged early in the novel.
When Fielding deprecates postimpressionism, the hy-
persensitive surgeon is offended, misinterpreting the
remark to imply "that he, an obscure Indian, had no
right to have heard of Post-Impressionism—a privilege
reserved for the Ruling Race." Only his awareness of
Fielding's "fundamental good will" prevents an outburst and early rupture. Similarly, when Fielding announces that he does not believe in God, Aziz and his
friends are scandalized: "The Indians were bewildered. The line of thought was not alien to them, but
the words were too definite and bleak. Unless a sentence paid a few compliments to Justice and Morality
in passing, its grammar paralyzed their minds."

Throughout the novel, personal and cultural differences lead to misunderstandings. Fielding finds
Aziz's emotionalism excessive, though it was the young
Indian's openness to emotion that revealed to the Englishman the presence of flowers among the desert
stones. Fielding finally complains, "Your emotions
never seem in proportion to their objects," attempting
to impose Western order on what he diagnoses as
Oriental muddle. In response, Aziz pointedly asks, "Is
emotion a sack of potatoes, so much the pound, to be
measured out? . . . If you are right, there is no point in
any friendship; it all comes down to give and take or
give and return, which is disgusting."[8]

When the men argue about Fielding's unwilling-
ness "to 'give in to the East,' as [Aziz] called it, and
live in a condition of affectionate dependence upon
it . . . something racial intruded—not bitterly, but inevitably, like the colour of their skins: coffee-colour
versus pinko-grey." The friendship of Aziz and Fielding
offers genuine solace to both men and spurs Fielding
to an act of heroism, but it is doomed by the very differences that attract the men to each other and that re-

flect the fissures of India. Even as Fielding throws in "his lot with Indians, he realized the profundity of the gulf that divided him from them," a gulf widened by the injustices of Anglo-India that embitter Aziz and increase his natural suspiciousness.

If Aziz is finally unable to connect fully with Fielding, he makes a lasting—if less personal and more mysterious—connection with Mrs. Moore. Although they are very different from each other, their bond of friendship expresses more purely the "secret understanding of the heart" than any other relationship in the book. From their first meeting, Mrs. Moore thinks highly of Aziz, and she frequently describes him as her friend, as when she interrupts one of Ronny's diatribes against Indians to interpose, "I like Aziz, Aziz is my real friend." Even as she succumbs to her devastating antivision and declines to continue the tour of the caves, she is solicitous of him: "'Yes, I am your friend,' she said, laying her hand on his sleeve, and thinking, despite her fatigue, how very charming, how very good he was, and how deeply she desired his happiness." Based on only three meetings with her, Aziz knows that his conviction of Mrs. Moore's "eternal goodness" amounts to "nothing, if brought to the test of thought." Yet he speaks sincerely when he tells Ralph Moore at the end of the book, "Your mother was my best friend in all the world." The communication of Aziz and Mrs. Moore has nothing to do with thought and everything to do with love, and it offers a reservoir of optimism that tempers the pessimism of the novel as a whole.

Mrs. Moore believes that "God . . . is . . . love." She abhors the racism of Anglo-India and penetrates beneath the logic of Ronny's defense of imperialism to see the self-satisfaction and complacency that motivate it. She realizes that "One touch of regret—not the canny substitute but the true regret from the heart—

would have made [Ronny] a different man, and the British Empire a different institution." At the heart of her humanism is the belief that "God has put us on the earth to love our neighbours and to show it, and He is omnipresent, even in India, to see how we are succeeding." Her belief in God's omnipresence enables her to transcend narrow sectarianism, as is apparent in her respect for the mosque as a holy place. When Aziz marvels at her courtesy in removing her shoes in the mosque—"so few ladies take the trouble, especially if thinking no one is there to see"—she replies: "That makes no difference. God is here."

Mrs. Moore's Christianity includes reverence for all life, as shown by her tender regard for the small wasp that she finds in her room. Throughout the novel, she is associated with wasps, and they symbolize the comprehensiveness of her love, especially as contrasted with the narrow perspective of orthodox Christianity. The narrower point of view is fairly represented by the devoted but ineffectual missionaries, who "made converts during a famine, because they distributed food; but when times improved they were naturally left alone again." Like Mrs. Moore, they reject the racism of Anglo-India and teach that "In our Father's house are many mansions . . . and there alone will the incompatible multitudes of mankind be welcomed and soothed." The two missionaries disagree as to the extent of divine hospitality, however. The younger and more advanced Mr. Sorley, who believes God's mercy to be infinite, would extend bliss to monkeys and perhaps to jackals. But even he "became uneasy during the descent to wasps, and was apt to change the conversation." He concludes that "We must exclude someone from our gathering, or we shall be left with nothing," thus both anticipating Mrs. Moore's antivision of nothingness and endorsing a doctrine of exclusion that links him with Anglo-India.

Mrs. Moore's most endearing characteristic is her capacity for empathy, her ability to escape the limitations of the self by interpenetrating other minds. "You understand me, you know what others feel," Aziz exclaims on their first meeting. To underline how rare this quality of understanding is among the "chilly English," he tells her, "you're an Oriental." Mrs. Moore's sympathetic understanding is at once her most natural and most mysterious quality. It springs from intuition rather than intellect, and it is as much a function of her apprehension of the unseen as her belief in ghosts. It not only inspires the devotion of Aziz and Adela, it also facilitates her putative role as spiritual guardian from beyond the grave, her metamorphosis into the Hindu goddess "Esmiss Esmoor."

Adela Quested lacks the spirituality of Mrs. Moore, but her liberal humanism also promises the possibility of friendship and understanding. Ironically, she finally achieves friendship not with Aziz, whom she hopes will "unlock his country for her," but with Fielding, who describes her early in the novel as a "prig." In many ways, Adela is a sympathetic character, intelligent, idealistic, and sincere. She is physically unattractive and sexually repressed, but she despises the superficiality and illiberal attitudes of Anglo-India. She fears that marriage to Ronny will restrict her to the isolation of club life, "while the true India slid by unnoticed." But Adela's theoretical fascination with India masks deep-seated ambivalence and fear.

Adela's self-consciously sympathetic response to India serves to contrast her with Ronny. She is spurred to break their tacit engagement by Ronny's rudeness at Fielding's party, particularly his "walking off in the middle of the haunting song" by Godbole, a song that has affected her more deeply than she realizes. But as she breaks the engagement, Forster comments: "Experiences, not character, divided them; they were not dissimilar, as humans go; indeed, compared with the people [i.e., the Nawab Bahadur and his Eurasian chauffeur] who stood nearest to them in point of space they became practically identical." This essential similarity of character suggests that India may affect Ronny and Adela similarly. Adela fears India in much the same way that Ronny does, and she fears most of all that India may transform her into an Anglo-Indian, a transformation very nearly accomplished by the incident in the Marabar Caves.

Significantly, the decision of Ronny and Adela to marry after all results more from their sense of isolation in a strange and incomprehensible land than from love. They become intensely aware of the strangeness of India—its resistance to labels and categories—when they are unable to identify the green bird in the dome of a tree. "It was of no importance," Forster writes, "yet they would have liked to identify it, it would somehow have solaced their hearts. But nothing in India is identifiable, the mere asking of a question causes it to disappear or to merge in something else." The pair's sense of isolation and disorientation draws them together.

As the couple travel along the Marabar Road in the Nawab Bahadur's automobile, they are disappointed in the inferior landscape, so different in scale from the "human norm" of Europe: "the countryside was too vast to admit of excellence. In vain did each item in it call out, 'Come, come.' There was not enough god to go around." This landscape reflects the loneliness so palpable in Professor Godbole's song to Krishna, and it heightens the couple's weak sexual attraction for each other. But their thrill of contact creates only a momentary transcendence: "a spurious unity descended on them, as local and temporary as the gleam that inhabits a firefly. It would vanish in a moment, perhaps to reappear, but the darkness is alone durable. And the night that encircled them, absolute as it seemed, was itself only a spurious unity, being modified by the gleams of the day." This description goes beyond merely noting the fleetingness of sexual desire to create a horrifying image of a universe isolated and meaningless, in which the apparently durable darkness of the night is itself exposed as a temporary and spurious unity engulfed by a more mysterious darkness beyond the sun.

Immediately following the spurious unity achieved in desperate reaction against the loneliness they feel in a land they cannot comprehend, Adela and Ronny are involved in a mysterious accident. Their rational reaction to the incident contrasts with the flustered bewilderment of the chauffeur and the "disproportionate and ridiculous" terror of the Nawab Bahadur. Ronny and Adela efficiently investigate and confidently diagnose the cause of the accident, a hyena or other hairy animal. They walk "a few steps back into the darkness, united and happy." When they return to the Anglo-Indian compound, they agree—quietly and without emotion—to be married. "Unlike the green bird or the hairy animal," Adela reflects, "she was labelled now." The couple's attraction to each other has little to do with love, being motivated by their need for Western order rather than by a more personal desire. Similarly, their scientific solution to the mysterious accident indicates not their superiority to superstitious Indians, as Ronny thinks, but their insensitivity to the unseen, as implied when Mrs. Moore and the Nawab Bahadur independently offer the unscientific explanation that the accident was caused by a ghost.

The inability of the English to comprehend India is most painfully demonstrated on the ill-starred expedition to the Marabar Caves, the event at the very center of the book's plot and at the core of all its multiple meanings. The outing is undertaken without enthusiasm and at the worst time of the year, the onset of the dreaded hot weather. In a country where, as Ronny says, the weather is "the Alpha and Omega of the whole affair," the hot season is ominous, separating man from nature in a manner particularly frightening to Westerners and accelerating the tendency toward reductiveness so characteristic of India. As the bad weather approaches, even Indians rush inside their bungalows "to recover their self-esteem and the qualities that distinguished them from each other."

April in this wasteland is the "herald of horrors," announcing the sun's return to his kingdom "with power but without beauty," dominating the overarching sky but failing to triumph. In his cruelty, the sun mocks the human desire for transcendence, increasing the frustration and loneliness of the human condition: "He was not the unattainable friend, either of men or birds or other suns, he was not the eternal promise, the never-withdrawn suggestion that haunts our consciousness; he was merely a creature, like the rest, and so debarred from glory." The sun in *A Passage to India* is both "the source of life" and the treacherous mocker of human aspirations: "no poetry adorns it because disillusionment cannot be beautiful. Men yearn for poetry though they may not confess it; they desire that joy shall be graceful and sorrow august and infinity have a form and India fails to accommodate them. The annual helter-skelter of April, when irritability and lust spread like a canker, is one of her comments on the orderly hopes of humanity."

Perhaps influenced by the debilitating rays of the cruel sun, the two English ladies experience painful crises in the Marabar Caves, but these crises are the culminations of processes that began earlier. For Adela, the experience is related to her unconscious fear of India, her susceptibility to Anglo-Indian values, and her lack of love for Ronny. For Mrs. Moore, the crisis is more profoundly spiritual. Although God "had been constantly in her thoughts ever since she entered India . . . oddly enough he satisfied her less. She must needs pronounce his name frequently, as the greatest she knew, yet she had never found it less efficacious."

India thwarts Mrs. Moore's desire for spiritual absolutes, as witnessed by her troubled response to Godbole's song, a response that anticipates her reaction to the message of the caves. When Krishna refuses to comply with Professor Godbole's plea, she gently asks the Hindu, "But He comes in some other song, I hope." Godbole replies, "Oh no, he refuses to come." To underline the disturbing effect of this negative answer on the Westerners, Forster adds: "there was a moment of absolute silence. No ripple disturbed the water, no leaf stirred." As the English ladies embark on their outing to the Marabar Caves, they still suffer the effects of disorientation caused by the haunting song: "Mrs. Moore and Miss Quested had felt nothing acutely for a fortnight. Ever since Professor Godbole had sung his queer little song, they had lived more or less inside cocoons."

The outing is a challenge to Aziz's desire to show courtesy to visitors from another country, "which is what all Indians long to do," and he successfully surmounts the logistical problems caused by different dietary customs and by "the spirit of the Indian earth, which tries to keep men in compartments." In dispensing hospitality to his guests, whom he loves especially because of the obstacles he has had to overcome in order to be able to share their company, Aziz imitates the generosity of his revered Mogul emperors. But though the Marabar Hills "look romantic in certain lights and at suitable distances," his friends "did not feel that it was an attractive place or quite worth visiting, and wished it could have turned into some Mohammedan object, such as a mosque, which their host would have appreciated and explained." Indeed, the one moment of true enthusiasm experienced by the English ladies occurs when Mrs. Moore, "suddenly vital and young," recalls her meeting with her friend in the mosque "And how happy we both were." Aziz and his guests are alike lost in the mysterious Marabar Hills without Professor Godbole.

But although Godbole may know the caves better than anyone else in the novel, the Marabar Hills are older than Hinduism, older than birds and gods and time itself. They antedate religion and ethics and all man-made categories: "To call them 'uncanny' suggests ghosts, and they are older than all spirit." Just as the sun mocks humanity's longing for the unattainable Friend, so this primal India of the Marabar Hills also signifies disappointment and disillusionment, for they are flesh of the sun's flesh: "They are older than anything in the world. No water has ever covered them, and the sun who has watched them for eons may still discern in their outlines forms that were his before our globe was torn from his bosom."

Rising "abruptly, insanely," they defy the human desire for order and proportion. Associated with the atheistic, world-rejecting Jain sect, the hills symbolize a renunciation of the world so absolute that even Buddha, "who must have passed this way . . . has left no legend of struggle or victory in the Marabar."[9] Although "Hinduism has scratched and plastered a few rocks . . . the shrines are unfrequented, as if pilgrims, who generally seek the extraordinary, had found too much of it here."

The caves are entered through a tunnel that connects a series of circular chambers, each about twenty feet in diameter, all barren of decoration and exactly alike: "Nothing, nothing attaches to them." They are dark, and there is little to see until the visitor strikes a match:

Immediately another flame rises in the depths of the rock . . . like an imprisoned spirit: the walls of the circular chamber have been most marvellously polished. The two flames approach and strive to unite, but cannot, because one of them breathes air, the other stone. A mirror inlaid with lovely colours divides the lovers, delicate stars of pink and grey interpose, exquisite nebulae, shadings fainter than the tail of a comet or the midday moon, all the evanescent life of the granite, only here visible. Fists and fingers thrust above the advancing soil—here at last is their skin, finer than any covering acquired by the animals, smoother than windless water, more voluptuous than love. The radiance increases, the flames touch one another, kiss, expire. The cave is dark again, like all the caves.

Beyond the caves connected by tunnels may be chambers that have no entrance at all. They mirror their own darkness infinitely: "Nothing is inside them, they were sealed up before the creation of pestilence or treasure; if mankind grew curious and excavated, nothing, nothing would be added to the sum of good or evil."

In describing the Marabar Hills and the caves within them, Forster proceeds from a vast, cosmic perspective in which human history is too insignificant to be mentioned to a narrow concentration on the caves themselves, in effect reducing the entire question of meaning in the universe to the contents of empty caves. This sudden contraction of the cosmos's expansive blur to the cave's nothingness is characteristic of the novel's persistent concern with perspective and reductiveness. Utterly without distinction, the caves are mysterious and horrifying because their egg shape and their curious beauty promise possibilities that are doomed to frustration. The eggs are hollow, and the mirrored walls reflect desires that can never be requited. The flames "touch one another, kiss, expire,"

poignantly dramatizing the inability to commune with
another, illustrating the loneliness and frustration of
the longing for the Friend who never comes.

As Wilfred Stone suggests, "The caves are the
primal womb from which we all come and the primal
tomb to which we all return; they are the darkness before existence itself."[10] Containing nothing, they imply
a stark truth about the universe more disappointing
than the sun's failure of apotheosis and more devastating than Krishna's repeated refusals to come. At the
core of the universe may be the primal void, nothingness itself. Not only may the Friend never come, he
may not even exist. At the same time, however, the
"imprisoned spirit" within the caves—perhaps the collective unconsciousness of the human race—represents
a need for union that transcends its impossibility of attainment. The dance of the flames—the eternal desire
for communion—may be more telling than their failure of union.

The most frightening feature of the caves is their
echo, the aural equivalent of the series of receding
arches that suggests meaning beyond the grasp of
human comprehension.[11] When disturbed by human
sounds, the caves emit a "terrifying echo . . . entirely
devoid of distinction":

Whatever is said, the same monotonous noise replies, and
quivers up and down the walls until it is absorbed into the
roof. "Boum" is the sound as far as the human alphabet can
express it, or "bou-oum," or "ou-boum,"—utterly dull. Hope,
politeness, the blowing of a nose, the squeak of a boot, all
produce "boum." Even the striking of a match starts a little
worm coiling, which is too small to complete a circle but is
eternally watchful. And if several people talk at once, an
overlapping howling noise begins, echoes generate echoes,
and the cave is stuffed with a snake composed of small
snakes which writhe independently.

It is this extreme reductiveness—the culmination
of India's tendency to blur all distinctions—that so disturbs Mrs. Moore:

The crush and the smells she could forget, but the echo
began in some indescribable way to undermine her hold on
life. Coming at a moment when she chanced to be fatigued,
it had managed to murmur, "Pathos, piety, courage—they
exist, but are identical, and so is filth. Everything exists,
nothing has value." If one had spoken vileness in that place,
or quoted lofty poetry, the comment would have been
the same—"ou-boum." If one had spoken with the tongues
of angels and pleaded for all the unhappiness and misunderstanding in the world, past, present, and to come, for all the
misery men must undergo whatever their opinion and position, and however much they dodge or bluff—it would
amount to the same, the serpent would descend and return
to the ceiling.

Confronted with the echo's reductiveness, its
revelation of a universe without meaning or value,
Mrs. Moore surrenders to spiritual despair. Her faith in
"poor little talkative Christianity"—even in its doctrine
of Agape, as expressed most movingly in I Corinthians
13—evaporates: "she knew that all its divine words
from 'Let there be light' to 'It is finished' only
amounted to 'boum.'"
Adela's crisis in the cave is similar to Mrs. Moore's
in that both are sparked by an echo from the primal
void; both are reactions to what Benita Parry describes
as "encounters between the civilized mind and the
primitive memories dormant in man."[12] Adela's is
more clearly a psychological breakdown inspired by
her inability to cope with the foreignness of India than
is Mrs. Moore's, but the psychological basis of Adela's
crisis may also help explain Mrs. Moore's antivision. If
the caves contain the collective unconsciousness, Mrs.
Moore's despair may be a psychological response to
the disappointment of an elemental human need to be-

lieve in the Friend who never comes. A world without
God as a guiding principle seems to her a petty and
contemptible nightmare, a negative vision that challenges her deepest instincts. Faced with the prospect
that the Friend does not exist, with the reduction of
Christianity's divine words to "boum," Mrs. Moore
suffers a breakdown as psychologically rooted as
Adela's. This reduction of the metaphysical to the psychological, which parallels the reduction of the metaphysical to the temporal and spatial dimensions of the
caves, is itself one of Forster's most chilling manifestations of nihilism, for it shrinks all meaning to the limitations of human consciousness.[13]

Adela's breakdown is a response to her own feelings of ambivalence toward India. It is linked to the
moment of "spurious unity" achieved on the Marabar
Road, for as she enters the cave, she suddenly acknowledges that she and Ronny do not love each
other, and she regrets their lack of physical attractiveness. She fears that in marrying Ronny, she may acquire the "mentality" of the Anglo-Indians, a mentality
that she has tried to avoid but which may express the
psychological ambivalence she shares with her fellow
exiles. The "shadow, or sort of shadow" that she sees in
the cave may be the Jungian shadow of her repressed
unconsciousness; this shadow may so threaten her persona—her social self—that she hallucinates a sexual assault, which expresses both a deep-seated fear and an
unacknowledged desire.[14] As a result of the alleged assault, Adela abandons her theoretical love for India
and embraces the familiarity of Anglo-India, a fate
that she may subconsciously desire. Forster allows the
possibility of explaining these breakdowns in psychological terms while maintaining their essential ambiguity, permitting such other explanations as sunstrokes
or fatigue or, less likely, an assault by the guide.

The picnic ends with Adela fleeing to Chandra-

pore in Miss Derek's automobile and with the rest of
the party, unaware of Adela's breakdown, huddled in
a train, described ominously as a cortege: "all resembled corpses, and the train itself seemed dead
though it moved—a coffin from the scientific north
which troubled the scenery four times a day." The
metaphor is particularly appropriate for Mrs. Moore, a
visitor from the scientific north whose interest in life
has vanished with her spiritual certainties. The picnic
leaves the elderly lady in retreat from life, Adela emotionally and physically injured, and Aziz threatened
with disgrace and imprisonment. The expedition also
leads to Fielding's surprising heroism and to the disappointment of his hope "to slink through India unla-
belled." In loyalty to his friend, he breaks his ties with
Anglo-India and earns the label "anti-British." The encounter with the extraordinary Marabar Caves leads to
racial and civil disturbances throughout the district
and spurs the Anglo-Indians to their own spurious
unity in hysterical reaction to "Oriental pathology."

The one person who fails to be troubled by the incident is the elusive Professor Godbole. In a discon-
certing conversation with Fielding shortly after Aziz's
arrest, he blandly declares, "I hope the expedition was
a successful one." He refuses to answer straightfor-
wardly Fielding's question as to whether he thinks
Aziz capable of the assault, insisting instead that
"nothing can be performed in isolation. All perform a
good action, when one is performed, and when an evil
action is performed, all perform it." Fielding is infur-
iated by this double-talk, which is later echoed in a
Western accent when the brutal Major Callendar remarks, "We are all to blame in the sense that we ought
to have seen the expedition was insufficiently guaran-
teed, and have stopped it." As always in *A Passage to
India,* every question can be answered in more than a
single way. Godbole's relativistic viewpoint is simply

another perspective, to be weighed alongside the Anglo-Indian assumption of Aziz's guilt and the Indian faith in his innocence.

Godbole is an enigmatic character, incompetent in the ways of the world, yet "all his friends trusted him, without knowing why." As Alan Wilde describes him, "He is 'Ancient Night'; he eludes the structures the Western minds have erected to accommodate reality to themselves."[15] He possesses a spirituality similar to Mrs. Moore's but deeper and more sophisticated. When he explains his inability to answer Fielding's query as to Aziz's guilt or innocence, the Hindu enunciates a philosophy capable of accommodating the apprehension of nothingness that so terrifies Mrs. Moore: "Good and evil are different, as their names imply. But, in my own humble opinion, they are both of them aspects of my Lord. He is present in the one, absent in the other, and the difference between absence and presence is great, as great as my feeble mind can grasp. Yet absence implies presence, absence is not non-existence, and we are therefore entitled to repeat, 'Come, come, come, come.'"

Godbole's view of the relationship of good and evil reflects Hinduism's comprehensiveness. The absence of God in the primal void does not disturb him, for "absence implies presence, absence is not non-existence." Godbole is more fully alert to the paradoxes of the unseen than is Mrs. Moore, for he is able to accept both good and evil as manifestations of God. Regarding the visible world as *maya*, or illusion, he preoccupies himself with the perception of the *Brahman*, or higher reality. As McConkey explains, "in the metaphysics of the Vedanta, the doctrinal basis of all Hinduism, Brahman . . . is without attributes, without distinctions. Nothing can be ascribed to it, nothing said of it: it is unknowable."[16] The distinction between *maya* and *Brahman* parallels the psychological distinction between consciousness and unconsciousness. The advantage of Godbole's comprehensive view is that it permits the expression of the elemental need to plead "Come, come, come, come" even while consciously aware that the Friend will never come. His calm contemplation of the abyss testifies that even the most horrible fears of humanity may be perceived from multiple perspectives.

Mrs. Moore's inability to accept the premise that absence implies presence leads to her rapid deterioration. She enters "the twilight of the double vision" where "horror of the universe and its smallness are both visible at the same time." In this state of spiritual muddledom in which the "undying worm" of eternity (cf. Isaiah 66:24 and Mark 9:44–48) appears to be "made of maggots," she becomes cynical, querulous, self-centered. Although convinced of Aziz's innocence, she exerts no conscious effort on his behalf: "she was actually envious of Adela. All this fuss over a frightened girl! Nothing had happened, 'and if it had,' she found herself thinking with the cynicism of a withered priestess, 'if it had, there are worse evils than love.' The unspeakable attempt presented itself to her as love: in a cave, in a church—Boum, it amounts to the same."

In her sorrow, Mrs. Moore repudiates the Christian doctrine of Agape that has guided her life, now finding the obligation to bear the burdens of others intolerable. She retreats into her card games of "patience," the ironically telling British term for solitaire. She clings to what is described in *Howards End* as "this ordered insanity, where the king takes the queen, and the ace the king." This addiction to card games reflects her desperate need to attach herself to a system of logical order—however artificial—in the face of the nothingness that obliterates all value.

But Mrs. Moore's despairing antivision is not her

final response to India. As she travels to Bombay to
board the ship for England, she gazes at a more hospitable landscape than the "hopeless melancholy of the
plain." She looks at the "indestructible life of man and
his changing faces" not solipsistically in terms of her
own troubles but as sights independent of herself. As
the train traces a semicircular route around Asirgarh, a
place with large and noble bastions and a mosque, the
town appears twice, from two different perspectives.
It seems to say, "I do not vanish," and to suggest once
again that everything can be assessed from more than
a single vantage point.

As she arrives in Bombay to board her steamer,
Mrs. Moore gazes at the thousands of coconut palms
that wave farewell to her: "'So you thought an echo
was India; you took the Marabar caves as final?' they
laughed. 'What have we in common with them, or
they with Asirgarh? Goodbye!'" India's final message
to Mrs. Moore emphasizes multiplicity and relativity.
It awakens her from the profound despair into which
she had lapsed, enabling her to place the cave's echo of
nothingness in a different perspective. The antivision
is as much a spurious and temporary unity as are the
various positive glimpses of transcendence in the
novel.

Mrs. Moore dies and is buried at sea. Her body
"was lowered into yet another India—the Indian
Ocean. . . . A ghost followed the ship up the Red Sea,
but failed to enter the Mediterranean." Her spirit remains in India and continues to influence the course of
the novel. In her continuing impact on the living, Mrs.
Moore is similar to Ruth Wilcox, who influences the
events of *Howards End* well after her death. Like
Ruth, Mrs. Moore functions on the mythic level as a
redemptive figure. She is transformed into a Hindu
version of Demeter, the goddess "Esmiss Esmoor,"
who atones for the British rape of India by sacrificing

her own life to save the innocent Aziz and who brings to the sere landscape soothing rains and renewed fertility.[17]

Other explanations of her influence range from the British verdict of mass hysteria when the chant "Esmiss Esmoor" convulses the courtroom to Adela's semiscientific suggestion of telepathy to Fielding's reluctant intuition—similar to Margaret Schlegel's conclusion in *Howards End*—that "we exist not in ourselves, but in terms of each others' minds." The question of how the dead influence the living is a familiar one in Forster's canon, especially prominent in *The Longest Journey* and *Howards End;* it is not answered definitely in *A Passage to India*—as with nearly everything else in the novel, the conflicting explanations are not mediated—but it is clear that Mrs. Moore's spirit does haunt the novel after her death. What is important is not how Mrs. Moore exerts her spiritual influence—whether as a goddess or a powerful memory or a projection of consciousness—but that such influence provides evidence of the unseen and a basis for belief in the Friend who never comes yet is not entirely disproved.

Mrs. Moore's influence is presented most dramatically during the trial scene when Adela finally recants her accusation against Aziz. As she enters the courtroom, she notices first of all the splendid punkah wallah, who "had the strength and beauty that sometimes comes to flower in Indians of low birth." One of the occasional gods that nature produces "to prove to society how little its categories impress her," the beautiful young man who pulls the rope that moves the fan is almost wholly oblivious to the court proceedings, embodying a state of unconsciousness that Adela must herself approximate in order to see beyond her deluded consciousness, beyond her hallucination. The punkah wallah's aloofness rebukes "the narrowness of her sufferings," and she longs for the presence of Mrs. Moore.

As Adela thinks of Mrs. Moore, the prosecution of Aziz begins. When the name of Mrs. Moore is mentioned, the trial erupts into a furor. Her name is repeated again and again: "people who did not know what the syllables meant repeated them like a charm." The magic of the name, Indianized into "Esmiss Esmoor," soothes Adela, and she takes the witness stand feeling more natural than she had since the disastrous picnic. Delving beneath her superficial consciousness to re-create the visit to the Marabar Caves from another perspective, she suddenly realizes that Aziz never followed her into the cave. She later credits this awareness, perhaps occurring simultaneously with the death of Mrs. Moore, to the elderly woman's telepathic communication. Aziz reports that "During the shouting of her name in court I fancied [Mrs. Moore] was present."

If the incident in the Marabar Hills does not dislocate the entire district, it profoundly affects the lives of Forster's characters. As a result of her exoneration of Aziz, Adela is ostracized by the British without earning the gratitude of the Indians. Her lack of emotion causes the Orientals to question her sincerity: "her behaviour rested on cold justice and honesty; she had felt, while she recanted, no passion or love for those whom she had wronged. Truth is not truth in that land unless there go with it kindness and kindness again, unless the Word that was with God also is God. And the girl's sacrifice—so creditable according to Western notions—was rightly rejected, because, though it came from her heart, it did not include her heart." She later agrees with Fielding's assessment—"you have no real affection for Aziz, or Indians generally"—a revelation that helps explain her ambivalence toward India as a failure of love.

Fielding alone befriends Adela in her outcast state, and he does so both because of his natural sympathy for the downtrodden and because she grows as a result of her suffering: "she was no longer examining life, but being examined by it; she had become a real person." They are drawn together because they recognize in each other a basic similarity. They share a vague but deep sense of dissatisfaction and a similar recognition of their limitations. Soon after Aziz's arrest, Fielding had gazed at the mysterious Marabar Hills and suddenly felt "dubious and discontented . . . and wondered whether he was really successful as a human being . . . he felt he ought to have been working at something else . . . he didn't know at what, never would know, never could know, and that was why he felt sad." This bewildering sense of inadequacy colors his relationship with Adela and joins them in a self-conscious friendliness "as though they had seen their own gestures from an immense height—dwarfs talking, shaking hands and assuring each other that they stood on the same footing of insight."

Their limitations reside in their rational approach to life, their achievement of a clarity that precludes experiencing something else. Their rationalism renders them unable to "give in to the East," to share intimacy, and to apprehend the unseen. Their inability to glimpse the transcendent is touchingly expressed as they meditate on Mrs. Moore's influence from beyond the grave, a notion that they finally dismiss: "Were there worlds beyond which they could never touch, or did all that is possible enter their consciousness? They could not tell. . . . Perhaps life is a mystery, not a muddle; they could not tell. Perhaps the hundred Indias which fuss and squabble so tiresomely are one, and the universe they mirror is one. They had not the apparatus for judging." This passage beautifully sums up the frustration that Westerners feel in the presence of India's mystery.

Fielding and Adela recognize the limits of the Western rationalism that they embrace, but this recognition only fuels their discontent. Although they seek no infinite goals beyond the stars, nevertheless "the shadow of the shadow of a dream fell over their clear-cut interests, and objects never seen again seemed messages from another world." Forster's point is that the desire for the Friend who never comes haunts the consciousness of even those who refuse to plead, "Come, come, come, come."

Fielding's intercession on Adela's behalf leads to his tragic misunderstanding with Aziz. Practicing "necromancy," Fielding finally persuades his friend that Mrs. Moore would wish him to spare Adela the compensation suit. These efforts arouse in Aziz the suspicion that Fielding intends to marry Adela for her money, which should rightfully be his. "Suspicion in the Oriental," Forster writes, "is a sort of malignant tumour, a mental malady, that makes him self-conscious and unfriendly suddenly; he trusts and mistrusts at the same time in a way the Westerner cannot comprehend. It is his demon, as the Westerner's is hypocrisy." In this novel where perception constitutes reality, where everything is subject to transformation by being seen from a different vantage point, where the central event of the plot proceeds from a hallucination, it is fitting that the disruption of its core relationship results not from verifiable reality but from a mistaken perception, from a tendency to trust and mistrust at the same time.

One of the many tangles that interrupt the communication of Fielding and Aziz—"A pause in the wrong place, an intonation misunderstood, and a whole conversation went awry"—the misunderstanding over Adela exposes the limits of their friendship, its fragility, and its frustrations. Fielding's reluctance to share confidences, his failure to take seriously the rumors linking him with Adela, and the indelicacy of his letter to Aziz all work to confirm the Indian's suspicion of betrayal. They are evidence of the cultural as well as personal differences that separate the two men, and the rift illustrates the difficulties of bridging these cultural gulfs.

India remains elusive even to a Westerner as receptive as Fielding. His awkwardness in the native costume he dons at Aziz's victory party vividly reveals his status as outsider even after his immersion in Indian life. Unlike Mrs. Moore and her son Ralph, Fielding is no Oriental. For all his good will and intelligence, he is finally unable to penetrate a "civilization which the West can disturb but will never acquire." The relief he feels when he escapes to the "human norm" of the Mediterranean is palpable. In Venice, he revels in the "harmony between the works of man and the earth that upholds them, the civilization that has escaped muddle, the spirit in a reasonable form, with flesh and blood subsisting." Fielding's eager embrace of Western order signals his retreat from the mystery as well as the muddle of India. The failure of his friendship with Aziz reveals the limits of his creed of personal relations in a "contradictory, echoing world."

The injustice visited upon Aziz narrows his response to the world, coarsens his character, and embitters him. He becomes politically committed for the first time in his life. He tells Fielding, "The approval of your compatriots no longer interests me, I have become anti-British, and ought to have done so sooner, it would have saved me numerous misfortunes." As Hamidullah notes early in the book, politics "ruin the character and the career, yet nothing can be achieved without them." Aziz's character and career are in fact damaged by his understandable bitterness and by his political activism, but such commitment is necessary in order to achieve the unity of India and to create the new social fabric that eventually will free the subcontinent of foreign domination. Ironically, however, India is so divided within itself that only the presence of the British provides a rallying point around which the union of its factions might be accomplished.

One positive effect of the prosecution of Aziz is a Hindu-Moslem entente, cemented by the selection of Amritrao, a fiercely anti-British Hindu, as chief counsel for Aziz's defense. Aziz attempts to overcome his prejudices against Hindus, and the Hindus similarly make a self-conscious effort to accept Moslems. The difficulty of connection between these factions is beautifully captured in the account of Aziz's meeting with Das soon after the trial, a meeting in which both men attempt to alter their habitual perceptions of the other:

They shook hands, in a half-embrace that typified the entente. Between people of distant climes there is always the possibility of romance, but the various branches of Indians know too much about each other to surmount the unknowable easily. The approach is prosaic. "Excellent," said Aziz, patting a stout shoulder and thinking, "I wish they did not remind me of cow-dung"; Das thought, "Some Moslems are very violent." They smiled wistfully, each spying the thought in the other's heart, and Das, the more articulate, said: "Excuse my mistakes, realize my limitations. Life is not easy as we know it on the earth."

Although he is "without natural affection for the land of his birth," Aziz makes a conscious effort to love India. "She must imitate Japan," he decides. "Not until she is a nation will her sons be treated with respect." He knows that if he is to help India achieve nationhood, he must look to the future of a united India instead of the past glories of Moslem conquest. "Of what help, in this latitude and hour, are the glories of Cordova and Samarcand?" he asks. "They have gone, and while we lament them the English occupy Delhi and exclude us from East Africa. Islam itself, though true, throws cross-lights over the path to freedom." He determines to leave Chandrapore and to settle in a Hindu state, where the British presence is less overbearing. "I think I could write poetry there," he reflects, knowing that "The song of the future must transcend creed." Despite the suspicions that divide Hindu and Moslem, they are more alike than they are different; the Moslem "restfulness of gesture . . . is the social equivalent of Yoga." In Mau, Aziz finally becomes "an Indian at last."

The visit to the Marabar Caves and its aftermath reveal the limitations of Forster's focal characters and expose their frustrations. They all flee Chandrapore in disillusionment and disappointment. Fielding marries in England and then returns to India, where he makes peace with Anglo-India. Aziz flees Chandrapore to become court physician at Mau, where Godbole incompetently administers the educational system. Adela makes a successful but limited life for herself in the familiar surroundings of London. All these characters are haunted by their inability to achieve the fuller connections they seek. *A Passage to India* offers little hope for the prospect of glimpsing a fully satisfying vision of wholeness, but in the reconciliations of the book's final section, all is not bleak. Haunted by the memory of Mrs. Moore, the final section intimates that the elderly lady who was so shattered by a vision of nothingness actually embodies the one belief that can solace the loneliness of life in the echoing, bewildering world.

The brief "Temple" section is set, two years later, in Mau, a village not far from Asirgarh, where Mrs. Moore had recuperated from her antivision. Here the subcontinent's divisiveness is expressed in the cleavage between Hindu castes: "Moslems and English were quite out of the running, and sometimes not mentioned for days." At a time "when all things are happy, young and old," Mau presents an India very different from the wasteland of the Marabar Hills. During a monsoon season that promises bumper crops, the "friendly sun" of Mau floods the world with color and everywhere are signs of harmony between man and nature. The great Mau tank, reflecting the evening clouds on its circular surface, creates an emblem of the world's overwhelming desire for wholeness and union, an image similar to the dance of the flames in the Marabar Caves but nonthreatening and even joyous: "earth and sky leant toward one another, about to clash in ecstasy." Even the presence of death does not bring sadness to the contented Indian evenings: "a compromise had been made between destiny and desire, and even the heart of man had acquiesced." The air thick with rain and religion, the time is propitious for reconciliation.

The section is dominated by the celebration of the birth of Krishna and the spirit of Hinduism. The celebration is muddled, dramatically inept, anticlimactic, repetitious, "a frustration of reason and form," and yet deeply satisfying to its participants. When the villagers of Mau glimpse the silver image of the infant Krishna, "a most beautiful and radiant expression came into their faces, a beauty in which there was nothing personal, for it caused them all to resemble one another during the moment of its indwelling, and only when it was withdrawn did they revert to individual clods." The presence of the god within the worshipers blurs their individuality and reflects yet another manifestation of India's reductiveness. Hinduism here responds to Indian divisiveness by creating a momentary unity, one belied perhaps by the return of the individual clods to their places among the infinite fissures of the Indian soil, but beautiful nevertheless.

The celebration has a scope broader than the worship services of most religions. It incorporates jollity as well as joy: "By sacrificing good taste, this worship achieved what Christianity has shirked: the inclusion of merriment. All spirit as well as all matter must participate in salvation, and if practical jokes are banned, the circle is incomplete." The ceremonies include roles for all social ranks, from the rajah to the untouchables, who provide the "spot of filth without which the spirit cannot cohere." Even the flies—a low but indestructible form of life that so annoyed Aziz in Chandrapore—here enjoy divine hospitality, freely claiming "their share of God's bounty."

At the climactic moment of the ceremony, "Infinite Love took upon itself the form of SHRI KRISHNA, and saved the world. All sorrow was annihilated, not only for Indians, but for foreigners, birds, caves, railways, and the stars; all became joy, all laughter; there had never been disease, nor doubt, misunderstanding, cruelty, fear." This rapturous vision of universal salvation, with joy extending to birds and caves and railways, is the obverse of the Marabar Caves' absence of value and an answer to it. The irrationality of the vision—"God is not born yet . . . but He has also been born centuries ago, nor can He ever be born, because He is the Lord of the Universe, who transcends human processes"—does not mitigate the validity of its reflection of a need at the very heart of human consciousness.

Compared with the other religions in *A Passage to India*, Hinduism is by far the most attractive. A living force to its adherents, it can "at certain moments fling down everything that is petty and temporary in their natures." Subsuming all matter and all spirit, its vision is more comprehensive than those of Christianity or Islam. More concerned with the difficulties of knowing God than with issues of ethics or behavior, it is less moralistic than other systems of belief, less susceptible to the petty prohibitiveness of suburban Christianity.

Moreover, it is refreshingly nondogmatic in its universality, absorbing into its own perspective the insights of other religions, as attested in Mau by the shrines erected to Moslem saints and by the English slogan, "God si Love," incorporated as part of the worship of Krishna. This absence of dogmatism makes it more truly international than Christianity or Islam, less able to be reduced to the narrowness of Anglo-Indian Christianity or the chauvinistic reveries of Aziz's Islam.

Even Hinduism's elusiveness—its imperviousness to rational explanations—is an appropriate reflection of the mysteriousness of the unseen and the irrationality of the collective unconscious. And its division into hundreds of sects mirrors the infinite fissures of India and the subcontinent's paradoxical tendencies toward simultaneous reductiveness and divisiveness: "Hinduism, so solid from a distance, is riven into sects and clans, which radiate and join, and change their names according to the aspect from which they are approached. Study it for years with the best teachers, and when you raise your head nothing they have told you quite fits."

Hinduism's recognition of the subjectivity of perception may frustrate Western expectations of order and logic, but it is precisely this recognition that renders Hinduism "less untrue" than other religions. As Benita Parry points out, "The eclecticism of Hinduism is all-important; because truth is not conceived as monolithic, varied beliefs are accepted as revealing different aspects of truth; thus contradictions do not exclude a fruitful coexistence."[18] The absolutism of Christianity and Islam cannot cope with the realities of the contradictory, echoing world that is India. Confronted with the nothingness of the Marabar Caves, all the divine words of "poor little talkative Christianity" amount only to "boum," and the symmetrical injunction of Islam, "There is no God but God," is "a religious pun, not a religious truth," failing to penetrate very deeply "the complexities of matter and spirit." Similarly, the rationalist faith of Adela and Fielding is also sharply limited. In the aftermath of her experience in the cave, Adela becomes uncertain whether the scientific aphorism, "In space things touch, in time things part," is a "philosophy or a pun."

Throughout the novel, the reduction of complex and subtle perceptions to neat formulations inevitably distorts them, as when Adela intends to endorse Aziz's dream of universal brotherhood "but as soon as it was put into prose it became untrue." Language in *A Passage to India* always threatens to lead to misunderstandings or distortions, and it is always inadequate to express accurately the complexities of the spirit.[19] In India, the grammar of sentences without compliments to justice and morality paralyzes minds and truth is not truth unless—as in the Christian doctrine of the Logos —the Word that was with God also is God. Hence, the Hindu misspelling of Mrs. Moore's slogan as "God si Love" may indicate not merely Hindu muddle in the outward forms of religion but also the expansion of a neat formula encapsulating Christian absolutism and exclusivity into a truer and more comprehensive expression. "God si Love" may be a more accurate spiritual insight than the neat and precise "God is Love," which may be a pun rather than a religious truth.

But for all the attractiveness of Hinduism, Forster stops far short of endorsing it as an accurate reflection of reality. If, as Fielding believes, the Hindus may have found "something in religion that may not be true, but has yet to be sung," the emphasis is as much on the uncertainty of the truth as on its need of expression. Hinduism embodies the human spirit's attempt "to ravish the unknown," but whether the attempt is successful eludes verification: "Not only from the unbeliever are mysteries hid, but the adept himself can-

not retain them. He may think, if he chooses, that he
has been with God, but as soon as he thinks it, it becomes history, and falls under the rules of time." After
the rapturous visions of transcendent unity, Hinduism
reverts to an inflexible social system, in which religious
injunctions render men literally untouchable. Moreover, the muddle of Hinduism approaches the very
chaos it attempts to explain, and its love for the universe is too abstract to be fully satisfying.

At the end of the celebration of Krishna's birth,
Forster writes: "at the Birth it was questionable
whether a silver doll or a mud village, or a silk napkin,
or an intangible spirit, or a pious resolution, had been
born. Perhaps all these things! Perhaps none! Perhaps
all birth is an allegory!" The glimpses of transcendence
provided by Hinduism may be as spurious and temporary as all the other fleeting perceptions of wholeness in the novel. Just as Ronny and Adela are momentarily deluded into believing that they are in love
and Aziz and his friends are temporarily convinced by
Ghalib's poem that all India is Moslem, so may the rap-
tures of Hinduism also be delusion. As Calvin Bedient
has observed, *A Passage to India* is at once Forster's
most belief-hungry and most skeptical novel.[20]

Religious certainty is impossible and skepticism
inevitable. What is clear, however, is that the spirit of
Mrs. Moore haunts the "Temple" section, making possible the limited but tender reconciliations with which
the novel concludes. Her presence is suggested in a
number of ways, and whether she is accepted finally
as a Hindu goddess or a "telepathic appeal" or merely
a memory held in common matters less than the recognition of her belief in love as the novel's positive
counterweight to the fear of nothingness.

Mrs. Moore first appears in the mind of Professor
Godbole as he sings a hymn in honor of Krishna. With
his colleagues in the choir, he attempts to escape the

transitory self and to love everyone and the entire universe, all matter and all spirit:

Chance brought her into his mind while it was in this heated
state, he did not select her, she happened to occur among the
throng of soliciting images, a tiny splinter, and he impelled
her by his spiritual force to that place where completeness
can be found . . . he remembered a wasp seen he forgot
where, perhaps on a stone. He loved the wasp equally, he
impelled it likewise, he was imitating God. And the stone
where the wasp clung—could he . . . no, he could not, he
had been wrong to attempt the stone, logic and conscious effort had seduced, he came back to the strip of red carpet and
discovered that he was dancing upon it.

This passage documents the limits of Godbole's
ability to love the universe. This love, necessarily unconscious and impersonal, is unable to encompass the
stone, and the completeness discovered in his unconsciousness may be as spurious as it is temporary. But
the chance presence of Mrs. Moore and her wasp
promises a possibility of bridging the chasms that separate individuals in the world of illusion even if wholeness remains impossible. Professor Godbole later imagines Mrs. Moore with "increasing vividness" and thinks:
"He was a Brahman, she Christian, but it made no difference, it made no difference whether she was a trick
of his memory or a telepathic appeal. It was his duty,
as it was his desire, to place himself in the position of
the God and to love her, and to place himself in her
position and to say to the God, 'Come, come, come,
come.'"

Mrs. Moore's function as an agent of reconciliation is apparent in the strained meeting of Fielding and
Aziz, precipitated by an attack of bees, who are at
least second cousins to the wasps associated with her.
The former friends have undergone many changes in
the two years since they parted, and intimacy cannot
easily be resumed. Fielding is older, sterner, and now

weighted with responsibility, while Aziz still nurses resentment against his former friend and hatred for the English.

When Aziz learns that Fielding married Stella Moore rather than Adela, the physician is ashamed and defiant. "I made a foolish blunder," he admits, and then declares, "My heart is for my own people henceforward." He rages against the British as a means of recovering his self-respect, but existing in his mind alongside the furies aroused by his admission of error is the possibility of affection's triumph once again. After declaring, "I want no Englishman or Englishwoman to be my friend," Aziz returns to his house "excited and happy. It had been an uneasy, uncanny moment when Mrs. Moore's name was mentioned, stirring memories. 'Esmiss Esmoor . . .'—as though she was coming to help him."

Mrs. Moore's presence is felt keenly in Aziz's encounter with her son Ralph. This meeting recapitulates the magic moment in which Aziz and Mrs. Moore achieved the "secret understanding of the heart" in the mosque. When Ralph asserts that he can always detect unkindness and can always tell whether a stranger is his friend, Aziz applies to him the same epithet he had earlier bestowed on the elderly lady: "Then you are an Oriental."

This title is justified when, as they row on the great Mau lake to observe the procession commemorating the birth of Krishna, Ralph directs Aziz to the one spot from which the tomb of the rajah's father is visible. The surgeon feels "that his companion was not so much a visitor as a guide," and as they near the palace and hear the chants of the worshipers, Aziz knows "with his heart that this was Mrs. Moore's son, and indeed until his heart was involved he knew nothing." Suddenly the chant "Radhakrishna Radhakrishna Radhakrishna Radhakrishna Krishnaradha" varies, "and

in the interstice he heard, almost certainly, the syllables of salvation that had sounded during his trial
at Chandrapore." The qualification—"almost certainly"—expresses the characteristic skepticism of the
narrative without tempering the significance of Mrs.
Moore's putative influence as spiritual guardian of the
conclusion.

The four outsiders at Mau—Aziz, Fielding, Stella,
and Ralph—are literally immersed in Mrs. Moore's
spirit of reconciliation at the climax of the Gokul Ashtami festival in a scene appropriately combining muddle and mystery. The festival ends with an image of
Krishna and a model of Gokul, the village of his birth,
thrown into the lake. The images dropped into the
water are emblems of passage: "a passage not easy, not
now, not here, not to be apprehended except when it is
unattainable." In short, they are emblems of the universal passage toward communion with the Friend
who never comes, the truest passage to India of all.

As the splendid servitor—like the punkah wallah
at the trial, "naked, broad-shouldered, thin-waisted," a
symbol of Indian vitality and primitivism—wades into
the water "to close the gates of salvation" and conclude the festival, the boats bearing Aziz and Ralph,
Stella and Fielding collide. These outsiders, falling
against each other and the servitor, are brought within
the Hindu circle of love. They are joined in the warm,
shallow water, baptized into the salvation implicit in
the sign "God si Love," a sign that expresses the muddle as well as the mystery of India and that foreshadows the difficulties as well as the possibilities of love.

After this comic baptism, the reconciliation of
Aziz and Fielding is possible. Bitterness and stiffness
recede, and the men bask in mutual affection. Aziz,
eager "to do kind actions all round and wipe out the
wretched business of the Marabar caves," writes a gracious letter to Adela, signifying his genuine forgive-

ness. Fielding confides to Aziz his marital difficulties, wonders why Stella and Ralph are so attracted to Hinduism, and betrays his own spiritual need. In an oblique response to his friend's metaphysical musings, Aziz—feeling something, perhaps a wasp, flit past him—adds a postscript to his letter to Adela: "For my own part, I shall henceforth connect you with the name that is very sacred in my memory, namely Mrs. Moore." The reconciliation of Aziz and Fielding is clearly made possible by the lasting impact on them of the apostle of love who shriveled into a withered priestess of nothingness only to flower finally as "Esmiss Esmoor."

But *A Passage to India* ends on a note of separation, not reconciliation. The union of the two friends is painfully incomplete, and even love cannot now heal the breach between India and Anglo-India. As Aziz tells Ralph, he may be Mrs. Moore's son but he is also Ronny Heaslop's brother, and "alas, the two nations cannot be friends." Fielding, having thrown in his lot with Anglo-India and having acquired some of its limitations, rejects Mrs. Moore's prescription of love, "meaning that the British Empire really can't be abolished because it's rude." He is surprised at his former greatness and wistfully acknowledges that such greatness is now beyond him.

Aziz cries, "Clear out, all you Turtons and Burtons. We wanted to know you ten years back—now it's too late." Willing himself into an unnatural reverence for the motherland, he shouts: "India shall be a nation! . . . Hindu and Moslem and Sikh and all shall be one!" When Fielding mocks at the image of India—"whose only peer was the Holy Roman Empire"—waddling in to take her seat among "the drab nineteenth-century sisterhood" of nations, Aziz "in an awful rage danced this way and that, not knowing what to do, and cried: 'Down with the English anyhow . . . if it's fifty-five hundred years we shall get rid of you.'" Half kissing Fielding, he adds: "and then . . . you and I shall be friends."

The novel ends in an extraordinarily moving re-capitulation of the difficulties of connection. These difficulties emanate from the infinite fissures of the Indian soil and from the poisoned air of imperialism, but they also mirror the loneliness of the human condition itself. "Why can't we be friends now?" Fielding asks. "It's what I want. It's what you want," he says, holding Aziz affectionately:

But the horses didn't want it—they swerved apart; the earth didn't want it, sending up rocks through which riders must pass single file; the temples, the tank, the jail, the palace, the birds, the carrion, the Guest House, that came into view as they issued from the gap and saw Mau beneath: they didn't want it, they said in their hundred voices, "No, not yet," and the sky said, "No, not there."

The novel thus ends with Aziz and Fielding parting if not forever at least for the foreseeable future. However tender their reconciliation, the reality of India frustrates the longing for connection. Fielding's good will and intelligence and Aziz's emotion and spontaneity are alike unable to transcend the differences that separate them, and even the power of love is limited. The early question as to whether Englishmen and Indians can be friends is answered. Friendship will be possible only when the two people can meet as equals, when imperialism's failure of love is rectified.

On a deeper level, the answer "not yet . . . not there" voices a longing that cannot be relieved in this life as we know it on earth. The answer expresses the frustration attendant upon the "never withdrawn suggestion that haunts our consciousness" yet never materializes. But "not yet . . . not there" does not mean "never, nowhere," and the novel is not without hope that the elemental need for communion will sometime, somewhere be satisfied. The quest for truth is "a passage not easy, not now, not here, not to be apprehended except when it is unattainable," but it is a quest that most fully expresses the human dilemma in a bewildering world.

A Passage to India offers no easy answers. The liberal humanism so potent in the earlier novels is here revealed as severely limited. Intellectual curiosity, personal relations, individualism, the harmony of man and nature, sexual love: all these Forsterian shibboleths are exposed as inadequate to the mystery and muddle of India. They are valuable in their own right, of course, and the novel never suggests otherwise. As John Sayre Martin observes, one reason *A Passage to India* is not depressing is that "despite its metaphysical and sociological implications, it communicates a sense that life is valuable for its own sake."[21] But the familiar Forsterian values fail to offer the prospect of transcendence that they promise in the early novels. Even the optimism afforded by Mrs. Moore's spirit of love is measured and suspect. Haunted by the possibility that at the core of the universe is nothingness, that meaning itself is so relative as to be merely a function of perception, the novel is obsessed with incompleteness, with the limitations of man's ability to understand either himself or the cosmos.

Forster described the novel as an attempt "to indicate the human predicament in a universe which is not, so far, comprehensible to our minds."[22] It affirms neither the negation of the caves nor the power of love nor the transcendental unity of matter and spirit. Like Whitman, Forster explores a passage to more than India, seeking "somewhere there the Comrade perfect," steering "for the deep waters only."[23] But he lacks Whitman's optimism, and the novel is permeated by a deep sadness that neither its comedy nor its guarded hopefulness nor its mythic transformations ever quite dispel. The book ultimately affirms only the universal longing for the Friend who never comes, a longing that transcends the limits of our capacities to comprehend the universe.

A large, intricate, elusive, and delicately balanced novel, *A Passage to India* integrates social comedy, biting satire, complex irony, and symbolism into a grand design mythic in scope and breathtaking in philosophical seriousness. It is remarkable for its subtle and sympathetic characterizations, its suggestive and poetic language, and its commanding intelligence and fundamental decency as well as for its brooding and unflinching exploration of the twentieth-century spiritual wasteland. Preoccupied with failure and frustration, the book is deeply moving in its documentation of life's incompleteness, yet it never succumbs to nihilism or despair. A profound study of the limitations of consciousness and the loneliness of the human condition, *A Passage to India* is also "perhaps the greatest English novel of this century as an esthetic accomplishment."[24] Forster's supreme achievement is both the culmination of his persistent concern with issues of wholeness and communion and a work of extraordinary beauty.

8

Other Kingdoms:
The Short Fiction

Forster is not a master of the short story. His importance as a writer rests on the novels and the nonfiction.
Yet the stories are not negligible. Some of them are
significant achievements in their own right, and taken
together, they help reveal the complexity of Forster's
art. They locate the source of some of his most characteristic effects in the tension generated by an imagination that is at once visionary and local, romantic and
realistic. They make obvious the romantic base of his
vision, tracing—in various ways and with varying degrees of success—the quest for a nostalgic wholeness,
glimpsed fleetingly during those Wordsworthian "spots
of time" in which the creative mind and external nature
intersect to yield an organic whole and to imagine other
kingdoms whose existence tellingly exposes the world
of local reality. As Judith Scherer Herz has observed,
the stories may indeed be "far closer to the sources of
Forster's imagination, even if we may finally value
more the transformation of that material into the novel's
social gesture than into the short fiction's parables, visions, and prophecies."[1]
    On first reading, the stories may seem whimsical
and light, more amusing than ambitious. Actually, the
stories are far more serious than they initially appear,
but this appearance calls attention to the balance of
realism and fantasy that characterizes the entire canon.

In the novels, realistic character study and social analysis prevail, whereas in the stories, fantasy and romance elements dominate. But just as the novels are themselves poetic in their emphases on symbolic moments, transfigurations, and metaphysical probings, so the stories also combine the passion with the prose. The fantasy is always anchored to the realistic, and the visionary illuminates the mundane.

In fact, the stories articulate the same social criticism that animates the novels. English insularity, materialism, class consciousness, indifference to art, and repression of natural instinct are all attacked. But in the stories, Forster does not so much analyze these social conditions as envision an escape from them into other kingdoms of his own imagining, frequently set in the past or the future. This is not to say that the stories are merely escapist but that they imagine romantically conceived alternatives to the realistically depicted worlds of complacency and convention. In some of the stories, the effect of this imagining is whimsical to the point of preciosity, but in the best—especially in "The Celestial Omnibus" and "The Life to Come"—the effect is wholly satisfying. In these, Forster beautifully juxtaposes worlds of bourgeois philistinism and kingdoms of the spirit. His self-conscious awareness that the stories are in fact fantasies actually serves to focus their social comment, just as the social realism of the novels provides the concrete background against which their mythic and symbolic counterplots reverberate.

The plots of nearly all the stories chronicle the breaking loose of characters, frequently children or adolescents, from the imprisonment of social conventions. The stories often pivot on *genius loci*, the apprehension of a particular spirit of place and the appreciation of elemental forces of nature. They are especially distinguished by their narrative techniques, sometimes employing obtuse narrators who fail to comprehend the import of the events that they relate, and by their lush prose. The use of untrustworthy narrators facilitates irony, placing the reader in a position superior to the characters, and it enhances mystery, making the reader aware that there is a story behind the story being narrated. The ecstatic prose functions to elevate the imagined worlds and eternal moments and to underline the contrast between the transcendent and the mundane, though sometimes this technique fails to convince and the prose seems merely strained or precious.

Spanning as they do more than fifty years, from "The Story of a Panic," which was written in 1902, to "The Other Boat," the final version of which was probably begun in 1957 and completed in 1958, the stories are especially important as evidence of Forster's consistent preoccupation with questions of wholeness, connection, and transcendence. The external subjects and the solutions vary, as does the quality of the individual explorations, but the Forsterian world view remains consistent. The visions of other kingdoms where connections can be made and wholeness thereby achieved mock the broken images and disconnected lives that animate Forster's art even as the imagined kingdoms transcend the restrictions of mundane reality. The stories offer fascinating insight into the issues that absorbed the man and helped shape the novelist.

The Celestial Omnibus

The Celestial Omnibus and Other Stories was published in 1911. It includes six stories and is dedicated "To the Memory of the Independent Review," the liberal journal in which three of the stories first appeared. The optimism of the stories—the conviction that the deadness of spirit so rampant in contemporary society can be imaginatively transcended—reflects the enthusiasm Forster felt for the journal. Indeed, the collection may be characterized in the same terms that Forster used to describe *The Independent Review* in his biography *Goldsworthy Lowes Dickinson:* "a light rather than a fire, but a light that penetrated the emotions." The most coherent of the three collections of short fiction, *The Celestial Omnibus* is also the most completely successful.

Placed first in the volume is "The Story of a Panic," Forster's earliest story and a central one in his canon. As Forster explains in his introduction to the *Collected Short Stories*, the tale resulted from a sudden revelation in May 1902, during a tour of Italy: "I took a walk near Ravello. I sat down in a valley, a few miles above the town, and suddenly the first chapter of the story rushed into my mind as if it had waited for me there. I received it as an entity and wrote it out as soon as I returned to the hotel." Published in 1904 in *The Independent Review*, "The Story of a Panic" satirizes English attitudes and celebrates the transforming power of nature, though not without acknowledging the danger of such transformations.

Narrated by the egregious Mr. Tytler, a snobbish prig, the story recounts an epiphanous moment—a visitation of Pan—in the chestnut woods above Ravello and its aftermath. This moment, set in a hollow that seemed like "a many-fingered green hand, palm upwards, which was clutching convulsively to keep us in its grasp," terrifies the adults in a party of English tourists but liberates fourteen-year-old Eustace Robinson. Previously listless and lazy, after this epiphany the adolescent bounds with animal vitality, embraces peasant women, and engages in "promiscuous intimacy" with Gennaro, a fisher boy doubling as a waiter. The night after the visitation of the great god Pan, Eustace leaves his room and gambols in the courtyard of the hotel, "saluting, praising, and blessing the great forces and manifestations of Nature." The boy sees the world with a new clarity. "I understand almost everything," he exclaims. "The trees, hills, stars, waters, I can see all. But isn't it odd! I can't make out men a bit." Eustace is captured and returned to his room. Gennaro, who had accepted a bribe to betray his friend, warns that the boy will die in confinement. When the smug adults dismiss his plea, the Italian rescues Eustace. But as the English adolescent escapes with shouts and laughter, Gennaro dies.

At the heart of the story are several related oppositions: youth and age, the natural and the artificial, the instinctual and the rational. Subsuming these contrasts is the larger opposition of Pan and Christ, or at least of primitive spirituality and modern religiosity. The appearance of Pan as a "cat's-paw of wind" is prompted by Eustace's whistle—a Pan pipe—which he blows just as the Christian adults pronounce the death of Pan. The curate, Mr. Sandbach, recounts the legend—from Plutarch via Eusebius—that at the time of Christ's birth sailors heard a loud voice proclaiming, "The great God Pan is dead." The events of the story refute the legend. Pan lives as a spirit of rebelliousness, sexuality, primal energy, and comprehensiveness. This spirit rebukes the conventional and the overcivilized, and it is felt most positively by the young.

In the adults, Pan induces sheer terror (or panic), for the pagan god reminds them of their animal natures, which they have struggled to repress. "I had been afraid," Mr. Tytler confesses, "not as a man, but as a beast." The younger characters accept the experience with equanimity. For instance, Tytler's daughter Rose, the youngest of the touring party except for Eustace, almost fails to be frightened: "I should have stopped," she explains, "if I had not seen mamma go." Gennaro understands the transformation of Eustace at once: "Ho capito," he murmurs. And Eustace himself announces, "I have been very happy." As young people, they are less rigidly civilized than their elders and closer to the stirrings of puberty.

Eustace's epiphany may indeed be regarded as a puberty rite, an initiation into sexuality. Certainly, his experience taps primitive instincts. He plays with a lizard, he whoops like a wild Indian, he pretends to be a dog, and he scurries like a goat. He freely violates artificial class barriers and sexual inhibitions, kissing an old woman on the cheek and leaping into Gennaro's arms. Most significantly, he apprehends the wholeness of nature, intuitively rather than rationally reaching an understanding "of the rain and the wind by which all things are changed, of the air through which all things live, and of the woods in which all things can be hidden," a description of nature that helps explain the function of the greenwood in *Maurice*. The fact that Eustace's vision of wholeness (Pan in the sense of "all") excludes human beings indicates both the distortion of human nature by society and the limits of his vision in the artificial world of repression. Precisely because he understands the interconnectedness of all aspects of nature, he cannot abide the confinement of a room without a view.

The pivotal character in the story is Gennaro. Suspended in age between the boy and the adults, he is the only character able to communicate with both. At Eustace's age, he too had experienced a mystical communion: "because I had neither parents nor relatives nor friends . . . I could run through the woods, and climb the rocks, and plunge into the water, until I had accomplished my desire!" Having grown older, however, he has grown susceptible to Tytler's bribe. The ideal friend of Eustace's longing, he functions as both a Judas and a Christ figure. Significantly, his decision to rescue the boy represents the triumph of his "ignorant animal nature" over "logic and reason." In saving Eustace, however, he dies, a "victim to his double vision," as Alan Wilde phrases it.[2] His apparently gratuitous death qualifies the ideal that Eustace's fantastic escape symbolizes and gives the story a hard edge. Indeed, the strength of "The Story of a Panic" resides in the ambiguity with which the vision of Pan is conceived. Without mitigating the force of the satire against his repressive society, Forster exposes the limitations of Pan even as he fantasizes an escape into primitivism.

"The Other Side of the Hedge," originally published in *The Independent Review* in 1904, is a simpler tale than "The Story of a Panic." Like the earlier story, it attacks modern attitudes, especially the belief in progress, competitiveness, and other Sawstonian catchwords but does so by means of a simple contrast, juxtaposing the monotony of contemporary life to an Edenic existence on the other side of the hedge, which functions as a kind of Möbius strip separating the outer and inner lives. The first-person narrator forces himself through the hedge into a deep pool, from which he emerges baptized into a paradisal garden, timeless and free. At first, he is disappointed with the lack of struggle and advancement and thinks that the "place was but a prison for all its beauty and extent." He learns, however, that the real prison is the road onto which opens the gate of ivory, the gate of false dreams. In contrast, the gate of horn, the gate of true dreams, opens inward. As the young man gazes at the gate of horn, he forgets the road and seizes a pot of beer from a passerby, whom he recognizes as his long-lost brother, who "had wasted his breath on singing and his strength on helping others" and is now a figure of easeful death.

"The Other Side of the Hedge" is a slight tale, charming but too obvious in its allegory and too bald in its attack on the idea of progress. Inverting Aesop's tale of the ant and the grasshopper, it is interesting primarily for its opposition of the inner and the outer lives and for its culmination in a union of brothers. In this tale, as in the novels, the modern emphasis on competitiveness and external achievement subverts fraternity and threatens the inner life. Thus, the narrator's reception into the congregation of the garden—his death to the world and his rebirth in the spirit—is completed by the communion of beer that he shares with his scythe-bearing brother. The other side of the hedge represents, in Wilfred Stone's words, the "geographical counterpart of an eternal moment, and an attempt to visualize a lost wholeness."[3] That it is conceived as a parody of the Christian heaven only increases the force of the story's indictment of modern society.

"The Celestial Omnibus," the collection's title story, also presents a parody of the Christian heaven. One of Forster's best stories, at once tough-minded and charming, concrete and expansive, it beautifully balances satire and fantasy, manipulating each to enhance the other. First published in 1908 in the *Albany Review*, the story recounts a small boy's escape from a confining suburban existence at Agathox Lodge, 28, Buckingham Park Road, Surbiton, into an unbounded world of imagination. Near the boy's house is a signpost whose faded letters read "To Heaven." Pointing up a deserted alley, the sign troubles the boy, who is loath to follow his elders in dismissing it as a cruel joke. His mother attributes the sign to a naughty young man who "wrote verses, and was expelled from the University and came to grief in other ways," thus immediately identifying Shelley as the story's presiding deity. The signpost recalls the wish that Rickie Elliot expresses about Madingley Dell in *The Longest Journey*: "If the dell was to bear any inscription, he would have liked it to be 'This way to Heaven,' painted on a sign-post by the high-road, and he did not realize till later years that the number of visitors would not thereby have sensibly increased."

In "The Celestial Omnibus," the Surbiton and Celestial Road Car Company provides free sunrise and sunset service to all who are willing to abandon self-importance and experience poetry and music directly and uninhibitedly. Despite the reasonable fare and the distinguished drivers—Sir Thomas Browne, Jane Austen, Shelley, and Dante—the omnibus service to heaven is rarely patronized. On his first journey, the boy is the sole passenger. Sir Thomas Browne conducts him into a realm of thunder and lightning and massive rainbows where Wagnerian Rhinemaidens "sport in the mancipiary possession of their gold" as the kindly conductor describes their play in the everlasting river. In this literary heaven, the boy romps with Tom Jones, Mrs. Gamp, the Duchess of Malfi, and other immortals.

When the boy returns to Agathox Lodge, his father punishes him for having run away and for telling preposterous lies. "It was the greatest day of his life," the boy thinks, "in spite of the caning and the poetry at the end of it." Part of his punishment consists of having to memorize Keats's "Sonnet to Homer," which aptly begins, "Standing aloof in giant ignorance." As he recites the poem to his eminent neighbor Mr. Bons, who presides over the literary society and owns seven copies of Shelley, the boy bursts into tears, "because all these words that only rhymed before, now that I've come back they're me. . . . All these things are true." When Mr. Bons, who prides himself on his finely honed sensibility, fails to credit the story, the boy is crushed. "I told them about you, and how clever you were, and how many books you had," he exclaims, adding: "and they said 'Mr. Bons will certainly disbelieve you.'" His vanity touched, the pompous but kindly neighbor agrees to meet the boy at sunset the next evening, expecting to expose his young friend's curious delusion.

At the appointed hour, however, the omnibus is waiting, its driver Dante, at whose sight Mr. Bons "gave a cry as if of recognition, and began to tremble violently." Over the door of the omnibus is written, "Lasciate ogni baldanza voi che entrate" ("Abandon self-importance all ye who enter here"), a tag that Mr. Bons corrects: "baldanza was a mistake for speranza." But the neighbor's pedantry is wrongheaded, for in "The Celestial Omnibus," as in conventional Christian wisdom, pride—not hope—is the foremost deadly sin. Thus, Mr. Bons's snobbery (as suggested by his anagrammatic name) condemns him to spiritual blindness and a savage death, the cause of which is a lack of faith. As the omnibus arrives at the rainbow bridge, Achilles raises the boy aloft on his wonderful shield. Mr. Bons, however, sees nothing of the "image of the Mountain that [the boy] had discovered, encircled with an everlasting stream." The terrified literateur pleads with Dante, "I have bound you in vellum. Take me back to my world." For all his smug profession of belief in "the essential truth of poetry," Mr. Bons lacks faith in imaginative reality. Whereas the boy is crowned with laurel leaves as he stands on the shield of Achilles, Mr. Bons crawls out of the omnibus and falls through a moonlit rock—whose existence he doubts—to the mundane reality of the earth, where his mutilated body is discovered the next day "in the vicinity of the Bermondsey gas-works."

"The Celestial Omnibus" is a richly resonant allegory that uses Christian dogma to celebrate the kingdom of poetry, which, as Dante tells Mr. Bons, "is a spirit; and they that would worship it must worship in spirit and in truth." To attain the kingdom of this heaven, one must approach it like a child, devoid of pride and open to the world of imagination. Just as it is difficult for a rich man to enter the Christian kingdom of heaven, so is it impossible for someone like Mr. Bons, who is pretentious and concerned with decorum and status, to attain the kingdom of poetry. Such a person is unable to accept its reality. The boy, on the other hand, has developed no worldly defenses against the transfiguring power of the imagination. He unaffectedly acknowledges a "queasy soul" when "the sun sets with trees in front of it, and you suddenly come strange all over." Thus, he stands solidly on Achilles's shield, that symbol of art encompassing an entire world of heroes and cities and vineyards and "every dear passion, every joy." He achieves an apotheosis as his reward for unpretentious faith.

The epilogue, detailing in flat, newspaper prose the discovery of Mr. Bons's body, effectively emphasizes the bizarre quality of everyday occurrences, thus rendering the kingdom of poetry less fantastic but even more wonderful. Similarly, when Dante echoes Jesus—"I am the means and not the end. I am the food and not the life"—he implies the ability of poetry to transfigure mundane existence. Hence, the story recommends not escapism but faith in the power of the imagination to create new worlds, a power that the story itself illustrates.

In its brilliant contrast of the world of Agathox Lodge and the realm of poetry, its sure control and pointed satire, its lightness of touch and playful irony, "The Celestial Omnibus" is a distinguished achievement, Forster's most successful fantasy. It perfectly embodies the romantic imagination that it celebrates, creating without affectation or archness a sense of wonder at the mystery of art. The playful parody of Christian dogma both sharpens the satire and deepens the irony. Executed without a false note, "The Celestial Omnibus" testifies to Forster's abiding faith in the imagination and in the doctrine of art for art's sake while

also graphically sketching the world of philistinism
that makes such faith so necessary.

The opposition of the world of poetry and a world
of philistinism also provides the tension in "Other
Kingdom," a story that begins in a translation class and
ends in a literal translation of a girl into a tree. First
published in 1909 in *The English Review*, "Other
Kingdom" both anticipates some details of *Howards
End*—especially the use of Hertfordshire folklore and
the themes of ownership and tradition—and recapitulates the story Rickie Elliot tells Agnes Pembroke in
The Longest Journey about the dryad who "flies out of
the drawing-room window, shouting 'Freedom and
Truth!'" and metamorphoses into a tree. "Other Kingdom" is not as fully satisfying as "The Celestial Omnibus," but it is distinguished by an especially intriguing
narrator, the sycophantic Mr. Inskip. Inskip is employed by Harcourt Worters to teach Latin to his fiancée
Miss Evelyn Beaumont and to his ward, a young man
named Ford. Ironically, the tutor cannot remember
the "perfectly sound" reasons for studying Latin, and
Harcourt and his mother are frankly dubious, considering it a luxury, important only for passing examina-
tions. But the story is witness to the living vitality of
mythology, to the fact that "Ah you silly ass, gods live
in the woods!" Indeed, the sense of continuity of the
past into the present gives the tale great evocativeness.

Harcourt functions in the story as a Midas figure.
Like Cecil Vyse in *A Room with a View*, he attempts
to own his fiancée, whom he "had picked . . . out of
'Ireland' and brought . . . home, without money,
without connexions, almost without antecedents, to be
his bride." He confidently expects that "in time Evelyn
will repay me a thousandfold." As her engagement gift,
he buys Other Kingdom Copse, a beech stand of
seventy-eight trees that he acquires suspiciously from a

widow. Evelyn's joy is bounded only by the knowledge that the copse has been leased for ninety-nine years rather than bought absolutely, a limitation that Harcourt soon remedies. But the idyllic freedom that Other Kingdom represents is circumscribed when the squire fences in the copse and constructs an asphalt path that links it to his estate.

The story comes to a crisis when Harcourt discovers Ford's "practically private" notebook. In the notebook are satiric sketches of Worters and love poems addressed to Evelyn. Despite her protests, Harcourt expels Ford from the estate. After a fierce storm, Evelyn runs into the woods and dances "away from our society and our life, back, back through the centuries till houses and fences fell and the earth lay wild to the sun." When he is unable to find her, Harcourt suspects that she and Ford have eloped. But Ford, discovered in a "squalid suburb" reading *Oedipus at Colonus*, tells the squire: "She has escaped you absolutely, for ever and ever, as long as there are branches to shade men from the sun."

Throughout the story, Forster opposes the practical and the absolute, and Evelyn's absolute escape into the apparently impractical world of mythology is devastatingly ironic. It exposes the limitations of the utilitarian ethos that governs even Harcourt's desire for "Everlasting Bliss!" in his union with Evelyn. Her Ovidian metamorphosis is the only means by which she can attain freedom. By subtly exposing Harcourt's sadism and gradually revealing Evelyn's decline from free-spirited youthfulness into modish languor, Forster imparts pathos to his brittle tale. He successfully depicts the young woman's affinity with nature and anticipates her transformation in the account of her dancing in a delicate green dress that quivers "with the suggestion of countless green leaves." Beautifully written and deliciously narrated, "Other Kingdom" never-theless suffers from self-conscious cuteness and obvious moralizing.

"The Curate's Friend," originally published in *Putnam's* magazine in 1907, is a slight tale of a young clergyman's encounter with a faun, an encounter that transforms his entire life, bringing him happiness and inner freedom. On first reading, it seems hardly more than an anecdote, yet concealed beneath its comic ve-neer is an account of homosexual recognition and ac-ceptance that is undoubtedly autobiographical. The story's celebration of the Wiltshire downs—"the land-scape, which is indeed only beautiful to those who admire land, and to them perhaps the most beautiful in England"—is reminiscent of *The Longest Journey*. Forster insists in "The Curate's Friend," as he demon-strates in *The Longest Journey* and in "Other Kingdom" as well, that the English countryside and "any country which has beech clumps and sloping grass and very clear streams" may reasonably produce fauns and other manifestations of the Greek spirit.

The faun appears to Harry during a picnic on the downs. The other members of the party—his fiancée Emily, her mother, and a young man—cannot see the faun, but the curate can, for he possesses "a certain quality, for which truthfulness is too cold a name and animal spirits too coarse a one." At first he is frightened, mistaking the faun for an evil spirit. But the benign creature reassures him. Harry tests the faun's powers by urging him to make Emily happy, supposing that the sprite will cause her to fall more deeply in love with him. Instead, however, the "great pagan figure" hovers above Emily and her young friend: "They, who had only intended a little cultural flirtation, resisted him as long as they could, but were gradually urged into each other's arms, and embraced with passion."

The new lovers enact a rhapsodic ballet that is both comically absurd and strangely moving.

Harry knows that he should be angry at this betrayal by his fiancée, but actually he is relieved and filled with joy. The faun tells him, "To the end of your life you will swear when you are cross and laugh when you are happy." Aided by his mythological friend, Harry goes on to a contented and useful life. He tries to share his joy with others, yet he can tell no one the source of his happiness: "For if I breathed one word of that, my present life, so agreeable and profitable, would come to an end, my congregation would depart, and so should I, and instead of being an asset to my parish, I might find myself an expense to the nation."

The story is a playful but serious exercise in tentative self-disclosure. It conceals its true subject—which demands "lyrical and rhetorical treatment"—in the disguise of "the unworthy medium of a narrative." In the process, author and narrator jointly delude the reader "by declaring that this is a short story, suitable for reading in the train," recalling Gwendolyn Fairfax's comment about her diary in Wilde's *The Importance of Being Earnest*: "One should always have something sensational to read in the train."[4] The delusion is only apparent, however, for the story betrays as well as conceals its true subject: self-discovery and, more specifically, self-acceptance of homosexuality. Like the lovers, Harry too can sing, "In the great solitude I have found myself at last." As a result of his self-acceptance, he rises beyond such concepts as guilt and sin and conformity. He saves himself from a loveless marriage and learns to commune with nature. "That evening, for the first time," he remarks, "I heard the chalk downs singing to each other across the valleys." His happy life is shadowed by the prospect of prison should he reveal the source of his transformation, but the clergyman's self-discovery is nonetheless rewarding. As part of the story's playful strategy of simultaneous disclosure and concealment, the prospect of prison is introduced ambiguously in order to permit a less explicitly homosexual reading, in which case the curate would be "an expense to the nation" by being confined in an insane asylum.

"The Curate's Friend" is unusual among Forster's stories in that it records a character's awakening to happiness within society. The tale is gentler than "The Story of a Panic," for Harry's recognition is less violent and desperate than Eustace's. The faun may be "second cousin" to Pan,[5] yet it is altogether a more benevolent creature. But although Harry prospers in society, he nevertheless understands the hollowness of his previous conformity, and he is constantly aware of the price society will exact should he reveal the homosexual root of his happiness. In its indirect and teasing way, "The Curate's Friend" indicts repression as thoroughly as does "Other Kingdom." At the same time that it unveils Harry's strategy of accommodation, the story also betrays Forster's awareness in 1907 of his own precarious position in a society that rewards him as author of *Where Angels Fear to Tread* and *The Longest Journey* but is nevertheless prepared to punish him for the secret desires that animate his art. The prison door threatens to swing shut on the author as well as on the narrator of "The Curate's Friend."

Like "The Story of a Panic," the final tale in *The Celestial Omnibus* was also inspired by a place. Forster received the inspiration for "The Road from Colonus" on his 1903 visit to Greece. Published in *The Independent Review* in 1904, the story is an ironic, modern reversal of Sophocles's *Oedipus at Colonus*, which recounts the tragic hero's old age and blessed death. Forster's aged protagonist, Mr. Lucas, experiences a symbolic moment in a small Greek village, but his daughter—a mock Antigone—drags him from the sacred place. He returns to a prosaic existence in London. At the end of the story, his daughter receives a parcel of asphodel bulbs from Greece. Reading the old newspapers in which the bulbs are wrapped, Ethel learns that a few hours after their brief visit to the village, a violent storm uprooted a large tree, which crushed the inhabitants of the inn where Mr. Lucas had wanted to stay. "Such a marvellous deliverance does make one believe in Providence," Ethel exclaims, as her doddering father complains about the noise of running water in his flat.

Mr. Lucas's failure to seize his symbolic moment and his realistic lapse into a querulous old age make "The Road from Colonus" seem less fanciful than the other stories in *The Celestial Omnibus*, thus earning it the admiration of those readers who find fantasy cloying. But Mr. Lucas's glimpse of coherent beauty in the universe is no less remarkable than the visions of Eustace in "The Story of a Panic," the boy in "The Celestial Omnibus," or Harry in "The Curate's Friend." Mr. Lucas's epiphanous moment reveals to him the unity of creation. As he stands in the votive tree, his ankles bathed in the mysterious spring that gushes from the tree's trunk, he discovers "not only Greece, but England and all the world and life." He knows suddenly that the "sun made no accidental patterns upon the spreading roots of the trees, and there was intention in the nodding clumps of asphodel, and in the music of the water." His heart floods with love for "everything that moved or breathed or existed beneath the benedictory shade of the planes," and "for the first time he saw his daily life aright." That his is an apprehension of wholeness is indicated by his desire "to hang within the tree another votive offering—a little model of an entire man." In this vision, Mr. Lucas achieves what Lionel

Trilling describes as "the romantic quest" for coherence, fulfilled in the contemplation of nature and ancient tradition.[6]

Mr. Lucas's experience promises a meaningful death, but this release is denied him by the force of society, here represented by his daughter and touring companions. He is condemned to a death in life, imprisoned within himself and his petty concerns. The meaninglessness of his existence is suggested by his sour complaints and total self-centeredness at the end of the story. His annoyances at the noise of running water, at his neighbors' dog and children, and at his abandonment by his daughter all contrast with the expansive understanding he felt in the Greek village. "There's nothing I dislike more than running water," Mr. Lucas remarks, having forgotten the mysterious stream whose healing powers had momentarily deepened his response to life. The "marvellous deliverance" of which Ethel speaks is not a deliverance at all but yet another example of society's tendency to trivialize experience and distance man from nature, presented here as both soothing and violent, healing and destructive. Written in spare but resonant prose, "The Road from Colonus" is rich yet unsentimental, marred only by the forced irony of its conclusion.

The Celestial Omnibus is Forster's most completely successful collection of short stories, but it is not entirely satisfying. "The Other Side of the Hedge" and "Other Kingdom" both suffer from sentimentality and obviousness. "The Curate's Friend," though intriguing and suggestive and fascinating as an exercise in self-disclosure, is nevertheless slight and understandably self-conscious. The title story, however, triumphantly combines romantic form and substance, while "The Road from Colonus" and "The Story of a Panic" convincingly suggest transcendent visions that are complex and ambiguous. These three stories are important achievements, yet even the less successful tales in *The Celestial Omnibus* repay careful reading. They reveal Forster's persistent yearning for wholeness, his faith in the inner life and in the unseen, and his profound dissatisfaction with the artificiality and alienation of his society.

The Eternal Moment

Although *The Eternal Moment and Other Stories* was published in 1928, all the tales it collects were written before World War I. The volume is dedicated to T. E. Lawrence "in the absence of anything else." More properly, the dedication should read "in the absence of anything else that I can publish at the present time," for by 1928 Forster had shared with Lawrence of Arabia the drafts of some of the short pieces that were to be published posthumously. English and American reviewers received *The Eternal Moment* respectfully, perhaps because Forster had established himself as an indisputably major voice with the publication of *A Passage to India* in 1924. Most reviewers took note of Forster's prefatory comment that he was unlikely to write more short stories and that the collection dates from a period early in his development.

The stories in *The Eternal Moment* recapitulate familiar Forsterian themes, but in general they lack the imaginative vitality of the tales collected in *The Celestial Omnibus*. The tone of the later volume is bleaker than that of the earlier one, reflecting a weariness of spirit and a sense of futility. This weariness pervades *The Eternal Moment*, dulling its satire and vitiating its irony. The moments of transcendence are few and generally unconvincing. The collection as a whole, containing as it does two extremely slight pieces, is inferior to *The Celestial Omnibus*. Still, two of the six pieces are impressive achievements, and two others are intriguing if not wholly successful.

"The Machine Stops," originally published in 1909

in the *Oxford and Cambridge Review*, is one of the two most successful tales in *The Eternal Moment*. A dystopia written in "reaction to one of the earlier heavens of H. G. Wells," as Forster explains in the preface to *Collected Short Stories*, "The Machine Stops" anticipates Huxley's *Brave New World* and Orwell's *1984* in its vivid sketch of a terrifying future. In this age of the Machine, men and women live underground in beehive cells, completely dependent on technology. They shun direct experience of all kinds, especially human contact. The Machine is elevated into a godhead, the Book of the Machine into a gospel, and the chant "How we have advanced, thanks to the Machine!" into a hymn of praise. Only Kuno, a rebellious young man who discerns mystery and continuity in the stars, challenges this brave new world. He attempts to recover his lost humanity and discovers the Forsterian moral: "Man is the measure. . . . Man's feet are the measure for distance, his hands the measure for ownership, his body is the measure for all that is lovable and desirable and strong."

Kuno shocks his conventional mother Vashti by recounting how he briefly escaped from the bowels of the Machine onto the surface of the earth. Hearing in his ears the voices of the dead, he exposes himself to fresh air and sunshine and is painfully but joyously reborn into the life of the earth. The low, colorless hills of Wessex seem to be alive: "the turf that covered them was a skin, under which their muscles rippled, and I felt that those hills had called with incalculable force to men in the past and that men had loved them." This experience gives Kuno insight into the nature of his society: "We created the Machine, to do our will, but we cannot make it do our will now. It has robbed us of the sense of space and of the sense of touch, it has blurred every human relation and narrowed down love to a carnal act, it has paralyzed our bodies and our wills, and now it compels us to worship it."

Kuno's brief escape teaches him as well the Machine's ruthlessness and power. The long white worm of the Mending Apparatus emerges from the vomitory shaft and forces Kuno underground. In the process, it castrates him and kills a young woman, an inhabitant of the earth's surface who attempted to aid him. In this horrible scene, the dehumanizing impulses of the Machine are unmistakably linked to its antisexuality. By emasculating Kuno and murdering the young woman, the Mending Apparatus attacks the basic human instinct toward sexual love, an instinct whose power threatens even the Machine. By limiting direct experience, enforcing isolation, and inhibiting desire, the Machine systematically erodes human relationships of all kinds.

Kuno is unable to evade the Machine, but gradually it breaks down of its own complexity: "Year by year it was served with increased efficiency and decreased intelligence. The better a man knew his own duties upon it, the less he understood the duties of his neighbor, and in all the world there was not one who understood the monster as a whole." The breakdown of the Machine culminates in an apocalyptic silence which kills thousands of people outright and induces worldwide panic. As their civilization collapses, Kuno and his mother embrace. "We die," he tells her, "but we have captured life." Weeping not for themselves but for humanity, Kuno and Vashti expire believing that there are still men and women on the earth's surface, "hiding in the mist and the ferns until our civilization stops."

As an assault on the notion of progress, "The Machine Stops" is altogether successful. It is especially interesting in its imaginative and convincing projection into the future of the dehumanizing trends that Forster consistently attacks in his own society: the distancing of human beings from direct experience by the imposition of social and religious conventions, by the alienation of man from nature, by the pursuit of comfort rather than joy, and by the devaluation of the body. The evocation of Orion as a symbol of primal humanity and of continuity recalls *The Longest Journey*, and the Machine's assault on the sense of space looks forward to the role of the automobile in *Howards End*, while the celebration of the body as the garment of the spirit recalls *A Room with a View* and anticipates *Maurice* and "What I Believe."

Forster's paean to the human body as the "measure for all that is lovable and desirable and strong" probably derives from Carlyle's *Sartor Resartus*, in which Teufelsdröckh endorses the view that the only temple in the world is the body of man: "Nothing is higher than this Form. . . . We touch Heaven, when we lay hands on a human body."[7] Carlyle's romantic philosopher formulates a clothes philosophy that insists that man "is by nature a *Naked Animal;* and only in certain circumstances, by purpose and device, masks himself in clothes" (pp. 5–6). He defines man as "A Soul, a Spirit, and divine Apparition. Round his mysterious Me, there lies, under all those wool-rags, a Garment of Flesh (or of Senses), contextured in the Loom of Heaven; whereby he is revealed to his like, and dwells with them in Union and Division [i.e., as a member of society and as an individual]; and sees and fashions for himself a Universe, with azure Starry Spaces, and long Thousands of Years" (p. 65).

Forster alludes to these passages from *Sartor Resartus* at the end of "The Machine Stops," when Kuno weeps for "beautiful naked man . . . strangled in the garments that he had woven. . . . Truly the garment had seemed heavenly at first, shot with the colours of culture, sewn with the threads of self-denial. And heavenly it had been so long as it was a garment and no more, so long as man could shed it at will and live by the essence that is his soul, and the essence, equally divine, that is his body." Thus, Kuno and Vashti weep for the Machine's sin against the flesh, "the centuries of wrong against the muscles and the nerves, and those five portals by which we can alone apprehend." With Carlyle, Forster trusts naked humanity and decries the accretions of society: "all these tubes and buttons and machineries neither came into the world with us, nor will they follow us out, nor do they matter supremely while we are here."

This last passage anticipates the conclusion of Forster's moving essay on the eve of World War II, "What I Believe." The essay and the earlier story share a muted optimism that springs from a willed belief in the impulse to resist regimentation. As in "The Machine Stops," in the 1938 essay, written with the world on the brink of global war and totalitarianism, Forster draws hope from man's nakedness, the symbol of individuality. "The dictator-hero can grind down his citizens till they are all alike, but he cannot melt them into a single man," Forster writes in "What I Believe," explaining that "they are obliged to be born separately, and to die separately, and, owing to these unavoidable termini, will always be running off the totalitarian rails. . . . Naked I came into the world, naked I shall go out of it! And a very good thing too, for it reminds me that I am naked under my shirt, whatever its color." This humanistic faith helps explain the optimistic ending of the bleak dystopia.

For all its apocalypticism, "The Machine Stops" is indeed an optimistic story. It affirms the enduring human spirit even as it envisions a terrifying era. Appropriately, the story ends with an affecting reunion of mother and son, the reestablishment of a basic human relationship, and a declaration of faith, a Carlylean belief in humanity's eventual phoenixlike resurrection from the ashes of a dehumanizing society. If this ending is sentimental, it nevertheless effectively dramatizes the points that man is the measure of civilization and that the human spirit will not easily be destroyed. The sentimentality is compensated for by a carefully controlled narration that presents an exaggerated but believable account of the likely results of tendencies already rampant in 1909. "The Machine Stops" is a powerful statement of the Forsterian ethos.

The second story in *The Eternal Moment* is "The Point of It," one of Forster's most intriguing tales. An allegory about the inevitable loss of life's "keen, heroic edge" as one grows older, the story was originally published in *The English Review* in 1911. It was "ill-liked when it came out by my Bloomsbury friends," Forster reports in his introduction to *Collected Short Stories:* "'What *is* the point of it?' they queried thinly, nor did I know how to reply." The point of the story seems to be the necessity to remember the visionary moments of youth as a charm against both the mediocrity of success and the disillusionment of failure. As the protagonist, Micky, comes to realize after his death, "the years are bound either to liquefy a man or to stiffen him, and . . . Love and Truth, who seem to contend for our souls like angels, hold each the seeds of our decay."

Those who live by love, like Micky and the "sentimentalists, the conciliators, the peacemakers, the humanists, and all who have trusted the warmer vision," earn a soft hell of barren sand. Those who live for truth, like Micky's wife and the "reformers and ascetics and all sword-like souls," lie among mountains of stone in an equally dark and cold afterlife. Only the young, and those who remember vividly those "magic years" between childhood and maturity, reach the "Happy Isles" sought in Tennyson's "Ulysses," the poem quoted by Micky in the story's brief opening scene as his friend Harold rows him across an estuary. Prompted by Micky's exhortations, Harold achieves the "mystic state that is the athlete's true though unacknowledged goal" and goes berserk and dies.

After the death of his friend, Micky plods onward to a long, comfortable life. He remembers Harold's final words—"Don't you see the point of it? Well, you will some day"—but the youthful vision gradually fades. With each passing year, "the business of life snowed him under" as he consistently chooses comfort rather than joy. He matures from Micky to Michael to Sir Michael. He pursues a successful career in the British Museum, marries, produces three children, grows "sweeter every day," and even gains modest fame as a sentimental essayist. His wife, a hard woman with a fierce manner, dies, and he survives her by more than ten years. On his deathbed, he realizes the failures of his relationship with his children and "the absurdity of love." He awakens from death into a surrealistic, "vast, yet ignoble" sandscape that he finally recognizes as hell.

From the perspective of this hell, he reviews his life, finding it mediocre and soft. But as he recalls "that once he had remembered . . . a country that had not been sand," he feels the presence of Harold, now a boy-angel who saves him in a reversal of the opening scene. Calling "Come to me all who remember," Harold reenacts the Castor-Pollux myth and rescues his friend from hell. He rows him across an everlasting river to a land of sunshine: "Micky heard the pant of breath through the rowing, the crack of muscles; then he heard a voice say, 'The point of it . . .' and a weight fell off his body and he crossed mid-stream."

Forster's curious allegory is sweeping in its understated but scathing indictment of the process of growing old. Mediocrity or disillusionment seem almost inevitable consequences of experience. But this pessimistic conclusion is balanced by the possibility of salvation after death through a vivid recollection of youth. "There is no abiding home for strength and beauty among men," the spirit of Harold announces: "The flower fades, the seas dry up in the sun and all the stars fade as a flower. But the desire for such things, that is eternal, that can abide, and he who desires me is I." Thus, Micky—like Tennyson's Ulysses, an old man who thirsts for adventure—is finally saved by his desire to recapture the sensations of youth. Forster's allegory is carefully constructed; the long middle section re-counting Micky's marriage and career is masterfully ironic; and myth and symbol, especially the evocation of Castor and Pollux, are effectively manipulated. But "The Point of It" fails either to convince or to move. It offers neither a persuasive account of youthful tran-scendence nor a compelling depiction of afterlife; hence, the resolution is unsatisfying. The story is inter-esting primarily as an example of Forster's radically romantic disaffection with the human plight.

The next story in *The Eternal Moment*, "Mr. An-drews," was originally published in *The Open Window* in 1911. Like "The Point of It," "Mr. Andrews" also imagines an afterlife, though primarily to parody anthropomorphism and, more generally, to expose the pettiness of conventional religiosity. The slight tale re-counts the joint ascension of two souls: Mr. Andrews, an orthodox, broad-church Christian, and a Turk, a true-believing Moslem "slain fighting the infidel." They float upward, hand in hand, each silently pitying the other. When they reach the Gate of Heaven, each cries out, "Cannot *he* enter?" Each is permitted access to his own version of heaven, but both are disap-pointed. Their conventionally conceived heavens ful-fill their expectations but not their inexpressible hopes. Mr. Andews is "conscious of no great happiness, no mystic contemplation of beauty, no mystic union with good. There was nothing to compare with that moment outside the gate, when he prayed that the Turk might enter and heard the Turk uttering the same prayer for him." The two souls abandon their unsatis-fying heavens to merge into the "world-soul": "they, and all the experience they had gained, and all the love and wisdom they had generated, passed into it, and made it better."

Lacking tension and conflict, "Mr. Andrews" is not a successful story, though it demonstrates clearly the romantic dissatisfaction that energizes Forster's more passionate work. The tale's interest lies in its celebration of brotherhood and its parody of anthropomorphic visions of heaven. The simple clasping of hands expresses the fraternity that transcends cultural and religious barriers and unites human beings of diverse backgrounds. Opposed to the insipid heavens of conventional religions is the Shelleyan world-soul that receives Keats in "Adonais." The mystical merger chosen by the two men is bought at the expense of personality and promises to make the world better. The story succeeds as a spoof of religion, but even this modest success is vitiated by the sentimentality implicit in the notion of the world-soul's improvement by the experience, love, and wisdom of Mr. Andrews and his friend. This depiction of the world-soul is no more expressive of infinity than the individualized heavens that the story rejects.

Even less successful than "Mr. Andrews" is "Co-ordination," which was originally published under the title "Cooperation" in *The English Review* in 1912. This slight tale resembles "The Celestial Omnibus" in its allegorical method and celestial machinery, but it never attains the concrete embodiment of the romantic imagination that distinguishes the earlier fantasy. "Co-ordination" contrasts the labored and artificial attempts to understand art by structuring the entire curriculum of a girls' school around a single theme and the spontaneous and direct apprehension of the "central sources of Melody and Victory." Burdened by an elaborate and silly plot, the fantasy is neither convincing nor interesting. The transcendent visions experienced by the music teacher Miss Haddon and the school principal are perfunctory and arbitrary, and the story is strained and cloying in its whimsy.

"The Story of the Siren," which was originally issued in 1920 as a pamphlet by Leonard and Virginia Woolf's Hogarth Press, suffers from none of the faults that mar "Co-ordination." Although composed as early as 1904, it anticipates the concerns of *A Passage to India*. Written in haunting yet restrained prose and employing an extreme distancing technique in its narration, "The Story of the Siren" is a richly suggestive though very brief tale. The story opens with the narrator, an English tourist in Sicily, observing his notebook on the deist controversy sink into the blue waters of the Mediterranean. After retrieving the notebook, a young Italian "child of nature" tells the English scholar the story of his brother Giuseppe, who dived beneath the sea and encountered a siren.

Giuseppe's experience leaves him unhappy: "unhappy because he knew everything. Every living thing made him unhappy because he knew it would die." He abducts and marries Maria, a young woman who reportedly had gone mad through bathing in the sea. They love each other but are not happy. When Maria becomes pregnant, the rumor spreads that their child would be Antichrist, "would always be speaking and laughing and perverting, and last of all he would go into the sea and fetch up the Siren into the air, and all the world would see her and hear her sing." Shortly before Maria is due to give birth, she is murdered by a priest, who pushes her over the cliffs into the sea. Giuseppe travels around the world searching for someone else who had seen the siren, and he finally dies in Liverpool.

Like the Wedding Guest in Coleridge's "Rime of the Ancient Mariner," the narrator is transfixed by the beautiful young diver's tale. He is gradually brought back from the magic world of the story, with "all its absurdity and superstition," to the "commonplaces that are called reality." He is left with the diver's faith that the siren eventually will rise from the sea, destroy silence, and save the world: "Silence and loneliness cannot last for ever. It may be a hundred or a thousand years, but the sea lasts longer, and she shall come out of it and sing." The story pivots on the contrast between the narrator, an intellectual tourist, and the "superstitious" young man who tells the story within the story. This contrast questions the efficacy of the rational mind to comprehend deep spiritual truths. It underlines the tendency of polite religion to trivialize powerful myths by focusing on such abstract and peripheral issues as the deist controversy while dismissing as absurd such concrete and immediate spiritual experiences as that of Giuseppe.

In "The Story of the Siren," Forster fuses classical and Christian myth to create his most apocalyptic vision. Similar to Homer's sirens in *The Odyssey*, Forster's siren embodies the collective human consciousness; she is the current of life that contains all individual deaths.[8] Although she has been exiled to the silence of the sea by orthodox religion, she will some day be summoned to the surface by a child hero. Then she will sing, destroying religion and expressing the human spirit that transcends death. Finally, she will marry the child, with whom she will rule the world forever. This vision is modeled on the Christian apocalypse, though with some key differences. Fittingly, Giuseppe and Maria bear the names of Christ's parents, and the child who will "fetch up the Siren from the sea" is a Christ figure.

Giuseppe's encounter with the siren is deeply disturbing, for she reveals to him a lesson of futility and death. This lesson proves as disruptive as Eustace's epiphany in "The Story of a Panic" and darker even than Helen Schlegel's glimpse of goblins stalking the universe in *Howards End*. Giuseppe's reaction anticipates the similar response of Mrs. Moore to the Marabar Caves in *A Passage to India*. Yet from Giuseppe's apprehension of futility and death springs a positive vision, just as Helen Schlegel comes to realize that "Death destroys a man: the idea of Death saves him." Thus, in its vision of salvation by a divine child who will release the human spirit from the bondage of death, "The Story of the Siren" presents the most comprehensive of all Forster's epiphanies. A tantalizing story, it fails to be entirely credible, yet even this failure may be part of its design, for it succeeds in suggesting meaning in the universe beyond the grasp of rationality.

The final story in the collection, "The Eternal Moment," originally appeared in 1905 in *The Independent Review*. Containing the best-drawn characters in Forster's early short fiction, the story resembles the novels in its psychological depth and ironic perspective. An account of the return of a middle-aged novelist to a resort she made famous by featuring it in one of her novels, "The Eternal Moment" explores the complexity of moral responsibility and the difficulty of self-knowledge. The story also confronts familiar issues of class and of transfiguration, those themes so prominent in the early novels. Complacent in her mild unconventionality and assuming an exaggerated sense of responsibility for having altered the life of a little village, Miss Raby recalls that twenty years ago a young porter fell in love with her in Vorta. The information shocks her traveling companion, Colonel Leyland, but gives her the opportunity to expound her theory that the "only thing worth giving away is yourself." She believes that "the only gate in the spiritual barrier that divided class from class" is self-exposure, making a fool of oneself "before your inferiors."

Miss Raby's encounter with the transformed village confirms her sense of guilt. Commercialized and
vulgar, Vorta is dominated by the tourist industry,
which has made it prosperous and greedy. The village
has lost its former dignity, kindness, and fraternity,
and it has become as class-conscious as the tourists
who flock to it. The Cantu family, Miss Raby's former
friends, has divided against itself, and she feels a personal responsibility for the bitterness expressed by the
aristocratic Signora Cantu against her son and his con-
cierge, who turns out to be the former porter who had
declared his love for Miss Raby some twenty years earlier. The novelist comes to believe that she "had done
much evil," and she determines to confront the con-
cierge, hoping that perhaps she can heal the divisions
she has unwittingly caused.

In the confrontation scene between Miss Raby
and her former lover, Feo Ginori, Forster skillfully
blends comedy and pathos into superbly controlled
irony. In her encounter with her former paramour now
grown stout and greasy, the lady does make a fool of
herself. Rather than bridging the social gulf that separates her from Feo, however, her self-exposure actually
unites Feo and Colonel Leyland, both of whom remain
as class-bound as ever in their embarrassment at Miss
Raby's unladylike display. More ironically still, she,
who had felt guilty for "transfiguring people's lives,"
discovers that she had not really touched Feo's life at
all, at least not in the sense she had hoped: "she realized
that he had forgotten everything; forgotten her, forgotten what had happened, even forgotten what he
was like when he was young." And most devastating of
all, she faces the knowledge that though she has not
touched Feo, he did in fact transfigure her: "the incident upon the mountain had been one of the great
moments in her life—perhaps the greatest, certainly
the most enduring . . . she had drawn unacknowledged

power and inspiration from it, just as trees draw vigour from a subterranean spring. . . . There was more reality in it than in all the years of success and varied achievement which had followed, and which it had rendered possible."

All Miss Raby's attempts to recompense Vorta for the damage she believes she has done end in failure. Her wild offer to adopt one of Feo's children is rebuffed. She is forced to recognize the kinship between Feo and Colonel Leyland and thus to reject her current suitor as well. But her self-knowledge is its own reward: "In that moment of final failure, there had been vouchsafed to her a vision of herself, and she saw that she had lived worthily. She was conscious of a triumph over experience and earthly facts, a triumph magnificent, cold, hardly human, whose existence no one but herself would ever surmise."

"The Eternal Moment" parodies Miss Raby's liberal guilt and self-conscious unconventionality, yet she is not merely a caricature on the model of Miss Lavish in *A Room with a View*. The self-knowledge Miss Raby achieves is ironic but genuine. In giving herself away, she does not transcend social barriers, but she comes to understand herself and how she has unknowingly validated her life by translating experience into art. The story's strength lies in its acknowledgment of the ambiguity of the eternal moment. Although her symbolic moment has enriched her life, she did not actually pursue the moment to fulfillment in marriage to Feo, and it is clear that she was wise in not doing so. And while she exaggerates her responsibility for transfiguring Vorta, her novel did contribute to the very vulgarity she despises, though the vulgarity was already present in the village, at least in potentiality. Precisely because the story recognizes the complexity of moral responsibility and the ambiguity of symbolic moments, it is among Forster's most successful efforts in short fiction.

The Eternal Moment as a whole is less satisfying than *The Celestial Omnibus*. Although four of its six stories are at least intriguing, the later collection lacks the vitality of the earlier one. The two disappointing tales—"Mr. Andrews" and "Co-ordination"—are imaginative as well as technical failures. And two others— "The Point of It" and "The Story of the Siren"—are beautifully written yet finally unconvincing, for they fail to create the imaginative worlds that might give substance to their visions. The most successful stories in the collection—"The Machine Stops" and the title piece—are significant achievements, yet even they suffer from a lack of passion and commitment. "The Machine Stops" is an important expression of Forsterian values, but it is more successful as an indictment of social trends than as an embodiment of positive vision. And "The Eternal Moment" is more interesting for its ironic perspective and character delineation than for imaginative vitality. Although the stories of *The Eternal Moment* span the most active period of Forster's career, they breathe a spirit of exhaustion, and their publication in 1928 seems in retrospect a fitting conclusion to Forster's efforts as a publishing writer of fiction.

The Life to Come

Although Forster published no more fiction after 1928, he continued to write short stories. *The Life to Come and Other Stories,* published in 1972, collects fourteen tales that date from 1903 to 1958, only two of which had been published during Forster's lifetime. An uneven collection, it includes both Forster's earliest fiction and his latest, both his slightest and his most accomplished. The tales in *The Life to Come* include both those which Forster believed unworthy of inclusion in his earlier volumes and those which he felt he could not publish because of their explicitly homosexual content. Not surprisingly, the range of the collection is wider than that of *The Eternal Moment* and *The Celestial Omnibus. The Life to Come* is not a coherent collection, yet it gains unity by a consistent focus on personal relations and other familiar Forsterian values. As Donald Salter observes, "Almost without exception, [the posthumously published tales] are concerned with the way in which people are destroyed when they abandon a trust in each other as individuals and choose instead through weakness or selfishness the morality of class, race, or organized religion."[9]

The first story in *The Life to Come*, "Ansell," is one of Forster's earliest surviving works of fiction, probably written in 1902 or 1903. Although it is not usually classified among the homosexual stories, "Ansell" anticipates *Maurice* by demonstrating how homosexuality can save one from the burdens of class. The narrator of the story, a priggish Greek scholar reminiscent of Philip Herriton, is finally awakened to the experience of real life by an encounter with a young gamekeeper similar to Alec Scudder and Stephen Wonham. The character of Ansell is based on an actual boy Forster knew and played with as a child and whom he recalls in *Marianne Thornton* as "a snub-nosed, pallid, even-tempered youth" who "probably did more than anyone towards armouring me against life."

The action of the story centers on the destruction of the books and notes necessary for the narrator to complete his dissertation on the Greek optative, a verb mood used to express a wish or a hypothetical situation. But in losing the books in the accident, the narrator is saved both literally and metaphorically, and by the end of the brief tale he has translated his unconscious wish for communion with Ansell into reality. He abandons his scholarly pursuits, which—like Rickie Elliot's literary Hellenism—are an escape from participation in life, and embraces the naturalness of Ansell, who like Stephen Wonham is an unconscious embodiment of the Greek spirit in England. The story's romantic anti-intellectualism can best be understood as an attack on society's perversion of education into a means of distancing men from one another and from a genuine response to life. Perhaps the tale's wittiest feature is the brilliant manipulation of tense to chronicle the gradual changes in the narrator, who progresses from the past tense to conclude in the continuous present.[10]

The second story in *The Life to Come* is Forster's earliest published work of fiction, "Albergo Empedocle," which appeared in *Temple Bar* in 1903. Although Forster initially planned to include it in *The Celestial Omnibus,* he subsequently decided against republishing it. The failure to reprint "Albergo Empedocle" during his lifetime may be due less to Forster's doubts about its quality than to its implied but unmistakable homosexual subtext. Indeed, the story—as James Malek has demonstrated—is also a precursor of *Maurice.*[11] Although "Albergo Empedocle" is not among Forster's best stories, it is not inconsequential.

Narrated by a young man named Tommy, the tale recounts the bizarre experience of Harold ("the man I love most in the world"), which culminates in his confinement in an insane asylum. Accompanying his fiancée, Mildred Peaslake, and her family on a European tour, Harold becomes convinced in Girgenti, Sicily, that he had lived there in the ancient past when the town was known by the Greeks as Acragas. Fittingly, Acragas was the birthplace of Empedocles, a disciple of Pythagoras and an exponent of reincarnation. Harold confides to Mildred, "I was a lot greater then than I am now. . . . I was better. . . . I loved very differently. . . . I loved better too."

Falsely romantic, Mildred interprets the revelation

to mean that in the past Harold had been a king, and she tries to convince herself that she too had lived in Acragas and that they had shared a glamorous love. But Harold, whose character "consisted of little more than two things, the power to love and the desire for truth," disputes her claim to have lived then. In retaliation, she calls him a charlatan, and in consequence, he retreats completely into the past, into that greater life where he had loved differently and better. The story ends with Tommy visiting Harold in the asylum. "I think he knows that I understand him and love him: at all events it comforts me to think so," Tommy concludes.

"Albergo Empedocle" is interesting for its combination of the realistic and the supernatural and for its demonstration of Forster's early mastery of social comedy. Unfortunately, however, the realistic and supernatural elements are not credibly fused, and the brilliance of the social comedy is vitiated by the strained conclusion. Still, the depiction of the English tourists in Sicily is assured, and the characterization of the Peaslakes is convincing. The contrast of Mildred's false romanticism and Harold's natural Greek spirit is effective, as is the understated but central contrast of Mildred and Tommy. Tommy suffers guilt for not having heeded Harold's plea to join him in Sicily, yet he passes the test of trust that Mildred fails. The implication is that had Tommy been with Harold in Sicily, the young man "might be living that greater life among us, instead of among friends of two thousand years ago, whose names we have never heard." The story may be read as a cryptic allegory about the modern world's refusal to accept homosexual love.

"The Purple Envelope," another early story, also blends the realistic and the supernatural, but with even less success than "Albergo Empedocle." Begun in 1904 and completed in 1905, "The Purple Envelope" was rejected both by *Temple Bar* and by the publisher of *The Celestial Omnibus*. A confusing and confused ghost story full of red herrings, it is interesting largely as an early epiphany of the natural man, in this instance a brutal youth named Howard who "loved to take life, as all those do who are really in touch with nature." Howard thus also anticipates Stephen Wonham and Alec Scudder, but he lacks their complexity of character, seeming merely crude and unfeeling. These qualities are played off against the spurious spirituality and bogus kindness of his uncle, who actually attempts to defraud the young man of his rightful inheritance. At the end of the story, Howard assumes his natural place as country squire, the earliest but least satisfying of Forster's heirs of England.

The other two early stories in *The Life to Come* are slight and anecdotal. "The Helping Hand," probably written in 1904 or 1905, recounts Lady Anstey's plagiarism of Mr. Henderson's dating theory in her book on the fifteenth-century artist Giovanni da Empoli. When Mrs. Henderson discovers what has happened, she alerts her friends—including an important journalist—only to be informed by her husband that his theory has just been proved wrong. The title thus reflects ironically on both Lady Anstey and Mrs. Henderson. Pivoting on a sudden reversal, the story is reminiscent of those by Saki. Forcefully written, it lacks substance.

"The Rock," on the other hand, possesses substance but lacks the development that might make it compelling. As Forster describes the story in his introduction to *Collected Short Stories*, it is "about a man who was saved from drowning by some fishermen, and knew not how to reward them. . . . He ended by giving them nothing, he lived among them, hated and despised." Forster adds: "It was a complete flop. Not an editor would look at it. My inspiration had been genuine but worthless, like so much inspiration. . . ." The story, probably dating from 1906, merely distances the intriguing dilemma rather than dramatizes it.

The remaining stories in *The Life to Come* are late, written between 1922 and 1958. Eight of these deal explicitly with homosexuality. Although they have been dismissed as frivolous and even pornographic,[12] the homosexual stories are among Forster's finest tales, ironic, witty, resonant, and angry. And though they have been condescendingly psychologized as their author's therapeutic attempt "to record his despair and to utter, via fictional indirection, his cry for help,"[13] they actually express a healthy rage against the injustices of a repressive society.

Vital protests against the heterosexual dictatorship, these stories make clear the fact that Forster's passionate denunciations of social conventions and class distinctions stem, at least in part, from his awareness of himself as a homosexual. As a group, the stories with explicitly homosexual dramatic situations illustrate Forster's greatest gifts as a writer of short fiction. Their fierce but rueful satire is comedy sharpened by pain; their prophetic strain is fantasy deepened by myth. Despite the homosexual plots, they are not "about" homosexuality but about the same concerns that shape all Forster's work: the quest for wholeness, the search for liberation, the exploration of the inner life, and the apprehension of the unseen.

"The Life to Come" weds satire and prophecy to tragedy and myth. Written in 1922, it recounts the conversion to Christianity of a primitive African chief, Vithobai, by a young English missionary named Paul Pinmay. Central to the conversion is a night of lovemaking shared by the two men, which leads Vithobai to believe the missionary's message of love and brings Pinmay to "an agony of grotesque remorse." Following the profession of faith, Vithobai (renamed Barnabas) and his tribe are systematically deceived and exploited

as the guilt-stricken Pinmay abandons the gospel of
love for the "gloomy severity of the Old Law." When
the newly baptized Barnabas asks Paul to repeat their
lovemaking in the forest, the hypocritical missionary
tells him, "Not yet." For five years, Barnabas waits for
his friend to come to him: "God continues to order me
to love you. It is my life, whatever else I seem to do."
But on the eve of his marriage to a medical missionary
whose brother owns a mining concession that exploits
and sickens Barnabas's tribe, Paul bluntly tells the doc-
ile and Westernized chief, "Never." The two men are
reunited five years later as Barnabas is dying. Reverting
to his original religion, the failing man looks forward
to real love after death and stabs the missionary through
the heart: "love was conquered at last and he was again
a king, he had sent a messenger before him to announce
his arrival in the life to come, as a great chief should."

"The Life to Come" anticipates *A Passage to India*
in its opposition of Eastern and Western values, in its
concern with the cultural barriers that separate individuals, and in its depiction of Vithobai's longing for
the friend who never comes. As in the novel, Christianity is tested from an Eastern perspective and found to
be narrow and small in its denial of the fullness of experience. This denial results from Christianity's refusal
to take literally the doctrine of love that it professes.
Paul Pinmay is the story's representative of this dichot-
omous mode of thought, and he is tellingly named for
St. Paul, who in I Corinthians both expounds a vision
of Agape, or universal love, and denounces erotic love,
enunciating an antisexual doctrine that has been crucial
in forming Western attitudes toward sexual expression
in general and homosexuality in particular. "The Life
to Come" satirizes Christian hypocrisy, exposing
Christian complicity in imperialism as a failure of
Agape as well as of Eros, and suggests that the repression of Eros perverts the expression of Agape.

But the story is not merely satirical. It implies an

alternative to the repression and exploitation that it documents. Proceeding from a holy joke—Vithobai's literal belief in Pinmay's slogan, "God is love"—the tale imagines a theology in which Vithobai is actually a fool in Christ. In such a theology, the profane is also the sacred, the literal also the true. In such a theology, God is love in all senses of the word.

"The Life to Come" has frequently been criticized as unbelievable—particularly the notion that Vithobai would harbor his desire for Paul Pinmay for ten years—and inflated in diction. But the concretely detailed story is a parable, mythic in inspiration and implication, whose events expand from local to universal significance. Questions as to the realistic credibility of Vithobai's devotion are thus beside the point. Blending Christian and classical mythology (particularly the myth of Pentheus and Dionysus as recounted in Euripides's *The Bacchae*), the story becomes, in Judith Scherer Herz's words, a "kind of sacred parody in which Paul's final punishment is a grotesquely inverted *imitatio Christi*. You don't play games with the gods is the conclusion that both Euripidean and Christian readings provide."[14] The resonant diction—the biblical syntax and language—calls attention to itself in order both to parody Christian orthodoxy and to reconsecrate the language of sacred mystery. As Herz declares, "'The Life to Come' is a scriptural fiction."

The 1927 story "Dr. Woolacott" is an intriguing psychomachia written in prose as haunting as that of "The Life to Come." Featuring a chronic invalid, a young squire named Clesant, the tale contrasts a prolonged but meaningless existence devoid of the pleasures and experiences that make life worth living with an eternal moment that may spell death but signifies fulfillment. In this respect, "Dr. Woolacott" is similar to "The Point of It." Into Clesant's boring existence enters a ghostly figure radiant with vitality and reminis-

cent of Robert in *The Longest Journey*, though he plays
a role analogous to that played by Harold the boy-angel
in "The Point of It." That the healthy young man, an
agricultural worker determined "to 'get down into the
manure' and feel people instead of thinking about
them," is a ghost—either literally or as a figment of
Clesant's imagination—is suggested by the story's epigraph from Shakespeare's *Cymbeline*, "For this, from
stiller seats we came," which is spoken by one of two
brothers who appear in the play "with wounds, as they
died in the wars."[15] The epigraph is appropriate, for
the young man of Forster's story died of wounds in the
Great War, refusing a physician's plea, "Let me patch
you up, do let me just patch you up."

After his real or imaginary encounter with this
mysterious young man, Clesant responds more fully to
life: "The park, the garden, the sounds from the tennis
all reassumed their due proportions, but it seemed to
Clesant that they were pleasanter and more significant
than they had been, that the colours of the grass and the
shapes of the trees had beauty, that the sun wandered
with a purpose through the sky, that the little clouds,
wafted by westerly airs, were moving against the
course of doom and fate, and were inviting him to follow them." On his second appearance, the young man
makes love to the invalid and urges him to dismiss Dr.
Woolacott. The physician keeps the squire alive but at
the cost of any experience of life. After a fierce internal
struggle, Clesant accepts the invitation of his ghostly
lover, "Come to me, and you shall be as happy as I am
and as strong." The story ends with Dr. Woolacott ar-
riving on the scene to discover Clesant's dead body
and to recall "dimly the sound of his own voice saying
to a mutilated recruit, 'Do let me patch you up, oh but
you must just let me patch you up.'"

T. E. Lawrence's praise of the story as "the most
powerful thing I ever read . . . more charged with the

real high explosive than anything I've ever met yet"
may be excessive,[16] but "Dr. Woolacott" is a work of
real interest, elusive yet forceful and haunting. It has
been misread by some critics as a parable "which
treats homosexuality as a disease that separates the suf-
ferer from life."[17] Such absurd misinterpretations
simply distort the story by inverting its value system,
as Judith Herz and James Malek have pointed out.[18]
The handsome young man in the story is a death figure, but he is also symbolic of experience and fulfillment, the agent of escape from a half life measured by
length rather than quality. The struggle within Clesant's soul is between the life of incompletion offered
by Dr. Woolacott and the moment of joy promised by
the ghostly lover. The life of incompletion is symbolized by the violin that never concludes a theme and the
moment of joy by the lovemaking that culminates in
an orgasmic release. There is no question that Clesant's
salvation lies in his embrace of the angel of death.

   "Arthur Snatchfold," written in 1928, also ranks
among Forster's best stories. Distinguished by an extraordinary control of nuance, the tale pivots on a brief
but fulfilling sexual exchange between Sir Richard
Conway, a successful speculator in aluminum, and Arthur Snatchfold, a young milkman. A weekend guest at
the country house of Trevor Donaldson, a business as-
sociate, Conway resigns himself to a dreary visit, elaborately orchestrated yet lacking real pleasure. But as
he gazes at his host's "dull costly garden" one morning,
he is awakened to an altogether more pleasing prospect by the sudden appearance of a young man walking
confidently down the amphitheater: "besides being
proper to the colour scheme he was a very proper
youth. His shoulders were broad, his face sensuous and
open, his eyes, screwed up against the light, promised
good temper." Delighted when the young man salutes
him without deference, Conway arranges to accost

him the next morning in the estate's adjoining wood, where they sport in the bracken. After a fully satisfying sexual bout, the wealthy businessman offers his handsome partner a gift of money, not as payment but as a token of appreciation. "The affair had been trivial and crude," the narrator explains, "and yet both had behaved perfectly."

The second half of the story is set some months later in Conway's London club, where he is entertaining his former host, now a business rival. In the course of their coversation, Donaldson remarks on an "extraordinary case" in his village: "Indecency between males." Worried that the milkman might be in trouble, Conway presses Donaldson for details of the story. He finally learns to his horror that the youth was arrested shortly after their early morning dalliance. Despite the promise of a reduced sentence for identifying his partner, the milkman bravely refused, claiming "it was someone from the hotel." Shaken by the fate of his anonymous lover and by the narrowness of his own escape, Conway asks for the name of the young man who saved him. He briefly flirts with the idea of confessing his own part in the affair but then realizes the futility of such a gesture of greatness: "He would ruin himself and his daughters, he would delight his enemies, and he would not save his saviour." The story ends with Conway writing into his notebook the name of his brief lover "who was going to prison to save him. . . . Arthur Snatchfold. He had only heard the name once, and he would never hear it again."

"Arthur Snatchfold" is a deeply moving story of great power. As Norman Page comments, it is "hard to fault."[19] Unified by subtle rhythms and narrated with unfailing control, the tale—with superbly reined bitterness—indicts a stupid and cruel society that criminalizes harmless pleasure and distances individuals and classes from each other. The sexual encounter at its center is neither romanticized nor trivialized. One of "the smaller pleasures of life," the erotic exchange revitalizes and humanizes Conway. When both men are pleasantly satiated, it becomes "part of the past. It had fallen like a flower upon similar flowers," a description that emphasizes the union's beauty and naturalness as well as brevity. The escapade has little significance beyond the considerable pleasure it provides the participants, yet it is distorted into a grave criminal offense by the barbarous prosecution of an engaging young man.

Arthur's defiant heroism in protecting his partner makes him a martyr to an unjust society. His loyalty contrasts with the disloyalty of the business world, as indicated by the shifting alliances of Conway and Donaldson. Arthur's martyrdom also reflects the larger social inequity of the class system. As Forster comments in the "Terminal Note" to *Maurice,* police actions against homosexuals mirror the class divisions that homosexuality can help bridge: "Clive on the bench will continue to sentence Alec in the dock. Maurice may get off." This unequal enforcement of unjust laws is suggested in the story when Arthur says, "We could get seven years for this, couldn't we?" and Conway replies: "Not seven years, still we'd get something nasty." The prosecution of either of them for their harmless activity is "Madness," as Conway remarks, but the class system affects even the dispensation of injustice. Although Arthur truly says, "we was each as bad as the other," their different social positions cause them to anticipate distinctly different fates at the hands of the law.[20]

It is in this context of social injustice that Sir Richard Conway must be judged as he ponders a difficult moral dilemma at the story's conclusion. He is the tale's protagonist but not its hero, that designation belonging to Arthur, as the title suggests and his valor verifies.

But Conway is by no means the villain that some critics think. J. I. M. Stewart, for instance, describes him as "a cold bisexual hedonist [who] seduces and thrusts money upon a young milkman," a description that is plainly inaccurate and partakes of the very attitudes that the story attacks; and Wilfred Stone, who asserts on no convincing literary or biographical evidence that the "homosexual engagement stirred violent, and violently ambivalent, feelings in Forster," finds Conway "morally disgusting."[21] These reactions to Conway have no basis in the story and reveal a gross misunderstanding of Forster's attitude toward homosexuality and society. Forster reveals no ambivalence or guilt about his homosexuality. On the contrary, he is justly indignant at the ignorance and cruelty of a society that criminalizes him.

Conway is, to be sure, a morally ambivalent character at the end of the story as he decides against a futile gesture of greatness. Like Aziz in *A Passage to India*, he believes that "There is no harm in deceiving society as long as she does not find you out, because it is only when she finds you out that you have harmed her; she is not like a friend or God, who are injured by the mere existence of unfaithfulness." He is guilty only to the extent that he—"a decent human being"—is complicitous in the society that condemns Arthur. Like the early *Maurice* and other upper-middle-class homosexuals who are protected by the class system, Conway "may get off," but the threat of disgrace and punishment remains very real. The point of the story is not to attack Conway for moral cowardice in refusing to sacrifice himself and his family but to expose the cruelty of a repressive system. As James Malek remarks, a more important issue than Conway's failure of greatness is the "spiritual bankruptcy of a society that inappropriately turns little things into great ones in the name of moral decency."[22]

Whereas in "Arthur Snatchfold" sexual dalliance
has tragic consequences, in "The Obelisk" the erotic
escapades of an unhappy married couple with a pair
of sailors lead to reconciliation and rejuvenation. The
two stories, so different in tone, are actually companion
pieces; both affirm the positive values of recreational
sex in an antisexual society. Written in 1939, "The Obelisk" is a comic triumph, interesting especially for Forster's ironic but affectionate narration from a bored
wife's point of view. An ex-typist trapped in a lifeless
marriage to a priggish pedant, her head filled with romantic images from sentimental movies, Hilda is easy
prey for a dashing sailor "so out-of-the-way handsome." Only in the delightful conclusion does she learn
that while she was dallying with one sailor, her husband
Ernest was similarly sporting with the other. This unexpected revelation liberates the young woman and
promises to revitalize her marriage: "Depth beneath
depth seemed to open. For if she couldn't have seen
the Obelisk he couldn't have seen it either, if she had
dawdled on the way up he must have dawdled too.
. . . She peeped at her husband, who was on the other
side of the coach, studying the postcard. He looked
handsomer than usual, and happier, and his lips were
parted in a natural smile."

"The Obelisk" is a comic story, but it is not merely
facetious. In the opening pages, Forster deftly sketches
the deadness of the married couple's relationship. By
the end of the story, however, both Hilda and Ernest
have been relaxed and refreshed by their brief but fulfilling encounters with the sailors, who represent joy
and freedom. Ernest is no longer obsessed with Hilda's
grammar and with such petty conventions as those
which prohibit ladies from smoking in public, and
Hilda comes to see her husband as more interesting
and complex than she had suspected. Previously so
preoccupied with her own lack of fulfillment in mar-

riage, she comes to recognize that Ernest too has secret desires. This understanding illustrates the potential for liberating growth in the escape from oppressive morality.

By concentrating on Hilda's seduction and telling the story from her point of view, Forster emphasizes the equivalence of heterosexual and homosexual expression. The happiness that Hilda feels as a result of her adventure enables her (and the reader) to appreciate the similar contentment obvious in her husband. By revealing only gradually details that cast the events of the story in a new light, Forster not only succeeds in surprising the reader, he also gains power and depth. For instance, the revelation that the obelisk has fallen effectively focuses attention away from an obvious but distant phallic symbol to the mundane but close reality of spontaneous joy in sexual exchanges that are unromantic but spiritually refreshing. "The Obelisk" is a deftly told comedy that is both humorous and wise.

"What Does It Matter? A Morality," an exuberant satire dating from the 1930s, translates the wisdom of "The Obelisk" into a political manifesto. Perhaps influenced by Auden and Isherwood's zany play *The Dog Beneath the Skin*, Forster's bedroom farce hilariously integrates political intrigue and sexual gymnastics. But as the subtitle indicates, the story is also quite serious. Detailing the transformation of the Republic of Pottibakia from a conventionally hypocritical state that breaks treaties and persecutes minorities into a utopian community where freedom reigns, the tale presents in comic form the familiar Forsterian indictment of sexual repression as the source of social disease and personal unhappiness. The secret of Pottibakia's metamorphosis is the discovery that, in God's eyes, "Poking doesn't count." Freed from oppressive morality, the Pottibakians convert natural impulses into national assets, accepting the pursuit of pleasure as a deeply human activity. The story thus attacks the antisexual attitudes that, paradoxically, exaggerate the importance of sex and distort true morality into moralistic prohibitions. Perhaps Forster's most amusing tale, "What Does It Matter" is a considerable achievement, enlivened by unusual energy and sharp wit.

"The Classical Annex" is not as amusing as "What Does It Matter," but it is written in the same jocular vein. A slight fantasy dating from 1930 or 1931, it forcefully juxtaposes Christianity and Hellenism in the opposition of a fastidious curator at the Bigglesmouth Museum and classical statues that miraculously come alive. The sexual antics of the statues shock the curator, who—despite his position—has no appreciation of the Hellenic spirit. He stills the statues by leaping into an early Christian sarcophagus while frantically making the sign of the cross. As James Malek comments, "This contrast between classical objects, whose activities express the joy of life, and Christianity, which kills joyful expression and whose representative is a receptacle for the dead, establishes an early framework for directing our sympathies in the story."[23]

In the comic conclusion, the curator hurriedly performs his ritual in the sarcophagus when he hears his son Denis responding with grunts and giggles to the amorous advances of a male statue. Thus, the curator unthinkingly freezes Denis and the statue in their posture of love, creating of their eternal moment "a Hellenistic group called The Wrestling Lesson [which] became quite a feature at Bigglesmouth."

"The Torque," Forster's only piece of historical fiction (except for the early fragment "The Tomb of Pletone," collected in *Arctic Summer and Other Fiction*), also contrasts Christianity and Hellenism. Perhaps composed as late as 1958, the story is set in early Christian Italy and identifies Christianity with deception, self-aggrandizement, and the suppression of natural instincts. In contrast, the spirit of Hellenism as embodied in a young man named Marcian is associated with truthfulness, respect for others, and the acceptance of sexual expression in all its variety.

The tale opens with the dedication of Marcian's sister Perpetua to a life of virginity after her narrow rescue from the Goths, who, the Bishop asserts, "are membered like horses." The assertion causes Marcian to laugh, for he is in a position to know the truth rather than to accept the Bishop's superstitious fear-mongering. In fact, the celebration is based on a self-serving lie: Perpetua's virginity was not preserved by a miracle but by Marcian's forced submission to Euric, the young leader of the Goths. Hence, Marcian's laugh at the Bishop's description of the Goths' sexual endowment. The rape was not traumatic—"What had happened was not serious," Marcian reflects—and it establishes a bond between the young men that helps them overcome the misunderstanding and bigotry fostered by the Church.

As a token of his affection, Euric presents Marcian a gleaming, golden necklace—the torque of the title. Perpetua grossly misrepresents this gift as a tribute to her virginity. In the story's strained conclusion, the primitive gods avenge themselves on Perpetua for her perversion of the golden torque. While Marcian dreams of sex with Euric, who this time offers himself "to be raped," the torque flickers "with intense luminosity," panicking the household into believing that the basilica is on fire. When the self-important Perpetua enters the church to destroy "the Enemy" and save her people, a thunderbolt reduces the basilica and the virgin to ashes. Marcian dutifully mourns his distinguished sister but thinks "what a relief not to have her about!" In consequence of this delivery, the farm prospers, joy returns, and Marcian and his family are freed from the shackles of Christianity, which decrees that "All fruitfulness and warmth are wrong." Skillfully narrated and boldly—but perhaps too broadly—satiric, "The Torque" is a witty and entertaining tale.

The longest of the late stories is "The Other Boat," which evolved from a novel that Forster began in 1913 and soon abandoned. The story's first section was published in late 1948 in *The Listener* under the title "Entrance to an Unwritten Novel" and in early 1949 in the *New York Times Book Review* as "Cocoanut & Co.: Entrance to an Abandoned Novel." Forster returned to the fragment in 1957 and completed the story in 1958. Despite this long and complicated evolution, "The Other Boat" is an organic whole, betraying no signs of fragmentation or false starts. Indeed, it is Forster's finest achievement in short fiction, the culmination of a lifelong preoccupation with the question of psychological wholeness.

The story recounts the struggle to fuse into wholeness the divided personality of Lionel March, a young army captain en route to India to marry and begin a career in the colonial service. This struggle comes to a crisis in his relationship with Cocoa, a "subtle, supple boy who belonged to no race and always got what he wanted." The two first met as children on "the other boat" returning Lionel with his mother and siblings from India, where they had been abandoned by his father, an army major who "went native somewhere out East and got cashiered."

In the interval between their reunion, Lionel has grown into a handsome soldier, "clean-cut, athletic, good-looking without being conspicuous," the hero of "one of the little desert wars that were becoming too rare." Cocoa, on the other hand, has matured from "a silly idle useless unmanly little boy," as Mrs. March described him on the earlier voyage, into a sensuous, mysterious, wealthy, but classless and effeminate young man. Having nursed his desire for Lionel for years, Cocoa bribes the officials of the *Normannia* to allow Lionel to share his cabin, where he proceeds to awaken the young officer's repressed sexuality. Lionel is shocked by Cocoa's first advances, but as the ship enters the Mediterranean, "resistance weakened," and "in the Red Sea they slept together as a matter of course." Under Cocoa's tutelage, Lionel responds fully to a life of "luxury, gaiety, kindness, unusualness, and delicacy that did not exclude brutal pleasure."

As the *Normannia* nears Bombay, Lionel is forced to choose between his conventional tribal identity and the newly awakened self that has been aroused by his affair with Cocoa, or, in the terms of James Malek's Jungian analysis, between his persona and his shadow.[24] The story pivots on the question of identity. Just as Cocoa has two passports with conflicting information, so does Lionel repress his full identity on his passport, which drops half his name to avoid connection with his disgraced father. When Lionel playfully tells Cocoa, "you're no better than a monkey, and I suppose a monkey can't be expected to know its own name," the mysterious "twister" of no tribal affiliation at all replies: "Lion, he don't know nothing at all. Monkey's got to come along to tell a Lion he's alive." The story in effect dramatizes Lionel's tragically unsuccessful struggle to accept the wholeness of his personality, to become "alive" and thereby escape the death in life of his narrow companions and repressive mother.

Self-fashioning is a difficult task in "The Other Boat," for it is dependent on so many different factors, from genetic predispositions and environmental conditions to socially induced self-images and tribal pressures. Cocoa is painfully aware of this lesson when Lionel departs after their quarrel over the unbolted door to their cabin. "When you come back you will not be you," Cocoa says. He knows that Lionel is still dependent for self-definition on the social approval to which he himself is indifferent, as their conflicting attitudes toward the unbolted door indicate. Cocoa's fear that Lionel will be altered by the social mores of his peers is justified, for the prospect of wholeness frightens Lionel. He knows full well that the discovery of his interracial, homosexual relationship will mean the obliteration of his social identity, just as his father's illicit liaison earned him the social status of a nonperson. As Lionel surveys the English travelers aboard the *Normannia*, he thinks: "How decent and reliable they looked, the folk to whom he belonged! He had been born one of them, he had his work with them, he meant to marry into their caste. If he forfeited their companionship he would become nobody and nothing."

The achievement of wholeness is a heroic quest, one made especially difficult by the conflict between Lionel's secret love for Cocoa and his self-definition as a member of a race-conscious society. The racism rampant on the *Normannia* militates against wholeness, forcing Lionel—whose "colour-prejudices were tribal rather than personal, and only worked when an observer was present"—into a duplicitous life, alternately enjoying sex with his "resident wog" in the magic circle of their cabin and shouting with laughter at racist jokes in the public rooms of the liner. This split in Lionel's personality is apparent when Colonel Arbuthnot remarks of the English sleeping section on the deck, "woe betide anything black that walks this way." Lionel initially replies, "Good night, sir," and then suddenly—unintentionally—blurts out, "Bloody rubbish, leave the kid alone," only finally to apologize to the colonel. These contradictory emotions reflect the conflicts within himself. Lionel's ripening but unwilled love for Cocoa Moraes is forbidden by the mores of his tribe and forces a crisis of identity.

Lionel's crisis is rooted in sexual as well as racial attitudes. Regarding homosexuality as "the worst thing in the world, the thing for which Tommies got given the maximum," his growing recognition of himself as a homosexual is deeply threatening to his sense of identity, especially his image of himself as a soldier. He has been reared to disdain all sexuality. "Hitherto he had been ashamed of being built like a brute," he reflects, relaxing in Cocoa's postcoital embrace: "his preceptors had condemned carnality or had dismissed it as a waste of time, and his mother had ignored its existence in him and all her children; being hers, they had to be pure."

But Lionel is his father's son as well as his mother's, and this dual inheritance reflects the irreconcilable divisions in his personality. He has rejected his father as "cruel and remorseless and selfish and self-indulgent," a description also appropriate to Cocoa, with whom he finds himself in love. But countering this love is his mother, in whose image Lionel has defined himself. The story's most forceful agent of repression and Cocoa's chief—and equally unscrupulous—rival for Lionel's soul, Mrs. March is a formidable figure. Whereas Cocoa represents personal fulfillment and dedication to the pleasure principle, Mrs. March embodies social conformity and adherence to the reality principle.[25] A Freudian carnivore who destroys her children, she is suggestive of the classical Fates, "blind-eyed in the midst of the enormous web she had spun—filaments drifting everywhere, she understood nothing and controlled everything. She had suffered too much and was too high-minded to be judged like other people, she was outside carnality and incapable of pardoning it." Lionel knows that the sight of him "topping a dago" would kill her.

The violent conclusion represents the simultaneous triumph and defeat of both Cocoa and Mrs. March and the tragic waste of Lionel. In the murder-suicide, Lionel desperately attempts to fuse the divisions of his personality into a single whole. What results is an irrational merging that yokes the opposing parts together without unifying them. Provoked by Cocoa's presence in his bunk and by his bite that draws blood, Lionel simultaneously makes love to Cocoa and reenacts his wartime experience "in the desert fighting savages." This double action at once pays tribute to his forbidden love and to the socially approved brutality that helped shape his self-conception. He strangles his lover and then takes his own life: "naked and with the seeds of love on him he dived into the sea."

Lionel's sad fate resolves the divisions between his social self and his real self without reconciling them, for both are unacceptable to him. Appropriately, when Cocoa's body is buried at sea, "It moved northwards—contrary to the prevailing current," and when Mrs. March learns of Lionel's death, "she never mentioned his name again." Unable to face either a life led contrary to prevailing currents or one without tribal identity, Lionel escapes both, a tragic victim of his conflicting impulses. He lacks the heroism necessary to achieve wholeness.

The last story Forster completed, "The Other Boat," is distinguished by consummate artistry. Incorporating the same social criticism that animates all the late tales, it explores with new profundity the psychological effects of racism and homophobia. Beautifully textured and psychologically acute, the story is unparalleled in Forster's short fiction in the depth of its characterization and the subtlety of its rhythms. As Norman Page concludes, "Throughout the entire story, the narrative complexities, symbolic subtleties, and modulations of tone are handled in a masterly fashion; and the struggle for possession of Lionel, involving at once the clash of east and west, upper-class and classless, male and female, is genuinely gripping. It seems to me to be not only Forster's finest story, but by any reckoning a remarkable achievement."[26]

The posthumously published collection concludes with "Three Courses and a Dessert: Being a New and

Gastronomic Version of the Old Game of Consequences," to which Forster contributed the second section of a frolicsome spy story published in *Wine and
Food* in 1944. The final contributor to the four-part
mystery, James Laver, resolves the absurd plot by revealing the murderer of a brigadier general to be none
other than "a sort of novelist" who "didn't like soldiers": E. M. Forster. He has eluded hanging, Laver
explains, because "These writing fellows . . . can get
away with anything."

As a collection, *The Life to Come* is too varied
and uneven to admit of generalizations. It is especially
enriched by the late stories, which reveal Forster as a
writer of great passion, indignant at injustice and un-
compromisingly committed to freedom. Even the apparently facetious tales contain sober truths and such
achievements as "The Life to Come" and "The Other
Boat" attain tragic intensity. Although the stories that
center on homosexual incidents have been scorned and
misread by some critics, they are among Forster's finest works of short fiction. *The Life to Come* contains
conspicuous failures as well as successes, but the posthumous volume is altogether welcome, enlarging as it
does the scope of Forster's accomplishment.

Arctic Summer

In 1980, Elizabeth Heine, with the aid of the late
Oliver Stallybrass, issued a collection of Forster's
fragments, including four unfinished novels. This volume, *Arctic Summer and Other Fiction*, is useful to
have in print, for it makes readily available the novels
and stories that Forster finally abandoned. Unfortunately, however, these fragments are astonishingly
mediocre, and their interest lies almost entirely in the
light they shed on the finished work and on Forster's
development as a writer. To be sure, the fragments

contain sporadic flashes of wit and occasional insights worthy of the completed novels, but such moments are rare, and in total *Arctic Summer and Other Fiction* is disappointing.

Three of the abandoned novels are very early, and they help establish 1904 as the pivotal year in Forster's development. "Nottingham Lace" may date from as early as 1899, when Forster was only twenty years old. A heavy-handed attack on middle-class values and conventions—as epitomized here in a public school suburb named "Sawstone"—the fragment presents a hero of the Philip Herriton-Rickie Elliot mold. The sensitive, dreamy young man is awakened to a new self-confidence and a wider vision by a young school-master of dubious social background. The abandoned work contains in embryo many of the issues later explored in *The Longest Journey*, and as the first effort of so young a writer it is surprisingly absorbing.

Less interesting are the other two early fragments, both of which are crude. "Ralph and Tony" is a violent tale of a weak youth's love for a mountain climber, who is finally revealed to be suffering from a bad heart. Written in the summer of 1903 and set in the Italian Alps, the fragment is faintly reminiscent of *Where Angels Fear to Tread*. The third abandoned novel is "The Tomb of Pletone," a piece of historical fiction set in the fifteenth century. Based on Sigismundo Malatesta's rescue of the tomb of Gemistus Pletho from Mistra, near Sparta, the unfinished novel dates from early 1904. Even more violent than "Ralph and Tony," it was eventually transformed into the elegant and interesting essay "Gemistus Pletho," which was published in *The Independent Review* in 1905. The ineptness of these early efforts is especially noticeable when contrasted with the sure control and polish of *Where Angels Fear to Tread*. This contrast suggests that Forster's development as a novelist was extraordinarily rapid. In less than a year he advanced from the awkward style and confused excesses of "The Tomb of Pletone" to the perfected voice and mastered irony of the first published novel.

Less understandable than the crudities of the early fragments—which are, after all, apprentice work—is the flatness of "Arctic Summer," a novel Forster began in 1910 or 1911, shortly after the publication of *Howards End*. "Arctic Summer" contrasts the heroic man, who lives for chivalry, and the civilized man, who hopes for an Arctic summer of social progress. Presumably Forster intended to connect the passion of an athletic and uneducated soldier, Clesant March, to the prose of an aesthetic and intellectual civil servant, Martin Whitby, and to explore such issues as feminism, militarism, and socialism in a milieu similar to that of *Howards End*. While it is competently written, the fragment never comes alive. In 1951, at the Aldeburgh Festival, Forster read the opening chapters and remarked: "I had got my antithesis all right. . . . But I had not settled what was going to happen, and that is why the novel remains a fragment."

Of the unfinished stories in *Arctic Summer*, only "Little Imber" is of much interest. Perhaps Forster's last effort at writing fiction, it was begun in November 1961, when he was almost eighty-three. A science-fiction fantasy set in the postwar future when most men have perished, it culminates in the successful generation of progeny from a homosexual union. A curiously moving tale, it returns to the question of the physical sterility of homosexuality that so disturbed Rickie Elliot in *The Longest Journey*. In total, the fragments published in *Arctic Summer* provide valuable evidence of Forster's development as a writer and of his failures of inspiration, but they are not of great interest in themselves.

As a writer of short fiction, Forster is uneven. Some of the stories collected in *The Celestial Omni-*

bus, *The Eternal Moment,* and *The Life to Come* are slight and sentimental, but most are at least intriguing, and a few are genuinely distinguished. The short fiction may be especially valuable for the insight it offers into the richness of Forster's imagination and the complexity of his art. Certainly, the stories illuminate the mythic and fantasy elements of the novels and help clarify the romantic base of Forster's vision. But the best of the stories need no defense: "The Celestial Omnibus," "The Road from Colonus," "The Machine Stops," "The Eternal Moment," "The Life to Come," and "The Other Boat" are significant achievements in their own right, and a number of others are only slightly less successful. Visions of other kingdoms, these haunting stories both illuminate the mundane world and imagine alternatives.

9

〰〰〰〰〰〰〰〰〰〰〰〰〰〰〰〰〰〰〰〰〰〰〰〰〰〰〰

Decency Touched with Poetry: The Nonfiction

Because Forster published no novels during the final four decades of his life, his canon is sometimes thought to be small. In fact, however, he was a prolific writer, though after *A Passage to India* he turned almost exclusively to nonfiction. His works of nonfiction include eight books that collectively chart a career remarkable for its breadth of interest and depth of commitment. In these books, Forster emerges as a sensitive and thoughtful critic, a charming yet unsentimental popular historian, a skillful biographer, and an essayist of rare power. As a defender of humane values in the dark days of World War II and the uncertain ones that followed, Forster established himself as a moral presence of continuing relevance, a steadying influence in an unstable world.

The liberal humanism so touchingly articulated in his collections of essays, the tribute to personal relations that is his biography of G. Lowes Dickinson, the aesthetic principles espoused in *Aspects of the Novel* and in the critical essays, the encounters with the East in the Alexandrian books and *The Hill of Devi,* and the account of his family background and early childhood in *Marianne Thornton*: all these help illuminate the novels in various ways. But Forster's nonfiction is valuable without reference to the novels. All of these books are written in the inimitable Forsterian voice, incorporating that elusive quality he discerned in *The Independent Review*: "decency touched with poetry."

Alexandria and *Pharos and Pharillon*

Forster's residence in Alexandria from 1915 to 1919 was a turning point in his life. There he enjoyed his first completely satisfying sexual relationship; met C. P. Cavafy, one of the great poets of the century; and discovered via Alexandria his own passage to India. His years in the fascinating city, so permeated with a sense of the past, where so many traditions—African, Jewish, Greek, and Arabic—mingle into a subtle civilization unique in the world, yielded two books, *Alexandria: A History and a Guide* (1922) and *Pharos and Pharillon* (1923). These books throw considerable light on Forster's preoccupations during a period in which *A Passage to India* was gestated, and they are remarkable in their own right. Forster's comment in *Alexandria* about Theocritus's Fifteenth Idyll is applicable to these works as well: "Only through literature can the past be recovered and here Theocritus, wielding the double spell of realism and of poetry, has evoked an entire city from the dead and filled its streets with men."

As its subtitle indicates, *Alexandria* is both a history and a guide. Since the "sights of Alexandria are in themselves not interesting, but they fascinate when we approach them through the past," Forster cross-references the guide and the history in order to help the reader connect the present and the past. For Forster, the latter is a means by which the former can be understood. Thus, the history is no mere accumulation of facts or simple narrative of events but an interpretation of the past in order to illuminate issues of enduring relevance.

The history of Alexandria covers some 2,250 years, and Forster does not pay equal attention to every era. He concentrates on two periods, the "Greco-Egyptian" (331 B.C.–30 B.C.), which is concerned primarily with Ptolemaic culture, and the "Christian" (30 B.C.–A.D. 641), which "begins with the rule of Rome, and traces the fortunes of Christianity, first as a persecuted and then as a persecuting power." He includes a fascinating interlude on "The Spiritual City," which considers Alexandrian philosophy and religion in terms quite pertinent to *A Passage to India*. The discussions of the Arab period (641–1798) and the modern era are perfunctory. This lack of proportion indicates the book's subjectivity. *Alexandria* provides not a balanced view of Alexandrian history but a record of Forster's own responses to the city. It is, in Wilfred Stone's words, "no impartial book but an Intelligent Tourist's Guide to Humanism, a marshaling of the past to discomfit Sawston and delight Bloomsbury."[1]

More pointedly, *Alexandria* is a meditation inspired by antiquity but focused on timeless questions of human achievement and aspiration. The book is especially interesting for its quick character sketches and firm judgments of historical figures and eras. Octavian, for instance, is summarized as "one of the most odious of the world's successful men," while Alexander and Cleopatra are linked by a quality that transcends all their differences: "the man who created and the woman who lost Alexandria have one element in common: monumental greatness; and between them is suspended, like a rare and fragile chain, the dynasty of the Ptolemies." Cleopatra is exquisitely eulogized as "the last of a secluded and subtle race . . . a flower that Alexandria had taken three hundred years to produce and that eternity cannot wither."

Part of Forster's charm as a historian is his ability to capture the humanity of his historical figures, to render them with the subtlety of literary characters. Perhaps his greatest triumphs in this regard are his presentations of two antagonists. The Emperor Heraclius, who lost Alexandria to Islam, is depicted as a tolerant, sensitive, intelligent leader, susceptible to immobilizing bouts of depression; while Amr, the Arab general who captured the city and then ushered in its decline by turning inland to found Cairo, is sympathetically portrayed as an able administrator and merciful conqueror. The account of Amr's death is especially poignant: "As he lay on his couch a friend said to him: 'You have often remarked that you would like to find an intelligent man at the point of death, and to ask him what his feelings were. Now I ask *you* that question.' Amr replied, 'I feel as if the heaven lay close upon the earth and I between the two, breathing through the eye of a needle.'"

Not surprisingly, Forster finds most congenial those periods in which tolerance, learning, diversity, and peace flourish. Thus he gives high marks to eras that less humanistic observers might dismiss as decadent. He prefers Imperial Rome—"who, despite her moments of madness, brought happiness to the Mediterranean for two hundred years"—to "harsh, ungenerous" Republican Rome, and he finds the dynasty of the Ptolemies possessed of "one element of greatness: it did represent the complex country that it ruled." Forster especially praises the Ptolemaic period's achievements in scholarship and science, declaring the third century B.C. the greatest era of scientific advancement that civilization has ever known: "It did not bring happiness or wisdom: science never does. But it explored the physical universe and harnessed many powers for our use." The Christian period, on the other hand, is characterized as intolerant, schismatic, and hateful. Alexandria provided Christianity with the philosophical sophistication the new religion needed to succeed, and then, ironically, the city paid a catastrophic price for its success.

The most important section of the book is the interlude, "The Spiritual City," which explores various answers to what is described as Alexandria's eternal question, "How can the human be linked with the divine?" This question is, of course, one that haunts Forster's early fiction and is to be central in *A Passage to India*. Philo's response to the question was to create the doctrine of the Logos, which made the Hebrew Jehovah intelligible to the Hellenized Alexandrian Jews. Plotinus, in whom the city finds her highest philosophical expression, answered the question by developing Neoplatonism, which holds that "We are all parts of God, even the stones, though we cannot realise it; and man's goal is to become actually, as he is potentially, divine."

Alexandria's posing of this question to Christianity led to Alexandrian Greek scholars providing sophistication and subtlety and universality to the simple faith of Palestine. Christ was finally offered as the link between God and man, but the interpretation of this link produced such heresies as Arianism and Monophysism and Monothelism, all of which Forster explains lucidly and irreverently. The discussion of Arianism is particularly interesting, for the belief that makes Christ inferior to God the Father and therefore closer to man has been particularly divisive, and its history gives Forster an opportunity to document the violence of Christian disputation. Despite the ultimate expulsion of Arianism from orthodox belief, "the strife still continues in the hearts of men, who always tend to magnify the human in the divine, and it is probable that many an individual Christian to-day is an Arian without knowing it," Forster concludes wistfully.

Alexandria's solution to the question by positing a link between the human and the divine reflects both

her weakness and her strength: "Her weakness: because she had always to be shifting the link up and
down—if she got it too near God it was too far from
man, and *vice versa.* Her strength: because she did cling
to the idea of Love, and much philosophic absurdity,
much theological aridity, must be pardoned to those
who maintain that the best thing on earth is likely to be
the best in heaven." As always, Forster's spirituality is
humanistic at base, centering on the value of love. His
great attraction to Alexandria is rooted in his conception of her as a city of love, and his animus against
Christianity proceeds from its perversion of the creed
of love in its persecution of others, both Christians and
non-Christians. Forster's neglect of the Arab period
stems from Islam's refusal to answer the question of
the link between the human and the divine. The faith
that swept Alexandria into the sea envisions a God who
never stoops to the weakness of love, and the question
is intelligible only to those who require God to be loving as well as powerful.

Forster's discussion of Alexandria as "The Spiritual City" is especially interesting for its anticipations of
A Passage to India, in which his humanistic doctrine of
love is most severely tested and his exploration of spiritual need is most extensive.[2] The novel's contrast of
Mrs. Moore's Christianity and Professor Godbole's
Hinduism is presaged in *Alexandria* by the contrast between Christianity and Neoplatonism: "The Christian
promise is that man shall see God, the Neo-Platonic—
like the Indian—that he shall be God. Perhaps, on the
quays of Alexandria, Plotinus talked with Hindu mer-
chants who came to the town." The history's depiction
of Islam as limited in its ability to penetrate spiritual
complexities also anticipates the novel. And as in the
novel, in *Alexandria* Forster treats all the competing
religious beliefs with a balance of irony and interest,
skepticism and fair-mindedness, tolerating every sys-

tem of belief and condemning only those who are intolerant of others.

The two parts of *Alexandria*—the history and the guide—are bridged by a poem by C. P. Cavafy, "The God Abandons Antony." The first publication of Cavafy in English, the poem is appropriate as an elaboration of Forster's earlier account of Cleopatra but most importantly as evidence of the living vitality of Alexandria's past in her present, particularly in the mind of her great poet obsessed with the past. The spirit of Cavafy, whose poems are haunted by history and by a pervasive sense of loss, permeates Forster's meditations inspired by Alexandria, both in the history and guide and in the companion volume *Pharos and Pharillon*, which includes an essay on the poet who—like Forster himself—always stands "at a slight angle to the universe."

Pharos and Pharillon, though published the year after the appearance of *Alexandria*, consists of Alexandrian vignettes, several of which were written between 1917 and 1919 for *The Egyptian Mail*, the city's English-language newspaper. *Alexandria* compresses the incidents treated at greater length in *Pharos and Pharillon*. Comparing the latter book with the former, the collection of vignettes seems more discursive, more reflective than the history. The collection is divided into two sections. The first—named for the famous lighthouse on Pharos, one of the wonders of the ancient world—consists of meditations on "a few antique events" and objects: the lighthouse, the deification of Alexander, the accession of Ptolemy V, the Jewish embassy to Caligula, and the controversies that embroiled the early Christian church. The second section—named for the obscure successor to Pharos, which slid unnoticed into the Mediterranean in the fourteenth century—concerns modern events and personal impressions of the modern city: the visit of an eighteenth-century lady traveler, Mrs. Eliza Fay; reactions to the cotton exchange; the search for a hashish den; the coming of spring to the desert; the vanished glory of the Rue Rosette; and the work of Cavafy.

The vignettes bear the influence of Lytton Strachey and of Cavafy himself. As Jane Lagoudis Pinchin observes, "Forster uses many Cavafian techniques to create a form that moves between the short story and the historical sketch."[3] Especially Cavafian is the attempt to "glimpse life through the very particular eyes of one human soul grounded in his own soil, at a peculiar—although not necessarily spectacular—moment in time." The vignettes are not equally successful; some are marred by an archness that approaches the precious, as, for example, in "Cotton from the Outside" and "The Den" in the "Pharillon" section. "Epiphany" in the "Pharos" section also suffers from this tendency toward cuteness, though not to the same extent. But the best of the sketches, such as "The Return from Siwa" and "The Solitary Place," are beautifully written and genuinely moving. All these pieces, even the ones employing a gossipy tone and a self-conscious lightness, are shadowed by a vague hint of sadness.

The account of the deification of Alexander, "The Return from Siwa," is an especially delicate blend of straightforward history, insightful characterization, and suggestive prose. The announcement of Alexander's divinity—itself perhaps the result of a priest's bad Greek—transforms the young conqueror from a Hellenist to a universalist: "He wanted not to convert but to harmonize, and conceived himself as the divine and impartial ruler beneath whom harmony shall proceed." Forster adds, "That way lies madness," but in madness Alexander "grows more lovable . . . than before. He has caught, by the unintellectual way, a glimpse of something great."

Forster conceives him finally as a voyager into the

realm of the infinite. The sketch ends by asking whether Alexander's death might not have been his greatest conquest:

When at the age of thirty-three he died, when the expedition that he did not seek stole towards him in the summer-house at Babylon, did it seem to him as after all but the crown of his smaller quests? He had tried to lead Greece, then he had tried to lead mankind. He had succeeded in both. But was the universe also friendly, was it also in trouble, was it calling on him, on him, for his help and his love? The priest of Amen had addressed him as 'Son of God.' What exactly did the compliment mean? Was it explicable this side of the grave?

In this beautifully poised conclusion, Forster's prose approaches the sublime.

The sketches centering on the controversies in the early Christian church contrast the vision of Clement of Alexandria, who "did more than even St. Paul to recommend Christianity to the Gentiles," with the narrow-minded schismatics who succeeded him. Clement hoped that the existing social fabric might pass from pagan to Christian without disruption, a hope that seems in retrospect naive: "Christianity, though she contained little that was fresh doctrinally, yet descended with a double-edged sword that hacked the ancient world to pieces. For she had declared war against two great forces—Sex and the State—and during her complicated contest with them the old order was bound to disappear." Forster's location of the source of antisexual attitudes in Christianity fuels his anger against the Church's intolerance and fanaticism.

The intolerance Forster so despises is perhaps best seen in the career of the ungenerous and violent hero of orthodoxy, St. Athanasius. In persecuting Arius and weaning "the Church from her traditions of scholarship and tolerance," Athanasius earned the Church's profound and characteristic gratitude: "she has coupled his name to a creed with which he had nothing to do—

the Athanasian." Forster's scathing account of Athanasius is provoked in part by a fondness for Arianism, which reflects his persistent concern with loneliness: "By declaring that Christ was younger than God Arius tended to make him lower than God, and consequently to bring him nearer to man—indeed to level him into a mere good man and to forestall Unitarianism. This appealed to the untheologically-minded—to Emperors, and particularly to Empresses. It made them feel less lonely."

The selections in the "Pharillon" section are in general less interesting than those in the first part. Modern Alexandria fails to stir Forster's imagination as vividly as does the ancient city. The long account of Mrs. Eliza Fay in Egypt is, however, lively and delightful. The catty lady, an eighteenth-century emissary from Sawston to the Orient, is a ready-made target for Forster's poisoned pen: she might well have come from one of his early novels. But beneath Forster's gleeful puncturing of her pretentiousness lies a grudging admiration for her exploits. Perhaps the best of the pieces on modern Alexandria is "The Solitary Place," a meditation on the flowers in the desert, on "the quiet persistence of the earth."

The brief essay on Cavafy that concludes the volume is of great historical importance. More than anyone else, Forster deserves credit for bringing this major poet to the attention of the English public. He presents Cavafy as a poet of extreme subjectivity and as a Hellenist but not a classicist: "He even looks back upon a different Greece. Athens and Sparta, so drubbed into us at school, are to him two quarrelsome little slave states, ephemeral beside the Hellenistic kingdoms that followed them, just as these are ephemeral beside the secular empire of Constantinople. He reacts against the tyranny of Classicism—Pericles and Aspasia and Themistocles and all those bores." Cavafy's complex view of history undoubtedly helped broaden Forster's own views of the past.

In Forster's writing about Cavafy there is the excitement of discovery and surprise. Rather than analyze Cavafy's poems, Forster quotes. But what now seems most striking about the essay is, in fact, what it does not say or quote. Forster is silent on the homoeroticism that pervades Cavafy's poetry, and he chooses for publication three poems on nonsexual subjects. This is understandable, of course, in light of Forster's inability to publish his own homoerotic novel, but their shared homosexuality was surely one of the ways in which Forster and Cavafy jointly stood "at a slight angle to the universe."

Forster's residence in Alexandria was probably a necessary prerequisite to writing his great novel. The Alexandrian books testify to a new breadth of interest in the East, in the past, in the philosophical and theological, all of which are developed in the masterpiece. But *Alexandria* and *Pharos and Pharillon* are significant beyond their interest as precursors of *A Passage to India*. They are not great books or even large ones, but they contain some superb writing, and they are a fitting tribute to the beguiling city that enlarged Forster's vision.

Aspects of the Novel

Aspects of the Novel (1927), the Clark lectures that Forster presented at Trinity College, Cambridge, in 1927, is Forster's most sustained critical statement. The colloquial style and extraordinary charm of the book, and its mask as a "ramshackle course," disguise its ambition. Choosing "the title 'Aspects' because it is unscientific and vague, because it leaves us the maximum of freedom, because it means both the different ways

we can look at a novel and the different ways a novelist can look at his work," Forster eschews critical systems and theoretical rigor in favor of a relaxed and
personal approach. But *Aspects of the Novel* is actually an ideological work, revealing the Forsterian aesthetic and implicitly defending his own practice in that
elusive medium the novel, a "spongy tract" of land
lying between the mountains of poetry and history and
bounded on a third side by the sea of prophetic song to
which it aspires but rarely achieves.

The novel's failure to attain the purity of music
haunts the book. Forster's rueful knowledge of the limitations of the novel colors all the lectures with a vague
sense of dissatisfaction, creating a complex tone of
voice not dissimilar to that of the novels, in which even
the comedy is shadowed by hints of sadness. Forster
actually employs several tones of voice in the lectures,
from the ironic to the mocking to the comic to the admiring, but they are tinged with a sadness that suggests
futility. This sense of futility is at the heart of the romantic ideology that informs both *Aspects of the
Novel* and Forster's own fiction; it reflects a disaffection with mundane life and a yearning for ontological
completeness. Thus, in *Aspects of the Novel*, Forster
devotes two interludes between the discussions of such
technical aspects as plot and pattern to kinds of novels
that transcend technique and demand the reader's responsiveness to visions of wholeness: fantasy and
prophecy. The romantic ideology espoused obliquely
here not only justifies the fantasy and prophetic elements so prominent in Forster's own work, it also represents the spiritual base of the eclecticism characteristic of *Aspects of the Novel*.

Forster's eclecticism combines humanism and
formalism in an uneasy alliance.[4] The lectures are
united by the idea "that there are in the novel two
forces: human beings and a bundle of various things

that are not human beings, and that it is the novelist's business to adjust these two forces and conciliate their claims." Throughout the series, Forster returns to this duality, hoping somehow to reconcile the fictive and the human in fiction. "In most literary works," he writes, "there are two elements: human individuals . . . and the element vaguely called art." Virginia Woolf and other readers have complained that Forster treats art slightingly, but the subordination of the "bundle of various things that are not human beings" is characteristic of his humanism.[5] For Forster, the novel's supreme goal is to transcend form and mediate the human and the divine, a goal finally revealed as prophecy.

Forster begins the book by rejecting literary history as a helpful approach to understanding the novel, offering instead a striking image of all the novelists sitting together in a circular room writing their novels at once. "History develops, art stands still," he declares. Unfortunately, however, the novel cannot escape time, for "as soon as fiction is completely delivered from time it cannot express anything at all." Indeed, the fundamental aspect of the novel is the story, "a narrative of events arranged in time sequence." Forster wishes that the fundamental aspect might be "melody, or perception of the truth" rather than "this low atavistic form," but he concludes ruefully, "Yes— oh, dear, yes—the novel tells a story." This regretful tone persists throughout the series as Forster notes the limitations of the novel bound by time and logic and people and art. The ideal novel would be beyond words and technique.

Not surprisingly, Forster speaks insightfully about problems of technique, but always he connects the technical to larger issues. For instance, in his two lectures on people in the novel, his discussion of literary characters is never divorced from his awareness of people in real life and his conviction that people are supremely important for a medium "sogged with humanity." The salient difference between "Homo Sapiens" and "Homo Fictus" is that we can know more about a fictional character than about a real person. We can never fully understand a fellow human being, but "people in a novel can be understood completely by the reader, if the novelist wishes; their inner as well as their outer life can be exposed. And this is why they often seem more definite than characters in history, or even our own friends." Because the secret lives of literary characters are visible, "novels, even when they are about wicked people, can solace us; they suggest a more comprehensible and thus a more manageable human race, they give us the illusion of perspicacity and power." This explanation of literature's ability to alleviate mankind's loneliness and bewilderment is deeply revealing of Forster's concerns in his own novels and of the humanistic bias in his criticism.

The second lecture on people in the novel is more technical than the first, and it culminates in Forster's famous distinction between flat and round characters. In their purest form, flat characters are constructed around a single idea or quality; they are easily recognizable and easily remembered, and they are usually comic. The test of a round character is "whether it is capable of surprising in a convincing way," whether it "has the incalculability of life about it." The novelist uses both kinds in his task of harmonizing "the human race with the other aspects of his work."

Forster next turns to plot, the novel in its "logical, intellectual aspect." Like a story, a plot is also a narrative of events, but with the addition of causality: "'The king died and then the queen died' is a story. 'The king died, and then the queen died of grief' is a plot. The time sequence is preserved, but the sense of causality overshadows it. . . . Consider the death of the queen.

If it is in a story we say 'and then?' If it is in a plot we ask 'why?' That is the fundamental difference between these two aspects of the novel." A story provokes our curiosity, but a plot demands intelligence and memory. The novel in its logical aspect is unsatisfying to Forster. "Cannot it grow? . . . Cannot it open out? . . . Cannot fiction devise a framework that is not so logical yet more suitable to its genius," Forster asks, longing for a more organic framework than that of conscious control. As Wilfred Stone remarks, these wistful questions "remind us of the spiritual ambitions behind Forster's esthetics. He wants the work of art to show God's handiwork, not man's."[6]

The consideration of technical aspects of fiction is interrupted by the interludes, "one gay, one grave," on the subjects of fantasy and prophecy. In the lecture on fantasy, Forster turns to a form of fiction that "asks us to pay something extra. It compels us to an adjustment that is different to an adjustment required by a work of art, to an additional adjustment." Fantasy includes not only time and people and logic but also an oddness of method or subject matter. Presided over by the small gods of muddle, fantasy implies the supernatural but need not express it. It unites "the kingdoms of magic and commonsense." As examples of fantasy, Forster cites novels as diverse as *Tristram Shandy, Zuleika Dobson,* and *Ulysses.*

Forster distinguishes between fantasy and prophecy by means of their different mythologies:

on behalf of fantasy let us now invoke all beings who inhabit the lower air, the shallow water, and the smaller hills, all Fauns and Dryads and slips of the memory, all verbal coincidences, Pans and puns, all that is medieval this side of the grave. When we come to prophecy, we shall utter no invocation, but it will have been to whatever transcends our abilities, even when it is human passion that transcends them, to the deities of India, Greece, Scandinavia and Judaea, to all that is medieval beyond the grave and to Lucifer son of the morning.

Clearly, Forster's critical interest here parallels the Alexandrian question, "How can the human be linked to the divine?"

It is prophecy's ability to harmonize the human and the divine that makes it the novel's highest achievement. Prophecy, which has nothing to do with foretelling the future, is "an accent in the novelist's voice, an accent for which the flutes and saxophones of fantasy may have prepared us." The prophet's theme is the universe, "but he is not necessarily going to 'say' anything about the universe; he proposes to sing, and the strangeness of song arising in the halls of fiction is bound to give us a shock." Prophecy "reaches back" beyond the phenomenal world, and "it gives us the sensation of a song or a sound. It is unlike fantasy because its face is toward unity." Forster's prophets are Dostoevsky, Melville, D. H. Lawrence, and Emily Brontë. Prophecy is achieved very rarely, and at the cost of the reader's pride and sense of humor and of the novelist's conscious art.

Following these interludes on kinds of fiction that demand "something extra" from the reader, Forster returns to a technical discussion, this time of pattern and rhythm. By pattern, he refers to the shape of the plot, such as the "hour-glass" shape of Anatole France's *Thaïs*, or the rigid pattern of James's *The Ambassadors*, bought—Forster alleges—at the expense of character. Pattern is an external and mechanical imposition of form, while rhythm is an internal and organic stitching that unifies the novel. More fluid than pattern and less rigid than symbol, rhythm can impart surprising beauty. Forster's chief example of rhythm is the recurring "little phrase" from the music of Vinteuil in Proust's *Remembrance of Things Past*, though his own novels provide excellent examples of the consummate practice of rhythm.

Aspects of the Novel is extraordinarily well-written, amusing and lively as well as rueful in tone. Throughout, the book is enlivened by sharp judgments and original insights on particular works and individual authors. Especially interesting are his comments on Lawrence and Austen and Meredith and Sterne, on *Billy Budd* and *Moby Dick* and *The Brothers Karamazov* and *Moll Flanders*. Even when his criticism is eccentric or unfair—as in the attack on James or the belittlement of Scott and George Eliot—it is intriguing and suggestive. Forster's comments on the technical aspects are always informed by his own practical experience as well as by thoughtful reflection, and his expositions on flat and round characters, pattern and rhythm, plot and story are justly well known. Yet the heart of the book is the discussion of fantasy and prophecy, a discussion that implicitly defends Forster's own works and reflects the romantic ideology that informs both his theory and his practice of fiction.

Goldsworthy Lowes Dickinson

Forster's 1934 biography of G. Lowes Dickinson is a graceful portrait of a "beloved, affectionate, unselfish, intelligent, witty, charming" friend, whose full but uneventful life provides the occasion for a tribute to the idealistic humanism that Dickinson and Forster jointly espoused and embodied. Of a slightly older generation than Forster, Dickinson was born in 1862 and died in 1932. He spent most of his life associated with Cambridge, where he developed into an extraordinary teacher of undergraduates and a significant influence. A minor poet and playwright, he is best known for several scholarly and political works, including *The Greek View of Life* (1896), *Letters from John Chinaman* (1901), *A Modern Symposium* (1905), *The European Anarchy* (1916), and *After Two Thousand Years*

(1930), as well as for his role in helping establish the League of Nations.

Forster judiciously assesses Dickinson's books and public life and concedes that they do not in themselves demand commemoration by a biography. But, he adds of his friend, "He was an indescribably rare being, he was rare without being enigmatic, he was rare in the only direction which seems to be infinite: the direction of the Chorus Mysticus. He did not merely increase our experience: he left us more alert for what has not yet been experienced and more hopeful about other men because he had lived."

Forster's biography is, in effect, an extended essay on the value of personal relations, on the incalculable impact of a relatively obscure don on the lives of his friends. Fittingly, the book is intensely personal without ever being cliquish. The tone is carefully controlled to maintain the semblance of objectivity, and Forster never exaggerates Dickinson's achievements in the public arena. The biography is finally a moving and generous assessment of a sensitive and sympathetic person, naturally gifted with the holiness of the heart's affections. The book's interest thus lies less in its careful chronicle of Dickinson's public life and varied accomplishments than in his emergence as a Forsterian hero. Dickinson and Forster share much in common—background, temperament, Cambridge, romanticism, and a penchant for mysticism as well as political and aesthetic interests—and the biography may be seen as a complex and oblique experiment in autobiography in which Forster portrays his friend in his own image.[7]

This autobiographical dimension may explain the book's central weakness as a biography of Dickinson: the suppression of its subject's strong and complex sexuality. Forster based his book on Dickinson's "Recollections," autobiographical materials that Dickinson left to Forster to use at his discretion. Now that this material has been published, it is possible to see how much Forster conceals.[8] In the biography, Forster tactfully hints at Dickinson's homosexuality, but he obscures its crucial role in Dickinson's life, a role pointedly emphasized in the "Recollections." The biography's reticence is understandable in 1934. Many of the men whom Dickinson loved—most prominent among them Roger Fry, the artist and critic—were still alive, as were members of Dickinson's family. But the concealment seriously mars the value of the book as an honest account of Dickinson's life, and it may be as attributable to Forster's own desire for privacy as to a concern to spare Dickinson's reputation.

The depictions of Dickinson's misery at public school and his liberation at Cambridge are reminiscent of Forster's own experiences, especially as distilled in *The Longest Journey*. When Forster writes of the Cambridge of Dickinson's day, he speaks movingly, conflating Dickinson's recollections with his own personal knowledge: "As Cambridge filled up with friends it acquired a magic quality. Body and spirit, reason and emotion, work and play, architecture and scenery, laughter and seriousness, life and art—these pairs which are elsewhere contrasted were there fused into one. People and books reinforced one another, intelligence joined hands with affection, speculation became a passion, and discussion was made profound by love." Cambridge is not the great world nor even "the world in miniature," but unlike Tibby Schlegel's Oxford, it offers not "the memory of a colour scheme" but a lasting radiance.

Similarly, the account of Dickinson's membership in the Apostles is informed by Forster's own experience in the society and helps explain how the author's undergraduate associations left so lasting an impact on him:

The young men seek truth rather than victory, they are willing to abjure an opinion when it is proved untenable, they do not try to score off one another, they do not feel diffi-

dence too high a price to pay for integrity; and according to
some observers that is why Cambridge has played, compar-
atively speaking, so small a part in the control of world affairs. Certainly these societies represent the very antithesis of
the rotarian spirit. No one who has once felt their power will
ever become a good mixer or a yes-man. Their influence,
when it goes wrong, leads to self-consciousness and super-
ciliousness; when it goes right, the mind is sharpened, the
judgment is strengthened, and the heart becomes less selfish.
There is nothing specially academic about them, they exist in
other places where intelligent youths are allowed to gather
together unregimented, but in Cambridge they seem to generate a peculiar clean light of their own which can remain
serviceable right on into middle age.

At the beginning of the century, Dickinson helped
found *The Independent Review*, a political and literary journal designed "as an appeal to Liberalism from
the Left to its better self—one of those appeals which
have continued until the extinction of the Liberal party."
In an important digression on the influence of the new
journal on his generation, Forster reveals how rampant
idealism was in the early years of the century as he
began his writing career, a hopefulness destined to be
dashed by the Great War.

We were being offered something which we wanted. Those
who were Liberals felt that the heavy, stocky body of their
party was about to grow wings and leave the ground. Those
who were not Liberals were equally filled with hope: they
saw avenues opening into literature, philosophy, human relationships, and the road of the future passing through not in-
surmountable dangers to a possible utopia. Can you imagine
decency touched with poetry? It was thus that the 'Independent' appeared to us—a light rather than a fire, but a light
that penetrated the emotions. Credit must be given to [Ed-
ward] Jenks, an able and a pernickety editor, and to his colleagues, but the inspiration was Dickinson's. The first
number lies on the table as I write: as fresh and attractive to

hold as when I bought it on a bookstall at St Pancras thirty
years back, and thought the new age had begun.

Forster accompanied Dickinson to India in 1912.
It was the first encounter of both men with the subcontinent, and the trip influenced Forster profoundly. The
account of their journey in *Goldsworthy Lowes Dickinson* sheds light on *A Passage to India* and suggests
that Dickinson's response to India helped shape the
novel. They visited the Maharajah of Chhatarpur, and
Forster's description of the maharajah in the biography evokes the novel's persistent concern with the
Friend who never comes: "The Maharajah was a tiny
and fantastic figure, incompetent, rusé, exasperating,
endearing. He lived for philosophy and love, and he
hoped that the two were one. . . . 'Tell me, Mr. Dickinson, where is God? Can Herbert Spencer lead me to
him, or should I prefer George Henry Lewes? Oh
when will Krishna come and be my friend?' I found
these questions grotesque, but Dickinson attuned them
to his own Platonism, and there was instant sympathy."

Dickinson finally came to find India incomprehensible and disorienting, especially the tendency of
nature to overwhelm distinctions between the human
and the animal. He wrote to an elderly lady, suggestively named Mrs. Moor, about a wasp and declared
that "If there's a God, or gods, they're beyond my ken.
I think perhaps, after all, the Hindus took in more of
the facts in their religion than most people have done.
But they too are children, like the rest of us." To
another correspondent he wrote: "Anglo-Indian society is the devil. . . . It's the women more than the
men that are at fault. There they are, without their
children, with no duties, no charities, with empty
minds and hearts, trying to fill them by playing tennis
and despising the natives." Dickinson's reactions to
India undoubtedly affected Forster's own response
and became transmuted into the novel.

The Great War profoundly depressed Dickinson and spurred him to work tirelessly for the establishment of a League of Nations. Forster dutifully records his friend's efforts but seems considerably more skeptical. He finally depicts Dickinson as memorable not for his scholarship and political activism but for the private virtues that motivated his work in the world: "What he cared for was love and truth. What he hoped for was a change in the human heart. He did not see how the civilisation which he had tried to help could be saved unless the human heart changed, and he meant by 'saved' not some vague apotheosis but salvation from aerial bombing and poison gas." Dickinson's desperate faith in the Audenesque imperative—"a change of heart"—is itself a public manifestation of the private devotion to love and truth that earns him his role as Forsterian hero.

The biography concludes with a selection of Dickinson's letters, including two interesting responses to Virginia Woolf's *The Waves* and several meditations on death. These letters, Forster remarks, "tend to exhibit him as merely sympathetic and kind"; they are a misleading substitute for his magical gifts of friendship: "When he spoke to his friends or spoke of them all altered at once; he vibrated to wave after wave, and as he turned his head from guest to guest at one of his lunch parties one felt that a new universe was seated on every chair. That was his strength, that was his glory, and if that could be communicated in a biography, he would appear for what he was: one of the rarest creatures of our generation."

Forster's life of Dickinson is seriously marred by the concealment of the strong sexual impulse that influenced many aspects of Dickinson's personality and work. But as a graceful tribute to a friend, as a meditation on friendship, as a review of the idealism and humanism that shaped the lives of both author and subject, *Goldsworthy Lowes Dickinson* is altogether successful. A revealing though oblique experiment in autobiography, the book tells us as much about Forster as about Dickinson.

Abinger Harvest

The 1936 collection of essays and reviews entitled *Abinger Harvest* is a rich mine of Forsterian insights and attitudes. Although it includes very early work as well as late, it may be most valuable as evidence of Forster's redirection of his career from novelist to essayist and literary journalist. Containing some eighty items that vary in quality and in ambition from the frivolous and the whimsical to the impressive and the serious, the volume as a whole is a remarkable miscellany. Witnessing to the vitality of Forster's liberalism even into the low, dishonest decade of the 1930s, *Abinger Harvest* is the record of a sensitive and courageous individual's broad interests and deep concern.

The collection is divided into five sections. The first is entitled "The Present" and includes essays on "passing events," on politics and the role of the artist in a troubled time. The section labeled "Books" collects criticism and appreciations of writers, mostly contemporary. "The Past" presents meditations on history and historical figures, similar in technique and imagination to those in *Pharos and Pharillon*, while "The East" collects essays and reviews concerned with the Orient. The final section presents "Abinger Pageant," a celebration of the Surrey village in which Forster lived most of his life and which provides the title for the volume as a whole.

Perhaps the strongest section of the book is the first, which reveals Forster as an acute and penetrating observer of his age. The items in this group excoriate

English insularity, prudery, class consciousness, hypocrisy, and imperialism. They state explicitly the political values that underlie the novels and that inform
Forster's entire career. The most important of these essays are "Notes on the English Character," "My Wood,"
"Me, Them and You," "Our Graves in Gallipoli," and
"Liberty in England."

The opening essay, "Notes on the English Character," is one of Forster's finest pieces, an incisive dissection of the limitations of the English upper middle
classes, who are ill equipped to "go forth into a world
that is not entirely composed of public-school men or
even of Anglo-Saxons, but of men who are as various
as the sands of the sea; into a world of whose richness
and subtlety they have no conception. They go forth
into it with well-developed bodies, fairly developed
minds, and undeveloped hearts." The Englishman is
finally diagnosed as incomplete in his inability to express emotion or to connect with the unseen. In "My
Wood," Forster ruminates gently and ruefully on the
psychological effects of owning property. For all its
charm and apparent slightness, this essay raises serious
issues that confront the liberal who believes both in socialism and in individuality.

"Me, Them and You" and "Our Graves in Gallipoli" are fierce denunciations of militarism. The first
and stronger piece was occasioned by Forster's visit to
John Singer Sargent's 1925 exhibit at the Royal
Academy. Displayed amid portraits of the powerful
and the socially prominent—"Them persons what
governs us, them dukes and duchesses and arch-
bishops and generals and captains of industry"—was a
large painting entitled "Gassed," which featured at its
center a lower-class soldier, the "You" of the title.
Forster finds this painting obscene, for it tidies up and
romanticizes war and the class divisions that war exploits: "You were of godlike beauty—for the upper

classes only allow the lower classes to appear in art on
condition that they wash themselves and have classical
features. . . . A line of golden-haired Apollos moved
along a duck-board from left to right with bandages
over their eyes. . . . No one complained, no one
looked lousy or overtired, and the aeroplanes over-
head struck the necessary note of the majesty of England. It was all a great war picture should be, and it
was modern because it managed to tell a new sort of
lie."

The companion piece, "Our Graves in Gallipoli,"
was occasioned by a 1922 Anglo-Turkish crisis. In a
bitter but sentimental dialogue between two dead
soldiers, one British and one Turkish, Forster attacks
the militarism on which imperialism rests. Satirizing
the attempt of Lloyd George and Winston Churchill—
the politician Forster most despised—to justify military action on the pretext of protecting the sanctity of
"our graves in Gallipoli," the dialogue reveals the hypocrisy of such sloganeering and its cynicism: "Nothing for schools, nothing for the life of the body, nothing for the spirit. England cannot spare a penny for
anything except for her heroes' graves."

"Liberty in England," an address delivered in
1935 to the International Writers Conference in Paris, is
a major statement on the precariousness of English
freedom and on the role of the artist in a perilous time.
Forster begins by acknowledging how race-bound and
class-bound English liberty is, conceding that "Freedom in England is only enjoyed by people who are
fairly well off." He distinguishes between fascism,
which "does evil that evil may come," and commu-
nism, which "does many things which I think evil, but
. . . intends good." Declaring himself a liberal, one
who cares about the past and about the preservation
and extension of individual freedom, he declares that
the threat to English liberty lies not in fascism but in

"the dictator-spirit working quietly away behind the
facade of constitutional forms, passing a little law (like
the Sedition Act) here, endorsing a departmental tyranny there, emphasizing the national need of secrecy
elsewhere, and whispering and cooing the so-called
'news' every evening over the wireless, until opposition is tamed and gulled."

Tellingly, Forster illustrates his point by focusing
not on an obvious erosion of political liberty such as
the Sedition Act but on the censorship of *Boy*, a homoerotic novel by James Hanley, which he admired. He
also cites the suppression of such works as Hall's *The
Well of Loneliness*, D. H. Lawrence's *Rainbow*, and
Joyce's *Ulysses*. "I want greater freedom for writers,
both as creators and as critics," he declares. "In England, more than elsewhere, their creative work is ham-
pered because they can't write freely about sex, and I
want it recognized that sex is a subject for serious
treatment and also for comic treatment."

Forster's concentration on sexual censorship is il-
luminating, and not merely because of his inability to
publish his own homoerotic novel and stories. It indicates his awareness of the political implications of sexuality. His determined posing of a question of freedom
that is so often obscured or dismissed as frivolous or irrelevant by the economic utopians of the left is both an
act of courage—especially since the conference was
dominated by communists—and a sign of Forster's
radical insight into the nature of repression.

Forster's courage is equally apparent when he acknowledges that the war looming on the world's horizon may sweep away "writers of the individualistic
and liberalizing type" but nevertheless asserts a central
tenet of his liberal humanism: "One must behave as if
one is immortal, and as if civilization is eternal. Both
statements are false—I shall not survive, no more will
the great globe itself—both of them must be assumed

to be true if we are to go on eating and working and travelling, and keep open a few breathing holes for the human spirit." This essay, written at a time when the ideals of liberalism and freedom were under attack from both the right and the left, illustrates Forster's own fulfillment of the writer's "public calling": to be sensitive and courageous. "Liberty in England" remains equally pertinent a half century later, when individual freedom and sexual expression are once again under attack by censors on all sides of the political spectrum.

The second section, "Books," opens strongly with "A Note on the Way," an essay similar in tone to "Liberty in England." Examining the utility of books and music in 1934, when the world was passing through "perhaps the roughest time that has ever been," Forster affirms that art, like the inner life in *Howards End*, actually pays. Art is "not enough, any more than love is enough," he admits, but he adds that "art, love and thought can all do something, and art, the most nervous of the three, mustn't be brushed aside like a butterfly." Part of "our outfit against brutality," literature can transport us into "a country where the will is not everything." This faith in art is not a form of escapism but a sophisticated refinement of Matthew Arnold's belief in literature's power to "prop" the mind. "Literature as a retreat is rightly discredited; it is both selfish and foolish to bury one's head in the flowers," Forster asserts, and then continues: "But herbs grow in the garden, too, and share in its magics, and from them is distilled the stoicism which we badly need today."

The considerations of individual writers are invariably interesting and sometimes brilliantly perceptive. Forster reads with great sympathy and fine intelligence, and his remarks on such important contemporaries as Eliot, Proust, Woolf, and Conrad are revealing. Equally interesting are his generous appreciations of

lesser writers and friends—Forrest Reid, Ronald Firbank, Howard Overing Sturgis, and T. E. Lawrence—
in whom he often discovers individual voices and genuine but insufficiently recognized achievements. The
essay on Reid celebrates the Belfast novelist's delicate
supernaturalism, while the account of Sturgis—"this
brilliant sensitive and neglected writer"—stresses the
psychological realism of *Belchamber*. The essay on
Lawrence is, fittingly, as personal as it is literary; he
finds his late friend possessed of "the three heroic
virtues: courage, generosity, and compassion" and
Seven Pillars of Wisdom a "sacred volume." His appreciation of Firbank is deliberately uncritical: "To
break a butterfly, or even a beetle, upon a wheel is a
delicate task," Forster writes, and concludes of Firbank's work: "It is frivolous stuff, and how rare, how
precious is frivolity! How few writers can prostitute all
their powers!" Firbank's prostitution consists of his
total absorption "in his own nonsense" and his consequent rejection of the "realistic lumber" of the modern
novel.

Forster hails Proust as the greatest artist of his day,
declaring that *Remembrance of Things Past* "expresses the spirit of our age." He questions whether
Proust makes "enough allowance for a certain good
sense that persists in the human organism even when it
is heated by passion? Does he not lay too much stress
on jealousy?" He concludes that the "curiosity of
Proust was not quite the same as yours and mine, but
then he was not as nice as you and me and he was also
infinitely more sensitive and intelligent." In a note on
Conrad, Forster suggests that the writer's obscurity
may proceed from a mistiness at the center of his vision.

The essays on Woolf and Eliot are penetrating and
exacting. Forster recognizes in these contemporaries
great ambition and consequently holds them to very
high standards. They are both praised as innovators,

but each is finally judged to be seriously deficient. Forster is deeply ambivalent toward Eliot, objecting to his deliberate obscurity, "his approval of institutions deeply rooted in the State," and "the inhospitality of his writing." Significantly, however, Forster recognizes what recent scholarship has confirmed: despite Eliot's theory of the impersonality of the poet, *The Waste Land* is a "personal comment on the universe, as individual and as isolated as Shelley's *Prometheus*." For his close friend Virginia Woolf, Forster feels great sympathy, but he questions whether she can create character. She has mastered the technique of getting inside her characters' minds, but they do not live continuously.

The section on "Books" concludes with a consideration of Jane Austen, in whose presence Forster abandons all attempts at objectivity. "I am a Jane Austenite, and therefore slightly imbecile about Jane Austen," he declares. "She is my favorite author! I read and re-read, the mouth open and the mind closed." He greets R. W. Chapman's new, scholarly edition of the six novels with enthusiasm, though he deplores the occasional appearance of pedantry. Reviewing Chapman's edition of the letters, he remarks, "Naturally, when one invests in a concern one comes to value it, and Mr. Chapman is not exempt from this sensible rule. He has contended with the subject manfully, like St. Paul at Ephesus; and would he have done so if it was not worth while?" No, Forster reluctantly confesses, the letters are not very good, being "catalogues of trivialities which do not come alive." Jane Austen is a superb novelist, but Miss Austen the letter writer "has not enough subject-matter on which to exercise her powers." Interestingly, Forster finds in the posthumously published fragment *Sanditon*, written during Austen's final illness, some evidence of a broadening concern with economic and geographic forces.

The third section, "The Past," begins with an engaging essay, "The Consolations of History," which explains why history is so attractive to the timid: "We can recover self-confidence by snubbing the dead." Forster himself rarely indulges in this practice; the sense of actuality is too strong to allow him to make history a vehicle for escapism or even to revel in the more exquisite pleasure of pitying the dead. Although frequently whimsical and ironic in his historical recreations, he never condescends to the past or romanticizes it.

Some of his best meditations on history are the early vignettes, "Macolnia Shops," "Cnidus," "Gemisthus Pletho," and "Cardan." In these pieces, he recreates earlier ages with the skill of a novelist and discovers in the ancient world wisdom relevant to the modern. In "Macolnia Shops," for instance, he deduces from the decorations on a beautiful bronze toilet case the Greek ideals of bodily fitness—"cherish the body and you will cherish the soul"—and of friendship, while in "Cnidus" he bears witness to the living vitality of mythology, specifically of the Demeter myth that so haunts his novels. In "Gemisthus Pletho" and "Cardan," Forster presents mini-biographies of fascinating eccentrics without ever making them seem merely odd.

The essays on Voltaire, Gibbon, Coleridge, and Keats evoke a more recent past than the earlier vignettes, but with the same gift of narrative and insight into character. Forster honors Voltaire as an early popularizer of science and Gibbon as a "genius who read, dreamed, and also knew—knew by direct contact, a fragment of the rough stuff of society, and extended his knowledge through the ages." The sketches featuring Coleridge and Keats playfully conceal their identities until the end, presenting each at an obscure but characteristic moment in his life. The Keats vignette, "Mr. and Mrs. Abbey's Difficulties," adopts the viewpoint of Keats's Sawstonian guardians and presents the poet only through letters to his sister Fanny. Coleridge appears under his assumed name Silas Tomkyn Comberbacke during his disastrous enlistment in the cavalry. The Keats and Coleridge pieces are amusing and interesting, but the technique of concealment induces a self-consciousness that approaches the cloying.

The final two essays in "The Past" are on subjects that impact on Forster's personal history, his family's Clapham Sect background. In "Mrs. Hannah More," he evaluates the lively and tireless woman who was the godmother of his equally active great-aunt Marianne Thornton. Hannah More epitomizes for Forster both the indubitable virtues and obvious limitations of his evangelical Christian heritage. Devoted to good works in the world, she lacks imagination and genuine love. Of her work with the poor, whom she helped but without real sympathy or respect, Forster writes with a great deal of irony: "If the destruction of instinct and the creation of an interest in the outside world are good things, then her work must be praised, for she effected the beginnings of both." In identifying the Clapham Sect with the destruction of instinct, Forster locates Sawston in his own background.

In "Battersea Rise," Forster meditates on the Thornton family home, which became the headquarters of the Clapham Sect. In the great oval library designed by William Pitt, such evangelical reformers as William Wilberforce, James Stephen, Zachary Macaulay, Thomas Babington, and Hannah More would gather to plan their philanthropies. "Riches, evangelical piety, genuine goodness, narrowness, integrity, censoriousness, clannishness, and a noble public spirit managed to flourish together in its ample bosom without mutual discomfort," Forster writes, adding up the movement's assets and liabilities. He admires his ancestors' commitment to such good causes as abolition of the slave trade, but he finds unattractive their obliviousness to the unseen (despite their religiosity) and their indifference to art and literature "unless it was of an intellectual or formative character." In 1907, the house itself fell victim to London sprawl, the fate that haunts Howards End itself. Of Battersea Rise, he concludes that "it has neither played a leading part in national life, nor has it produced any outstanding individual. It was just the abode of an unusually upright and intelligent middle-class family. . . . London knocked and everything vanished—vanished absolutely, for the Thorntons do not approve of ghosts."

The penultimate section, "The East," opens with a "Salute to the Orient," which emphasizes the complexity of the East and the legacy of mistrust engendered by Western insincerity and exploitation. This opening essay is especially interesting for its review of Western literature about the East, for a discussion of the role of women in the Orient, and for its shrewd political analysis. In a revealing contrast of Moslem and Hindu religious ideals, Forster explains the importance of personal relations to Moslems, for whom the self is precious. Whereas Hindus long for union with God, Moslems "do not seek to be God or even to see Him. Their meditation, though it has the intensity and aloofness of mysticism, never leads to abandonment of personality." This contrast helps explain some key differences in the characterizations of Professor Godbole and Dr. Aziz in *A Passage to India*.

Other essays in the section on the Orient consider the architecture and function of the mosque, the exploits of such Westerners in the East as Wilfrid Blunt and Marco Polo, the scandalous theft of Egyptian antiquities by the British Museum, the work of Rabindranath Tagore, the Bhagavad-Gita's ideal of non-attached action, and Aziz's revered Emperor Babur, whose career was "not only successful, but artistic!" The long and wandering account entitled "Adrift in India" documents the contradictions of modern Indian life and includes a dissertation on the etiquette of Pan, the ritual that serves as "a nucleus for hospitality" in Indian social life. In "The Mind of the Indian Native State," Forster draws on his own experience as secretary to the Maharajah of Dewas Senior to sketch the political dilemmas of the princes of India.

The volume concludes with "The Abinger Pageant," an episodic celebration of English rural life and a protest against the destruction of the greenwood. The epilogue asks whether hotels, restaurants, roads, and petrol pumps are going to be England: "Are these man's final triumph? Or is there another England, green and eternal, which will outlast them? . . . this land is yours, and you can make it what you will. If you want to ruin our Surrey fields and woodlands it is easy to do, very easy, and if you want to save them they can be saved." The pageant featured music by Vaughan Williams and was very well received.

Despite the diversity of subject matter, *Abinger Harvest* is a coherent collection. It is unified by recurrent themes and by an unwavering commitment to the liberal humanism that values individuality, personal relations, art and literature, the apprehension of the unseen, and rural tradition. The book is a valuable miscellany of insights and information that helps illuminate the novels, but it represents a considerable achievement in its own right, providing concrete evidence of

Forster's successful transition from creative writer to thoughtful critic and shrewd analyst of politics and culture.

Two Cheers for Democracy

Between 1936 and 1951, when *Two Cheers for Democracy* was published, the transition is completed and Forster emerges as one of the most articulate defenders of humane values in the language. In this second volume of essays, he exposes his liberal humanism to the tests of the twentieth-century political upheavals and confronts a mass culture indifferent to art and tradition. He responds to the challenges of totalitarianism and social disruption with a vigorous defense of liberty and a searching analysis of liberalism. He neither despairs nor wavers in his humanistic faith in the value of the individual and the true utility of art. The book is urbane and civilized but deeply committed.

Containing more than sixty essays, broadcasts, and reviews, the collection is unified by a consistent preoccupation with questions of personal freedom and the role of culture in modern life. Although a few of the pieces are slight, the volume generally maintains a very high level of quality; considered in its entirety, it is an exceptional record of political and cultural activity. Despite the diversity of subject matter, the collection is carefully organized into a coherent whole. "A chronological arrangement would have been simplest," Forster explains in the prefatory note, "But I was anxious to produce a book rather than a time-string, and to impose some sort of order upon the occupations and preoccupations, the appointments and disappointments of the past fifteen years." The first section, "The Second Darkness," presents responses to World

War II: "The climate is political, and the conclusion
suggested is that, though we cannot expect to love one
another, we must learn to put up with one another.
Otherwise we shall perish." The next section, "What I
Believe," opens with the classic essay of that title and
then focuses on the arts, both in theory and in practice.
The final section, "Places," presents responses to locales as various as the United States and London, India
and Abinger.

The rise of totalitarianism in the 1930s shadows
the entire book. In the opening section, Forster mounts
a frontal assault on the forces of darkness. He sca-
thingly ridicules anti-Semitism and exposes the absurdity of claims to racial purity; he excoriates dictators
and attacks brutality; he regrets collectivism and
pleads for tolerance. Always he recognizes that the
threat to freedom lies within as well as without: the
hope for true liberty can be realized only in our
dreams of Swinburne's Love, the Beloved Republic.
But he is never sentimental. "Love is a great force in
private life; it is indeed the greatest of all things: but
love in public affairs does not work," he admits wistfully. The surest foundation for a civilized world is the
negative virtue of tolerance, which is dull and boring,
"And yet it entails imagination. For you have all the
time to be putting yourself in someone else's place.
Which is a desirable spiritual exercise."

Tellingly, even in broadcasts delivered in the
darkest days of the war, Forster is never jingoistic. He
supports the war not because Germany is a hostile
country but because Nazism is a hateful and destructive principle: Hitler's Germany "stands for a new and
bad sort of life, and if she won, would be bound to
destroy our ways. There is not room in the same world
for Nazi Germany and for people who don't think as
she does." He believes that a truly national culture as-

pires toward internationalism and desires to share cultural achievements with the world. Hence, he is as suspicious of English attempts to limit the freedom
necessary for art or to create an official government-
sponsored culture as he is of German efforts in the
same arena.

In "Post-Munich," written on the eve of the war,
Forster states the dilemma to which he returns again
and again in the pieces composed during the conflict:
"All is lost if the totalitarians destroy us. But all is
equally lost if we have nothing left to lose. . . . Looking at the international scene, [sensitive people] see,
with a clearness denied to politicians, that if Fascism
wins we are done for, and that we must become Fascist to win." Thus, in an anti-Nazi broadcast, he warns
that "as soon as the war is won people who care about
civilisation in England will have to begin another war,
for the restoration and extension of cultural freedom."
He pointedly observes in an essay occasioned by the
tercentenary of *Areopagitica* that Milton's subject "is
not tyranny abroad but the need, even in wartime, of
liberty at home. Not the beam in Dr. Goebbels' eye,
but the mote in our own eye. . . . Is there as much
freedom of expression and publication in this country
as there might be? That is the question which, on its
tercentenary, this explosive little pamphlet propounds."

The fullest expression of the Forsterian credo is
"What I Believe," a meditation that he describes as
"the reflections of an individualist and a liberal who
has found liberalism crumbling beneath him and at
first felt ashamed." Written in 1938 on the eve of the
war, the essay is a stunning yet unsentimental, tender
but tough-minded profession of faith in values that
were endangered by the excesses of the period and
that continue to be attacked by ideologues of right and
left alike. The Forsterian tenets outlined here are the
deeply felt beliefs of a decent, thoughtful, and cour-

ageous man. They continue to inspire confidence even in a world now more gravely threatened by the possibility of annihilation than Europe was in 1938.[9]

Forster begins "What I Believe" by declaring, "I do not believe in Belief." His lawgivers are Erasmus and Montaigne, not Moses and St. Paul, and he disavows any faith in Christianity's ability to cope with the world crisis: "such influence as it retains in modern society is due to the money behind it, rather than to its spiritual appeal." He places his hope in personal relations and bravely and forthrightly asserts that "if I had to choose between betraying my country and betraying my friend, I hope I should have the guts to betray my country." When love and loyalty to an individual run counter to the claims of the state, then "down with the State say I, which means that the State would down me."

Given this radical yet fundamentally conservative premise that elevates personal relations beyond the regulations of the state, it follows that Forster prefers democracy to other forms of government. Democracy is "less hateful . . . and to that extent it deserves our support." It merits two cheers because it admits variety and permits criticism. "Two cheers are quite enough," he explains, "there is no occasion to give three. Only Love the Beloved Republic deserves that." Another merit of democracy is that it does not encourage hero worship or "produce that unmanageable type of citizen known as the Great Man." This measured endorsement of democracy reflects both a distrust of the mass psychology that produces dictators and a fear of movements that sacrifice individualism on the altar of the communal good.

Forster next considers the question of force and violence, "the ultimate reality on this earth." The state of true civilization—what the worshipers of violence label decadence—occurs only during those intervals when force is locked away in its box. "It gets out sooner or later and then it destroys us and all the lovely things which we have made," Forster writes, "But it is not out all the time, for the fortunate reason that the strong are so stupid." Those interludes when force is absent are "the chief justification for the human experiment." He refuses to despair even though the world may well get worse in the immediate future: "What is good in people—and consequently in the world—is their insistence on creation, their belief in friendship and loyalty for their own sakes; and though Violence remains and is, indeed, the major partner in this muddled establishment, I believe that creativeness remains too, and will always assume direction when violence sleeps."

Forster's optimism stems from his faith in personal relations, as exemplified most fully in his concept of a spiritual aristocracy:

I believe in aristocracy, though—if that is the right word and if a democrat may use it. Not an aristocracy of power, based upon rank and influence, but an aristocracy of the sensitive, the considerate and the plucky. Its members are to be found in all nations and classes, and all through the ages, and there is a secret understanding between them when they meet. They represent the true human condition, the one permanent victory of our queer race over cruelty and chaos. Thousands of them perish in obscurity, a few are great names. They are sensitive for others as well as for themselves, they are considerate without being fussy, their pluck is not swankiness but the power to endure, and they can take a joke.

Since the revelation of Forster's homosexuality, much nonsense has been written about this crucial passage, alleging it to be an allusion to homosexual exclusivity, a declaration "about bedmates."[10] In fact, however, there is no reason to suppose that Forster's aristocracy is confined to homosexuals, and certainly it extends beyond his lovers. Even ascetics may join, and it numbers such sensitive, considerate, and plucky characters who share "a secret understanding when they meet" as Stephen Wonham and Stewart Ansell, Lucy Honeychurch and George Emerson, Maurice Hall and Alec Scudder, and Mrs. Moore and Dr. Aziz. These aristocrats—invincible but not victorious—shine their lights in the darkness, "reassuring one another, signalling: 'Well, at all events, I'm still here. I don't like it very much, but how are you? . . . Come along—anyway, let's have a good time while we can.' I think they signal that too."

Forster doubts that humanity will heed Auden's 1929 plea for "New styles of architecture, a change of heart,"[11] but he hopes that "by ordering and distributing his native goodness, will Man shut up Force into its box, and so gain time to explore the universe and to set his mark upon it worthily." Appropriately, the faith that Forster clings to here provided Auden a reservoir of optimism as he observed "the clever hopes expire / Of a low dishonest decade" in "September 1, 1939," the despairing poem written as the war began. Auden concludes the poem by saluting the novelist and asking to be counted among the unquenchable lights of the Forsterian aristocracy:

> Defenceless under the night
> Our world in stupor lies;
> Yet, dotted everywhere,
> Ironic points of light
> Flash out wherever the Just
> Exchange their messages:
> May I, composed like them
> Of Eros and dust,
> Beleaguered by the same
> Negation and despair,
> Show an affirming flame.

In an essay written soon after the war, Forster confronts directly "The Challenge of Our Time," the question of how to reconcile individualism and collectivism. The question is difficult, for Forster's loyalties are painfully divided: he is suspicious of claims of progress, he lacks a mystic faith in the people, he is fearful for the individual in a centralized state, yet he recognizes the need for social planning. "I belong to the fagend of Victorian liberalism, and can look back to an age whose challenges were moderate in their tone, and the cloud on whose horizon was no bigger than a man's hand," he confesses with an air of bewilderment. He is grateful for having received an education that made him "soft"—"for I have seen plenty of hardness since, and I know it does not even pay"—but regrets that it failed to address questions of economic and social injustice.

Forster acknowledges the necessity of "planning and ration books and controls, or millions of people will have nowhere to live and nothing to eat," but he fears that individualism will be lost in the process. The doctrine of laissez faire will not work in the material world, he concedes, but insists that it "is the only one that seems to work in the world of the spirit; if you plan and control men's minds you stunt them, you get the censorship, the secret police, the road to serfdom, the community of slaves." Confronting the classic liberal dilemma of the mid-twentieth century, he calls for planning for the body but freedom for the spirit; when there is a conflict between the community and the individual, he favors personal freedom at the expense of the community. Forster here is a libertarian in the realm of personal relations and a socialist in economic matters, though his economic socialism is qualified by his love of rural tradition, which he fears will be eroded by insensitive state planning.

Describing himself as "a writer, who cares for men and women and for the countryside," he admits to feeling uncomfortable and sometimes miserable and indignant in contemporary society yet nevertheless "convinced that a planned change must take place if the world is not to disintegrate, and hopeful that in the new economy there may be a sphere both for human relationships, and for the despised activity known as art." Forster concludes this important essay by endorsing "art for art's sake." He declares that "Art is valuable not because it is educational (though it may be), not because it is recreative (though it may be), not because everyone enjoys it (for everybody does not), not even because it has to do with beauty. It is valuable because it has to do with order, and creates little worlds of its own, possessing internal harmony, in the bosom of this disordered planet."

Forster's concept of art's ability to create self-contained worlds of internal order is his central aesthetic principle and helps explain his conviction—as stated in "The *Raison D'Etre* of Criticism in the Arts"—that "music is the deepest of the arts and deep beneath the arts." He repeats the defense of art as the "only material object in the universe which may possess internal harmony . . . the one orderly product which our muddling race has produced" in his lecture "Art for Art's Sake," delivered at the American Academy of Arts and Letters in 1949. In this lecture, he points out that the phrase "art for art's sake" does not mean that only art matters—such an aestheticism ensures sterility—but that a work of art "is a self-contained entity, with a life of its own imposed on it by its creator." He also declares that "the artist will tend to be an outsider in the society to which he has been born," a romantic conception that he uses to counter the official view that "treats the artist as if he were a particularly bright government advertiser and encourages him to be friendly and matey with his fellow citizens, and not to give himself airs."

Forster's romanticism is also evident in the emphasis he places on inspiration in "Anonymity: An Enquiry" and "The *Raison d'Etre* of Criticism in the Arts." In "Anonymity," he distinguishes between the artist's surface consciousness—the personality—and the unconsciousness, or lower personality, which is creative. Declaring that "all literature tends towards a condition of anonymity," he imagines it as the product of a well of unconsciousness that the artist dips into for inspiration: "The lower personality is a very queer affair. In many ways it is a perfect fool, but without it there is no literature, because unless a man dips a bucket down into it occasionally he cannot produce first-class work. There is something general about it. . . . What is so wonderful about great literature is that it transforms the man who reads it towards the condition of the man who wrote, and brings to birth in us also the creative impulse." In "Does Culture Matter?" he makes a similar claim: "Works of art do have this peculiar pushful quality; the excitement that attended their creation hangs about them, and makes minor artists out of those who have felt their power."

Forster's essays on and reviews of particular writers and works include important considerations of John Skelton, George Crabbe, Virginia Woolf, and "English Prose Between 1918 and 1939," as well as brief tributes to such admired figures as Proust, Tolstoy, Gide, Gibbon, and Samuel Butler. The section on applied art also collects graceful salutes to such friends as Forrest Reid, Auden and Isherwood, Edward Carpenter, and Syed Ross Masood. The section includes as well historical vignettes such as "Voltaire and Frederick the Great" and commentary on popular culture such as "Mrs. Miniver," a critique of the upper-middle-class heroine of the Jan Struther novel and Greer Garson film.

Like the pieces in *Abinger Harvest*, the practical criticism in *Two Cheers for Democracy* is nearly always interesting and insightful. Here, Forster identifies Butler's *Erewhon* as "A Book That Influenced Me" and Proust's *Remembrance of Things Past* as "Our Second Greatest Novel," outranked only by Tolstoy's *War and Peace*. He admires Gide's "pagan outlook" and devotion to truth, concluding that he "had not a great mind. But he had a free mind, and free minds are as rare as great, and even more valuable at the present moment." He nominates Voltaire as one of two people he would choose to speak for Europe at the Last Judgment: "Shakespeare for his creative genius, Voltaire for his critical genius and humanity."

The longer essays in the volume reveal Forster at his discursive and discriminating best, combining telling quotation and firm judgment. The piece on Skelton charmingly brings alive the early Tudor poet laureate, who was "also a clergyman, and . . . extremely strange." In "George Crabbe and Peter Grimes," Forster analyzes the influence of place on the eighteenth-century poet and the motives of the character Peter Grimes, the subject of Benjamin Britten's opera. In the Rede Lecture on Virginia Woolf, he rescues her from the charge of aestheticism and again laments her inability to create character. He credits her with reminding "us of the importance of sensation in an age which practises brutality and recommends ideals" but finds her limited by an "old-fashioned feminism" and a lack of sympathy for the working class. He summarizes her achievement with genuine feeling: "Virginia Woolf got through an immense amount of work, she gave acute pleasure in new ways, she pushed the light of the English language a little further against darkness." The essay on English prose between the wars examines the effects of the economic upheaval and the psychological revolution on the prose of the period, paying particular homage to T. E. Lawrence's *Seven Pillars of Wisdom* and Lytton Strachey's *Queen Victoria*.

The tributes to friends are predictably generous

and deeply felt. Especially important are the characterizations of Edward Carpenter—whose work and
example so profoundly influenced Forster—and Syed
Ross Masood. In a sketch occasioned by Masood's
death, the novelist movingly credits his Indian friend
with helping him penetrate the mysteries of the Orient:

There never was anyone like him and there never will be
anyone like him. He cannot be judged as ordinary men are
judged. My own debt to him is incalculable. He woke me up
out of my suburban and academic life, showed me new horizons and a new civilisation and helped me towards the understanding of a continent. Until I met him India was a
vague jumble of rajahs, sahibs, babus, and elephants, and I
was not interested in a jumble: who could be? He made everything real and exciting as soon as he began to talk, and seventeen years later when I wrote *A Passage to India* I dedicated it to him out of gratitude as well as out of love, for it
would never have been written without him.

The final section of *Two Cheers for Democracy* is
a celebration of the *genius loci*. Places have always
been important to Forster and his fiction is distinguished by his sensitivity to them. In these accounts of
widely different places, he not only reacts to the spirit
of particular locales but contrasts one with another, as
in his fascinating vignette in the form of a letter addressed to Madan Blanchard, which is inspired by the
death of an abducted Polynesian prince in London and
the decision of an English sailor—Blanchard—to remain in the Pelew Islands in 1783. In "India Again," the
contrast is between the subcontinent of his memory
and postwar India. "I was back in the country I loved,
after an absence of twenty-five years," he remarks.
The essay comments on the changing status of women,
the language problem, and the political situation.
"Goodwill is not enough" to surmount the barriers that
separate the English and the Indians, Forster warns:

"The only thing that cuts a little ice is affection or the possibility of affection."

"America is rather like life," Forster explains. "You can usually find in it what you look for." What he found on his 1947 visit to the United States was scenery and friends. The Berkshires he describes as homely, the Grand Canyon as gigantic; the people he found charitable but obsessed with Russia. In the United States he did encounter "hints of oppression and of violence, and of snobbery. But the main verdict is favourable, and I do beg anyone who happens to have fallen into the habit of nagging at America to drop it." Visiting the Shaker community at Mount Lebanon, Massachusetts, he comments on his friends' romantic nostalgia at the sight of homemade chairs: "It was part of the 'dream that got bogged,' the dream of an America which should be in direct touch with the elemental and the simple. America has chosen the power that comes through machinery but she never forgets her dream."

The accounts of English places are almost as various as the ones of foreign visits. In "Clouds Hill" Forster meditates on T. E. Lawrence's cottage in Dorsetshire, where he spent many hours in "happy casualness" with his friend. In "Cambridge," he alternately celebrates the beauty of the university town and attacks the snobbery of the guidebook under review. His attitude toward London mellowed somewhat as he grew older, he reveals in an essay entitled "London Is a Muddle": "I used to loathe London when I was young. Living an immense distance away (to be precise, in Hertfordshire), I used to denounce her for her pomp and vanity, and her inhabitants for their unmanliness and for their unhealthy skins. Like Blake, I went too far. Time has tamed me, and though it is not practicable to love such a place (one could as easily embrace both volumes of the Telephone Directory at once), one

can love bits of it and become interested in the rest."
Like *Abinger Harvest*, Forster's second miscellany
concludes with a tribute to Abinger. "The Last of
Abinger" consists of commonplace book notes on the
village he loved and finally left in 1946.

   Two Cheers for Democracy is Forster's fullest expression of the political and aesthetic ideals that nur-
tured his art and sustained him during the bleak years
of World War II. Containing some of his finest essays
and some of his most revealing remarks, the book is a
valuable collection of a novelist's "occupations and
preoccupations." More than this, it is the extraordinary
record of a sensitive and thoughtful individual's response to the dangers and difficulties of his time. A
powerful testimony of faith in liberal values and a bold
declaration of the fundamental human need for art,
Two Cheers for Democracy is a brave and wise and
reassuring book.

The Hill of Devi

The Hill of Devi (1953) re-creates Forster's two visits
to the state of Dewas Senior in central India, first in
1912–13—on his tour with Dickinson—and then in
1921, when he served as private secretary to the ruling
maharajah. With a minimum of commentary, Forster
forges his carefully edited letters from India into an
absorbing narrative, followed by a retrospective account of the catastrophe that was later to befall the
maharajah. Thus the book preserves the immediacy of
a Westerner's bewildered but sympathetic response to
a beguiling and stimulating land while also framing it
in the controlling and tempering perspective of hind-
sight. *The Hill of Devi* is at once a memoir of a fascinating individual, a "record of a vanished civilisation,"
and a curiously poignant comedy of errors.

The focus of the book is Forster's beloved maharajah, referred to as "H. H." or "His Highness." Flamboyant, intelligent, charming, and devout, he emerges as a complex character embroiled in a world of petty intrigue and constant muddle. Distinguished by an enormous capacity for giving and receiving love, he is generous and sensual and exciting. Preeminently for Forster, he is an apostle of the creed of personal relations. "It is only for the sake of those who love us that we do things," he remarks. "Affection, all through his chequered life, was the only force to which [he] responded. It did not always work, but without it nothing worked," Forster writes. "Affection and its attendants of human warmth and instinctive courtesy—when they were present his heart awoke and dictated his actions."

Forster describes H. H. as "a genius and possibly a saint." He was passionately devoted to Krishna: "His religion was the deepest thing in him." He believes "that we—men, birds, everything—are part of God, and that men have developed more than birds because they have come nearer to realising this. . . . Salvation, then, is the thrill which we feel when God again becomes conscious of us, and all our life we must train our perceptions so that we may be capable of feeling when the time comes." Although the maharajah frequently extols the ideal of retirement from the world, he condemns asceticism. When he learns that Forster "worried because the post-war world of the '20's would not add up into sense," the maharajah sends him a message through a friend: "tell him from me to follow his heart, and his mind will see everything clear." As Forster remarks: "to remember and respect and prefer the heart, to have the instinct which follows it wherever possible—what surer help than that could one have through life?"

Forster presents his maharajah as a saint, someone

"who was never simple, never ordinary, never deaf to the promptings which most of us scarcely hear." But he concedes that when measured as a politician and administrator, H.H. "will go down in history as a failure." The catastrophic conclusion to his life—marked by family squabbles, allegations of poisonings, the bankruptcy of the state, the failure of sympathy by British officials, disgraceful publicity, death in exile—gives in retrospect a curious poignancy to the comedy of muddle at the court. This complexity of tone emerges as well from the depiction of Dewas as a dying civilization, haunted by memories of past glory and fears of an uncertain future.

An Alice-in-Wonderland kingdom plagued by chronic inefficiency and constant confusion, Dewas is recognized by Forster as an anachronism even in 1921. Although he at first regards the muddle of the court with amused tolerance, viewing it as a Gilbert and Sullivan operetta, his assessment gradually grows more ominous. His Moslem friend Syed Ross Masood is shocked when he visits, thus helping shake Forster's complacency and reminding him that Dewas is not typical of all India: "After three days of Hinduism Masood retired with his clerks and his files to Hyderabad. Our incompetence distressed him more than it could me because he saw it as an extreme example of his country's inefficiency."

Dewas's ancient and rich civilization is symbolized by the Hill of Devi—the "sacred acropolis"—that dominates the landscape, by the "numinous" Old Palace in the heart of the village, and by the royal tombs and elaborate religious ceremonies. This civilization is increasingly threatened by the forces of change at work in India, both those changes espoused by the faint stirrings of nationalism and by the British government of India. The maharajah seeks to preserve the old traditions even as he strives to modernize his chaotic domain. The tokens of modernization are comically yet poignantly engulfed in muddle: the New Palace, under construction for years, is never completed; electrical gadgets fall into disrepair even before they are installed; the elaborate gardens planned by Forster's predecessor as private secretary, Colonel Leslie, die for lack of a proper irrigation system; the mock constitution improvised for the proposed visit of the Prince of Wales is unsuccessful. Life at the court is a series of real or imagined insults from British political agents and intrigues from rival courts and slights from more powerful princes. Caught between the remote threat of nationalist agitation and the immediate reality of British pressure, the maharajah fails to cope successfully with the chaos that surrounds him and finally falls victim to the "wheels of Western righteousness."

Forster's love for the maharajah colors the book with a sense of regret that despite all H. H.'s intelligence and devotion, Dewas seems doomed to mismanagement. But *The Hill of Devi* is not an apology for the princely states of India. Forster knows that beyond Dewas the forces of nationalism are gaining strength and that the days of British domination in India are numbered. In a letter warning about the proposed visit of the Prince of Wales, he reveals his awareness of the difficult political position of the British in India: "I have been with pro-Govt and pro-English Indians all this time, so cannot realise the feeling of the other party; and am only sure of this—that we are paying for the insolence of Englishmen *and* Englishwomen out here in the past. I don't mean that good manners can avert a political upheaval. But they can minimise it, and come nearer to averting it in the East than elsewhere." In a passage strikingly reminiscent of the ending of *A Passage to India*, he adds: "But it's too late. Indians don't long for social intercourse with Englishmen any longer. They have made a life of their own."

The Hill of Devi is indeed a valuable companion

to *A Passage to India,* for the novel reflects many of the attitudes Forster formed in Dewas and many of his experiences there. He began the novel before his 1921 visit and took to Dewas the opening chapters, "But as soon as they were confronted with the country they purported to describe, they seemed to wilt and go dead and I could do nothing with them. The gap between India remembered and India experienced was too wide. When I got back to England the gap narrowed, and I was able to resume."

The Hill of Devi confirms that many details of the novel were suggested by Forster's personal experiences in India and his direct observation of the countryside, especially that represented in the "Temple" section. For instance, the palace at Mau in the novel is based on the Old Palace at Dewas, and the mysterious royal tombs glimpsed by Ralph Moore correspond to the mausoleum at Dewas, though Mau itself is located in the neighboring state of Chhatarpur. The incident of the snake that is actually a tree and the automobile accident caused by an animal that may be a ghost are also based on actual events. Most important, Forster's ideas about Hinduism were profoundly influenced by the maharajah, and the novel's festival of Gokul Ashtami is clearly modeled on the Dewan celebration of the birth of Krishna.

The letters about the Gokul Ashtami festival are, Forster writes, "the most important of my letters home, for they describe (if too facetiously) rites in which a European can seldom have shared." As in the novel, the festival as recorded in the letters is at once a muddle and a mystery:

What troubles me is that every detail, almost without exception, is fatuous and in bad taste. The altar is a mess of little objects, stifled with rose leaves, the walls are hung with deplorable oleographs, the chandeliers, draperies—everything bad. Only one thing is beautiful—the expression on the faces of the people as they bow down to the shrine, and he himself [the maharajah] is, as always, successful in his odd role. I have never seen religious ecstasy before and don't take to it more than I expected I should, but he manages not to be absurd. Whereas the other groups of singers stand quiet, he is dancing all the time, like David before the ark, jigging up and down with a happy expression on his face, and twanging a stringed instrument that hangs by a scarf round his neck.

It is clear that Forster's observance of the maharajah's participation in the festival inspired the similar transport of Professor Godbole, though Godbole is not actually based on the maharajah. The novel's appreciation of the jollity of the Hindu celebration as opposed to the solemnity of Christian observances is.also rooted in Forster's response to the Dewan festival. "One was left," he writes, "aware of a gap in Christianity: the canonical gospels do not record that Christ laughed or played. Can a man be perfect if he never laughs or plays? Krishna's jokes may be vapid, but they bridge a gap."

Forster characterizes his stay in Dewas as "the great opportunity of my life," an opportunity that he translated into one of the great novels of the century and into one of the most valued friendships of his life. Like *Goldsworthy Lowes Dickinson, The Hill of Devi* is also an essay on personal relations and an oblique self-portrait, and it is similarly marred by the necessity of sexual reticence. The maharajah's acceptance of Forster's homosexuality actually sealed their bond of friendship and provided the real basis for the Englishman's regard of him as a saint, yet this is never mentioned in the book. Still, *The Hill of Devi* successfully captures the fineness as well as the strangeness of Dewas, while also presenting fascinating—if necessarily limited—portraits of the maharajah and of Forster himself. As John Colmer notes, the author emerges as a man with a remarkable ability "to enter into the lives and thoughts of people utterly unlike himself and to refrain from applying inappropriate Western standards to the beauty, mystery, and muddle that surrounded him."[12] By responding fully to the maharajah's affectionate spirit, Forster earns the tribute accorded him by a participant in the Gokul Ashtami festival: "We have not met an Englishman like you previously."

Marianne Thornton

Forster's final book, published in 1956 when he was seventy-seven years old, is the lively biography of his great-aunt. As its subtitle suggests, *Marianne Thornton: A Domestic Biography 1797-1887* analyzes English domestic life during a period made increasingly remote by the rapid social changes of the twentieth century. Based on family papers and letters, the book is a genuine contribution to social history. It vividly re-creates the past in terms of domestic details rather than public events. At its heart are an imposing house—Battersea Rise—and an unusual family, finally dominated by an energetic though essentially private woman. But more emphatically even than *Goldsworthy Lowes Dickinson* and *The Hill of Devi*, *Marianne Thornton* is an experiment in autobiography, an attempt both to discover the roots of the self in the past and to trace amid the changes of almost two centuries a line of continuity. Appropriately, Forster's final book is characterized by a valedictory air, a brooding thoughtfulness that is very affecting.

With extraordinary poise, Forster presents his great-aunt as a charming and intelligent and forceful woman who is nevertheless quite limited. She embodies the attitudes of her class and era so completely that she functions as a representative figure even while maintaining a distinctive personality. But though she is conventional, she is never merely a caricature. He constructs her biography in terms of the family roles she performs—daughter (1797-1815), sister (1815-1852), aunt (1852-1879), and great-aunt (1879-1887)—but he does not neglect her interests beyond the home that helped make her so formidable a presence, particularly her educational schemes and her relationship with Hannah More and William Wilberforce. Without exaggerating her importance or overlooking her limitations, Forster depicts Marianne Thornton as an interesting product of a society now vanished yet still exerting a powerful influence.

The book's novelistic plot is the rise and fall of Battersea Rise, the Thornton family home in Clapham Common in which Marianne lived for over fifty years and from which she was finally exiled. The opening chapter describes the destruction of the "sacred shrine" in 1907 and establishes the house as a symbol of "that longing for a particular place, a home, which is common amongst our upper and middle classes, and some of them transmitted that longing to their descendants, who have lived on into an age where it cannot be gratified." Indeed, the frustrated longing for a place is finally revealed as a line of continuity linking Marianne Thornton and her nephew. The destruction of the great house mocks the sentimental Clapham Sect notion of immortality as a "changeless background for family life as it was at Battersea Rise" and poignantly symbolizes the triumph of London over Howards End, the twentieth-century homelessness that Forster feels so deeply.

The crisis of Marianne Thornton's life was her expulsion from Battersea Rise in 1852. The crisis, occasioned by her brother Henry Sykes Thornton's scandalous marriage to his deceased wife's sister, tested her strength of character as well as her love of place.

Thwarted in his attempts to change the law prohibit-
ing such a marriage in England, her brother finally
moved his children and new wife to the Continent and
abandoned the family home to servants. Shocked by
the scandal, Marianne reacted with admirable good
sense and empathy. Disapproving of her brother's attachment, she regarded the marriage as "not a sin but a
shame" and foresaw that the next generation will
"wonder at our scruples." Forster remarks of this
comment: "We do wonder at them, but we wonder
much more at the greatness of her character and the
goodness of her heart. The rest of her family were
ready to be hostile but she, with the most to bear, par-
dons and hopes to endure."

Despite her greatness of character, Marianne is
not presented as a heroine. In fact, she partakes of
many of the conventions that Forster finds hateful.
Mildly anti-Semitic and anti-Catholic and insensitive
to the poor, she is also snobbish toward tradespeople
and basically anti-intellectual. Indeed, she embodies
many of the Sawstonian attitudes that are attacked in
the early novels. Nevertheless, Forster treats her with
surprising sympathy and real understanding. For instance, he remarks of her anti-Semitism that "Not until
the present century did the British middle classes realise what jokes about Jews can lead to." He does not
judge a woman born in the eighteenth century by
twentieth-century standards, but he also never forgets
the differences between the two ages or the lessons so
painfully learned in the twentieth century. Indeed, an
important but submerged theme of the book is the
idea that the past and the present illuminate each other.

Marianne Thornton is thus as much a critique of
twentieth-century life as it is of nineteenth-century
values. Forster avoids the assumption of a superior attitude toward the past, and frequently he sees change
as accompanied by loss, as illustrated in the following

comment contrasting nineteenth- and twentieth-century mourning rituals:

The twentieth-century observer has to remind himself that inside all this cocoonery of words there was love, there was pain. It was the technique of the age and of a section of the middle class; it lasted, as far as my own family were concerned, into the 1850s. After that the technique of mourning shortens, it is now very brief and some sensible people cut out mourning altogether. With it they cut down pain, which has practical advantages, and with pain they cut down love. People today love each other from moment to moment as much as ever their ancestors did, but loyalty of soul, such as the elder Thorntons possessed, is on the decrease.

Forster's tolerance toward the past also influences his assessment of his Clapham Sect heritage, the background that he connects with Sawston yet never repudiates completely. Affectionate, intelligent, public-spirited, the evangelical Christians lacked imagination and breadth of vision. Their religion was narrowly moral rather than mystical, and even their philanthropy was tinged with self-interest. The Thorntons, for instance, were passionately concerned with such projects as the Church Missionary Society and the Free Bible Society and committed to the abolitionist cause. But they were indifferent to issues of social injustice and capitalist exploitation in England, and they never questioned the basic structure of their society.

Typically, Forster does not merely condemn the Thorntons for their hypocrisy or attack Clapham Sect blindness to social injustice. Instead, he attempts to place these failings in the contexts of the age and of his knowledge of character. For instance, he admits that Marianne's devotion to education was motivated both by a hatred of ignorance and by a desire to produce servants and governesses of good quality. "If this second motive is accented, she can be shown as craftily defending her own class, and as breeding up servitors for it," Forster observes, but adds: "The accent (I believe) should be on the first motive."

Similarly, he recognizes the discrepancy between the Clapham Sect's opposition to slavery abroad and their indifference to the exploitation of the working class at home: "When the slavery was industrial they did nothing and had no thought of doing anything; they regarded it as something 'natural,' to encounter it was an educational experience, and an opportunity for smug thankfulness. Misery might be alleviated at the soup-kitchen level, but to do more might make the workers unruly and even un-Christian." Forster does not excuse this narrowness of vision, but he refuses to share the moral indignation sometimes directed against the Clapham Sect. "The really bad people," he declares, "are those who do no good anywhere and help no one either at home or abroad."

The book's autobiographical impulse is obvious in the final section, in which Forster himself is a character in the Thornton family saga. His arrival is an incident in his great-aunt's life, and his recollections are evidence on which the biography is constructed. But Forster's personal presence is felt throughout *Marianne Thornton*, dominating the narrative, mediating doubtful incidents, connecting the past with the present. This intrusion of himself into the biography frequently creates moments of tender emotion and always serves the thematic purpose of allowing the past and the present to illuminate each other.

For example, when Henry Sykes Thornton elopes, Forster comments in autobiographical terms on the bewilderment of the Thorntons as to the disposition of Battersea Rise, brilliantly turning his own experience into a means to understand the past and illuminate the changes wrought by the contemporary world:

It was the loss of Battersea Rise that distressed them most and exacerbated their genuine moral distress. They had been accustomed to return to it and to show it to their children, or at any rate to think of it as functioning. Now they were excluded for ever—unless they bent the knee to immorality, which was unthinkable. Their outlook wavered; they did not know whether they wished Henry to return at once or after an interval or never. They did not know whether they wished the house to be sold and to vanish off the spiritual face of the earth, or to stand as it was, an empty and dishonoured shell. I understand many of their feelings: it has so happened that I have been deprived of a house myself. They will not be understood by the present generation.

Similarly, after describing Marianne's disappointment when her estranged brother's children are prevented from visiting her, Forster intrudes with a comment moving in its beauty and directness and obviously informed by personal experience: "Anyone who has waited in vain for a beloved person will understand what she felt. A wound has been inflicted which no subsequent reunion quite heals. The insecurity against which we all struggle has taken charge of us for a moment—for the moment that is eternity. The moment passes, and perhaps the beloved face is seen after all and the form embraced, but the watcher has become aware of the grave." Less tender but equally informed by personal pain is the comment on the trouble caused by the prohibition against marrying a deceased wife's sister as "yet another example of the cruelty and stupidity of the English law in matters of sex."

The final chapters of *Marianne Thornton* provide valuable information about Forster's early life and reveal the intensely personal motivation for the book. When he was born in 1879, his great-aunt was eighty-two years old and something of a domestic tyrant. Forster's father was her favorite nephew, and when he died in 1880, his infant son succeeded in that role, receiving the "deplorable nickname of The Important One." Marianne's interest in her great-nephew was compounded by her love for Forster's mother Lily, who had been her trusted protégée. Marianne had prepared Lily for a career as a governess; but when Forster's father—a promising architect—fell in love with the young woman, Marianne led the way in welcoming her into the Thornton family, despite reservations about the appropriateness of the union. Given this background, it is not surprising that in her final years Marianne developed a tiresomely proprietary attitude toward the young widow and her son: "Her thirst for youth had become cannibalistic."

Forster's own allegiances as a child were with his maternal grandmother, "a lovely, lively woman, most amusing and witty, fond of pleasure, generous and improvident, and by no means inclined to regard trials as blessings." In some ways the Whichelos were the antithesis of the Thorntons—"Anyhow the Whichelos muddled through. They had no enthusiasm for work, they were devoid of public spirit, and they were averse to piety and quick to detect the falsity sometimes accompanying it"—and Mrs. Whichelo captured her grandson's heart: "How I adored my grandmother!—we played for hours together. In later life I became high-minded and critical, but we remained friends and it is with her—with [the Whichelos]—that my heart lies."

But if Forster's heart lies with his mother's side of the family, he also recognizes a profound debt to the Thorntons. He shares with them the reverence for place that constitutes a recurring theme in the book. In his case, the place is Rooksnest, the Hertfordshire house that provided the model for Howards End: "From the time I entered the house at the age of four and nearly fell from its top to its bottom through a hole ascribed to the mice, I took it to my heart and hoped, as Marianne had of Battersea Rise, that I should live and die there. We were out of it in ten years." The loss of his childhood home, which has haunted his life and his fiction, enables him to interpret acutely Marianne's strange deathbed request for milk from her estranged sister-in-law then in residence at Battersea Rise: "The milk was a sacrament. She knew she was dying and before it happened she wished to be in physical touch with Battersea Rise."

Forster owes to the Thorntons his particular slant on society and history, a "middle-class slant, atavistic, derived from the Thorntons, and it has been corrected by contact with friends who have never had a home in the Thornton sense, and do not want one." He also is indebted to Marianne for a more tangible bequest. In her will, she left him £8,000, a legacy "which has been the financial salvation of my life. Thanks to it, I was able to go to Cambridge. . . . After Cambridge I was able to travel for a couple of years, and traveling inclined me to write." He wonders whether "in so stormy an age as ours" his life has been "a reputable sequence," but he has no doubt about his gratitude to Marianne Thornton: "for she and no one else made my career as a writer possible, and her love, in a most tangible sense, followed me beyond the grave."

An interesting and vivid book that is at once social history, biography, and autobiography, *Marianne Thornton* is also a token of reconciliation between a rebellious nephew and a generous aunt. An attempt to discover continuity between the past and the present, it re-creates with tact and understanding—but without indulgence—the social milieu of an earlier age, and it portrays a woman whose long life was outwardly uneventful yet inwardly rich. The narrative of Marianne Thornton's biography is lively and unfailingly absorbing, but the great pleasure of the book lies in the personality of Forster himself. As he brings his own experience to bear on the interpretation of the past and meditates on the links that connect him with a heritage

increasingly anachronistic in the twentieth century,
Forster provides an oblique self-portrait as telling as
the explicitly autobiographical account of his childhood: the portrait of the artist uncomfortable in the
contemporary world yet open to experience in a way
that his ancestors would find incomprehensible.

In addition to the eight books discussed at some
length here, Forster's nonfiction includes many essays
and reviews and broadcasts and tributes that he did
not collect in his two miscellanies; his introduction to
The Government of Egypt (1919); a pageant play entitled *England's Pleasant Land*, originally performed
in 1938 and published in 1940; a war pamphlet, *Nordic
Twilight* (1940); the libretto, written in collaboration
with Eric Crozier, for Benjamin Britten's opera based
on Melville's *Billy Budd* (1951); and scores of prefaces
and forewords to books. These miscellaneous contributions number hundreds of items.

Some of the fugitive essays have been conven-
iently gathered by George Thomson in *Albergo Empedocle and Other Writings* (1971). This volume contains mostly slight pieces, such as contributions to the
Cambridge student magazine *Basileona*, and brief reviews. But a few of the essays are genuinely important,
especially "Pessimism in Literature" and "Dante,"
while others provide interesting background on the
novels, as for example the reviews of books on Indian
subjects, published between 1913 and 1915. Like "The
Abinger Pageant," *England's Pleasant Land* celebrates
rural England and pleads for conservation. *Nordic
Twilight*, similar to the "Three Anti-Nazi Broadcasts"
included in *Two Cheers for Democracy*, considers the
dim prospects for human dignity and freedom should
Germany win World War II. The Crozier-Forster libretto for *Billy Budd* is an interesting psychological in-

terpretation of Melville's story, though it is frequently faulted for a lack of dramatic tension.

Forster's nonfiction is an important achievement, representing the novelist's altogether successful transition to new modes of expression. The eight major books of nonfiction vary in quality, with *Two Cheers for Democracy, Marianne Thornton,* and *Aspects of the Novel* being the most completely successful. But they are all genuinely worth reading, embodying the peculiarly Forsterian combination of tough-mindedness and sensitivity, the "decency touched with poetry" that distinguishes the entire canon. These books incorporate many of the qualities that characterize the novels—a distinctive prose style, a sensitivity to nuance, a towering intelligence, a commitment to enduring values—but they also evidence an unusual range of interest and a political and cultural activism expressed most appropriately in nonfiction. Forster's essays, criticism, and biographies are a significant fraction of an important literary career.

10

Afterword

There is no other writer quite like E. M. Forster. He expresses in a voice unmistakably his own a vision that uniquely combines passion and intelligence, romanticism and skepticism. A curiously old-fashioned modernist, linked both with the novelistic traditions of Jane Austen and Henry James and with the modernism associated with D. H. Lawrence and Virginia Woolf, he deftly combines social comedy in the manner of Austen and prophecy in the vein of Lawrence. At once a symbolist and a realist, a fantasist and a satirist, he is always the humanist in search of wholeness.

Forster ranks among the finest novelists of the century. His six novels—each of them quite individual—maintain an extraordinary level of quality. *Where Angels Fear to Tread* is a minor masterpiece, a perfectly controlled homage to the complexity of life, while *The Longest Journey* is a powerful and passionate if not completely successful expression of the mythopoeic imagination. A bold hybrid of domestic comedy and sexual celebration, *A Room with a View* assimilates into a heterosexual plot the ideology of homosexual comradeship, while *Howards End*—among the finest works produced in Edwardian England—presents a comprehensive social vision, one that includes metaphysical as well as political dimensions. *Maurice*, Forster's most undervalued novel, beautifully articulates

357

the pain and joy of personal growth in a repressive society. Finally, *A Passage to India*—the novelist's supreme achievement—is both the classic study of imperialism in English literature and a brooding and unflinching exploration of the twentieth-century spiritual wasteland.

Forster is less impressive as a writer of short fiction than as a novelist. But his short stories include some distinguished achievements—as, for example, "The Celestial Omnibus" and "The Road from Colonus" and "The Other Boat" and "The Life to Come"—and they are especially valuable for their help in revealing the complexity of Forster's art and the richness of his imagination. The fantasies, parables, and prophecies make obvious the romantic base of his vision.

Forster's special place in literary history depends not merely on his achievement in fiction but also on a career spent in defense of humane values. His political and historical and critical essays and books are never narrow or parochial, solemn or dogmatic. They are always informed by a large and urbane perspective, by a quality that can best be defined as wisdom.

Forster faced the dangers and difficulties of his time with uncommon courage and sensitivity. Hence, he continues to function as a moral presence, and his liberal humanism, expressed with such disarming honesty and touching conviction, remains a viable faith. What W. H. Auden wrote of him in 1938 is still true some forty-five years later:

> As we run down the slope of Hate with gladness
> You trip us up like an unnoticed stone,
> And just as we are closeted with Madness
> You interrupt us like the telephone.[1]

Notes

1. THE MIRROR TO INFINITY:
A Biographical Sketch

1. The standard account of Forster's life is P. N. Furbank's authorized biography, *E. M. Forster: A Life*, 2 vols. (London: Secker and Warburg, 1977-78; reprint, 2 vols. in 1, New York: Harcourt Brace Jovanovich, 1978), to which this chapter is heavily indebted. All subsequent references are to the American reprint, hereafter cited as *Life*.
2. On the Clapham Sect, see Noel Annan, "The Intellectual Aristocracy," in *Studies in Social History: A Tribute to G. M. Trevelyan*, ed. J. H. Plumb (London: Longmans, Green, 1955), pp. 241-87.
3. Forster, "Breaking Up," *Spectator*, July 28, 1933; quoted in Furbank, *Life*, I, 48.
4. Quoted in "Editor's Introduction," *Arctic Summer and Other Fiction*, ed. Elizabeth Heine (New York: Holmes & Meier, 1981), p. xxx.
5. Furbank, *Life*, I, 191; the diary entry for December 8, 1910 also appears on this page.
6. Lionel Trilling, *E. M. Forster* (Norfolk, Conn.: New Directions, 1943), p. 9.
7. Quoted in Furbank, *Life*, I, 199.
8. On Forster's three trips to India, see Robin Jared Lewis, *E. M. Forster's Passages to India* (New York: Columbia University Press, 1979).
9. Furbank, *Life*, I, 259.

10. D. H. Lawrence, letter to Bertrand Russell, February 12, 1915; quoted in Furbank, *Life*, II, 10.

11. Lawrence, letter to Forster, February 19, 1924; quoted in Furbank, *Life*, II, 163.

12. On Forster's influence on Lawrence, see, e.g., John Beer, "'The Last Englishman': Lawrence's Appreciation of Forster," in *E. M. Forster: A Human Exploration*, ed. G. K. Das and John Beer (New York: New York University Press, 1979), pp. 245–68; and Dixie King, "The Influence of Forster's *Maurice* on *Lady Chatterley's Lover*," *Contemporary Literature* 23 (1982): 65–82.

13. Forster, letter to the *Nation and Athenaeum*, March 29, 1930; quoted in Furbank, *Life*, II, 163. Forster's letter precipitated a controversy with T. S. Eliot and Clive Bell.

14. On Forster's Bloomsbury connection, see, e.g., J. K. Johnstone, *The Bloomsbury Group: A Study of E. M. Forster, Lytton Strachey, Virginia Woolf, and Their Circle* (New York: Noonday, 1954); and *The Bloomsbury Group: A Collection of Memoirs, Commentary, and Criticism*, ed. S. P. Rosenbaum (Toronto: University of Toronto Press, 1975).

15. The exchange between Russell and Forster took place in *The Listener* in 1952; it is reprinted in *The Bloomsbury Group*, ed. Rosenbaum, pp. 402–407.

16. Virginia Woolf, *Diary*, ed. A. O. Bell (London: Hogarth, 1977), I, 310–11; see also H. K. Trivedi, "Forster and Virginia Woolf: The Critical Friends," in *E. M. Forster: A Human Exploration*, ed. Das and Beer, pp. 216–30.

17. Furbank, *Life*, II, 40.

18. Forster, letter to (London) *Times*, December 28, 1937; quoted in Furbank, *Life*, II, 220.

19. Furbank, *Life*, II, 148.

20. See May Buckingham, "Some Reminiscences," in *E. M. Forster: A Human Exploration*, ed. Das and Beer, pp. 183–85.

21. W. H. Auden, "To E. M. Forster," in W. H. Auden and Christopher Isherwood, *Journey to a War* (New York: Random House, 1939), p. 11.

22. Christopher Isherwood, *Down There on a Visit* (New York: Simon and Schuster, 1962), p. 162; the previous Isherwood quotation is from *Christopher and His Kind* (New York: Farrar, Straus, Giroux, 1976), p. 105.

23. Forster, letter to J. R. Ackerley; quoted in Furbank, *Life*, II, 217.

24. Quoted in Furbank, *Life*, II, 278n.

25. Quoted in Furbank, *Life*, II, 305.

26. J. R. Ackerley, *E. M. Forster: A Portrait* (London: Ian McKelvie, 1970), p. 12.

2. HOMAGE TO THE COMPLEXITY OF LIFE: *Where Angels Fear to Tread*

1. C. F. G. Masterson, Review of *Where Angels Fear to Tread*, (London) *Daily News*, November 8, 1904, p. 4; reprinted in *E. M. Forster: The Critical Heritage*, ed. Philip Gardner (London: Routledge & Kegan Paul, 1973), pp. 52–55.

2. Forster, letter to Lily Forster, August 18, 1905; quoted in "Editor's Introduction," *Where Angels Fear to Tread*, Abinger Edition, ed. Oliver Stallybrass (London: Edward Arnold, 1975), p. xii.

3. Alexander Pope, "An Essay on Criticism," 1. 625, in *Poetry and Prose of Alexander Pope*, ed. Aubrey Williams (Boston: Houghton Mifflin, 1969), p. 54.

4. Forster, *Aspects of the Novel*, p. 240.

5. Ibid., p. 239.

6. Frederick C. Crews, *E. M. Forster: The Perils of Humanism* (Princeton, N.J.: Princeton University Press, 1962), p. 79.

7. Forster, *Aspects of the Novel*, pp. 103–104, 118.

8. Lionel Trilling, *E. M. Forster*, p. 58.

9. Cf. Forster's remarks in "Notes on the English Character": The English go forth into the world "with well-developed bodies, fairly developed minds, and undeveloped hearts. And it is this undeveloped heart that is largely responsible for the difficulties of Englishmen

abroad. An undeveloped heart—not a cold one" (*Abinger Harvest*, p. 13).

10. Wilfred Stone, *The Cave and the Mountain: A Study of E. M. Forster* (Stanford, Calif.: Stanford University Press, 1966), p. 165.

11. Translation by Dorothy Sayers, quoted in the Abinger Edition of *Where Angels Fear to Tread*, p. 179. See also Forster's lecture on Dante read to the Working Men's College Literary Society on November 21, 1907, included in *Albergo Empedocle and Other Writings*, pp. 146–68; and John Sayre Martin, *E. M. Forster: The Endless Journey* (Cambridge: Cambridge University Press, 1976), pp. 22–23. In the lecture on Dante, Forster criticizes the medieval poet for attempting to "draw a distinct line" between the body and soul and praises modern thinkers—like Goethe and Whitman—for attempting to harmonize the dualities (*Albergo Empedocle*, p. 155). But, as F. P. W. McDowell points out, Dante "also experienced the revelation that brought him peace" (*E. M. Forster*, rev. ed. [Boston: Twayne, 1982], p. 31).

12. Stone, *The Cave and the Mountain*, pp. 176–77.

13. Alan Wilde, *Art and Order: A Study of E. M. Forster* (New York: New York University Press, 1964), p. 19.

14. Martin, p. 17.

15. Cf. Charles Martel on the Bersaglieri: "Great care is taken that the men chosen for these celebrated light infantry corps possess good constitutions, are broad and deep in the chest, quick and active in their step" (*Military Italy* [London, 1884], quoted in the Abinger Edition of *Where Angels Fear to Tread*, p. 178).

16. The fresco Forster describes is actually Ghirlandaio's "St. Gregory Announces the Death of Santa Fina" in the Collegiate Church of Santa Fina in San Gimignano. See Jeffrey Meyers, *Painting and the Novel* (Manchester: Manchester University Press, 1975), pp. 31–38.

17. Forster, letter to R. C. Trevelyan, October 28, 1905; reprinted as "An Exchange between Forster and R. C. Trevelyan" in the Abinger Edition of *Where Angels Fear to Tread*, p. 149.

3. BUBBLES ON AN EXTREMELY ROUGH SEA: *The Longest Journey*

1. For a grossly overstated account of the novel's sentimentality and confusion, see John Harvey, "Imagination
   and Moral Theme in E. M. Forster's *The Longest Journey*," *Essays in Criticism* 6 (1956): 418–33. For a discussion that finds the book "an intricately and systematically worked out philosophical novel," see P. N.
   Furbank, "The Philosophy of E. M. Forster," in *E. M.
   Forster: Centenary Revaluations*, ed. Judith Scherer
   Herz and Robert K. Martin (Toronto: University of Toronto Press, 1982), pp. 37–51.
2. "*The Longest Journey* is the least popular of my five
   novels but the one I am most glad to have written,"
   Forster declared in 1960. See "Aspect of a Novel," *The
   Bookseller*, September 10, 1960, pp. 1228–30.
3. J. K. Johnstone, *The Bloomsbury Group*, p. 176.
4. George Gordon, Lord Byron, *Don Juan*, ed. Leslie A.
   Marchand (Boston: Houghton Mifflin, 1958), Canto 15,
   Stanza 99, p. 425. The subsequent quotation from Canto
   1, Stanza 194, also follows this edition, p. 53.
5. James McConkey, *The Novels of E. M. Forster* (Ithaca,
   N.Y.: Cornell University Press, 1957), p. 8.
6. Percy Bysshe Shelley, "Epipsychidion," 11. 159, 153–54,
   151–53, 156, and 158; quoted from *John Keats and Percy
   Bysshe Shelley: Complete Poetical Works* (New York:
   Modern Library, n.d.), pp. 468–69.
7. John Sayre Martin, *E. M. Forster: The Endless Journey*,
   p. 34.
8. Wilfred Stone, *The Cave and the Mountain*, p. 193. For
   another discussion of homosexuality in the novel, see
   Judith Scherer Herz, "The Double Nature of Forster's
   Fiction: *A Room with a View* and *The Longest Journey*," *English Literature in Transition* 21 (1978): 254–65.
9. For a discussion of brotherhood and fraternity in the
   novel, see Bonnie Blumenthal Finkelstein, *Forster's
   Women: Eternal Differences* (New York: Columbia
   University Press, 1975), pp. 36–63.

10. Forster, "Aspect of a Novel," p. 1229.
11. John Magnus, "Ritual Aspects of E. M. Forster's *The Longest Journey,*" *Modern Fiction Studies* 13 (1967): 195–210. On the novel's symbolism, see also George H. Thomson, *The Fiction of E. M. Forster* (Detroit: Wayne State University Press, 1967), pp. 134–59; Elizabeth Heine, "Rickie Elliot and the Cow: The Cambridge Apostles and *The Longest Journey,*" *English Literature in Transition* 15 (1972): 116–34; and S. P. Rosenbaum, "*The Longest Journey:* E. M. Forster's Refutation of Idealism," in *E. M. Forster: A Human Exploration,* ed. Das and Beer, pp. 32–54. On the significance of Orion, see Judith Scherer Herz, "The Narrator as Hermes: A Study of the Early Short Fiction," and John Beer, "'The Last Englishman': Lawrence's Appreciation of Forster," in *E. M. Forster: A Human Exploration,* pp. 19 and 250–52, respectively. In his 1904 essay "Cnidus," Forster writes of Demeter that she "alone among gods has true immortality. The others continue, perchance, their existence, but are forgotten, because the time came when they could not be loved. But to her, all over the world, rise prayers of idolatry from suffering men as well as suffering women, for she has transcended sex. And Poets, too, generation after generation, have sung in passionate incompetence of the hundred-flowered Narcissus and the rape of Persephone, and the wanderings of the Goddess, and her gift to us of corn and tears" (*Abinger Harvest,* p. 201). Forster's concepts of Demeter and of the relationship of Demeter and Dionysus are undoubtedly influenced by the *Greek Studies* of Walter Pater; on this point, see Robert K. Martin, "The Paterian Mode in Forster's Fiction," in *E. M. Forster: Centenary Revaluations,* ed. Herz and Martin, pp. 99–112. For his insistence on the continuing vitality of ancient gods and myths, Forster may also be indebted to Edward Carpenter's *The Art of Creation* (1904), which may also have influenced Forster's attitude toward the existence of objects. On this latter point, see Tony Brown, "Edward Carpenter and the Discussion of the Cow in *The*

Longest Journey," *Review of English Studies* NS 33 (1982): 58–62.

12.   Frederick C. Crews, *E. M. Forster: The Perils of Humanism,* pp. 66–67.

13.   See Magnus, "Ritual Aspects of E. M. Forster's *The Longest Journey,*" p. 209; and McDowell, *E. M. Forster,* p. 55.

14.   P. N. Furbank and F. J. H. Haskell, "E. M. Forster: The Art of Fiction I," *Paris Review* 1 (1953): 38. For discussions of other autobiographical elements in *The Longest Journey,* see Stone, *The Cave and the Mountain,* pp. 184–214; and Heine, "Rickie Elliot and the Cow," pp. 116–22.

4.   THE HOLINESS OF DIRECT DESIRE:
A Room with a View

1.   For an account of the early versions of *A Room with a View,* see Elizabeth Ellem, "E. M. Forster: The Lucy and New Lucy Novels: Fragments of Early Versions of *A Room with a View,*" *Times Literary Supplement,* May 28, 1971, pp. 623–26.

2.   For Forster's remark about Austen, see P. N. Furbank and F. J. H. Haskell, "E. M. Forster: The Art of Fiction," p. 40. Cf. Virginia Woolf's comment in her essay "The Novels of E. M. Forster": "His old maids, his clergy are the most lifelike we have had since Jane Austen laid down the pen. But he has into the bargain what Jane Austen had not—the impulses of a poet" (*Collected Essays,* I [London: Hogarth Press, 1966], 344). On the debt of *The White Peacock* to *A Room with a View,* see, e.g., Dixie King, "The Influence of Forster's *Maurice* on *Lady Chatterley's Lover,*" especially pp. 72–75.

3.   Frederick C. Crews, *The Perils of Humanism,* p. 82.

4.   All references to and quotations from Carlyle's *Sartor Resartus* follow the edition of Charles Frederick Harrold (New York: Odyssey, 1937) and are cited parenthetically by page number in the text. Forster later came to believe

that Carlyle "had something of the Nazi about him: he despised individualism and liberty and worshipped the dictator-hero" ("Three Anti-Nazi Broadcasts," in *Two Cheers for Democracy*, p. 42), but this assessment rests on Carlyle's *On Heroes and Hero-Worship*, not *Sartor Resartus*.

5. For a discussion of the importance of this fresco to the novel, see Jeffrey Meyers, *Painting and the Novel*, pp. 38–45.

6. A. E. Housman, "From far, from eve and morning," *A Shropshire Lad*, poem XXXII, in *The Collected Poems of A. E. Housman* (New York: Holt, Rinehart, and Winston, 1965), p. 49. *A Shropshire Lad* was originally published in 1896.

7. For a discussion of the scene in the Piazza Signoria as "a symbolic fountainhead in which all the later images and motifs find their source," see Zohreh T. Sullivan, "Forster's Symbolism: *A Room with a View*, Fourth Chapter," *Journal of Narrative Technique* 6 (1976): 217–23.

8. Alan Wilde, *Art and Order: A Study of E. M. Forster*, p. 50.

9. For a discussion of Forster's indebtedness to Butler, see Lee Elbert Holt, "E. M. Forster and Samuel Butler," *Publications of the Modern Language Association* 61 (1946): 804–19.

10. "A Pronouncing Vocabulary of Common English Given Names," in *Webster's New Collegiate Dictionary* (Springfield, Mass.: Merriam, 1959), p. 1131. The subsequent identification of the meaning of "George" is also from this source.

11. Cecil's aestheticism is modeled on the criticism of Walter Pater. The qualities that Cecil perceives in Lucy are similar to those Pater discerned in "La Gioconda," which, he declared, is "Leonardo's masterpiece, the revealing instance of his mode of thought and work. In suggestiveness, only the *Melancholia* of Durer is comparable to it; and no crude symbolism disturbs the effect of its subdued and graceful mystery" (*The Renaissance: Studies in Art and Poetry* [London: Macmillan,

1910], p. 123). *The Renaissance* was first published in 1873.

12. Walt Whitman, "Song of Myself," 1. 200, in *Walt Whitman: The Complete Poems,* ed. Francis Murphy (Harmondsworth, Middlesex, England: Penguin, 1975), p. 73. Among the late nineteenth-century homoerotic paintings of bathing scenes are "The Swimming Hole" by Thomas Eakins and "August Blue" by H. S. Tuke. On the prevalence of the bathing scene motif in homoerotic poetry, see *Sexual Heretics: Male Homosexuality in English Literature from 1850 to 1900,* ed. Brian Reade (London: Routledge & Kegan Paul, 1970). On the homoerotic dimensions of Forster's bathing scene, see Jeffrey Meyers, *Homosexuality and Literature 1890-1930* (London: Athlone Press, 1977), pp. 91-95. It is appropriate that Forster should juxtapose Whitmanesque ideals to the medieval ideals associated with Cecil, for in his 1907 lecture on Dante, Forster cites Whitman as an example of modern thinkers who oppose the medieval world view by proposing a harmony of body and soul (see *Albergo Empedocle,* pp. 154-56).

13. Forster, "What I Believe," *Two Cheers for Democracy,* p. 73.

14. Judith Scherer Herz, "The Double Nature of Forster's Fiction," p. 258.

15. Glen Cavaliero, *A Reading of E. M. Forster* (London: Macmillan, 1979), p. 99. On Mr. Beebe's homosexuality, see also Meyers, *Homosexuality and Literature,* pp. 91-99. Meyers errs, I believe, in asserting that Mr. Beebe is in love with George. He is unquestionably wrong to think that Forster "is essentially sympathetic to Beebe's views of celibacy and sex" (p. 99).

16. According to Oreste Ferrari, the *ignudi* "symbolize the endless resurgence of youth and vigour in the human race" (*Masterpieces of the Vatican,* tr. Geoffrey Webb [New York: Abrams, 1971], p. 170). See also Charles de Tolnay, *Michelangelo: Sculptor, Painter, Architect* (Princeton, N.J.: Princeton University Press, 1975), p. 31. One of the nudes may be particularly relevant to

George's early "world sorrow" and to the novel's pervasive imagery of light and shadow: placed in a panel "next to the *Separation of Light from Darkness* one of the nudes carries his garland like a gigantic burden which weighs him down, casting his face in shadow" (Frederick Hartt, *Michelangelo* [New York: Abrams, 1964], p. 126).

17. John Milton, *The Complete Poetry of John Milton,* ed. John T. Shawcross, rev. ed. (Garden City N.Y.: Doubleday, 1971), p. 419.

18. See P. N. Furbank, *Life,* I, 159n. Below the list reprinted by Furbank is another list that includes the names of Tuke, Signorelli, and Michelangelo. The lists are described by Robert Martin, "Edward Carpenter and the Double Structure of *Maurice,*" *Journal of Homosexuality,* 8 (Spring/Summer 1983): 35–46. Although he did not recognize the significance of the lists for *A Room with a View,* Martin richly deserves credit for having first noted the existence of the second list and for having first suggested that the lists consist of writers and artists whom Forster believed to be homosexual. The absence from the lists of the most famous homosexual writer of Forster's lifetime—Oscar Wilde—may be attributed to Wilde's notoriety: his homosexuality was so well known, Forster did not need to include his name on the lists. In any case, *A Room with a View* occasionally sounds a Wildean note, as in the description of Lucy's piano playing: "her runs were not at all like strings of pearls, and she struck no more right notes than was suitable for one of her age and situation."

19. John Colmer, *E. M. Forster: The Personal Voice* (London: Routledge & Kegan Paul, 1975), p. 51.

20. Quotations from *Homogenic Love* are from *Sexual Heretics,* pp. 324, 327.

21. Forster, "Edward Carpenter," *Two Cheers for Democracy,* p. 212.

22. [John Addington Symonds], "The Song of Love and Death," in *Studies in Terza Rima, Etc.* (Privately printed, 1875?), pp. 5–6.

23. K. W. Gransden, *E. M. Forster* (New York: Grove Press, 1962), p. 34.

5. HOPE THIS SIDE OF THE GRAVE:
Howards End

1. On this point, see Cyrus Hoy, "Forster's Metaphysical Novel," *Publications of the Modern Language Association* 75 (1960): 126–36.
2. On Forster's liberal humanism, see, e.g., Frederick C. Crews, *E. M. Forster: The Perils of Humanism*, pp. 19–36; and H. A. Smith, "Forster's Humanism and the Nineteenth Century," in *Forster: A Collection of Critical Essays*, ed. Malcolm Bradbury (Englewood Cliffs, N.J.: Prentice-Hall, 1966), pp. 106–16.
3. For an interesting account of the inner weaknesses and contradictions of liberalism as presented in the novel and in the historical circumstances from which the novel grows, see Peter Widdowson, *E. M. Forster's Howards End: Fiction as History* (London: Chatto & Windus for Sussex University Press, 1977).
4. James McConkey, *The Novels of E. M. Forster*, p. 124.
5. For an elaborate and informative discussion of the novel's symbolism, see George Thomson, *The Fiction of E. M. Forster*, pp. 170–200.
6. For appreciative discussions of the novel's domestic comedy, see James Hall, "Family Reunions: E. M. Forster," in *The Tragic Comedians* (Bloomington: Indiana University Press, 1963), pp. 11–30; and Malcolm Bradbury, "*Howards End*," in *Forster: A Collection of Critical Essays*, ed. Bradbury, pp. 128–43.
7. Forster's phrase echoes Arnold's description of Sophocles, "Who saw life steadily, and saw it whole," in the sonnet "To a Friend." *Howards End* is informed as well by Arnold's concept of culture. On this point, see, among others, Wilfred Stone, who in *The Cave and the Mountain* asserts that the novel "can be read as the most explicit test of Arnold's notion of culture in our lit-

erature" (p. 239); and Peter Widdowson, *E. M. Forster's Howards End*, pp. 39–45, 66–72. In a 1944 review of William Arnold's Indian novel *Oakfield*, Forster remarks that "Matthew Arnold is of all the Victorians most to my taste: a great poet, a civilised citizen, and a prophet who has managed to project himself into our present troubles" (*Two Cheers for Democracy*, p. 197).

8. See Wilfred Stone, "Forster on Love and Money," in *Aspects of E. M. Forster*, ed. Oliver Stallybrass (New York: Harcourt, Brace & World, 1969), pp. 107–21.

9. See Crews, *E. M. Forster: The Perils of Humanism*, p. 119.

10. See John Edward Hardy, "*Howards End:* The Sacred Center," in *Man in the Modern Novel* (Seattle: University of Washington Press, 1964), pp. 40–41.

11. Thomas Carlyle, *Sartor Resartus*, p. 53.

12. The sense of the aphorism is attributed to Michelangelo in John Addington Symonds, *The Life of Michelangelo Buonarroti*. See Thomson, *The Fiction of E. M. Forster*, pp. 174, 287n.

13. Wallace Stevens, "Sunday Morning," in *The Collected Poems of Wallace Stevens* (New York: Knopf, 1977), p. 68.

14. See, e.g., F. R. Leavis, "E. M. Forster," in *The Common Pursuit* (London: Chatto & Windus, 1952), pp. 261–67; Alan Wilde, *Art and Order: A Study of E. M. Forster*, pp. 112–13; and John Sayre Martin, *E. M. Forster: The Endless Journey*, pp. 122–23.

15. For a feminist approach to the novel, see Bonnie Blumenthal Finkelstein, *Forster's Women: Eternal Differences*, pp. 89–116.

16. Hardy, "*Howards End:* The Sacred Center," p. 48. On the child as heir, see also R. N. Parkinson, "The Inheritors; or A Single Ticket for Howards End," in *E. M. Forster: A Human Exploration*, ed. Das and Beer, pp. 55–58.

17. In a study of Forster's successive manuscript revisions of *Howards End*, J. H. Stape finds a coherent pattern of alterations in the depiction of sexual relationships: "original impulses to describe physical attraction graph-

ically were regularly replaced by an impulse toward greater vagueness and less physicality in such descriptions." Stape speculates that these revisions were motivated both to enhance the theme of comradeship and to avoid giving offense to a prudish public. See J. H. Stape, "Leonard's 'Fatal Forgotten Umbrella': Sex and the Manuscript Revisions to *Howards End*," *Journal of Modern Literature* 9 (1981–82): 123–32.

6. THE FLESH EDUCATING THE SPIRIT: *Maurice*

1. For an excellent account of the novel's evolution and complex manuscript history, see Philip Gardner, "The Evolution of E. M. Forster's *Maurice*," in *E. M. Forster: Centenary Revaluations*, ed. Herz and Martin, pp. 204–23. Even in manuscript, *Maurice* exerted a great deal of influence, most notably helping shape D. H. Lawrence's *Lady Chatterley's Lover;* see Dixie King, "The Influence of Forster's *Maurice* on *Lady Chatterley's Lover*."

2. Cynthia Ozick, "Forster as Homosexual," *Commentary* 52 (December 1971): 85. Homophobia may also be detected in, e.g., Frank Kermode, "A Queer Business," *Atlantic Monthly* 227 (November 1971): 140–42, 144; and Paul Theroux, "Forster's Fantasy of Liberation," *Washington Post Book World*, October 3, 1971, pp. 1, 3. Joseph Epstein's review in the *New York Times Book Review*, October 10, 1971, is dismissive and condescending rather than explicitly homophobic, but the choice of Epstein to review *Maurice* may itself reflect sexual politics. A year earlier, Epstein proudly revealed himself as a virulent homophobe in a repugnant essay, "Homo/Hetero: The Struggle for Sexual Identity," *Harper's* 241 (September 1970): 37–51. In this irrational and painfully autobiographical piece, Epstein proclaims his deep-seated aversion to homosexuals, describes homosexuality as an "anathema," and declares that "If I had the power to do so, I would wish homosexuality off

the face of the earth." The choice of such a person to review a novel of homosexual love is analogous to asking an avowed white supremacist to evaluate a novel about the Black experience or a self-proclaimed anti-Semite to discuss a book about Jewish life. Perhaps anticipating an even more hostile review than Epstein actually produced, the *New York Times Book Review* balanced his dismissal of *Maurice* with an affectionate reminiscence of Forster by Glenway Westcott, "A Dinner, A Talk, A Walk with Forster."

3. See Judith Scherer Herz, "The Double Nature of Forster's Fiction"; and Jane Lagoudis Pinchin, *Alexandria Still: Forster, Durrell, and Cavafy* (Princeton, N.J.: Princeton University Press, 1977), pp. 86-98. Other discussions that place *Maurice* in the context of the entire canon include Alan Wilde, *Horizons of Assent: Modernism, Postmodernism, and the Ironic Imagination* (Baltimore: Johns Hopkins University Press, 1981), pp. 50-89; and Philip Gardner, "E. M. Forster and 'The Possession of England,'" *Modern Language Quarterly* 42 (1981): 166-83. The failure to consider *Maurice* (and the homosexual stories) as an integral part of the canon vitiates an otherwise competent recent book, Barbara Rosecrance's *Forster's Narrative Vision* (Ithaca, N.Y.: Cornell University Press, 1982). Rosecrance's discussion of the novel is astonishingly obtuse. Although her book is a specialized study of Forster's narrative voice, she fails utterly to understand the complex narrative technique of *Maurice* and consequently misses the book's irony and distorts its meaning. Her interpretation—constructed by perversely wrenching quotations out of context and proceeding from the belief that the theme of sexual fulfillment is essentially trivial—ludicrously alleges Clive Durham to be the novel's "architect of the ideal homosexual love" (p. 167). The point is not merely that Rosecrance egregiously misreads a particular novel, but that her misreading also renders highly suspect all her conclusions about Forster's development, an issue at the heart of her book.

4. James S. Malek, "Tackling Tribal Prejudices: Norms in Forster's Homosexual Fiction," unpublished essay, p. 32.

5. See Alan P. Bell, Martin S. Weinberg, and Sue Kiefer Hammersmith, *Sexual Preference: Its Development in Men and Women* (Bloomington: Indiana University Press, 1981). On the homosexual milieu of Edwardian England, see Ira Bruce Nadel, "Moments in the Greenwood: *Maurice* in Context," in *E. M. Forster: Centenary Revaluations*, ed. Herz and Martin, pp. 177-90.

6. Plato, *The Symposium*, trans. Walter Hamilton (Harmondsworth, England: Penguin, 1951), pp. 46-47.

7. Prominent as a biographer of Sir Philip Sidney (1886), Sir Thomas Browne (1886), Benvenuto Cellini (1888), and Michaelangelo (1893), and as an essayist and critic, Symonds wrote two distinctly different kinds of apologia for homosexuality, directed toward two distinct audiences. In his commercial publications, such as *Studies of the Greek Poets* (1873, augmented 1876), *Renaissance in Italy* (1877-1886), his collection of poetry *Many Moods* (1888), and his translation of the *Sonnets of Michaelangelo* (1878), he is circumspect and evasive, frequently treating homosexual subjects but nearly always platonizing the homoerotic or otherwise concealing physical passion. In his privately printed publications—sometimes issued anonymously and in very small editions—Symonds is more explicit. These privately printed works include two important prose treatises, *A Problem in Greek Ethics* (1883) and *A Problem in Modern Ethics* (1891); a collection of essays, *In the Key of Blue* (1893); his collaboration with Havelock Ellis, *Sexual Inversion* (issued anonymously in 1897); and numerous volumes of poetry. Carpenter's works include a long Whitmanesque poem, *Towards Democracy* (1883, augmented 1885, 1892, 1895) and such books as *Homogenic Love* (1894), *Ioläus: An Anthology of Friendship* (1902), and *The Intermediate Sex* (1908). For an account of the Uranian movement and Symonds's and Carpenter's roles in it, see Brian Reade's introduction to *Sexual Heretics: Male Homosexuality in English Literature from 1850 to 1900*. Although he applies the term "*Uranian*" too narrowly to designate only a group of pederastic poets who wrote sentimental celebrations of boyhood, see also Timothy d'Arch

Smith's *Love in Earnest: Some Notes on the Lives and Writings of English 'Uranian' Poets from 1889 to 1930* (London: Routledge & Kegan Paul, 1970).

8. Robert K. Martin, "Edward Carpenter and the Double Structure of *Maurice.*"

9. *De Profundis* was first published in England in the abridged version of 1905; the complete text was not published until 1962. My subsequent quotations from *De Profundis* are from the version published in London by Methuen in 1905 and are cited parenthetically by page numbers. In the April 1905 issue of *The Independent Review*—immediately following Forster's essay "Cardan"—G. Lowes Dickinson reviewed *De Profundis*, vigorously attacking the philistinism of society for persecuting Wilde and remarking that "suffering has crowned his life" (*The Independent Review* 5 [1905]: 375–77). Wilde and *De Profundis* were much in the news in 1913, the year Forster began work on *Maurice*. In 1912 Arthur Ransome published *Oscar Wilde: A Critical Study*, in which he alleged that Wilde blamed his erstwhile lover Lord Alfred Douglas for his ruin. Douglas promptly sued Ransome for libel; the trial was heard in April 1913. As justification for his allegations, Ransome produced the unpublished full version of *De Profundis*, portions of which were read aloud in court. The jury found in Ransome's favor. Widely reported, the trial served to rehash the Wilde scandal of 1895 and to focus attention on *De Profundis*. Like most homosexuals of the day, Forster undoubtedly followed the case with great interest. For an account of the Ransome libel action, see H. Montgomery Hyde, *Cases that Changed the Law* (London: Heinemann, 1951), pp. 164–76.

10. The quotation is from Wordsworth's 1814 Preface to the *Excursion;* Wilde slightly misquotes line 139 of Book IV, which actually reads: "Heights which the soul is competent to gain." Whether Forster was influenced directly by the *Excursion* is difficult to determine, but his celebration of childhood in *Maurice*—"the precocious clearness of the child which transfigures and ex-

plains the universe"—probably derives from Wordsworth's "Intimations" ode.

11. Thomas Carlyle, *Sartor Resartus*, pp. 53–54.
12. See "Alexis" in "A Pronouncing Vocabulary of Com-
     mon English Given Names," p. 1131.
13. Martin, "Edward Carpenter and the Double Structure
     of *Maurice*." See also Kathleen Grant, "*Maurice* as Fan-
     tasy," in *E. M. Forster: Centenary Revaluations*, ed.
     Herz and Martin, p. 200.
14. The color blue was frequently evoked by Uranians,
     and Forster's use of the Blue Room as the scene of Mau-
     rice's exchange with Clive fittingly links their relation-
     ship with the apologia of Symonds, whose collection of
     essays is entitled *In the Key of Blue*. Certainly Forster
     intends a contrast between the spiritual communion in
     the Blue Room and the later physical communion in the
     Russet Room. As Bonnie Blumenthal Finkelstein writes,
     "Maurice's cool, platonic affair . . . in the Blue Room
     . . . is finally superseded by a more complete, hot, pas-
     sionate, and physical love in the Red" (*Forster's Women:
     Eternal Differences*, p. 172).
15. This description of Dickie Barry is similar to the de-
     scription of Forrest Reid's dream friend in his autobiog-
     raphy: "And presently, out from the leafy shadow he
     bounded into the sunlight. I saw him standing for a
     moment, his naked body the colour of pale amber
     against the dark background—a boy of about my own
     age, with eager parted lips and bright eyes. But he was
     more beautiful than anything else in the whole world,
     or in my imagination" (*Apostate* [London: Constable,
     1926], p. 73). A friend of Forster's, Reid read *Maurice*
     in manuscript. Forster very much admired Reid's novels
     about boyhood, and one of them—*Following Darkness*
     (1912), which is dedicated to Forster—probably influ-
     enced the account of Maurice's boyhood.
16. On this point, see Norman Page, *E. M. Forster's Post-
     humous Fiction*, ELS Monograph Series 10 (Victoria,
     B.C.: University of Victoria, 1977), pp. 93–94; and Mar-
     tin, "Edward Carpenter and the Double Structure of
     Maurice."

17. Malek, "Tackling Tribal Prejudices," p. 38.

18. See Alan Wilde, "The Naturalisation of Eden," in *E. M. Forster: A Human Exploration*, ed. Das and Beer, p. 202.

19. This incident may have been inspired by an 1838 letter from Thomas Carlyle to his mother in which he recounts having seen Queen Victoria driving through a park: "Yesterday, going through one of the Parks, I saw the poor little Queen. She was in an open carriage, preceded by three or four swift red-coated troopers; all off for Windsor just as I happened to pass. . . . It seemed to me the poor little Queen was a bit modest, nice sonsy little lassie; blue eyes, light hair, fine white skin; of extremely small stature: she looked timid, anxious, almost frightened; for the people looked at her in perfect silence; one old liveryman alone touched his hat to her: I was heartily sorry for the poor bairn" (*New Letters of Thomas Carlyle*, ed. Alexander Carlyle [London: John Lane, 1904], I, 119).

20. Malek, "Tackling Tribal Prejudices," p. 38. On the flawed ending of *Maurice*, see also Stephen Adams, *The Homosexual as Hero in Contemporary Fiction* (New York: Barnes & Noble, 1980), pp. 116–19. For an account of the importance of the greenwood in Forster's fiction, see Elizabeth Wood Ellem, "E. M. Forster's Greenwood," *Journal of Modern Literature* 5 (1976): 89–98. In an interesting but perverse and inattentive reading that refuses to accept the novel's political and psychological realities, Wilfred Stone denies that the ending is really happy at all, finding it not sentimental but fantastic ("'Overleaping Class': Forster's Problem in Connection," *Modern Language Quarterly* 39 [1978]: 386–404). Crucial to Stone's strained argument are his unsubstantiated assumptions that Forster was guilt-ridden about his homosexuality and that he really loathed the lower classes. Both the novel and the evidence of Forster's life suggest precisely the opposite.

21. Glen Cavaliero, *A Reading of E. M. Forster*, p. 137.

22. Jeffrey Meyers, *Homosexuality in Literature*, p. 102. Meyers' discussion of *Maurice* is particularly offensive, containing not only an abysmally insensitive reading of

the novel but also an ill-informed and contemptuous account of Forster's personal life. For a rebuttal to Meyers' objections to *Maurice*, see Adams, *The Homosexual as Hero*, pp. 118–19.

23. Martin, "Edward Carpenter and the Double Structure of *Maurice*."

24. Joseph Cady, "Oscar Wilde and the Homosexual Potential for 'Imagination,'" unpublished paper presented at the 1974 Gay Academic Union Conference, p. 12.

25. P. N. Furbank, "Introduction," *Maurice* (London: Edward Arnold, 1971). p. ix.

7. THE FRIEND WHO NEVER COMES:
A Passage to India

1. The classic study of the novel's rhythmic technique is E. K. Brown, *Rhythm in the Novel* (Toronto: University of Toronto Press, 1950), pp. 33–59, 89–115. See also the discussions in James McConkey, *The Novels of E. M. Forster*, pp. 132–60; and Wilfred Stone, *The Cave and the Mountain*, pp. 298–346.

2. On the novel's structure, see, e.g., Reuben A. Brower, *The Fields of Light: An Experiment in Critical Reading* (New York: Oxford University Press, 1951), pp. 182–98; Hugh Maclean, "The Structure of *A Passage to India*," *University of Toronto Quarterly* 22 (1953): 157–71; Gertrude M. White, "*A Passage to India*: Analysis and Revaluation," *Publications of the Modern Language Association* 68 (1953): 641–57; Glen O. Allen, "Structure, Symbol, and Theme in *A Passage to India*," *Publications of the Modern Language Association* 70 (1955): 934–54; and V. A. Shahane, "Symbolism in E. M. Forster's *A Passage to India*: 'Temple,'" *English Studies* 44 (1963): 422–31.

3. On the social and political background of the novel, see, e.g., Benita Parry, "Passage to More than India," in *Forster: A Collection of Critical Essays*, ed. Bradbury, pp. 160–74; K. Natwar-Singh, "Only Connect . . . : Forster and India," in *Aspects of E. M. Forster*, ed. Stal-

lybrass, pp. 37–50; Benita Parry, *Delusions and Discoveries: Studies on India in the British Imagination 1880–1930* (Berkeley: University of California Press, 1972), 260–320; Jeffrey Meyers, *Fiction and the Colonial Experience* (Ipswich, England: Boydell, 1973), pp. 29–53; M. M. Mahood, *The Colonial Encounter* (London: Rex Collings, 1977), pp. 65–91; and G. K. Das, *Forster's India* (London: Macmillan, 1977). For an account of Forster's visits to India, see Robin Jared Lewis, *E. M. Forster's Passages to India.*

4. Walt Whitman, "Passage to India," 1. 165, in *Walt Whitman: The Complete Poems,* ed. Francis Murphy, p. 434. On Whitman's influence on the novel, see, e.g., Maclean, "The Structure of *A Passage to India*"; and Benita Parry, "*A Passage to India:* Epitaph or Manifesto," in *E. M. Forster: A Human Exploration,* ed. Das and Beer, pp. 129–41. Parry links Forster's idea of India with Edward Carpenter's "India, The Wisdom-Land" as well as with Whitman, and remarks suggestively: "It is interesting that Forster's perceptions are in the tradition of Walt Whitman and Edward Carpenter, the one a passionate believer in popular democracy, the other a romantic socialist, both mystics and homosexuals disassociated by temperament and conviction from the conventions of their respective societies. Instead of the bizarre, exotic and perverse world made out of India by Western writers in the late nineteenth and early twentieth centuries, a compilation serving to confirm the normality and excellence of their own systems, Whitman and in his wake Carpenter found in that distant and antique civilisation expressions of transcendent aspects to experience and access to gnosis, predicting that, when connected with the secular, these would open up new vistas to democratic emancipation, international fellowship and progress" (p. 135).

5. McConkey, *The Novels of E. M. Forster,* p. 82.

6. McBryde's theory of climatic zones—"All unfortunate natives are criminals at heart, for the simple reason that they live south of latitude 30"—is probably intended to parody Sir Richard Burton's theory of a "'Sotadic Zone,' bounded westwards by the northern shores of the Medi-

terranean (N. Lat. 43°) and by the southern (N. Lat. 30°)" in which pederasty flourishes, a vice Burton considered "geographical and climatic, not racial." Burton's theory is expounded in his "Terminal Essay," appended to his translation of *The Arabian Nights* (1885), reprinted in *Sexual Heretics*, ed. Brian Reade, pp. 158–93; the quotations are from p. 159.

7. On the metaphor of invitation, see Frederick C. Crews, *E. M. Forster: The Perils of Humanism*, pp. 148–50; and John Colmer, "Promise and Withdrawal in *A Passage to India*," in *E. M. Forster: A Human Exploration*, ed. Das and Beer, pp. 117–28.

8. In the 1920 essay, "Notes on the English Character," Forster recounts an anecdote in which he tells an Indian friend—Syed Ross Masood, to whom *A Passage to India* is dedicated—that the amount of emotion he expresses on their parting is inappropriate: "The word 'inappropriate' roused him to fury. 'What?' he cried. 'Do you measure out your emotions as if they were potatoes?'" The friend tells Forster: "your whole attitude toward emotion is wrong. Emotion has nothing to do with appropriateness. It matters only that it shall be sincere" (*Abinger Harvest*, p. 14).

9. On the Jain sect, see the discussion in Parry, *Delusions and Discoveries*, pp. 286–90.

10. Stone, *The Cave and the Mountain*, p. 307. For a discussion of the various interpretations of the caves, see June Perry Levine, *Creation and Criticism: A Passage to India* (Lincoln: University of Nebraska Press, 1971), pp. 133–39.

11. On the significance of the echo, see Keith Hollingsworth, "*A Passage to India*: The Echoes in the Marabar Caves," *Criticism* 4 (1962): 210–24.

12. Parry, *Delusions and Discoveries*, p. 294.

13. On this point, see Alan Wilde, *Horizons of Assent*, p. 61.

14. On Adela's psychological breakdown, see, e.g., Louise Dauner, "What Happened in the Cave? Reflections on *A Passage to India*," *Modern Fiction Studies* 7 (1961): 258–70; and Stone, *The Cave and the Mountain*, pp. 334–39.

15. Wilde, *Art and Order: A Study of E. M. Forster*, p. 129.

For two divergent—and equally extreme—accounts of Godbole, see McConkey, *The Novels of E. M. Forster*, pp. 140-44; and David Shusterman, "The Curious Case of Professor Godbole: *A Passage to India* Reexamined," *Publications of the Modern Language Association* 76 (1961): 426-35.

16. McConkey, *The Novels of E. M. Forster*, p. 138. McConkey's argument that the emptiness of the cave actually contains the absolute *Brahman* and his equation of "ou-boum" with the mystical symbol "OM" are suggestive but unconvincing. The Hindu symbolism associated with the caves permits them to be accepted by Godbole as an emblem of *Brahman*, but Forster certainly does not indicate that Godbole's perceptions are accurate.

17. On Mrs. Moore's function as Hindu goddess, see, e.g., Ellin Horowitz, "The Communal Ritual and the Dying God in E. M. Forster's *A Passage to India*," *Criticism* 6 (1964): 70-88; and Frederick P. W. McDowell, *E. M. Forster*, rev. ed., pp. 109, 129-30. But, for a dissenting view, see Edwin Nierenberg, "The Withered Priestess: Mrs. Moore's Incomplete Passage to India," *Modern Language Quarterly* 25 (1964): 198-204. On the limits of myth criticism, see Robert L. Selig, "'God si Love': On an Unpublished Forster Letter and the Ironic Use of Myth in *A Passage to India*," *Journal of Modern Literature* 7 (1979): 471-87.

18. Parry, "Passage to More than India," p. 165.

19. See Michael Orange, "Language and Silence in *A Passage to India*," in *E. M. Forster: A Human Exploration*, ed. Das and Beer, pp. 142-60.

20. Calvin Bedient, *Architects of the Self: George Eliot, D. H. Lawrence, and E. M. Forster* (Berkeley: University of California Press, 1972), p. 251. On Forster's ambivalence toward Hinduism, see, e.g., Crews, *E. M. Forster: The Perils of Humanism*, pp. 151-55; and Wilde, *Art and Order*, pp. 150-55.

21. John Sayre Martin, *E. M. Forster: The Endless Journey*, p. 162.

22. Forster, Program Note to Santha Rama Rau's Dramati-

zation of *A Passage to India,* quoted in the Abinger Edition of *A Passage to India,* p. 328.

23. Whitman, "Passage to India," ll. 200, 248.
24. Stone, *The Cave and the Mountain,* p. 345.

8. OTHER KINGDOMS:
The Short Fiction

1. Judith Scherer Herz, "From Myth to Scripture: An Approach to Forster's Later Short Fiction," *English Literature in Transition* 24 (1981): 206.
2. Alan Wilde, *Art and Order: A Study of E. M. Forster,* p. 77.
3. Wilfred Stone, *The Cave and the Mountain,* p. 147.
4. Oscar Wilde, *The Importance of Being Earnest,* in *The Portable Oscar Wilde,* ed. Richard Aldington (New York: Viking, 1946), p. 481.
5. Alan Wilde, "The Naturalisation of Eden," in *E. M. Forster: A Human Exploration,* ed. Das and Beer, p. 197. In his 1964 book, *Art and Order: A Study of E. M. Forster,* Wilde first suggested a homosexual dimension to "The Curate's Friend."
6. Lionel Trilling, *E. M. Forster,* p. 40.
7. Thomas Carlyle, *Sartor Resartus,* ed. Harrold, p. 239. Subsequent quotations from *Sartor Resartus* are from this edition and are cited parenthetically by page numbers.
8. George H. Thomson, *The Fiction of E. M. Forster,* p. 85.
9. Donald Salter, "'That is My Ticket': The Homosexual Writings of E. M. Forster," *London Magazine* 14 (1975): 7.
10. See Robert K. Martin, "Forster's Greek: From Optative to Present Indicative," *Kansas Quarterly* 9 (1977): 69–73.
11. James S. Malek, "Forster's 'Albergo Empedocle': A Precursor of *Maurice,*" *Studies in Short Fiction* 11 (1974): 427–30.
12. For instance, Donald Salter, in an otherwise sympathetic survey, regards several of the stories as pornographic;

see "'That is My Ticket': The Homosexual Writings of
E. M. Forster," pp. 16–22. But Salter bases this judgment
on a misunderstanding of the "facetious tales" and on a
too literal interpretation of Forster's remark in a diary
entry about some stories that he destroyed in 1922:
"They were written not to express myself but to excite
myself." It is questionable whether a story written to
"excite" the author is necessarily pornographic, but in
any case Forster's remark does not refer to the stories in
The Life to Come. Furbank reports that Forster was
excited while writing "The Story of a Panic" and the
scene in *Where Angels Fear to Tread* in which Gino
twists Philip's broken arm (*Life*, I, 114); these scenes
reverberate with sexuality, but they certainly are not
pornographic. Neither are the posthumously published
tales. Any definition of pornography that would encompass Forster's stories would be tortuous indeed.

13. Wilfred Stone, "'Overleaping Class': Forster's Problem
in Connection," p. 404. Equally inaccurate is Barbara
Rosecrance's smug assertion: "The homosexual stories
concern themselves not with the meaning of life but
with a byway of experience, the thrills and punishments
of homosexual passion. . . . Their orgies of rape, mutilation, and death project anguish, but also a questionable
pleasure in violence, self-punishment, and destruction"
(*Forster's Narrative Vision*, pp. 182–83). Such assertions
reflect remarkable innocence of complex psychological
issues and apparently willful misreadings of the fiction.
Because they reduce the important social and political
and sexual issues at the heart of Forster's gay fiction to
symptoms of neurosis and to "a byway of experience"
irrelevant to "the meaning of life," such assertions are
also fundamentally (though perhaps unintentionally)
homophobic.

14. Herz, "From Myth to Scripture," p. 210; the subsequent
quotation is from p. 209.

15. *Cymbeline*, V.iv.69 and stage directions. See Norman
Page, *E. M. Forster's Posthumous Fiction*, p. 43.

16. Lawrence's encomium is in a letter to Forster dated October 27, 1927, quoted in Oliver Stallybrass's Introduction to *The Life to Come and Other Stories*, p. xv.

17. "Now They Can Be Told," *Times Literary Supplement*,

October 13, 1972, p. 1215; see also Stone, "'Overleaping Class': Forster's Problem in Connection," pp. 399–405.

18. Herz, "From Myth to Scripture," p. 207; and James S. Malek, "Salvation in Forster's 'Dr. Woolacott,'" *Studies in Short Fiction* 18 (1981): 319–20.

19. Page, *E. M. Forster's Posthumous Fiction*, p. 49.

20. The accuracy of Forster's perception of the class system's effect on criminal prosecutions for homosexual activities is attested by the famous trials of Oscar Wilde. As Robert Keith Miller observes of them, "the transcripts reveal an obsession with the distinctions of social class. . . . The prosecution did not hesitate to name the grooms and coachmen with whom Wilde had been involved, but it took pains to keep other names from public record. When it seemed as if Wilde was about to mention having shared a hotel room with the nephew of the solicitor-general, he was passed a sheet of paper and instructed to write out the name of the man in question but not say it out loud. And it is worth noting that despite a wealth of evidence against him, no charge was ever made against [Wilde's lover] Lord Alfred Douglas, son of one of the most powerful families in England" (*Oscar Wilde* [New York: Ungar, 1982], pp. 20–21).

21. J. I. M. Stewart, "Old and Gay," *Spectator*, October 21, 1972, p. 629; Stone, "'Overleaping Class': Forster's Problem in Connection," p. 397.

22. James S. Malek, "Forster's 'Arthur Snatchfold': Respectability Vs. Apollo," *Notes on Contemporary Literature* 10 (September 1980): 9.

23. James S. Malek, "Forster's 'The Classical Annex': The Triumph of Hellenism," *Notes on Contemporary Literature* 5 (November 1975): 4–6.

24. James S. Malek, "Persona, Shadow, and Society: A Reading of Forster's 'The Other Boat,'" *Studies in Short Fiction* 14 (1977): 21–27.

25. On the contrast of the reality and pleasure principles, see Sigmund Freud, *Beyond the Pleasure Principle,* in *The Complete Psychological Works of Sigmund Freud,* vol. 18, trans. James Strachey et al. (London: Hogarth, 1955).

26. Page, *E. M. Forster's Posthumous Fiction*, p. 60.

9. DECENCY TOUCHED WITH POETRY:
The Nonfiction

1. Wilfred Stone, *The Cave and the Mountain*, p. 293.
2. On the importance of this section of the history to *A Passage to India*, see Jane Lagoudis Pinchin, *Alexandria Still: Forster, Durrell, and Cavafy*, pp. 137–46; Mohammad Shaheen, "Forster's Alexandria: The Transitional Journey," and John Drew, "A Passage via Alexandria?" in *E. M. Forster: A Human Exploration*, ed. Das and Beer, pp. 79–88 and 89–101, respectively. On Forster's Egyptian experience and its impact on *A Passage to India*, see also Martin Quinn and Safaa Hejazi, "E. M. Forster and *The Egyptian Mail*: Wartime Journalism and a Subtext for *A Passage to India*," *English Literature in Transition* 25 (1982): 131–45.
3. Jane Lagoudis Pinchin, *Alexandria Still: Forster, Durrell, and Cavafy*, p. 125. The quotation immediately following is from p. 126. On Cavafy's influence on Forster, see also G. D. Klingopulos, "E. M. Forster's Sense of History: and Cavafy," *Essays in Criticism* 8 (1958): 156–65.
4. On Forster's critical eclecticism, see S. P. Rosenbaum, "*Aspects of the Novel* and Literary History," in *E. M. Forster: Centenary Revaluations*, ed. Herz and Martin, pp. 55–83. For an overview of Forster's criticism, see Donald Watt, "The Artist as Horseman: The Unity of Forster's Criticism," *Modern Philology* 79 (1981): 45–60.
5. On the critical relationship between Forster and Woolf, see Robert Gish, "Mr. Forster and Mrs. Woolf: Aspects of the Novelist as Critic," *Virginia Woolf Quarterly* 2 (1976): 255–69; H. K. Trivedi, "Forster and Virginia Woolf: The Critical Friends," in *E. M. Forster: A Human Exploration*, ed. Das and Beer, pp. 216–30; and Rosenbaum, "*Aspects of the Novel* and Literary History," in *E. M. Forster: Centenary Revaluations*, ed. Herz and Martin, especially pp. 73–81.
6. Stone, *The Cave and the Mountain*, p. 115.
7. On this point, see Judith Scherer Herz, "Forster's Three

Experiments in Autobiographical Biography," *Studies in the Literary Imagination* 13 (1980): 51-67. The other two experiments referred to in her title are *The Hill of Devi* and *Marianne Thornton*.

8. See *The Autobiography of G. Lowes Dickinson*, ed. Dennis Proctor (London: Duckworth, 1973).

9. On the continuing relevance of Forster's humanism, see Wilfred Stone, "E. M. Forster's Subversive Individualism," in *E. M. Forster: Centenary Revaluations*, ed. Herz and Martin, pp. 15-36.

10. Cynthia Ozick, "Forster as Homosexual," p. 85. For a more subtle yet equally homophobic assessment, see George Steiner, "Under the Greenwood Tree," *New Yorker*, October 9, 1971, where he remarks that in light of Forster's homosexuality some of his "most famous dicta—it is better to betray one's country than a friend, 'only connect'—take on a more restricted, shriller ambience" (p. 169).

11. W. H. Auden, "Sir, no man's enemy, forgiving all," in *The English Auden*, ed. Edward Mendelson (New York: Random House, 1977), p. 36. The following quotation from "September 1, 1939" also follows this edition (p. 247).

12. John Colmer, *E. M. Forster: The Personal Voice*, p. 152. See also J. Birje-Patil, "Forster and Dewas," in *E. M. Forster: A Human Exploration*, ed. Das and Beer, pp. 102-108.

10. AFTERWORD

1. W. H. Auden, "To E. M. Forster," in W. H. Auden and Christopher Isherwood, *Journey to a War*, p. 11.

Bibliography

I. PRINCIPAL WORKS BY E. M. FORSTER
(Arranged chronologically)

Where Angels Fear to Tread. Edinburgh: William Blackwood
and Sons, 1905.
The Longest Journey. Edinburgh: William Blackwood and
Sons, 1907.
A Room with a View. London: Edward Arnold, 1908.
Howards End. London: Edward Arnold, 1910.
The Celestial Omnibus and Other Stories. London: Edward
Arnold, 1911.
Alexandria: A History and a Guide. Alexandria: Whitehead
Morris, 1922.
Pharos and Pharillon. London: Hogarth Press, 1923.
A Passage to India. London: Edward Arnold, 1924.
Aspects of the Novel. London: Edward Arnold, 1927.
The Eternal Moment and Other Stories. London: Sidgwick
& Jackson, 1928.
Goldsworthy Lowes Dickinson. London: Edward Arnold,
1934.
Abinger Harvest. London: Edward Arnold, 1936.
The Collected Tales of E. M. Forster. New York: Knopf, 1947.
Two Cheers for Democracy. London: Edward Arnold, 1951.
The Hill of Devi. London: Edward Arnold, 1953.
Marianne Thornton. London: Edward Arnold, 1956.
Maurice. London: Edward Arnold, 1971.
"Albergo Empedocle" and Other Writings. Ed. George H.
Thomson. New York: Liveright, 1971.

The Life to Come and Other Stories. London: Edward Arnold, 1972.

The Abinger Edition of E. M. Forster. Ed. Oliver Stallybrass et al. London: Edward Arnold, 1975–

II. WORKS ABOUT E. M. FORSTER

(Only book-length studies are included here. Readers should also consult important essays cited in the notes.)

Bibliographies

Kirkpatrick, B. J. *A Bibliography of E. M. Forster.* London: Rupert Hart-Davis, 1965; rev. ed., 1968.

McDowell, Frederick P. W. *E. M. Forster: An Annotated Bibliography of Writings about Him.* DeKalb: Northern Illinois University Press, 1977.

Selected Biographical and Critical Books, Monographs, and Essay Collections

Ackerley, J. R. *E. M. Forster: A Portrait.* London: Ian McKelvie, 1970.

Adams, Stephen. *The Homosexual as Hero in Contemporary Fiction.* New York: Barnes & Noble, 1980.

Bedient, Calvin. *Architects of the Self: George Eliot, D. H. Lawrence, and E. M. Forster.* Berkeley: University of California Press, 1972.

Beer, J. B. *The Achievement of E. M. Forster.* London: Chatto & Windus, 1962.

Bradbury, Malcolm, ed. *E. M. Forster: A Passage to India.* Casebook Series. London: Macmillan, 1970.

———, ed. *Forster: A Collection of Critical Essays.* Englewood Cliffs, N.J.: Prentice-Hall, 1966.

Brander, Laurence. *E. M. Forster: A Critical Study.* London: Rupert Hart-Davis, 1968.

Brower, Reuben A. *The Fields of Light: An Experiment in*

Critical Reading. New York: Oxford University Press, 1951.

Brown, E. K. *Rhythm in the Novel*. Toronto: University of Toronto Press, 1950.

Cavaliero, Glen. *A Reading of E. M. Forster*. London: Macmillan, 1979.

Colmer, John. *E. M. Forster: The Personal Voice*. London: Routledge & Kegan Paul, 1975.

Cox, C. B. *The Free Spirit: A Study of Liberal Humanism in the Novels of George Eliot, Henry James, E. M. Forster, Virginia Woolf, Angus Wilson*. London: Oxford University Press, 1963.

Crews, Frederick C. *E. M. Forster: The Perils of Humanism*. Princeton, N.J.: Princeton University Press, 1962.

Das, G. K. *Forster's India*. London: Macmillan, 1977.

——— and John Beer, eds. *E. M. Forster: A Human Exploration*. New York: New York University Press, 1979.

Finkelstein, Bonnie Blumenthal. *Forster's Women: Eternal Differences*. New York: Columbia University Press, 1975.

Furbank, P. N. *E. M. Forster: A Life*. 2 vols. London: Secker and Warburg, 1977–78. Reprint, 2 vols. in 1. New York: Harcourt Brace Jovanovich, 1978.

Gardner, Philip. *E. M. Forster*. Harlow, Essex: Longman Group, 1978.

———, ed. *E. M. Forster: The Critical Heritage*. London: Routledge & Kegan Paul, 1973.

Godfrey, Denis. *E. M. Forster's Other Kingdom*. Edinburgh: Oliver and Boyd, 1968.

Gowda, H. H. Anniah, ed. *A Garland for E. M. Forster*. Mysore, India: The Literary Half-Yearly, 1969.

Gransden, K. W. *E. M. Forster*. New York: Grove Press, 1962.

Hall, James. *The Tragic Comedians: Seven Modern British Novelists*. Bloomington: Indiana University Press, 1963.

Hardy, John Edward. *Man in the Modern Novel*. Seattle: University of Washington Press, 1964.

Herz, Judith Scherer, and Robert K. Martin, eds. *E. M. Forster: Centenary Revaluations*. Toronto: University of Toronto Press, 1982.

Johnstone, J. K. *The Bloomsbury Group: A Study of E. M.*

Forster, Lytton Strachey, Virginia Woolf, and Their Circle. New York: Noonday, 1954.

Joseph, David I. *The Art of Rearrangement: E. M. Forster's Abinger Harvest.* New Haven, Conn.: Yale University Press, 1960.

Kelvin, Norman. *E. M. Forster.* Carbondale and Edwardsville: Southern Illinois University Press, 1967.

King, Francis. *E. M. Forster and His World.* London: Thames and Hudson, 1978.

Levine, June Perry. *Creation and Criticism: A Passage to India.* Lincoln: University of Nebraska Press, 1971.

Lewis, Robin Jared. *E. M. Forster's Passages to India.* New York: Columbia University Press, 1979.

Macaulay, Rose. *The Writings of E. M. Forster.* London: Hogarth Press, 1938.

Martin, John Sayre. *E. M. Forster: The Endless Journey.* Cambridge: Cambridge University Press, 1976.

Martin, Richard. *The Love that Failed: Ideal and Reality in the Writings of E. M. Forster.* The Hague: Mouton, 1974.

McConkey, James. *The Novels of E. M. Forster.* Ithaca, N.Y.: Cornell University Press, 1957.

McDowell, Frederick P. W. *E. M. Forster.* New York: Twayne, 1969. Rev. ed., Boston: Twayne, 1982.

Meyers, Jeffrey. *Fiction and the Colonial Experience.* Ipswich, England: Boydell, 1973.

———. *Homosexuality and Literature 1890–1930.* London: Athlone Press, 1977.

———. *Painting and the Novel.* Manchester: Manchester University Press, 1975.

Natwar-Singh, K., ed. *E. M. Forster: A Tribute with Selections from His Writings on India.* New York: Harcourt, Brace & World, 1964.

Oliver, H. J. *The Art of E. M. Forster.* London: Cambridge University Press, 1960.

Page, Norman. *E. M. Forster's Posthumous Fiction.* ELS Monograph Series, No. 10. Victoria, B.C.: University of Victoria, 1977.

Parry, Benita. *Delusions and Discoveries: Studies on India in the British Imagination 1880–1930.* Berkeley: University of California Press, 1972.

Pinchin, Jane Lagoudis. *Alexandria Still: Forster, Durrell, and Cavafy*. Princeton, N.J.: Princeton University Press, 1977.

Rose, Martial. *E. M. Forster*. London: Evans Brothers, 1970.

Rosecrance, Barbara. *Forster's Narrative Vision*. Ithaca, N.Y.: Cornell University Press, 1982.

Russell, John. *Style in Modern British Fiction: Studies in Joyce, Lawrence, Forster, Lewis, and Green*. Baltimore: Johns Hopkins University Press, 1978.

Rutherford, Andrew, ed. *Twentieth Century Interpretations of A Passage to India*. Englewood Cliffs, N.J.: Prentice-Hall, 1970.

Shahane, Vasant A. *E. M. Forster: A Study in Double Vision*. New Delhi: Arnold-Heinemann, 1975.

————, ed. *Perspectives on E. M. Forster's A Passage to India: A Collection of Critical Essays*. New York: Barnes & Noble, 1968.

Shusterman, David. *The Quest for Certitude in E. M. Forster's Fiction*. Bloomington: Indiana University Press, 1965.

Stallybrass, Oliver, ed. *Aspects of E. M. Forster: Essays and Recollections Written for His Ninetieth Birthday*. London: Edward Arnold, 1969.

Stone, Wilfred. *The Cave and the Mountain: A Study of E. M. Forster*. Stanford, Calif.: Stanford University Press, 1966.

Thomson, George H. *The Fiction of E. M. Forster*. Detroit: Wayne State University Press, 1967.

Trilling, Lionel. *E. M. Forster*. Norfolk, Conn.: New Directions, 1943.

Widdowson, Peter. *E. M. Forster's Howards End: Fiction as History*. London: Chatto & Windus for Sussex University Press, 1977.

Wilde, Alan. *Art and Order: A Study of E. M. Forster*. New York: New York University Press, 1964.

————. *Horizons of Assent: Modernism, Postmodernism, and the Ironic Imagination*. Baltimore: Johns Hopkins University Press, 1981.

Index